Murder and Mayhem

Edited by David Nash and Anne-Marie Kilday

Murder and Mayhem

Crime in Twentieth-Century Britain

 palgrave

First published 2018 by
PALGRAVE

Palgrave in the UK is an imprint of Macmillan Publishers Limited, registered in England, company number 785998, of 4 Crinan Street, London, N1 9XW.

Palgrave® and Macmillan® are registered trademarks in the United States, the United Kingdom, Europe and other countries.

ISBN 978–1–137–29044–1 hardback
ISBN 978–1–137–29043–4 paperback

This book is printed on paper suitable for recycling and made from fully managed and sustained forest sources. Logging, pulping and manufacturing processes are expected to conform to the environmental regulations of the country of origin.

A catalogue record for this book is available from the British Library.

A catalog record for this book is available from the Library of Congress.

For Bella Nash, with love, as she continues her journey as a historian and a scholar!

Contents

Acknowledgements   ix

Notes on Contributors   xi

1   Introduction: Crime and Punishment in
Twentieth-Century Britain   1

2   Britain's 'Most Wanted': Homicide and Serial Murder
since 1900   31

3   Serious Property Offending in the Twentieth Century   65

4   Racial Hate Crime in Modern Britain   91

5   Offences Against the Person: Child Sexual Abuse   125

6   Anarchism, Assassination and Terrorism in Modern Britain   149

7   'Hope I Die Before I Get Old': Social Rebellion and Social
Diseases   177

8   Organised Crime, Criminality and the 'Gangster'   213

9   Punishment: The Death Penalty and Incarceration   243

10   Law Enforcement: Policies and Perspectives   271

Further Reading   303

Index   311

Acknowledgements

The editors would like to thank the numerous people who have helped in the writing of this book. Firstly, we would like to express our thanks to staff at the National Archives, the National Archives of Scotland, Manchester Central Library and the Bodleian Library, Oxford for their patience and helpful advice. Anne-Marie Kilday would like to thank Daniel Vicars for the research work that he carried out in relation to her chapter of this volume. We would also like to thank each of the contributors to this volume for their hard work and, in particular, their patience and grace when dealing with our many queries.

We would also like to thank those involved at Palgrave publishing in the production of this book from embryonic idea to published work. Thanks go to our commissioning editor and to editorial contact Rachel Bridgewater. We would also like to thank our anonymous reviewers for their helpful and important contributions.

Notes on Contributors

Neil Davie is Professor of British History at Université Lumière Lyon 2, France. He is the author of *Tracing the Criminal: The Rise of Scientific Criminology in Britain, 1860–1918* (2005) and *The Penitentiary Ten: The Transformation of the English Prison, 1770–1850* (2015). He is currently working on a history of Parkhurst children's convict prison.

Johannes Dillinger is Professor of Early Modern History at Oxford Brookes and Honorary Professor of Modern and Regional History at Mainz (Johannes Gutenberg Universität). Dillinger won the Friedrich Spee Award for outstanding contributions to the history of witchcraft. His publications include ten English and German monographs on terrorism, witchcraft, treasure hunting, the political representation of the peasantry and on concepts of alternate history. Dillinger's main research interests include state building, constitutional history, the history of political crime, church history and the history of folk belief, magic and witchcraft.

Barry Godfrey is Professor and Associate Pro Vice Chancellor (Research) in the Faculty of Humanities and Social Sciences at the University of Liverpool. He has authored or co-authored 14 books on the history of crime. His research interests include private policing, desistance, biographical historical methods, digital methodologies, longitudinal studies of sentencing, ethics and historical research, and changes to the operation of criminal justice in the nineteenth and twentieth centuries.

Helen Johnston is Senior Lecturer in Criminology at the University of Hull. Her publications include *Crime in England, 1815–1880: Experiencing the Criminal Justice System* (2015, Routledge); *Punishment &*

Control in Historical Perspective (editor, 2008, Palgrave Macmillan) and she also co-edited *Prison Readings* with Yvonne Jewkes (2006, Willan).

Anne-Marie Kilday is Professor of Criminal History at Oxford Brookes University. She has published widely on the history of violence and the history of female criminality in Britain, Europe and North America from 1600 to the present. She is currently working on two monograph projects: one on the history of homicide in Britain and one on the history of violence in Scotland.

David Nash is Professor of History at Oxford Brookes University. He has written and published on the secular movement in Britain, the history of blasphemy, the history of secularisation and the history of shame. He has given expert advice on the issue of blasphemy to the British, Australian and Irish governments as well as the European Parliament. He is currently researching for a book on the history of hate crime.

Heather Shore is a Reader in History at Leeds Beckett University. She has published extensively on the history of crime. She is the author of *Artful Dodgers: Youth and Crime in Early Nineteenth-Century London* (Boydell and Brewer, 1999); (with Pam Cox) *Becoming Delinquent: British and European Youth, 1650–1950* (Ashgate, 2002); (with Tim Hitchcock) *The Streets of London: From the Great Fire to the Great Exhibition* (Rivers Oram Press, 2003); and *London's Criminal Underworlds, c. 1720–c. 1930* (Palgrave, 2015). She is currently working (with Professors Barry Godfrey and Pam Cox) on a Leverhulme funded project, Aftercare: Youth Justice and Its Impact, 1850–1945, which explores the long-term impact of nineteenth- and twentieth-century youth justice interventions.

Kim Stevenson is Professor of Socio-Legal History at Plymouth University and is co-founder of and director of SOLON: Interdisciplinary Studies in Law, Crime and History. She has published widely on historical and contemporary aspects of crime and the criminal law with particular emphasis on sexual offences, specifically rape and child sexual abuse. Recent publications include *Public Indecency in England 1857–1960* with D. Cox, C. Harris and J. Rowbotham (Routledge, 2015) and *Crime News in Modern*

Britain: Press Reporting and Responsibility 1820–2010 with J. Rowbotham and S. Pegg (Palgrave, 2013).

Lucy Williams is a postdoctoral researcher in the Department of Sociology, Social Policy and Criminology at the University of Liverpool specialising in women, gender and crime in the nineteenth and early twentieth centuries. Her research uses a range of interdisciplinary approaches drawing from history, criminology and digital humanities.

Clifford Williamson is Senior Lecturer in Contemporary British and American History at Bath Spa University. His research interests and publications include work on 'The Teddy Boys', the development of private practice in the NHS in the 1950s and 1960s and the religious history of contemporary Scotland. He is currently working on a monograph on deviance and disorder in popular music.

1

Introduction: Crime and Punishment in Twentieth-Century Britain

Anne-Marie Kilday and David Nash

This book is an attempt to bring together some of the recent research on the history of modern twentieth-century criminality for an undergraduate and general readership. In the past, this period has not received this overall treatment from scholars and we are delighted to offer a single volume which focuses on a range of aspects and themes related to twentieth-century crime, law, policing and punishment.[1] It remains something of a considerable surprise that the history of crime in twentieth-century Britain is still spectacularly under-researched and relatively ignored. Criminologists have brought a range of social science disciplines to bear on the study of criminality over this period. However, historical approaches still lag significantly behind this venture. This book takes the first steps in seeking to address this oversight and neglect of the modern British historical context.

This work represents the findings of research undertaken by various key scholars throughout Britain and beyond over a number of years. This would normally be very difficult to gather together in any other form than conference proceedings. However, our inspiration for the production of this volume has come from the success and reception of our previous volume for Palgrave, *Histories of Crime: Britain 1600–2000.*[2] This earlier volume covered many of the central themes in the history of

1

crime and punishment. It surveyed these over a period of three to four centuries, tracing the much longer term evolution of practices, mechanisms, institutions and attitudes. Whilst this has provided help for survey courses in the history of crime, law and criminology, there has been a clear and obvious need for a more specialised volume that would shed light on the more focussed time period of the twentieth century. Such a book would more readily assist those requiring more detailed knowledge of a more concise historical period. This book also has the advantage of more readily addressing the needs of students and readers from the legal, policing, social, caring and journalistic professions. This is realised through its consistent use of a rigidly structured approach to the study of crime and punishment in the modern era and its employment of case studies to illuminate particular aspects of the scholarship and chronology relating to the topics included.

A focus on the twentieth century brings with it an observation that the history of crime in this period, more so than the eighteenth and nineteenth centuries, breaks down more obviously into coverage of specific offences. This coverage has produced both advantages and drawbacks for the study of these crimes in the modern era and beyond.[3] Obviously, it is a great advantage for scholars to be able to consult a wide variety of well-researched and well-respected research monographs that provide in-depth knowledge, insight and interpretation. Likewise such works, covering the twentieth century, have also been able to take advantage of a number of factors that assist in the study of this particular period. The growing power of government to collect and process information has, since the last years of the nineteenth century, ensured that a considerable array of primary sources exist for sustained use by the historian interested in this period. Alongside this, we might argue that the gradual, sometimes episodic, development of cultures of transparency and accountability have themselves added a new dimension to the potential for fruitful study of this century. Indeed, the fruits of such developments are demonstrated in some of the chapters in this volume. Such transparency and accountability have themselves produced a growing tradition of both positive and negative reflection and criticism of the workings of everything from the creation and operation of the law in practice to policing methods and detention and punishment regimes. This book does not aim at exhaustive chronological coverage of every crime, event and legislative change important to the history of twentieth-century murder and mayhem. Instead, the authors have highlighted important periods of change and development that have shaped the overall history of each of the themes covered in the volume. Thus, it has provided in-depth analysis and explanation, rather than a simple chronological account of each theme. Starting this book in 1900 and ending it in 1999 would be an unhelpful and artificial periodisation. Allowing the chapters to have a degree of leeway in their chronological coverage is something we view as important for conveying a wider and more useful history and a fuller analysis of the themes discussed.

Similarly, mechanical discussions of the different histories of crime and criminality across all the different constituent parts of the United Kingdom in each chapter of this book would be unhelpful, bland and cursory. This is not to dismiss the distinct variations that do occur in these different countries such as distinctive legislative histories and practices. Indeed, many of these are alluded to and discussed. Nevertheless, our concentration on themes, more often than not, serves to emphasise the commonality of experience in Britain and the ripple effect of many events, policies and ideas across its constituent countries.

1. The Changing Face of Modern Policing and Detection – Professionalisation, Efficiency and Accountability

Whilst the twentieth-century perception of law and order views the police service as a normal and visible presence, it is worth remembering that society's acceptance of this institution remains relatively recent.[4] What is perhaps even more surprising is that acceptance of the police service and its work still remains somewhat conditional. Some of this is a perception of the task it has to undertake and how this has an impact on the criminal world. Groups within society that subsist on the margins of criminality have for a long time been resistant to the police and their constant presence. Others noted that the police were capable of over-zealous methods and sometimes of outright corruption – the latter of which would occasionally appear in tabloid newspapers. On other occasions, the actions and attitudes of the police would be readily identified with the particular personality of their chief constable, and the twentieth century exhibits a number of instances of this particular phenomenon, where police work occasionally shaded into political lobbying.

Minority groups certainly had their misgivings about their perception that police interference in their lives was targeted, unwarranted and out of all proportion. As some instances within this book demonstrate, the mechanisms and procedures of particular constabularies would regularly be shown to be antiquated and unfit for purpose – especially as the service was required to undertake more and more duties as the century wore on. Thus, the activities of the police service now went beyond upholding the law and keeping the peace to include showing sensitivity and awareness to a general public increasingly cast as 'consumers' of the institution in the more modern era. Like the prison service discussed below, a successful and functioning police service does not readily attract newspaper headlines. Likewise, the stories of conscious and sustained adaptation to changed circumstances, changed roles and a vastly changed social landscape do not get so easily told. Conscious steps have been taken to make procedures more sensitive, to ensure that the composition of the service is more diverse and considerably modernised and that improved training regimes to cement these efforts have been instigated and implemented throughout the country.

However, these aspects of the modern police force do tend to appear under the media heading 'lessons learned', rather than invoking an appreciation of the genuine attempts of serving officers to modernise their practices in harmony with changes in society and its expectations. Police competence could also regularly be called into question by the media's regular concerns about slow, unsuccessful and apparently bungled police actions or investigations. This whole area itself opened up levels of accountability as never before, so that serving officers would regularly note how the reputation and confidence the public had in particular constabularies would sink or swim on this particular tide.[5]

From its comparative infancy, the twentieth century has also witnessed the spectacular growth and development of ways of investigating and studying crime at the hands of specialists and experts.[6] These were increasingly recognised, as the century wore on, as important auxiliary services which aided the practice of crime detection and prosecution. Experts were increasingly involved in the investigation of crimes and the apprehending of criminals, with forensic and other scientific advisors increasingly called upon in court to offer expert testimony, which itself grew in stature and importance as the century progressed. Yet, it would be wise to remember here that not all such developments were smooth and even, and such innovations could be discredited when the failure of expert evidence produced unsafe convictions, such as in the miscarriage of justice that wrongfully imprisoned the 'Birmingham Six'.[7] Experts were also involved in supplying the police service with other methods of detecting and catching criminals in the ever-expanding race to out-think felonious activity. Whilst graphologists examined handwriting and police artists created more sophisticated images of suspects, the arrival of the criminal profiler and their work was another tool by which a bridge was built with the media and the general public at large.[8] Other policing methods began to see crime prevention as an important element within an overall strategy. This also spawned a security industry that offered both technology and manpower to an ever-growing and anxious client base.

Crime and crime prevention came together in the development of a relatively new branch of scholarship during the twentieth century – criminology. Although well-established on the Continent, this discipline grew in importance in the British context only during this period. Criminals themselves have also been subject to a greater level of scrutiny at the hands of psychologists and psychiatrists who were consulted, as never before, about the motivations of these individuals and their modes of behaviour. Although a psychological understanding of aspects of criminality was evident in the nineteenth century, it was the merging of various scientific disciplines such as psychology, psychiatry and sociology that brought this area into focus. This systematised over the course of the twentieth century to study the nature, extent, control, consequences and prevention of criminal behaviour (in terms of both the individual and society) as the discipline of criminology.[9] The discipline chose to look at the phenomena of crime from both a micro and a macro perspective. At the micro level, the propensity for individuals to offend and the factors that make this likely, offered solutions and initiatives to policing agencies increasingly preoccupied with bringing crime levels down.

One aspect of crime prevention involved tackling precisely the factors that led to offending – often with mixed results.

Occasionally, the primary focus of criminology would shift from a concern about high levels of property crime to an investigation of the relationship between crime and forms of violence and how and why individuals employed such violence. However, it also operated at a macro level in its consideration of criminal statistics and offender profiles over time. These potentially offered in-depth studies of individuals and their crimes that would identify patterns and places where society and its policing agencies might seek to take action. Criminology's macro focus also offered more grandiose and overarching theories about how crime functioned within society and its relationship to issues of class, gender and identity. The subject then became a valuable training ground for all individuals likely to be involved in policing and the work of ancillary agencies such as the remand and probation services. By the end of the twentieth century, criminology courses were common in academic faculties within most of Britain's universities, where the preparation of the next generation of practitioners went hand in hand with an intensive and fluid research agenda which constantly had to adapt to new developments, new theories and new categories of criminal activity.

2.   Development of Law and the Courts

The twentieth century has also seen conceptions of the law itself alter considerably since the nineteenth century. The previous century has been considered spectacularly notable for the rise in government interest and activity throughout many areas of life, although this did overshadow the fact that many crimes had individual victims. One aspect of government involvement, which reached a maturity over the course of the twentieth century, was the gradual extension of its function in the area of criminal justice to pay greater attention to the damage done to society by criminality and criminal behaviour. Consequently, the needs and requirements of the individual as victim became paramount and this agenda gave birth to the concept of victim support. In addition, courts themselves have had to reform their procedures and approaches as they sought to deal with crimes that had attracted public notoriety amid perceptions that society, police and the courts had 'failed' the victims of certain crimes.[10]

Perhaps the most obvious example of this is to consider how the ways in which the police and the courts deal with the crime of rape has been utterly transformed over the course of the century. At the start of this period it was an exceptionally brave woman who brought a rape accusation against a male assailant. Significant levels of proof were required and the odds were dramatically stacked in favour of the defendant, who often benefited considerably from the opaque nature of consent as a legal concept. This was often compounded by the vulnerability of the victim in a charged courtroom situation. This became an intimidating place where her personal conduct and intimate history were both openly and implicitly scrutinised. Yet, by the end of the twentieth century, the Home Office, the police service and the Crown Prosecution Service had responded to calls for structural changes in procedure which had been lobbied for by law reform and women's pressure groups. This lobbying produced enhanced levels of specialised training and new courtroom practices which were aimed at restoring a much more legitimate balance between plaintiff and defendant. Despite continued criticism, these did much to enable society to deal more justly with the crime of rape and to alleviate the suffering of its victims.[11]

Legislation in the modern era was also charged with moving more into line with contemporary attitudes and thus it also had to address social developments in the realm of sexuality. In the 1960s, for instance, abortion was decriminalised in England and Scotland, as was homosexuality. Access to abortion in Northern Ireland was, in contrast, severely restricted and up to this date remains available only if the life of the mother is threatened. The extent of this restriction is evident in the fact that in 2014/15 Northern Ireland permitted only 16 abortions whilst 184,571 took place in England and Wales.[12]

From initially policing various aspects of sexuality and labelling them as both deviant and predatory, the law was transformed into one which offered protection to individuals and minorities who remained vulnerable to hostile attitudes from other members of society. In the resultant conception of this overt hostility as hate crime, this form of protection was also eventually extended to transgendered individuals as well as to ethnic minorities and the disabled.[13] The situation in Northern Ireland lagged behind these changes with respect to the laws against homosexuality, with decriminalisation only coming in 1982. Lowering the age of consent for homosexuals was only enacted after pressure from the European Court of Human Rights and eventually harmonised with the rest of the United Kingdom in 2008.

Occasionally, the adaptation to change witnessed in twentieth-century Britain was indecently rapid and represented a hasty retooling of established justice and policing measures, rather than a concerted and careful series of planned developments. Certainly the history of policing, detention and punishment policies that were extant in Northern Ireland in the two decades since 'The Troubles' broke out in 1968 represents a not entirely successful example of this.[14] Internment without trial and the Diplock courts were simply two of the emergency measures that left a part of the United Kingdom locked into a justice system that had hastily been revised to adapt to extraordinary circumstances. These measures were always considered less than ideal, but became emergency initiatives that would leave lasting resentment and a legacy of problems.

As well as responding to the needs of newly enfranchised social and identity groups, the law itself was tasked throughout the century with responding adequately to the pace of social and economic change. New concerns and requirements meant that the police and criminal justice system had to remain alert, dynamic and adaptable. Technological developments created new types of fraud and cybercrime – the advent of a wholly new arena of crime where new crimes arose alongside new ways in which older crimes could be reinvented and could flourish once more.[15] It was also recognised that social change and the realisation of past inertia or blindness allowed heinous crimes to go unnoticed or escape discovery. For example, the twentieth century saw knowledge and action around the crime of child abuse grow to be recognised as a crime that requires its own pathology, criminological investigation and range of prevention and detection strategies. The recent focus upon individuals in positions of power who have been suspected or found to be guilty of child abuse, grooming, indecency and sexual assault, provides a constant reminder that the law needs to evolve regularly in order to protect the powerless from the powerful.[16]

3. The Punishment Debate

As many books covering the nineteenth century testify, the issue of punishment was one that preoccupied theorists, legislators, prison administrators, practitioners and reformers throughout the Victorian era.[17] In many respects, the nature of these debates remained unaltered into the twentieth century, although some elements of context and emphasis did change. The perennial argument about the purpose and function of punishment endured into the later twentieth century and even beyond as debates over the use of the death penalty testify.[18] It was during the nineteenth century, however, that British society gradually became aware that certain forms of punishment that had been inherited from previous eras no longer seemed fit for purpose and had been victims of changing sensibilities. This provided the inspiration for the gradual displacement of transportation, corporal punishment and capital punishment, by incarceration.[19] Thus, in the twentieth century, incarceration in the form of the prison survived the period intact, but not without some challenges to both its underlying principles and its precise makeup.

Throughout the twentieth century there was a persistent debate regarding the precise function of punishment. Whilst the twin ideological pillars of revenge/retribution and rehabilitation have undoubtedly supported the edifice of the prison, they have not always seemed linked to one another across the decades of the modern era. Both of these pillars have sought to create or build alternative structures which claim an exclusive role in the delivery and management of punishment. Convention argued in the twentieth century that the prison was a meeting point of these two ideological approaches. Whilst inmates were incarcerated as a form of punishment, aspects of their rehabilitation within the prison system were also catered for. Access to educational opportunities, psychiatric and religious counselling and instruction, voluntary and compulsory elements of community service and, finally, remission of sentences for good behaviour, all became part of the prison experience in the modern era. Aspects of rehabilitation as a punishment philosophy were also evident in the attempts to create alternatives to prison. These saw the development of less regimented and disciplined establishments – the so-called open prison – for those convicted of non-violent offences.[20]

These reactions represented only one response to the prison and its purposes which has to be balanced with occasional calls from politicians, commentators and the general public for still more disciplined and draconian punishment regimes. These were eventually encapsulated in the so-called 'boot camp' or 'short, sharp shock' ideas which regularly resurfaced during the century.[21] Whilst some politicians saw this crude motif as a populist touchstone, the interested public were also regularly treated, as the twentieth century wore on, to the much more problematic motif of the 'overcrowded prison'.[22] This image had a number of layers and narratives that problematised the prison system, its aims and its accomplishments. Prisons were arguably overcrowded because of the apparent 'success' of policing measures, although alternatively, these could appear to demonstrate the failure of deterrence in its widespread and varied forms. Prisons also seemed overcrowded because there were few alternatives to their logic and their apparently universal acceptance as the preferred form of punishment. Conservative voices frequently countered this criticism by suggesting that one of the prison's virtues was that it constituted a familiar and 'known quantity' form of deterrent amongst the public at large, thus fulfilling the long sought-after goal of predictability and certainty of punishment. But prisons also seemed to be overcrowded because the prison system was regularly deemed to be functioning in an inadequate fashion, constituting places where resources were being routinely squandered.

Overcrowding, at different moments, seemed to damn both the draconian and liberal approaches. Draconian commentators thought that prisons had failed because they had degenerated into 'soft' options, as their severity had been diluted by misguided enlightenment and kindness. This made it difficult for them to function as institutions which instilled discipline and foregrounded its virtues. Liberal opponents argued that unforeseen high levels of recidivism marked the prison out as a bankrupt institution, rooted in the utilitarian severity of the Victorian era – often (literally) clinging to the Victorian structures in which this kind of approach had been conceived. Such a system seemed anachronistic, especially when compared to the evolution that had occurred elsewhere in several European countries, and it also seemed to condemn inmates to almost permanent membership of a criminalised underclass.

In this sense the prison system always seemed a failure to the society it was supposed to serve. It was by turns too lenient for its draconian detractors whilst too old-fashioned, severe and outmoded for its liberal opponents. Both perspectives oversaw its significant growth in size, and the almost exponential growth in resources devoted to it, throughout the twentieth-century era – a development which arguably pleased no one. It was also disappointing for successive governments to note that, despite mushrooming levels of investment from the Home Office, the growth in prison populations led to frequent headlines about unsatisfactory Victorian conditions in the country's prisons.[23] This story would also receive further credence from the growth of the celebrity prisoner memoir which would either turn a convicted felon into a narrator of the system's operation in a 'warts and all' manner, or would describe the genteel prisoner's unpleasantly abrupt confrontation with the official and unofficial regimes within such prisons.[24]

In some respects Britain's prison system would never be treated fairly by the media or public opinion during the course of the twentieth century. A functioning prison was not newsworthy, and it was inevitable that evidence of systematic dysfunction (in the shape of overcrowding, poor conditions, suicides, sit-ins, protests and occasional prisoner escapes) would ensure the public would always be critical of prisons for the wrong reasons.[25] Nonetheless, the problems facing the prison system in Britain over the century were very real and could not be ignored. The growing concerns created by the system and its operations seemed to dwarf any assessment of its apparent effectiveness and these, at times, would metamorphose into a recurring narrative of 'the prison is broken' or 'the prison is not working'.[26] This was especially pertinent when the levels of resources poured into these institutions were taken into account. Criminologists, penologists, social commentators and the Home Office were eventually persuaded to commence the debate about alternatives.[27] The liberal wing of such investigations would periodically put its weight behind versions of the 'community service' idea. This was intended to rehabilitate offenders by enabling them to do work which assisted in developing or improving facilities in the community at large.[28] Such an approach emphasised rehabilitation and, quite apart from its apparent cost benefit over simple imprisonment, it also answered the call that society should not be allowed to simply forget those it had incarcerated.

Other related experiments in managing punishment led to reinventions of the infamous 'ticket of leave' idea whereby individuals were on license or warrant for good behaviour – sometimes enforced by the controlled use of surveillance techniques such as electronic tagging. Another extra-custodial development in punishment, or arguably simple restraint, was the later twentieth century's development of the Anti-Social Behaviour Order (ASBO). This represented a new departure which removed individuals from locations or situations where breach of the peace or disorder would probably result. As such it was a part of newer thinking which saw a combination of factors being responsible for the perpetration of crime, rather than the previously accepted simple reductionist view that culpability lay solely with the perpetrator.[29]

In addition, alternative forms of punishment came to be suggested over the course of the modern era which involved the exploration of various species of shame penances, which seemed to be cheap and easy to dispense. Although liberal regimes in the first third of the nineteenth century rejected the value and humanity of inflicting shame punishments several commentators, but most notably the criminologist John Braithwaite, began to actively contemplate them as a viable alternative to the 'failed' prison. Whilst it would be devolved justice at county level in the United States that would explore the outer edges of these ideas, some elements did emerge in British penal thinking. For instance, innovative victim reconciliation strategies came to be developed in areas where rehabilitation, integration and reconciliation seemed paramount, and they also appeared to be strategies relevant to a modern society. Such strategies also involved a retooling of traditional shame punishments and a renewed appreciation of the social and cultural ostracism that three centuries earlier had appeared potent and effective.[30]

Another punishment-related preoccupation that ebbed and flowed over the course of the twentieth century was a concern about the treatment and eventual fate of the young offender. This problem led to the creation of a separate system dealing with juvenile offenders that departed from the nineteenth-century obsession with prisons as 'universities of crime'. Thus, institutions like the approved school (created in 1933 from the Victorian Reformatory School and eventually superseded in 1969 by the community care home concept) and the borstal (initiated in 1902 and extended by the 1908 Prevention of Crime Act) were episodic, and often short-lived, attempts at separate solutions to the problem of juvenile crime.[31]

Whilst the punishment debate around minor offending continued in a circle, the twentieth century also saw a significant change in approaches to capital punishment. The nineteenth century had seen the retributive act of capital punishment concealed behind prison walls. By the twentieth century there was an active and effective abolition lobby flourishing as the middle of the century arrived.[32] This punishment, so it was argued, was not in keeping with the notion of a civilised nation, as society itself became increasingly divided over the questionable application of the ultimate punishment in several high-profile cases. Many of these such as those against Ruth Ellis, Derek Bentley and Timothy Evans exhibited elements which meant the logic of the ultimate punishment was less than straightforward.[33] Occasionally the abolition lobby would even increase the potency of their arguments by seeking to identify apparent 'victims' of miscarriages of justice, such as James Hanratty, a man condemned to death when the evidence did not warrant his conviction.[34]

Even when the death penalty was abolished in Britain in 1965, and gradually thereafter in former colonial possessions, this emphatically did not end the discussion of the issue. From a debate around the inhumanity of applying the ultimate sentence, arguments developed around the idea that British justice was no longer firm enough to deter or to adequately punish serious offenders. Such thoughts became crystallised by the unfortunate coincidence of abolition occurring at the same time as one of the century's most notorious high-profile cases – the Moors Murders. The issue was exacerbated by the apparent and blatant inhumanity of the two perpetrators, Myra Hyndley and Ian Brady. Their stalking, kidnap, torture and murder of five child and adolescent victims seemed to be the unleashing of a new barbarism. In the wake of this, some claimed that society could no longer deal adequately with such inhuman crimes after the abolition of capital punishment.[35] As we will see in subsequent chapters, such calls would resurface in the face of the terrorist atrocities which afflicted the British mainland and Northern Ireland after the impact of

'The Troubles' at the end of the 1960s. Such events sometimes became an occasion for seeking the restitution of the death penalty for all murders, and at other times a request that it be reserved for terrorism or the murder of a member of the police or security forces. Despite the ongoing debate, the attitudes of social elites and the campaigns of pressure groups, such as Amnesty International, to eradicate the death penalty across the globe have probably ensured that the reintroduction of the death penalty in European countries is highly unlikely.

4.   The Media and Its Messages about Crime

What is by now becoming obvious is that public interest and knowledge in practically all areas of crime, policing, punishment and the law became a constant presence that influenced thinking, planning and action in relation to these issues over the course of the twentieth century. A tradition of accountability grew hand in hand with the development of the media and the popular interest in numerous aspects of criminality and illegality. It is an enduring truism that crime and law-breaking sell newspapers. This has been evident since the very inception of popular publishing. But the historian would be unwise to ignore the sustained growth of the popular press in the closing decades of the nineteenth century, and likewise its impact on public perceptions of crime and criminal behaviour. As several of the following chapters demonstrate, the media's influence became a tide that was unstoppable during the twentieth century. Before its middle decades, newspapers and periodicals were joined by radio and eventually by television. By the last years of the century, these media were augmented by the arrival of the Internet which carried with it a promise of accessibility, alongside its function as a repository of both current and professionally archived information and opinion. Although parts of this latest media development have educated and informed, other parts have created platforms for all shades of opinion, and even spawned new areas of criminality.

As we know from the Victorian period, the printed media soon established a series of agendas where it 'accompanied' the police in the act of questioning, investigating and suggesting possible outcomes in high-profile public cases.[36] This inter-relationship grew in power and sophistication as the twentieth century developed and it was, at least partly, fed by a flourishing public interest in all things deviant, gory and mysterious. Criminality became important news and the media's role in tracking down criminal suspects (as well as sometimes turning them into celebrities) became something of a self-appointed duty amongst newspaper editors. Newspapers almost became another branch of policing and justice as the public was invited, at least tacitly, to participate in the series of processes related to the detection and punishment of crimes and the criminals who perpetrate them. Hence newspaper news and opinion acted like an additional, and sometimes alternative, form of justice within British society. Television itself was scarcely far behind this trend, with a plethora of programmes such as *Police Five, Crime Desk* and *Crimewatch* which encouraged the public to assist in the investigation of crimes, alongside a growing fashion for crime reconstruction documentaries and dramas based on true-crime stories.[37]

All these media were capable of sustaining public debate on the nature of real crime, policing and punishment, yet there was also a parallel development which had its roots in the last years of the nineteenth century. Fictionalised portrayals of the world of crime, criminals and policing had existed as early as the advent of the Bow Street Runners. Likewise, it could be argued that both broadside narratives and ballads, which had criminals and crime as their subject matter, were an early form of fictionalisation of the act of crime and its committal. Newspapers, for a long time, had carried reports of crimes, and the actions of the authorities in combatting and suppressing these, but it was the nineteenth century which saw the fictionalisation of crime and criminality and the creation of new genres to narrate and portray these.[38]

Although newspapers carried stories about the Bow Street Runners and later publications like the *Illustrated Police News* took this fictionalisation further, the middle of the century saw the advent of detective fiction which eventually blossomed into the public obsession with the exploits of Sherlock Holmes and Dr Watson. Like factual reporting of crime, criminality and policing, the world of fictional representations of the same phenomena mushroomed throughout the twentieth century. Holmes was joined by a plethora of contemporaries, with some eventually being imported from across the Atlantic. In their content such writings generally displayed an in-built Whig assumption of hope surrounding the triumph of civilisation and progress. However before reaching this denouement, they often touched raw public nerves about the various menaces that were set to transform society for the worse – if they were ever allowed to prevail.

Likewise, depictions of such phenomena that existed in popular novels were joined later in the twentieth century by cinema, fictional radio drama and eventually television. Once again the variety could be staggering with pictures of low-life sub-cultures in both book and film (such as those portrayed in Graham Greene's *Brighton Rock* which was later immortalised in Sir Carol Reed's film adaption) rubbing shoulders in the public consciousness with the moral righteousness and didacticism of Jack Warner's Sergeant Dixon. The latter was a creation who first appeared in Basil Dearden's 1950 film *The Blue Lamp* and rapidly took on an afterlife of its own. It is testament to the public taste for such narratives that, in response to popular demand, Sergeant Dixon was subsequently transformed into a long-running television character that became an icon of policing for audiences and the police themselves – only finally leaving television screens in 1976. Alongside cosy didactic portrayals of commonsense policing, such as Dixon, twentieth-century Britain saw a burgeoning of other police and crime genres that alternatively portrayed, to varying degrees, sleaze, dysfunctionality, corruption, incompetence and amorality. These developments problematised the Whig liberal moral universe, where on occasion, the optimistic resolution of plots gave way to a darker message that stressed aspects of the minimisation of harm. By the end of the twentieth century, the arrival of the 'True Crime' depiction on television and in the cinema had taken over from the printed word. Such genres sometimes showed real police tackling real situations, but endeavoured to turn these into sensationalised drama-laden narratives with a conclusion and a message. Some hybrid genres mixed the factual with fictional reconstruction and sometimes fictional material to augment and sustain the narrative power of the story, thereby transforming both knowledge about individual cases and their treatment.[39]

The impact of fictional moving pictures about policing and crime (including those that mix this with fact) is largely beyond the scope of this book. Yet the transformation these wrought upon the public consciousness in Britain about policing, punishment, crime and government was, to say the least, considerable and remains an inherent theme within this volume. In the second decade of the subsequent century, the production of such genres, public taste for these and sustained interest in the themes they contain, shows absolutely no sign of abating. However, we might also remember that the growing number of such portrayals and their apparent immediacy have the potential to dilute or even deaden public consciousness of the issues being portrayed. At the very least, it seems that the impact of such discussions is becoming more fleeting and transitory – especially with the increasing pace of news coverage and experiences for the viewing and reading public to digest and engage with.

The various media involved in creating these portrayals also firmly have their own agendas that are not typically driven by motives associated with civilisation, good order and the flourishing of society. Media interest and the processes which surround and underpin it produces a cult of celebrity which has been developed around aspects of crime and criminality. The media treatment of some individuals such as Myra Hyndley, Ian Brady, Peter Sutcliffe and Rose and Fred West, fall one side of a line marked by ghoulish repugnance and informed fascination in equal measure. An equally ambivalent phenomenon, perhaps, was the creation and quasi-glorification of a cult of the celebrity criminal that encompassed public fascination with the Kray twins, the Great Train Robbers, the Brink's-MAT heist thieves and, most latterly, the Hatton Garden jewellery gang.[40]

5. The Structure of This Volume

Within this new work we have chosen to continue our reliance upon the structure which informed our previous collection. Each individual chapter commences with an outline of the main developments in each of the subjects covered. These will give readers an account of the events, policies and legislation that had significant impact on these topics during the twentieth century. The chapters are referenced with guidance on sources which inform the conclusions portrayed and directions for further reading. The next section in each chapter is devoted to the scholarship of the particular issue being examined. As well as outlining the key arguments and debates surrounding a given topic, this section also indicates any lacunae in research and invites future scholars to fill in these gaps. This account is followed in each chapter by an in-depth case study, which offers an opportunity to appreciate the whole context of a particular area, alongside the dilemmas and imperatives that concern all individuals, institutions and stakeholders involved. Such case studies bring such dry issues around legislation and policy to life, by enabling readers to see how decisions in all areas of policing, punishment and crime have direct consequences in real (and even sometimes imaginary) situations. After this introduction, the volume's individual chapters cover various aspects of the changing nature of crime and punishment in twentieth-century Britain and society's reactions to them. The analysis provided aims to reflect the development of legal thinking about each topic, but also the approach adopted by government, policing authorities, the media and the public at large.

The first chapter, by Anne-Marie Kilday, outlines the history and scholarship on homicide and serial murder and the variants of this type of crime. It also examines how these related crimes have altered significantly over the course of the twentieth century. Over this period the perception that murder was perpetrated by person or persons unknown has mushroomed – yet hard evidence demonstrates that this was emphatically not the case, and that such events still predominantly happen between individuals known to one another. Through this subject we glimpse a range of wider cultural and social concerns about the nature of violent crime and its perceived escalation, in particular British society's growing obsession with fatal violence. Likewise the apparent safety of the public seems to be compromised, by perceptions that the justice system continuously failed to deal adequately with the mentally unstable perpetrators of violence – those who, within the narrative of moral panic, appear released to prey on an unsuspecting public. Such fears of homicide, and the panic associated with instances of fatal violence, seemed wholly justified to a public who witnessed a steady, but sustained, statistical increase in unlawful deaths in Britain after 1960. Our specific interest in these crimes emerges as surprisingly unpredictable and piecemeal and the chapter offers an explanation of why this was and still is the case. It surveys the criminological theories that explain this through its concluding case study of the Mancunian killer Trevor Hardy. The chapter suggests that these theories overlook historical context which adds new dimensions of explanation. Only by appreciating these together can the history of crime explain why some murders attain spectacular notoriety whilst others remain relatively obscure and unnoticed.

Following on from this, Chapter Three, by Lucy Williams and Barry Godfrey, examines serious property offences over the course of the twentieth century. It investigates the nature of crimes such as burglary, breaking and entering, robbery and serious fraud, alongside statistical trends in offending over the course of the century. These are analysed and explained through the examination of the context around patterns of offending, including such factors as the impact of warfare, unemployment and poverty. The twentieth century's growth and boom in technology, as well as social and spatial mobility, are revealed to have their dark side in their multiplication of opportunities for the pursuit and perpetration of these types of crimes. Because such crimes appeared less serious than the aforementioned violent and fatal ones, they sometimes spawned the phenomenon of the property criminal as folk/popular hero who indulges in some quasi-redistribution of wealth and perceived popular moral restitution. This is a theme that, in particular, emerges from the chapter's concluding case studies of the Great Train Robbery and the exploits of the Kray twins and Richardson brothers, where the tone of popular opinion regarding their actions occasionally emerges as surprisingly ambivalent.

Chapter four, by David Nash, investigates hate crime targeted against minorities. This emerges as a newly defined crime over the course of the twentieth century, and the chapter charts this as a vehicle for a range of legal, social and policing developments and reforms. From its coining as a vague concept, the chapter outlines how the definition of this type of criminality, and the supposed cordon of protection that it afforded religious and ethnic minorities, burgeoned over the century as agendas of rights and protection similarly expanded. The history of hate crime is examined by focussing upon its single most important driver over the century – racial hate crime. Although the government had conceived of ethnic minorities in the nineteenth century as a problem, this attitude had been utterly transformed by the last quarter of the twentieth century. The growing awareness of human rights and perceptions of responsibility meant that government agencies were increasingly tasked with ensuring peace and personal protection for ethnic minority groups and individuals. However, in offering such protection for minorities, other areas, such as blasphemy laws and religious hate crime, also introduced the more complicated and conflicting requirement to safeguard freedom of expression. The case study that concludes this chapter is the long drawn out cause célèbre of the Stephen Lawrence case. The horrific facts of the cruel murder of an innocent young man have acted as a lightning rod that exposed late twentieth-century Britain's failings around hate crime in an almost unbelievable number of areas. Its resonating power exposed the failings of the police and other agencies and illuminated, to a shocked media and public, the alienation of whole communities. Moreover, institutional racism became identified not simply with active hate but also with surprisingly mundane behaviours such as inertia, inattention, poor practice and serial procedural ineptitude. The eventual inquiry into the case, and its report, grew into a work of literature that told British society how it had failed – yet it finished by offering lessons for the future that are still being digested, learned and implemented.

The Sixth chapter of the volume by Johannes Dillinger investigates terrorism in the twentieth century and commences with the question of establishing a satisfactory definition of the phenomenon. This definition had altered from the nineteenth century to ally this crime with new social and cultural fears that stalked the later twentieth-century landscape. In particular, the chapter demonstrates that terrorism was, in the early twentieth-century mind at least, perpetrated by those outside of society – that is, interlopers who brought alien and destructive ideas into more stable societies to effectively prey on and terrorise these. By the latter twentieth century, however, societies had to confront the fact that such settled and secure enclaves were now producing their own worrying range of dangerous opponents, refuseniks and discontents who were radicalised to become the previously unnoticed enemy within.

After cataloguing the activities of a number of examples of terrorist organisations, the chapter chooses to examine the IRA in considerable detail. It investigates how this organisation was tackled by policing methodologies but also importantly, it identifies how, in particular, the law constantly developed to combat terrorists and their evolving methods. When outrages occurred, and attracted the 'oxygen of publicity', populations were terrorised and governments always appeared unprepared and negligent as the nature of each outrage increased concern. Whilst the IRA demonstrated that terrorism was an horrific extension of political aims, in other hands this violent activity straddled the period into the first years of the twenty-first century and appeared to be the inevitable outcome of earlier trends in terrorist violence. This suggestion is best demonstrated by the case study of 7/7 which concludes this chapter. The scale of terrorist atrocity and its practice without warning by indigenous 'insiders' ensured that the potential for terrorism was constant. All the necessary security to prevent this, and the radicalisation which caused it, have become lingering and constant threats as Britain has been forced into becoming a full-time 'vigilant' and surveillance society.

The seventh chapter, written by Clifford Williamson, traces the moral panics associated with the interaction between popular music and deviance over the twentieth-century period. Commencing with the pre–rock 'n' roll era, through the youth movements of the 1960s and '70s, it looks at the relationship between popular music and disorder as conceived of by social institutions and the media. Through a detailed investigation of this, the chapter highlights the paucity of serious academic studies of the history of popular music and its relationship to concepts of deviance. This theme, and others, are emphasised by the chapter's case study which looks at the 'pay party' movement of the rave era. This scene associated music and dance with juvenile delinquency, public disorder, casual recreational drug use and episodic attempts by government agencies to try and curb this basket of illicit and deviant behaviours.

After this analysis, the chapter by Heather Shore examines organised crimes and their impacts upon wider society over the course of the modern era. It begins by discussing the comparative dearth of detailed work upon the subject. The early twentieth century was precisely the period when organised crime came to public attention through popular discourses (chiefly from the entertainment industry) about gangsterism, which itself reflected a strong American influence. Yet this was at odds with Britain's own experience, which was less about high-profile gangster figures and far more about the hidden underworld of networks and other profitable links which enabled this phenomenon to flourish. By the middle of the century, the chapter notes a shift towards a more modern conception of the career criminal had occurred. This was an individual most frequently engaged in what Shore describes as 'project crime'. These were elaborate episodes that involved substantial planning, alongside reliance on the older networks which had previously supported more petty and more regular 'ongoing' crime, something which the early century more readily identified with a criminal underworld.

In the early part of the twentieth century, 'ongoing' crime was represented by gambling, prostitution and protection racketeing. This was later replaced by such criminals pursuing longer term objectives such as major bank robberies, spectacular heists, ambitious drug trafficking and widespread organised frauds. The two sections of case studies map this transition precisely. The first is an examination of the activities of the Sabini brothers whose racecourse gambling racket involved the routine dispensing of violence to those who stood in their way. The analysis of their activities demonstrates the link between organised crime and the use of violence as a tool to further illicit activity. The second group of studies examines a collection of 'project crimes' which demonstrates both their increased ambition and variety over the course of the twentieth century. These emerge as projects which could arguably only be conducted in the modern era by groups who demonstrate recently evolved characteristics, which appear so strongly identified with the whole notion of modern organised crime.

The penultimate chapter in the volume, by Helen Johnston, moves away from the examination of forms of crime to look at the experience of punishment regimes throughout the twentieth century. Attitudes to this area evolved significantly over the century and this process also displays many of the themes which drove debate about this aspect of the criminal justice system during the more modern era. The early twentieth-century punishment system clearly had to address a number of legacies which it had inherited from the nineteenth century. The problem of how and why to punish delinquent youths was one of these that remained a constant issue throughout the period and indeed was not wholly resolved by the end of the period.

Undoubtedly, as the chapter indicates, the function and composition of the prison altered in the second half of the twentieth century as a result of the abolition of capital punishment. This was to have an impact upon the size, scale and need to provide for a growing prison population. The pathway to the various changes that occurred is picked up in the chapter's first case study relating to the sentencing and execution of Peter Anthony Allen and Gwynne Owen Evans in 1964. The establishment of incarceration as the central tenet of Britain's penal policy by the end of the 1960s ensured that prisons became objects of study and criticism, as is demonstrated by the chapter's key theme which highlights the impetus behind, and evidence which argued for, reform. This theme emerges in the second case study outlining the findings of the Mountbatten Report of 1966, which focussed on the issue of prison security after an unprecedented volume of escapes and a noted atmosphere of unrest within the nation's prisons. The Mountbatten analysis was representative of many later reports which would regularly highlight deficiencies in everything from prison security to aspects of the accommodation and treatment of inmates – issues that continued to be discussed at regular intervals into the twenty-first century.

The final chapter of this book, by Neil Davie, addresses the issue of law enforcement in twentieth-century Britain. It examines both organisational and operational changes, such as the introduction of women police officers and policy initiatives aimed at making the service more ethnically diverse. It also highlights the history of the introduction of modern tools, procedures and technologies to aid the detection and apprehension of criminals. Alongside this is a story of greater centralisation and government control of the police service and its remit over time. This, in turn, made the service into a more obvious servant of government and particularly of Home Office imperatives. It also incited something of a national obsession with statistics regarding the perpetration, detection and clear-up rate of crimes at any given time. Several of these themes become clear in the case study which concludes this chapter.

Davie's analysis looks at how the Royal Commission on Criminal Procedure, which reported in 1981, ushered in a period in which police procedure, its credibility and its effectiveness was under particularly close scrutiny. Its deliberations were swiftly followed by an unprecedented wave of rioting and civil disorder which broke out across Britain in 1981. The magnitude of these led to an even deeper examination of police activities and community relations in the shape of the Scarman Report. The outcome of these three events was to lead to the construction and implementation of the Police And Criminal Evidence act (PACE) of 1984. Davie's case study concludes with an examination of the workings of PACE and assesses its relative success or failure in the immediate aftermath of these events. As such, the conclusion of this story ties in well with the discussion of the subsequent events and issues which form part of the earlier chapter by Nash.

Taken together, these chapters do not bring the history of crime and punishment in the twentieth century either up to date or to a conclusion. Much is still unknown, and significant avenues of research are yet to be fully explored. What the chapters of this volume do offer, however, is a stepping stone between the nineteenth century and our own time. Many of the issues that society had to confront in the early part of the twentieth century remain contentious into the twenty-first century.

Notes

1. There are numerous works that offer insights into twentieth-century crime in the British context, but they relate to specific aspects of criminal history, rather than providing a broad overview of experiences and how they have changed over the course of the modern era – see for instance P. Adey (2016) *Crime, Regulation and Control During the Blitz: Protecting the Population of Bombed Cities* (London: Bloomsbury); D.J. Cox, K. Stevenson, C. Harris and J. Rowbotham (2015) *Public Indecency in England 1857–1960* (London: Routledge); V. Bailey (2014 edition) *Order and Disorder in Modern Britain: Essays on Riot, Crime, Policing and Punishment* (London: Breviary Stuff Publications); M. Roodhouse (2013) *Black Market Britain: 1939–1955* (Oxford: Oxford University Press); K. Laybourn and D. Taylor (2011) *Policing in England and Wales, 1918–39: The Fed, Flying Squads and Forensics* (Basingstoke: Palgrave) and L. Seal (2014) *Capital Punishment in Twentieth-Century Britain: Audience, Justice, Memory* (London: Routledge). The one exception to this is notably C. Emsley (2011) *Crime and Society in*

Twentieth-Century England (Harlow: Pearson) which focuses on the English experience of criminality. Although this work does not adopt a systematically structured approach, it is nonetheless an excellent introduction to the criminal history of the period. Other works relating to crime in the twentieth century have more of a criminological or sociological focus than a historical one such as E. Carrabine, P. Cox, M. Lee and N. South (2002) *Crime in Modern Britain* (Oxford: Oxford University Press); R. Gartner and B. McCarthy (eds) (2014) *The Oxford Handbook of Gender, Sex and Crime* (Oxford: Oxford University Press) and P. Knepper and A. Johansen (eds) (2016) *The Oxford Handbook of the History of Crime and Criminal Justice* (Oxford: Oxford University Press). Nevertheless, they are indicative of the potential to be gained from interdisciplinary collaborations between scholars interested in the relationship between crime, the law and public opinion. Finally, there are other works of a more 'popular' nature which can, despite their typical concentration on sensationalised cases or notorious individuals, augment our understanding of criminality in the twentieth-century era. Examples include J. Pearson (2015 edition) *The Profession of Violence: The Rise and Fall of the Kray Twins* (London: William Collins); E. Williams (1992 edition) *Beyond Belief: The Moors Murders – The Story of Ian Brady and Myra Hindley* (London: Pan) and J. Morris (2015) *The Who's Who of British Crime* (Stroud: Amberley Publishing).

2. A.-M. Kilday and D.S. Nash (eds) (2010) *Histories of Crime: Britain 1600–2000* (Basingstoke: Palgrave).

3. In addition to those works cited in the first part of note 1 above, see also B. Godfrey and D.J. Cox (2014) *Policing the Factory: Theft, Private Policing and the Law in Modern England* (London: Bloomsbury); H. Croall (2001) *Understanding White Collar Crime* (London: Open University Press); C. Emsley (2013) *Soldier, Sailor, Beggarman, Thief: Crime and the British Armed Services Since 1914* (Oxford: Oxford University Press); L. Bland (2013) *Modern Women on Trial: Sexual Transgression in the Age of the Flapper* (Manchester: Manchester University Press) and P. Cox (2003) *Gender, Justice and Welfare: Bad Girls in Britain, 1900–1950* (Basingstoke: Palgrave).

4. See C. Emsley (2004 edition) *The English Police: A Political and Social History* (London: Routledge); D. Jones (1996) *Crime and Policing in the Twentieth Century: The South Wales Experience* (University of Wales Press) and especially C.A. Williams (2011) *Police and Policing in the Twentieth Century* (London: Routledge).

5. G. McLagan (2007) *Bent Coppers: The Inside Story of Scotland Yard's Battle against Police Corruption* (London: Orion) and M. Gillard and L. Flynn (2004) *Untouchables: Dirty Cops, Bent Justice and Racism in Scotland Yard* (London: Cutting Edge Press).

6. See for instance K.D. Watson (2010) *Forensic Medicine in Western Society: A History* (London: Routledge); T. Golan (2007) *Laws of Men and Laws of Nature: The History of Scientific Expert Testimony in England and America* (Cambridge, MA: Harvard University Press); C.D. Adam (2016) *Forensic Evidence in Court: Evaluation and Scientific Opinion* (Chichester: John Wiley and Sons) and A. Adam (2015) *A History of Forensic Science: British Beginnings in the Twentieth Century* (London: Routledge).

7. See C. Mullins (1990) *Error of Judgement: The Truth about the Birmingham Bombings* (Dublin: Poolbeg Press).

8. See for instance P. Britton (2013 edition) *The Jigsaw Man: The Remarkable Career of Britain's Foremost Criminal Psychologist* (London: Transworld Publishers) and J. Olsson (2009) *Wordcrime: Solving Crime through Forensic Linguistics* (London: Continuum).

9. For further discussion of these developments in a modern British context see the pertinent references in note 1 above as well as P. Rock (ed.) (1988) *A History of British Criminology* (Oxford: Clarendon Press); M. Maguire, R. Morgan and R. Reiner (eds) (2012 edition) *The Oxford Handbook of Criminology* (Oxford: Oxford University Press); T. Newburn (2012 edition) *Criminology* (London: Routledge); S. Jones (2013 edition) *Criminology* (Oxford: Oxford University Press) and C. Hale, K. Hayward, A. Wahidin and E. Wincup (eds) (2013 edition) *Criminology* (Oxford: Oxford University Press).

10. For further discussion see for instance P. Davies, P. Francis and C. Greer (eds) (2007) *Victims, Crime and Society* (London: Sage) and S. Walklate (ed.) (2007) *Handbook of Victims and Victimology* (Cullompton: Willan).

11. For further discussion see K. Stevenson (2010) '"Most Intimate Violations": Contextualising the Crime of Rape', in A.-M. Kilday and D.S. Nash (eds) *Histories of Crime: Britain 1600–2000* (Basingstoke: Palgrave), pp. 80–99; S. Lees (2002) *Carnal Knowledge: Rape on Trial* (London: The Women's Press); J. Temkin (1996) *Rape and the Legal Process* (Oxford: Oxford University Press) and H. Jones and K. Cook (2008) *Rape Crisis: Responding to Sexual Violence* (London: Russell House Publishing).

12. 'Why are Northern Ireland's abortion laws different to the rest of the UK?' *BBC News Magazine*, 8th April 2016. Available at http://www.bbc.co.uk/news/magazine-35980195 (Accessed 8th October 2017).

13. For further discussion see David Nash's chapter in this volume as well as A.-M. Kilday and D.S. Nash (2017) *Shame and Modernity in Britain: 1890 to the Present* (Basingstoke: Palgrave); M.A. Walters (2014) *Hate Crime and Restorative Justice: Exploring Causes, Repairing Harms* (Oxford: Oxford University Press) and N. Chakraborti and J. Garland (2015) *Hate Crime: Impact, Causes and Responses* (London: Sage).

14. See for instance G, Ellison and J. Smyth (2000) *The Crowned Harp: Policing Northern Ireland* (London: Pluto Press); C. Ryder (2004) *The Fateful Split: The Failure of Policing in Northern Ireland* (London: Methuen Publishing); J. Jackson and S. Doran (1995) *Judge Without Jury: Diplock Trials in the Adversary System* (Oxford: Clarendon Press) and J. Moran (2008) *Policing the Peace in Northern Ireland: Politics, Crime and Security after the Belfast Agreement* (Manchester: Manchester University Press).

15. For further discussion see R.G. Smith, P. Grabosky and G. Urbas (eds) (2004) *Cyber Criminals on Trial* (Cambridge: Cambridge University Press).

16. For further discussion see Kim Stevenson's chapter in this volume as well as M. O'Brien (2006) 'The Witchfinder-General and Will-o'-the-Wisp: The Myth and Reality of Internet Control', *Information and Communications Technology Law*, Vol. 15, No. 3, pp. 259–73; A.A. Gillespie (2011) *Child Pornography: Law and Policy* (London: Routledge) and D.C. Wilson and I. Silverman (2002) *Innocence Betrayed: Paedophilia, the Media and Society* (London: Polity Press).

17. See for instance V. Gatrell (1996 edition) *The Hanging Tree: Execution and the English People 1770–1868* (Oxford: Oxford University Press); H. Johnston (2015) *Crime in England 1815–1880: Experiencing the Criminal Justice System* (London: Routledge); D. Taylor (2010) *Hooligans, Harlots and Hangmen: Crime and Punishment in Victorian Britain* (Westport: Praeger) and R.W. Ireland (2007) *A Want of Good Order and Discipline: Rules, Discretion and the Victorian Prison* (Cardiff: University of Wales Press).

18. This debate is especially pertinent and enduring in the North American context, see for instance L. Wall (2016) *The Death Penalty Debate: Exploring the Hidden Costs of Capital Punishment* (New York: Real Clear Politics); J. Bren Guernsey (2009) *Death Penalty: Fair Solution or Moral Failure?* (New York: Twenty-First Century Books) and E. Van den Haag (1983) *The Death Penalty: A Debate* (New York: Springer).

19. See D.D. Gray (2015) *Crime, Policing and Punishment in England, 1660–1914* (London: Bloomsbury); H. Potter (2013) *Hanging in Judgment: Religion and the Death Penalty in England from the Bloody Code to Abolition* (London: SCM Press); D. Garland (1985) *Punishment and Welfare: A*

History of Penal Strategies (Aldershot: Gower) and A. Brown (2003) *English Society and the Prison: Time, Culture and Politics in the Development of the Modern Prison* (London: Boydell Press).

20. For further discussion see various essays in C. Emsley (ed.) (2005) *The Persistent Prison: Problems, Images and Alternatives* (London: Francis Boutle); P. Priestly (1989) *Jail Journeys: The English Prison Experience Since 1918* (London: Routledge) and C. Harding, B. Hines, R. Ireland and P. Rawlings (1985) *Imprisonment in England and Wales: A Concise History* (London: Croom Helm).

21. See J. Muncie (1990) 'Failure Never Matters: Detention Centres and the Politics of Deterrence', *Critical Social Policy*, Vol. 10, No. 28, pp. 53–66.

22. See various articles on the British experience in M. Tonry (ed.) (1991) *Penal Reform in Overcrowded Times* (Oxford: Oxford University Press) and Sir D. Ramsbotham (2005) *Prisongate: The Shocking State of Britain's Prisons and the Need for Visionary Change* (London: Simon and Schuster).

23. See the references in note 21 above as well as various essays in Y. Jewkes (ed.) (2007) *Handbook on Prisons* (Cullompton: Willan).

24. See for instance J. Boyle (1977) *A Sense of Freedom: An Autobiography* (London: Ebury Press); J. McVicar (1979) *McVicar by Himself* (London: Arrow Books). For a celebrity prisoner's multifaceted view of different prison regimes see J. Archer (2000–2004) *Prison Diaries* (3 vols) (London: Pan Books).

25. For further discussion see the references in notes 21 and 22 above as well as R. Adams (1994) *Prison Riots in Britain and the USA* (London: Macmillan); A. Brown (2013) *Inter-war Penal Policy and Crime in England: The Dartmoor Convict Prison Riot, 1932* (Basingstoke: Palgrave) and E. Player and M. Jenkins (1994) *Prisons after Woolf: Reform through Riot* (London: Routledge).

26. See the references in notes 21 and 22 above.

27. For a discussion of both the achievements of the prison system, and its setbacks, in the first half of the twentieth century see R. Cross (1971) *Punishment, Prison and the Public* (London: Hamlyn).

28. For an elaboration of the terms of the debate related to this in more recent times see 'Community or Custody? A Tough Question', *BBC News*, 12th September 2011 at http://www.bbc.co.uk/news/uk-14886720 and 'David Cameron: We Must Make Prisons Work for Offenders', *BBC News*, 22nd October 2012 at http://www.bbc.co.uk/news/uk-politics-20022794 and 'Now Even Criminals Say Community Sentences Are a Soft Option', *Daily Mail*, 14th April 2014. (Accessed 15 October 2017)

29. For more on these types of non-custodial approaches see T. Vass (1990) *Alternatives to Custody* (London: Sage) and Y. Jewkes and J. Bennett (eds) (2008) *Dictionary of Prisons and Punishment* (Cullompton: Willan).

30. For further discussion see A.-M. Kilday and D.S. Nash (2017) *Shame and Modernity in Britain: 1890 to the Present* (Basingstoke: Palgrave).

31. For further discussion see V. Bailey (1997) *Delinquency and Citizenship: Reclaiming the Young Offender, 1914–48* (Oxford: Clarendon Press); Cox (2003) *Gender, Justice and Welfare*; J. Muncie (1999 edition) *Youth and Crime* (London: Sage); R. Smith (2013 edition) *Youth Justice: Ideas, Policy and Practice* (London: Routledge) and R.J. Lundman (2001) *Prevention and Control of Juvenile Delinquency* (Oxford: Oxford University Press).

32. For further discussion see B.P. Block and J. Hostettler (1997) *Hanging in the Balance: A History of the Abolition of Capital Punishment in* Britain (London: Waterside Press); H. Potter (2013) *Hanging in Judgment: Religion and the Death Penalty in England from the Bloody Code to Abolition* (London: SCM Press); S. Webb (2011) *Execution: A History of Capital Punishment in England* (London: The History Press); R. Clark (2009) *Capital Punishment in Britain* (London: Ian Allen Publishing) and J. Rowbotham (2010) 'Execution as Punishment in England: 1750–2000', in A.-M. Kilday and D.S. Nash (eds) *Histories of Crime: Britain 1600–2000* (Basingstoke: Palgrave), pp. 180–202.

33. See J.J. Eddleston (2000) *Blind Justice: Miscarriages of Justice in Twentieth-Century Britain* (London: Clio).

34. *The Daily Telegraph*, 11th May 2012.

35. See for instance A. Hammel (2010) *Ending the Death Penalty: The European Experience in Global Perspective* (London: Springer), p. 111.

36. For further discussion see for instance T. Boyle (1990) *Black Swine in the Sewers of Hampstead: Beneath the Surface of Victorian Sensationalism* (London: Hodder and Stoughton); J. Flanders (2013) *The Invention of Murder: How the Victorians Revelled in Death and Detection and Created Modern Crime* (London: Thomas Dunne Books) and L.P. Curtis (2001) *Jack the Ripper and the London Press* (New York: Vail-Ballou Press).

37. For further discussion of the relationship between crime and the media which stems from the Victorian era see A.-M. Kilday (2016) 'Constructing the Cult of the Criminal: Kate Webster – Victorian Murderess and Media Sensation', in A.-M. Kilday and D.S. Nash (eds) *True Crime Histories: Micro-Studies in Law, Crime and Deviance Since* 1700 (London: Bloomsbury), pp. 210–50. See also S.E.H. Moore (2014) *Crime and the Media* (Basingstoke: Palgrave); Y. Jewkes (2015 edition) *Media and Crime (Key Approaches to Criminology)* (London: Sage) and D. Wilson (2011) *Looking for Laura: Public Criminology and Hot News* (London: Waterside Press).

38. For further discussion of this see D. Cox (2016) 'Hand in Glove with the Penny-a-liners': The Bow Street "Runners" in Factual and Fictional Narrative', in A.-M. Kilday and D.S. Nash (eds) *True Crime Histories: Micro-Studies in Law, Crime and Deviance Since* 1700 (London: Bloomsbury), pp. 251–89.

39. For further discussion see for instance B. Forshaw (2016) *Brit Noir: The Pocket Essential Guide to British Crime Fiction, Film & TV* (Harpenden: Old Castle Books); J. Earwalker (2002) *Scene of the Crime: A Guide to the Landscapes of British Detective Fiction* (London: Aurum Press); P. Elliott (2016) *Studying the British Crime Film* (Leighton Buzzard: Auteur) and S. Chibnall and R. Murphy (eds) (1999) *British Crime Cinema* (London: Routledge).

40. See for instance the chapter by A.-M. Kilday in this volume as well as I. Madoc-Jones, C. Gordon, S. Dubberley and C. Hughes (2014) 'From Celebrity Criminal to Criminal Celebrity: Concerning the "Celebrification" of Sex Crime in the UK', *British Journal of Community Justice*, Vol. 12, No. 3, pp. 35–48.

2

Britain's 'Most Wanted': Homicide and Serial Murder since 1900

Anne-Marie Kilday

1. Introduction

There are various reasons why a volume on the history of criminal activity in twentieth-century Britain should feature a chapter on homicide. First of all, homicide has always been regarded as the most serious and extreme criminal offence that can be committed. Throughout history and across cultures, homicide has had an extensive reach and a lasting significance for those individuals affected by its perpetration.[1] In addition, unlawful fatal violence is worthy of scholarly attention as it has been a ubiquitous feature of human societies. Its incidence has been well documented too, particularly during the modern era, and certainly in comparison with other manifestations of violent criminality.[2] This is certainly the case in Britain, where it is perfectly possible to trace homicidal activity over the course of the twentieth century (as we will see in due course) and make some significant observations about trends in its nature and associated characteristics.

However, a study of homicide can reveal much more than this. As Pieter Spierenburg has argued:

Killing always affects the fundamental values of those who participate in and witness the act, thus providing valuable information about culture, social hierarchy, and gender relations. In turn, a consideration of broad social change over the long terms increases our understanding of the history of killing. Hence, the subject lies at the crossroads of historical scholarship and criminology.[3]

Certainly then, a history of homicide in twentieth-century Britain can inform us about individuals who kill, the victims they affect and how the characteristics of homicide have changed over time. But it can also act as a prism onto wider social concerns relating to a given historical context. In part, this relates to the third and final reason for the inclusion of a study of homicide in this work: the unrelenting fascination that popular audiences have for this particular type of violent crime.[4] Some scholars have likened the interest in murder amongst the British public to an addiction and have described it as 'virtually insatiable'.[5] The evidently fascinating and pervasive link between unlawful killing, legal attitudes and public opinion has ensured that homicide has retained a powerful relevance over time, and has resulted in the crime being regarded as a microcosm for various aspects of social tension and social change. This chapter will try to determine why homicide was such a 'national obsession' in Britain throughout the twentieth century and, indeed, why that fixation largely continues unabated to this day.[6]

In studying the chronology of homicide, the next section of this chapter will outline the ways in which the definition of this type of offence changed over the course of twentieth-century British history. It will also address the legal context for the offence and the trends in homicidal activity since 1900 in order to assess whether the modern moral panic about unlawful fatal violence, especially since the 1970s, has been justified. This will then be followed by an outline of the historiography relating to homicide, which will identify the extent to which trends in scholarship have mirrored the popular fascination with murder. The case study for this chapter is an analysis of the crimes of the peculiarly obscure Manchester serial killer Trevor Hardy in order to ascertain why some twentieth-century murderers achieve notoriety and significant media attention whilst others do not. The concluding section of the chapter will highlight various avenues for future historical research.

2.   Chronology

a)   Definition and Legal Context

Homicide is a legal category of behaviour which involves the killing of another person, whether lawful (e.g. death caused by military combat) or unlawful. There are three recognised types of unlawful killing: murder, manslaughter and infanticide. Rather surprisingly, the crime of murder has never been statutorily defined in Britain. The accepted definition of murder in England and Wales was laid down in the early seventeenth century by the celebrated jurist Sir Edward Coke, and although heavily criticised as being 'misleading' and 'out-of-date' by many, it is still held in high regard by legal commentators and found to be persuasive amongst judges in the present day.[7] Coke explained that murder occurred

> when a person of sound memory, and the age of discretion, unlawfully killeth within any country of the realm any reasonable creature in *rerum natura* under the Kings peace, with malice aforethought, either expressed by the party or implied by law, so as the party wounded, or hurt, etc., die of the wound or hurt, etc., within year and a day after the same.[8]

The phrase *rerum natura* means 'in being' and was included by Coke to distinguish between the killing of a human being and that of an unborn child. During the twentieth century in England and Wales, much of Coke's initial definition was still applicable in law – a killing could only be defined as such if the evidence pointed to *actus reus* (an unlawful act) and to *mens reas* (a guilty mind). The killing also had to take place within the jurisdiction of the monarch. The only evident change to Coke's definition came in 1996 with the Law Amendment Act which abolished the 'year and a day' clause and left the determination over the periodicity of a killing to the Attorney General, based on the circumstances of how the victim had died.[9]

In 1957, the Homicide Act laid out three defences for murder which could result in the alternative, lesser charge of manslaughter. The first of these was diminished responsibility, where an individual evidently suffered from an abnormality of the mind which 'substantially' impaired his or her responsibility in terms of the act of killing in question. The second defence was provocation, where an individual lost self-control by things said or done by another person. Crucially in these instances, the jury had to determine whether the provocation was such that a 'reasonable man' would have behaved in the same way as the defendant. The final defence to murder was if a killing occurred in the pursuance of a suicide pact.[10] Both before and after 1957, if there were no appropriate defences to murder and the defendant was convicted of that crime, the death penalty could be imposed until its suspension in 1965 and abolition in 1969.[11] After that time a mandatory life sentence was given. Criteria to determine the exact duration of life sentences was clarified in the Criminal Justice Act 2003, a piece of legislation which had a notable impact on the subject of our case study in this chapter, Trevor Hardy.[12]

These three legal defences to murder remain with us today and as can be seen, the key consideration which separates a crime of murder from one of manslaughter relates to the notion of *mens rea* or, as Sir Edward Coke would have it, 'malice aforethought' – the state of mind of the defendant at the time of the killing. Did the individual intend to kill or to inflict grievous bodily harm on the victim? In England and Wales there are two types of manslaughter. Voluntary manslaughter applies when one (or more) of the three defences to murder have been proven. Involuntary manslaughter, on the other hand, applies when a defendant did not intend to kill or cause serious injury but blame of some sort can still be apportioned to the cause of death of the victim. For instance, the death might have occurred as the unintended consequences of another criminal act (deemed constructive manslaughter) or it might have occurred due to carelessness or incompetence (deemed reckless or gross negligence manslaughter).[13]

The final category of unlawful killing after murder and manslaughter is infanticide. This species of homicide was defined for England and Wales in the twentieth century by the Infanticide Act of 1922 and clarified by further legislation in 1938. The offence is described as the killing of a new-born child (aged 12 months or less) by its mother when the balance of her mind was disturbed due to the effects of giving birth.[14] Most scholars choose to separate infanticide from their consideration of types of unlawful killing as its definition is so specific and distinct from murder and manslaughter.[15] This chapter will not consider infanticide in any detail, although its incidence will be acknowledged as part of the trends in unlawful killing in twentieth-century Britain outlined below.

In Scotland, there is no separate offence of infanticide. Rather, the killing of a new-born infant by its mother is classed as either murder or as the Scottish equivalent of manslaughter – common law 'culpable homicide'.[16] Historically, having a definition for the broad term of homicide, rather than that of any associated sub-categories, appears to have been more important to Scottish jurists. This may have been because Scottish Law has largely been founded on common law (more so than in England and Wales) and as such, its basis lies more with tradition than with statute. This has meant that throughout history Scottish Law has often been more concerned with the practicalities of the prosecution of an indictment rather than a complex legal definition on which an indictment might be founded. In the eighteenth century, Baron David Hume defined homicide, simply, as a crime 'by which life is taken away, and the person of a human creature is destroyed.'[17] Interestingly, he makes no reference in this to the issue of 'malice aforethought' which was such a perennial concern of English legal authorities. Hume recognised four categories of homicide which he related in descending order of severity: aggravated murder, murder, culpable homicide and murder free from all blame. It was left to the courts' discretion (rather than the information contained in any statutory directive) to determine which of the four charges should apply based on the particular circumstances of a given case.[18]

Over time, however, these four categories of unlawful killing blended together so that just two remained: murder and culpable homicide, and slightly more detailed definitions of these offences began to appear. By 1948, for instance, a clearer definition of murder was provided which described it as

> Any wilful act causing the destruction of life, whether intended to kill, or displaying such wicked recklessness as to imply a disposition depraved enough to be regardless of the consequences.[19]

During the twentieth century, there were two partial defences to murder in Scottish law. The first of these was provocation, which could take the form of violence or the discovery of infidelity (where the expectation of fidelity was reasonable). The response made by the defendant in instances such as this had to be both immediate and proportionate. The second defence to murder was diminished responsibility where a mental disorder of some description caused a substantial impairment of the defendant's ability to employ self-control.[20] As can be seen, these defences are not that dissimilar from their English equivalents, although the Scottish versions are more related to applying the law in practice and as such are more narrow and succinct. Further similarities between English and Scottish Law appear when we consider descriptions of culpable homicide in the twentieth century. A charge of culpable homicide could be incurred if a death resulted from an unlawful act, from recklessness or in instances where either provocation or diminished responsibility were proven defences to murder.[21] This description compares well with the English equivalent of manslaughter, but, once again, the Scottish description appears more condensed. It should be added that in Scotland between 1900 and 1965, murder could result in the death penalty. Effectively, after that date it carried a mandatory life sentence.[22] In cases of culpable homicide, judges have complete discretion in the sentencing of any individual convicted, as was the case with manslaughter in the English context.[23]

b) Trends in Incidence and Explanations Offered

Scholars are generally in agreement that there has been a persistent decline in homicidal violence since the early modern period. As Manuel Eisner describes 'homicide rates declined significantly across Europe from the Middle Ages to the nineteenth century, but … there were significant differences in the timing and speed of that decline.'[24] The main reason given by historians, sociologists and criminologists for the downturn in violent behaviour over time relates to Norbert Elias's celebrated theory of the so-called 'civilising process'.[25] This theory suggests that across several centuries individuals have developed personalities which increasingly enable them to employ rationality and self-control in a variety of situations. By deploying greater self-control, everyday interactions become more conciliatory and this in turn manifests itself in lower levels of violent behaviour and violent criminality.[26]

The historic downward trend in homicide recorded by scholars in many European countries has also been evident in relation to Britain more specifically. Moreover, as far as the twentieth century is concerned, scholars have described how the decline in unlawful killing continued until the 1950s period, at which point there is evidence of a sharp rise in indictments for this type of offence.[27]

Figure 2.1 traces indictments for murder, manslaughter or culpable homicide and infanticide for Scotland, England and Wales over the course of the twentieth century, using judicial statistics recorded in the House of Commons Parliamentary Papers.[28] Although this material provides an interesting picture of the trends in unlawful killing between 1900 and 1999, we need to bear in mind deficiencies in the data and socio-economic factors which might affect the recording of statistics. For instance, as we have already seen, the changing legal definition of what constitutes an instance of 'murder' as opposed to an instance of 'manslaughter' was changed and clarified over the course of the twentieth century. This means that a killing classified as a murder before the Homicide Act was passed in 1957 might be deemed a manslaughter if it occurred after that date. We might also want to think about how trends in homicidal

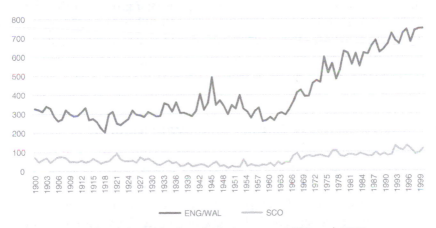

Figure 2.1 Unlawful Deaths in Britain between 1900 and 1999

activity compare with demographic change in Britain over the course of the twentieth century, or the extent to which the development of medicine and medical provision impacted upon homicide levels by improving survival rates for violent and aggravated assault.[29]

Although there is no real evidence of a deepening decline in homicidal activity in the first half of the century from the data series in Figure 2.1 as some scholars have indicated was the case, it is true to say nevertheless, that the incidence of unlawful killing was low during this period in Britain as a whole (and in Scotland in particular) up until 1960. According to Terence Morris and Louis Blom-Cooper, writing in 1964, the first half of the twentieth century was a period where by and large unlawful killing was 'not only a rare phenomenon but one characterised by a stability which is most marked when comparisons are made with other types of serious crimes.'[30]

The graph does bear out the suggestion that the homicide rate increased sharply in the second half of the century, particularly after 1960, although this incline is not quite so marked north of the Tweed.[31] Various explanations for this increase have been offered by historical criminologists, and they centre around contextual factors which prevailed in many European countries at this time. These include the growing importance of evening recreational activities; immigration and related ethnic, cultural and religious tensions; de-industrialisation; a waning of certain aspects of the 'civilising process' such as deference to superiors; a growth in the prevalence of firearms and in the consumption of alcohol and illegal drugs; and a significant expansion in organised crime.[32] More research needs to be done to assess the extent of the applicability of these explanations to the British context during the modern era.

c)   The Paradoxical Moral Panic over Homicide

Despite the evident increase in homicidal activity after 1960, the figures for this kind of violent criminality in Britain for the second half of the twentieth century still compare favourably with that of many other countries during the same period.[33] As scholars regularly point out, murder, in modern Britain, is a 'comparative rarity'.[34] Yet, ever since the

Victorian era, we have become increasingly fascinated with fatal violence and increasingly fearful of its incidence.[35] Facilitated by rapid changes in forms of modern media and fuelled by expanding commercial interests which capitalised on evident popular interest in the macabre, a particular 'frenzy' over homicidal activity developed in modern Britain.[36] However, the resulting 'moral panic' associated with murder in particular was evidently exaggerated and inappropriate. As scholar Paul Rock argues: 'British criminologists have tended to describe murder as statistically uncommon, socially contained and morally equivocal, a mundane problem whose gravity has been somewhat overblown by popular and press misconceptions centred on the reporting of egregious cases.'[37]

One of the reasons homicide became such a focus for attention in twentieth-century Britain was the growing importance of new categories or types of murder. In the main, descriptions and definitions of these new murder types were provided by American criminologists and law enforcement experts in the 1970s, and were widely discussed and reported across the Atlantic. Mass murder, for instance, was said to be committed when an assailant killed several people in public, at the same geographical location over a short period of time. Spree murder, on the other hand, also resulted in multiple victims being killed in public, but not necessarily at the same geographical location and there might be a time lag in between offences. Finally, serial murder (formerly called 'stranger killing') occurred when an individual or individuals murder more than one victim but on separate occasions, in private, and with a cooling-off period in between.[38] Unquestionably, it was this latter murder type in particular that aroused the most interest.

Serial murder became something of an unhealthy fascination for many individuals in Britain during the second half of the twentieth century. Again, and as with homicide more generally, this emergent preoccupation was completely disproportionate to the frequency of the actual activity in England, Scotland and Wales between 1900 and 1999.[39] The interest in serial killing and serial killers lies at one extreme end of the well-established pleasure in things ghastly and ghoulish mentioned above. For those individuals who found descriptions of homicide to be both repellent and compelling at the same time, serial murder offered a whole new level of terror, especially after killers such as George Joseph Smith (active

1912–1914), John Reginald Halliday Christie (active 1943–1953) and John George Haigh (active 1944–1949) had initially piqued public and media interest in multiple victim stranger homicides. Individuals increasingly clamoured for detail about the gory, ritualised methodology used to carry out this form of homicide. They wanted to learn more about the unfathomable addiction to murder that these perpetrators appeared to have. Most of all, they enjoyed revelling in the notion that serial killers were unpredictable, and as a result, everyone in society was their potential prey.[40] As Brian Masters explains, serial killers

> strike fear into the heart, for they are somewhere among us, unseen and unsuspected. They use the same shops, catch the same buses and appear in every sense normal. ... But their subterranean lives are a florid expression of Hell, and the damage they wreak is a repellent blot upon human nature ... [they] ... open a window on the nature of evil.[41]

The British preoccupation with serial murder, which evidently burgeoned from the last three decades of the twentieth century onwards, has done much to influence the content and direction of scholarship on the subject of homicide, as we will now discover.

3.   Historiography

It is evident that in terms of scholarship, homicide has been a rather neglected subject of study, particularly in relation to the modern era, and especially with reference to the post-war period.[42] Whilst various scholars have pointed to the importance of understanding the context within which fatal violence occurs as it allows us to better understand the motivation behind this kind of crime and therefore could aid various agencies in future prevention strategies, historians have largely ignored the study of homicide.[43] Arguably, according to sociologist Kevin D. Haggarty, this has resulted in the study of homicide appearing 'a-historical and a-cultural.'[44] Indeed, this area of scholarship has been dominated not by historians, but by criminologists, sociologists and by the work of significant numbers of popular, non-academic writers who have responded to the growing (and seemingly unremitting) public interest in episodes of murder and individuals who kill.

When historians *have* become engaged in the study of British homicide, it has been largely in relation to the calculation of long-term data series.[45] As we have already seen, this information has been collected in a variety of ways by individuals including Paul Hair, Ted Gurr, Lawrence Stone, James Cockburn and Manuel Eisner in an attempt to prove or disprove the notion that modern society is less violent in comparison with earlier periods.[46] Criminologists on the other hand have four areas that dominate their interests in relation to the study of homicide: methodology, gender, the rise of stranger killing and 'victimology'.

Discussions of methodology have largely centred upon whether the evident increase in homicide after 1960 was related to an increase in the availability of firearms in Britain. In the main, this suggestion has been dispelled, and it has been concluded instead that the majority of unlawful killings in modern Britain have occurred after a physical fight of some sort where the victim was cut, kicked or punched to death. Firearms, whilst more prominent in affluent areas compared to more impoverished locations since mid-century, have been used relatively minimally.[47]

Criminologists and sociologists have given far more attention to the nature and characteristics of offenders in homicide cases. In the main this work has resulted in three conclusions about twentieth-century British homicide. First, that male protagonists predominated (although female killers were not insignificant in either number or the degree of brutality they employed) and second, that the number of male victims significantly increased over time.[48] Finally, it was concluded that although killing had become less intimate and domestically based than in previous centuries, it was still more likely for killer and victim to know each other. Media reports of an inexorable rise in predatory stranger-killings in Britain since the 1960s have evidently been grossly exaggerated.[49]

Much more recently, scholars have become very interested in knowing more about the victims of homicide in an attempt to understand why certain types of individuals have been far more vulnerable to this kind of criminal activity than others. When trying to determine causal factors for the trends in homicidal activity in twentieth-century Britain, there surely has to be a better explanation than simply more individuals disposed to behaviour of that kind existed at certain time periods and not others.[50] Rather, it has become clear that understanding how a given historical context can alter an individual's circumstances to make them more 'socially vulnerable' to murderous assault is as important as trying to understand the contextual factors which may have encouraged, or facilitated, an intent to kill within a given individual at a particular time and place.[51] Both of these areas of study are in their academic infancy as far as historians are concerned. However, initial (tentative) insights from a few research studies have revealed interesting results. In relation to serial killing more specifically for instance, babies and young infants, vulnerable teenagers, homosexuals, individuals with ethnic minority backgrounds, prostitutes and the elderly have been identified as the most likely social groups to have been targeted in this kind of homicide in twentieth-century Britain. However, their vulnerability was not fixed or uniform over this period. It was highly complex and dependant on a myriad of political, socio-economic and personal circumstances which regularly operated in a state of flux.[52] Clearly, we have much more to learn about homicide and its inter-relationship with the historical context in which it occurs.

There have been some notable scholarly works on serial killing and serial killers such as those by Peter Vronsky and David Wilson.[53] Although these studies have engaged with historical detail and context to some extent, they have been far more preoccupied with offering the definitive definition of serial murder and associated serial killer types. The accepted typology of serial killing has constructed five types: 'Visionaries' who respond to voices or hallucinations such as Robert Maudsley (active 1973–1978); 'Missionaries' who believe that by their actions they are ridding the world of perceived problems such as Peter Sutcliffe (active 1975–1980); 'Hedonists' or 'Lust Killers' who kill for sexual pleasure such as Dennis Nilsen (active 1978–1983); 'Thrill Killers such as Fred and Rose West (active 1967–1987) who are excited by the terror/pain they inflict on their victims; and, finally, 'Power and Control Killers' such as Ian Brady and Myra Hindley (active 1963–1965) who kill in order to enjoy determining the decision over life and death. Individuals can manifest more than one of these typologies and indeed, in some cases, arguably all five typologies apply.[54]

Aside from these texts however, the vast majority of literature on the subject of serial murder is much more 'popular' in tone and content, mirroring much of the media output on the subject.[55] As has already been argued, the attention given to serial homicide in Britain (and elsewhere) has been overblown and disproportionate to the actual incidence of that kind of offence. Media interest has unnecessarily exposed the public to the grisly details of serial killings, which are exceedingly rare instances in reality, and only appear significant due to the prevailing low rate of homicides in Britain during the modern era.[56] One might argue that to some extent the insatiable addiction to the provision of macabre detail mirrors the addiction to kill amongst the offenders concerned. Anna Gekoski, for instance, likens the interest in serial killing in Britain during the second half of the twentieth century to 'an Olympic event, with its own heroes and records.'[57] To put it another way, the more killings an individual perpetrates, the more the media frenzy and the more potent the cultural ramifications will be in terms of the production of films and writings (both fictional and non-fictional) on the subject.[58]

Often, scant thought appears to have been given to the victims concerned and the families they have left behind in such brutal and tragic circumstances. Few of these works, for instance, aim to better understand serial murder in order to prevent it in the future. Few have considered whether the nature and characteristics of this type of homicide have changed or evolved over time and what clues that might give to crime detection personnel. Few examine the historical context for a given episode of murder and whether that might have influenced the killer and his or her actions with a view to crime prevention. Instead, this voluminous literature prefers to titillate with gory recreations of murder scenes and hyperbolic descriptions of ghoulish fiends who maraud unfettered around us, ready to pounce on unsuspecting prey.

In recent years, we have even seen the fascination with serial homicide develop a stage further as a commercial interest, with objects relating to serial killers and their crime scenes being bought and sold for significant sums by collectors. We have also witnessed the advent of 'dark tourism' where holidays are organised to 'celebrated' murder sites or locations where death and tragedy have occurred.[59] Moreover, and most disturbingly, some serial killers have even reported that the guarantee of 'celebrity' which serial murder evidently provides in the modern era was a key factor which motivated them to kill an innocent victim in the first instance. Moreover it encouraged them to make their offence as gruesome as physically possible so as to be more memorable and also to escalate the frequency and the brutality of their murderous activity over time.[60] The 'popular' fascination with homicide in the modern era, and the fetishisation of serial killing in particular, appears to have developed into something of a symbiotic relationship and, for many, it is something that is inappropriate, insatiable and out of control.

4. Case Study

The preoccupation with homicide, and with serial killers in particular, is certainly a key development of the history of crime in twentieth-century Britain. However, this fascination and attention has not been applied in equal measure to every instance that has occurred. It is evident that since 1900, some killers have received far more attention than others and it is interesting for us to consider why that might have been the case.[61] Trevor Joseph Hardy (1945–2012), for instance, is one serial killer who has achieved less notoriety than many others. This is especially curious if we consider the details of his crimes and compare the media's ignorance of Hardy with the arguably unprecedented frenzy over other serial murderers who also operated in the 1970s, such as the infamous American Theodore (Ted) Bundy (1946–1989) and the British killer Peter Sutcliffe, referred to more commonly as 'The Yorkshire Ripper'.[62]

Fifteen-year-old Manchester schoolgirl (Janet) Lesley Stewart went missing on New Year's Eve, 1974.[63] During the prolonged and extensive police search for Lesley, workmen found the body of a young woman on a building site in Moston and the authorities assumed that they had discovered Lesley's remains.[64] Forensic examinations, however, revealed that the victim found was in fact an 18-year-old barmaid called Wanda Skala. Local newspapers reported in July of 1975 that Wanda had been sexually attacked and then clubbed to death and also noted that her handbag and one of her platform shoes were missing.[65] Interestingly, the day after this was reported in the press, the missing shoe was found on a rubbish tip which had previously been searched by police, indicating that the killer had (somewhat brazenly) returned to the scene of his crime.[66] However, and despite a detailed police investigation, including a reconstruction of the victim's last movements, there seemed to be few clues as to a likely suspect.[67]

Some eight months after this episode, in March 1976, the naked body of a teenage girl was found in a disused lock on the Rochdale Canal. The victim had been strangled. She was later identified as 18-year-old Sharon Mossoph.[68] The details of these two murders, set alongside two other unsolved killings of young girls in the Manchester area and the still unknown whereabouts of Lesley Stewart, began to generate some panic in the community which was reflected in one local press headline: 'GIRLS IN FEAR OF SHARON'S KILLER'.[69] This panic subsided to some extent, however, on the 21st of July 1976, when newspapers revealed that a 31-one-year-old bachelor of no fixed abode, Trevor Joseph Hardy, had been arrested for the murders of both Wanda Skala and Sharon Mossoph: crimes which, up until this point in time, had been seemingly unconnected.[70]

Then, on the 2nd of September 1976, police unearthed the skeleton of a teenage girl on waste ground in the Newton Heath area of Manchester. The skeleton was headless and dismembered, so formal identification was impossible. Nevertheless, police believed the remains to be that of Lesley Stewart who had disappeared nearly two years before. They police were able to be fairly confident in their statement regarding victim identification as they had been given information on where to look for Lesley's body by a man they already had in police custody: Trevor Hardy.[71]

At the time of his arrest, Trevor Hardy was well known to police. In part, this was because of his extensive criminal record which dated back to when he was just eight-years-old.[72] In addition, however, the police had suspected Hardy's involvement in the Wanda Skala murder long before he had confessed to the actual crime. This was because they knew that Hardy had admitted committing the brutal assault and killing of Wanda to his brother Colin, just days after the event, when the two were drinking in a local pub. Hardy's confession to his sibling differed to what he later told police. He said to his brother:

> I did it! I didn't mean to kill her – I was going to mug her. I only wanted her handbag. I hit her with a brick; she must have had a thin or weak skull.[73]

Hardy went on to explain that there had been no sexual motive to the attack as far as he was concerned, but that as he had read a book about the murderous activities of the serial sadist Neville Heath (active 1946), Hardy thought he ought to make the murder *look* sexual so as to hide the fact that it had been a failed robbery of which he might be suspected due to his previous convictions. Thus, Hardy explained, he had bitten off Wanda Skala's right nipple.[74] Trevor Hardy then went back to his brother's flat, where he proceeded to viciously assault Colin and threatened to kill him if he ever repeated what he had been told.

Although clearly petrified, Colin was encouraged by his wife to go to the police and tell them what he knew.[75] Hardy was subsequently arrested and the police demanded an impression of his teeth so as to compare with the bite marks found on Wanda Skala's breast. Whilst pondering their request, however, Hardy managed to persuade his lover Shelagh Farrow to smuggle a file into his cell and he duly used the implement to sharpen his teeth into points, rendering any dental impression useless. Hardy also persuaded Farrow to give him an alibi for the night of the Skala murder and so he had to be released without charge. In the minds of the authorities, however, Trevor Hardy was the prime suspect for that brutal crime.[76]

Upon his later arrest, Trevor Hardy submitted a 40-page handwritten confession to police officers which detailed the three murders he had committed. He explained how anguish over how he had been treated by a former friend (who Hardy had in fact assaulted with a pickaxe) and an ex-girlfriend called Beverley Driver (who had initially been infatuated with Hardy) had resulted in him getting drunk and approaching Lesley Stewart, mistakenly thinking she was his ex-girlfriend. He punched and kicked Lesley till she was subdued on the ground and then cut her throat with a knife before partially burying her. He then returned to her body on several occasions in the weeks that followed to dismember her corpse and dispose of the body parts. He said he did this in order to prevent her identity being established, but it has also been theorised that these return visits were for the purposes of sexual gratification. Hardy took Lesley's watch and her ring, and he gave them to his new lover, Shelagh Farrow, as gifts.[77]

Hardy claimed that Wanda Skala's murder was different to that of Lesley Stewart's in that Wanda had disturbed him in the process of a robbery and he had been forced to kill her as otherwise she would have been able to identify him. Claiming to have been intoxicated with liquor once again, Hardy had brutally beaten Wanda about the face and head with a paving stone which had shattered her skull. A ligature made from her own socks had been tied around her neck. She had been sexually assaulted and mutilated as previously described.[78]

Shortly after his release from police custody where he had avoided being charged with the Skala murder, Trevor Hardy next assaulted a young woman called Christina Campbell in a Manchester pub. He gripped the victim's throat so tightly in this attack that she bit off part of her tongue. Christina Campbell survived the incident and was able to give the police a good description of the assailant. The police began to hunt for Trevor Hardy in connection with the pub incident, but could not locate him. Three days after that assault, Trevor Hardy killed Sharon Mossoph. He had strangled her using her tights, had stabbed her in the stomach with a screwdriver and had mutilated her body by biting off her left nipple. Once again, he claimed to have been drunk at the time of the killing. Hardy had tried to disguise the bite marks left on Sharon's breast by slashing at the wound some 64 times with a large rivet.[79]

The prosecution of Trevor Hardy, which began at Manchester Crown Court on the 20th of April 1977, attracted sustained *local* publicity largely due to his antics in the courtroom in various pre-trial hearings. Hardy had been charged with three murders and a further indictment for indecent assault and wounding. Seemingly craving attention and trying to prolong the proceedings for as long as possible, Trevor Hardy continually changed his plea and repeatedly sacked his legal team, preferring instead, to defend himself despite having no legal training.[80] Eventually, and by the time the trial against him had been properly initiated, Hardy pled guilty to manslaughter on the grounds of diminished responsibility. Aside from the damning evidence provided in court by Colin Hardy and (especially) Shelagh Farrow, the prosecution also had forensic evidence which directly linked Trevor Hardy to the murder sites of Wanda Skala and Sharon Mossoph.[81] In addition, forensic psychiatrists testified that Hardy did not display any mental illness like schizophrenia or depression which would facilitate a defence of diminished responsibility. Rather, they described how Hardy had told them that he had enjoyed 'happy dreams' about the girls that he had killed; that he felt no particular distaste when dismembering Lesley Stewart's body; and that he was fully aware that what he did to the young women was criminal. They concluded that Trevor Hardy was a pathological sexual deviate and that for them, 'he illustrated remorseless brutality in action.'[82]

Hardy's plea of manslaughter on the grounds of diminished responsibility was subsequently rejected by the court in the face of the evidence presented, and when faced with the indictment again, on the 27th of April 1977, he pled not guilty to the three murder charges but admitted to unlawfully killing the girls. He also pled guilty to unlawfully wounding a fourth woman.[83] On the 2nd of May 1977, Trevor Joseph Hardy was convicted of the three murders of Lesley Stewart, Wanda Skala and Sharon Mossoph and was sentenced to life imprisonment. He was also found guilty of wounding Christina Campbell and was jailed for five years concurrent with the other sentence.[84] Hardy was described in court as 'a hopelessly evil, dangerous man who could kill again.'[85] On sentencing Hardy, the judge, Mr Justice Caulfield, told the prisoner, 'This area is a happy place. But it will be a happier place without you.'[86]

According to some scholars, certain criteria have to be fulfilled in order for a crime to be considered newsworthy. Of course, the importance placed on a given crime story can be undermined (sometimes unexpectedly) by other events, such as episodes of national or international political significance. Nonetheless, essentially for a crime to make the headlines it has to appeal to a national audience; it has to be a relatively simple story which has an element of 'human interest' to it; it has to show a risk or threat to the audience; and it has to contain elements of sex and/ or violence which can facilitate opportunities for spectacle and graphic imagery for the interested reader or viewer.[87] Although these criteria seem perfunctory and insensitive to many of us, and may be regarded as symptomatic of the media-led modern age, as early as 1946, writer George Orwell (1903–1950) also pointed to certain elements that needed to be present in a homicide in order for the public to be interested. He argued that in order to be deemed a 'good murder', a homicide had to involve sex; a desire for reputation and/or respectability; it had to be set in the familiarity of the domestic context; to involve a slow crescendo of information from the investigation appearing in the press; and it had to contain a dramatic element of some sort in order to make it memorable.[88]

An analysis of the Trevor Hardy case indicates various elements which suggest that not only should his crimes have been considered 'newsworthy' but they also had the potential to create the kind of media frenzy afforded to other modern day killers. Hardy killed multiple victims and the police believed he was responsible for other murders.[89] He used a memorable and gruesome methodology and took 'trophies' from his victims.[90] He had a female accomplice. He was given the pseudonyms 'The Beast of the Night' and 'The Beast of Manchester' by local pressmen.[91] He went on the run and managed to taunt the police on several occasions such as when he moved evidence around crime scenes, filed his teeth down to points to avoid forensic odontology and built a secret hiding place in his accommodation in order to evade the police when they came looking for him.[92] There was also a mystery relating to the motives for the murders: Hardy's crimes seemed unfathomable.

Trevor Hardy's trial also had sensational elements to it, such as his decision to defend himself which enabled him to cross-examine his accomplice, Shelagh Farrow, who appeared as a witness for the prosecution.[93] Even in the aftermath of his sentencing, the Hardy case was arguably still made highly newsworthy due to the fact that the killer managed to smuggle out a letter from his prison cell to the parents of his final victim, Sharon Mossoph. In this so-called 'dossier of death' sent during the Christmas period in 1981, Hardy sickeningly went into great detail about the savage crimes he committed and said that the poor upbringing he received from his parents was to blame for his criminality.[94] The incident was considered to be a serious breach of prison security and was even discussed in Parliament.[95]

In 2008, Trevor Hardy surfaced once again in the public domain when his case was reviewed as part of considerations relating to the setting of minimum terms for mandatory life sentences under the aforementioned Criminal Justice Act 2003. Hardy asked that his minimum jail term be set at 30 years, which would effectively have resulted in his release after time served. However, this plea was rejected by Mr Justice Teare at the High Court who described Hardy as 'utterly wicked' and said that he 'did not accept his guilt and showed no remorse. For him, life should mean life.'[96]

Interestingly, much of the details of the Hardy case echo those of American serial killer Ted Bundy (active 1961–1978), who was first brought to trial in Miami, Florida, two years after Trevor Hardy, but who went on to be one of the world's most infamous and most talked about killers. However, aside from a flurry of reports in the local press and a few fleeting comments in a few national newspapers, Trevor Hardy's crimes have never received any significant attention from scholars, the media, the public or from true-crime obsessives. This is remarkable when we consider that his case file was not simply limited to the years he was an active killer. Instead this continued because of his lengthy prison record for minor offences since his youth, his repeated attempts to interact with legal authorities and with the public at large since his final conviction, and several aggravated attacks on him by fellow prison inmates over the years, his 'story' effectively spans a time period of over five decades until his death in prison from a heart attack in September 2012, at the age of 67.[97]

According to criminological researchers at Birmingham City University, led by David Wilson, there are several reasons the crimes of Trevor Hardy were largely ignored by the mainstream media at the time. After interviewing journalists who worked at the time of Hardy's murder and prosecution, Wilson and his team concluded that six factors were involved. First, because of the timing of events, no linkage was made between the three murders and so the killings were not considered the work of a serial offender. Second, there were few visual aids for the media to use. There were few pictures of Trevor Hardy in existence at the time and no pictures of his accomplice Shelagh Farrow. Third, Hardy never really gave any motive for the killings, so it was difficult for a story to be built around his actions. Fourth, the pseudonyms given to Hardy by the press were weak and forgettable. Fifth, the victims were 'too nice' to arouse public interest and finally, as the crimes occurred in the north of England, the mainstream press and media were largely uninterested.[98]

From the detailed evidence presented in this chapter regarding the crimes of Trevor Hardy, some of these suggestions hold more validity than others and need to be considered in comparison with the activities of other modern killers whose crimes *did* achieve a lot of media attention. In general, the arguments put forward about the timing of events and the lack of visual cues and motive do seem to be crucial factors which determine how a case is reported and regarded by both the media and by the public more widely. However, Wilson's argument regarding the weakness of the pseudonyms given by the press seems far more scurrilous, especially if we consider that some notorious serial killers such as Ted Bundy, Dennis Nilsen, Robert Black (active 1981–1986) or Dr Harold Shipman (active 1978–1998) were never assigned an alias. In addition, his point about the background of the victims can be similarly undermined. Surely if the victims were innocent, 'nice' girls, then the press attention given to the offences would increase not decrease, as by Wilson's own argument, the media relies on its ability to panic the public by suggesting that they might be at risk. Indeed, this tactic is well-established as one of the key tools used by the media to pique audience interest and to sell a given story. Also problematic is the notion that because the murders committed by Trevor Hardy occurred outside of London, the press was not interested in what had transpired. This particular suggestion can be challenged if we consider the momentous nationwide press reaction to the murders committed by Peter Sutcliffe in Leeds and Bradford, some of which were concurrent with the homicides committed by Hardy.

Clearly other factors, in addition to some of the points raised by the Birmingham research team, must explain the lack of interest in Trevor Hardy and his crimes. The inability to find and then identify Lesley Stewart's body certainly hampered the police's ability to link her disappearance to the murders of Wanda Skala and Sharon Mossoph. As a result, there was never a suggestion made that a lone offender might be responsible for all three murders until after Trevor Hardy had been arrested. Consequently, there was no real opportunity for any media frenzy to begin, and the story could not gain momentum as it was effectively over by the time the press and the public first came to know the details.[99]

Moreover, we should not forget that at the time of the murders, the term 'serial killer' and the theories and characteristics associated with that type of homicide were in their infancy and not fully developed or understood. The media were not able to describe Hardy as a 'serial killer' as they were unfamiliar with the concept. The police too were unaware of this new typology of homicide. Despite this, it is fair to say that the police investigation into the murders was very thorough and indeed the judge in Hardy's trial commended the investigative team for their efforts. Some 23,000 people were interviewed by the authorities in connection with the murders and these exertions no doubt limited the number of victims Hardy attacked, thereby stunting his notoriety in terms of body count 'achieved'.[100]

The fact that the victims' families were reluctant to talk to the media must have also made the story more difficult to expose in any great depth at the time.[101] Hardy's lack of emotion or remorse, as well as his evident and substantial history of petty and serious offending, may also have made his story less interesting to the public and to the media, in the sense that his actions almost had a sense of inevitability about them, rather than an air of mystery.[102] By the time of his arrest for the murders at the age of 30, Trevor Hardy already had some 147 convictions to his name for other offences (including indecent exposure, wounding with intent and violent robbery) and had been in and out of borstals and prisons for most of his life.[103] The escalation of violence that he employed may not have come as that much of a surprise to the Mancunian communities in which he had resided, nor to the authorities who had so strenuously tried to keep him off the streets for so many years. Arguably, the most tragic element of the crimes of Trevor Hardy is that they were almost predictable, given his past history and his predilection for trouble.

Finally, we should also consider the impact that the aforementioned crimes of Peter Sutcliffe might have had in terms of interest in the murders committed by Trevor Hardy. Although Hardy's killings were initiated at the same time as those of the Yorkshire Ripper, as we have already noted, Trevor Hardy was arrested far more quickly than his killer contemporary. Peter Sutcliffe, by contrast, went on to kill at least 13 women and attempted to murder 7 others over a 5-year period until his arrest in 1980. The scale and extent of his attacks, the fear that engulfed women in the

Yorkshire area and the desperate police search which ensued, commanded significant and unprecedented national and global media attention for a prolonged period of time and either relegated 'lesser' stories to the small print or made them redundant altogether.[104] Arguably, this contextual factor, more than any detail relating to the specifics of Trevor Hardy's crimes, explains the dearth of interest in him as a serial killer: his story was considered relatively unimportant when compared to the 'competition'.

5.   Conclusion

Twentieth-century Britain is a fascinating period in which to study the history of homicide as it is one where the traditional long-term downward trend in fatal violence is reversed, and an increase in that type of criminality can be observed from the 1960s period onwards. The modern era is also marked by a series of legal attempts to better define what was meant by the term 'homicide' and its associated categories, with efforts to determine what possible defences should be open to an individual facing such a charge. Furthermore, the post-war period saw clearer typologies of murder develop, including categories such as spree killing and serial killing, and this in turn instigated a seemingly insatiable fascination amongst the public – fuelled by the media – for details of especially egregious murders. Yet, as this chapter has shown, the modern British history of fatal violence has been largely neglected by academics and by historians in particular. Moreover, this neglect has flown in the face of repeated calls amongst scholars from other disciplines including sociology, psychiatry and criminology, for us to better understand the context in which serious crime takes place in order to better prevent it happening in the future.

This chapter in itself has taken a first tentative step in showing the value of understanding the historical context for instances of homicide. In analysing why the case of Trevor Hardy did not attain the same media prominence as other modern serial killings had done for instance, it becomes evident that the context within which the crime took place was central to determining the levels of 'popular' attention afforded a given case. This conclusion, whilst of course limited to the case study to which it relates, is indicative nonetheless of the kind of significant insight that a detailed history of homicide in Britain could provide. As one scholar has put it 'Murder is a social marker.'[105] Historians are yet to fully recognise that a study of homicide can tell us much about different aspects of society and how they have changed over time.[106] By better understanding homicide in the past, we can offer much to the various disciplines and agencies working on its prevention in the present.

Notes

1. For further discussion of how seriously homicide has been regarded throughout history see P. Spierenburg (2010 edition) *A History of Murder: Personal Violence in Europe from the Middle Ages to the Present* (Cambridge: Polity Press), p. 1; D. Dorling (2006) 'Prime Suspect: Murder in Britain', *Prison Service Journal*, Vol. 166, pp. 3–10 at p. 3 and F. Brookman (2005) *Understanding Homicide* (London: Sage), p. 1.

2. For further discussion on the longevity of homicidal activity through history see M. Eisner (2013) 'What Causes Large-Scale Variation in Homicide Rates?', in H.-H. Kortüm and J. Heinze (eds) *Aggression in Humans and Other* Primates (Berlin: De Gruyter), pp. 137–62 at p. 137 and Spierenburg (2010 edition) *A History of Murder*, p. 1. For further discussion of its accurate recording in comparison with other forms of criminal activity see J.S. Cockburn (1991) 'Patterns of Violence in English Society: Homicide in Kent 1560–1985', *Past and Present*, Vol. 130, pp. 70–106 at p. 76; L. Stone (1983) 'Interpersonal Violence in English Society 1300–1980', *Past and Present*, Vol. 101, pp. 22–33 at p. 22; M. Eisner (2001) 'Modernization, Self-Control and Lethal Violence: The Long-Term Dynamics of European Homicide Rates in Theoretical Perspective', *British Journal of Criminology*, Vol. 41, pp. 618–38 at p. 634 and Eisner (2013) 'What Causes Large-Scale Variation?', p. 137.

3. Spierenburg (2010 edition) *A History of Murder*, p. 1.

4. For further discussion see S. D'Cruze, S. Walklate and S. Pegg (2011 edition) *Murder* (Abingdon: Routledge), pp. 22–23 as well as Chapter 2; Brookman (2005) *Understanding Homicide*, p. 1 and E. Carrabine (2008) *Crime, Culture and the Media* (Cambridge: Polity Press). One indication of the strength of this fascination can be seen by looking at the publications list of just one independent publisher – Wharncliffe Books – who specialises in case study texts relating to murder cases in England during the twentieth century. This series currently consists of 64 volumes.

5. B. Masters (1994) *On Murder* (London: Hodder and Stoughton), p. 178.

6. Historian Lucy Worsley emphasises the preoccupation with homicide in Britain, describing it as a 'national obsession' in the title of her work on the subject: L. Worsley (2013) *A Very British Murder: The Story of a National Obsession* (London: BBC Books).

7. For further discussion of these criticisms see The Law Commission (2005) *A New Homicide Act for England and Wales? Consultation Paper No. 177* (London: The Law Commission), especially Part I. Available at http://lawcommission.justice.gov.uk/docs/cp177_Murder_Manslaughter_and_Infanticide_consultation_.pdf (Accessed 11th November 2017); The Law Commission (2006) *Murder, Manslaughter and Infanticide – Project 6 of the Ninth Programme of Law Reform: Homicide* [Law COM No. 304] (London: The Law Commission), especially Part I. Available at http://lawcommission.justice.gov.uk/docs/lc304_Murder_Manslaughter_and_Infanticide_Report.pdf (Accessed 11th November 2017) and A. Ashworth and B. Mitchell (eds) (2000) *Rethinking English Homicide Law* (Oxford: Oxford University Press).

8. Sir Edward Coke (1628) *The First Part of the New Institutes of the Lawes of England* (London: Adam Islip), STC 15784, p. 9. Accessed from Early English Books Online via: http://www.jischistoricbooks.ac.uk/Search.aspx (Accessed 11th November 2017).

9. Parliamentary Papers, Law Reform (Year and a Day Rule) Act 1996, c. 19. For further discussion of the definition of murder in the twentieth-century English legal context see D'Cruze, Walklate and Pegg (2011 edition) *Murder*, pp. 1–4 and that provided by the Crown Prosecution Service. Available at http://www.cps.gov.uk/legal/h_to_k/homicide_murder_and_manslaughter/#definition (Accessed 11th November 2017).

10. For further discussion see Parliamentary Papers, 5 & 6 Eliz.2 c.11 (1957), Part I.

11. Parliamentary Papers, Murder (Abolition of Death Penalty) Act 1965, c. 71 and Hansard: House of Commons Debates, 793, 16th December 1969: 1148–297.

12. Parliamentary Papers, Criminal Justice Act 2003, c. 44, s. 21.

13. For further discussion of the definition of manslaughter in the twentieth-century English legal context see Brookman (2005) *Understanding Homicide*, pp. 8–13 and that provided by the Crown Prosecution Service. Available at http://www.cps.gov.uk/legal/h_to_k/homicide_murder_and_manslaughter/#definition (Accessed 12th November 2017). It should be noted that in 2007, a new offence of Corporate Manslaughter was introduced across Britain via the Corporate Manslaughter and Corporate Homicide Act 2007, c. 19.

14. Parliamentary Papers, 12 & 13 Geo. 5, c. 18 (1922) and Parliamentary Papers, 1 & 2 Geo. 6, c. 36 (1938).

15. For further discussion of the twentieth-century history of this particular type of homicide see A.-M. Kilday (2013) *A History of Infanticide in Britain c.1600 to the Present* (Basingstoke: Palgrave), especially Chapter 7.

16. See The Law Commission (2005) *A New Homicide Act for England and Wales?* Appendix D, section D.1.

17. Baron D. Hume, *Commentaries on the Laws of Scotland, Respecting Crimes Volume I*, Edinburgh originally 1797, 1844 edn., 1986 reprint, Chapter VI, p. 179 [National Library of Scotland H.27.a.10].

18. *Ibid.*, p. 179 and pp. 181–82. For further discussion of the early Scottish legal context for homicide see A.-M. Kilday (2008) *Women and Violent Crimes in Enlightenment Scotland* (Woodbridge: Boydell), Chapter 3.

19. This modern definition was modified from an 1867 version. For the modern definition see J.H.A. Macdonald, J. Walker and D.J Stevenson (1948 edition) *A Practical Treatise on the Criminal Law of Scotland* (Edinburgh: W. Green), p. 89 [Bodleian Law Library KM500. S3. MAC1948].

20. See The Law Commission (2005) *A New Homicide Act for England and Wales?* Appendix D, section D.8 and D.9.

21. See *ibid.*, D.1.

22. See the references at note 11 above.

23. See The Law Commission (2005) *A New Homicide Act for England and Wales?* Appendix D, section D.1.

24. Eisner (2013) 'What Causes Large-Scale Variation?', p. 154. See also M. Eisner (2003) 'Long-Term Historical Trends in Violent Crime', in M. Tonry (ed.) *Crime and Justice: A Review of Research*, Vol. 30, pp. 83–142 and Spierenburg (2010 edition) *A History of Murder*, p. 4.

25. N. Elias (2000) *The Civilizing Process* (trans. E. Jephcott) (Oxford: Wiley Blackwell).

26. For further discussion of the 'civilising process' in relation to homicidal activity in particular see E. Leyton (1995) *Men of Blood: Murder in Modern England* (London: Constable), especially Chapter 10; Eisner (2003) 'Long-Term Historical Trends', pp. 123–25; Spierenburg (2010 edition) *A History of Murder*, pp. 5–10 and Eisner (2001) 'Modernization, Self-Control and Lethal Violence', p. 619 and pp. 630–31.

27. For further discussion of British homicide trends through history and with reference to the twentieth century see Leyton (1995) *Men of Blood*, especially Chapter 5; Cockburn (1991) 'Patterns of Violence in English Society',

pp. 76–77; S. D'Cruze (2010) 'Murder and Fatality: The Changing Face of Homicide', in A.-M. Kilday and D.S. Nash (eds) *Histories of Crime: Britain 1600–2000* (Basingstoke: Palgrave), pp. 100–119 at p. 101.

28. It should be noted that the prevailing counting rules applicable in any given year were adopted in the collection of data. No judicial statistics were recorded in 1939 in England and Wales as a result of the Second World War.

29. For further consideration of issues affecting homicide data see T.R. Gurr (1981) 'Historical Trends in Violent Crime: A Critical Review of the Evidence', in M. Tonry (ed.) *Crime and Justice: A Review of Research*, Vol. 3, pp. 295–353 at p. 302 and pp. 344–46; Eisner (2001) 'Modernization, Self-Control and Lethal Violence', p. 628 and Stone (1983) 'Interpersonal Violence', p. 24.

30. T. Morris and L. Blom-Cooper (1964) *A Calendar of Murder: Criminal Homicide in England since 1957* (London: Michael Joseph), p. 277. The rarity of homicide in Britain at this point in history is also a point picked up by P.E.H. Hair (1971) 'Deaths from Violence in Britain: A Tentative Secular Survey', *Population Studies*, Vol. 25, No. 1, pp. 5–24 at p. 17 and G. Honeycombe (2009) *Murders of the Black Museum 1875–1975: The Dark Secrets behind More than a Hundred Years of the Most Notorious Crimes in England* (London: John Blake), p. xiii and Leyton (1995) *Men of Blood*, p. 9.

31. For further evidence of a rise in homicide rates in the second half of the twentieth century see for instance P. Vronsky (2004) *Serial Killers: The Method and Madness of Monsters* (New York: Berkley), p. 4; Eisner (2003) 'Long-Term Historical Trends', p. 88 and p. 106; Cockburn (1991) 'Patterns of Violence in English Society', p. 77 and p. 106 and Gurr (1981) 'Historical Trends in Violent Crime', p. 311 and p. 340.

32. See in particular Spierenburg (2010 edition) *A History of Murder*, pp. 207–8 and pp. 216–18.

33. See 'Report on UK Crime', *The Independent*, 15th November 1997.

34. See Leyton (1995) *Men of Blood*, p. 9 and Morris and Blom-Cooper (1964) *A Calendar of Murder*, p. 277.

35. For the nineteenth-century origins of this see J. Flanders (2011) *The Invention of Murder: How the Victorians Revelled in Death and Detection and Created Modern Crime* (London: Harper Press) and Worsley (2013) *A Very British Murder*, passim.

36. For further discussion see Spierenburg (2010 edition) *A History of Murder*, p. 196; Morris and Blom-Cooper (1964) *A Calendar of Murder*, pp. 271–72 and Worsley (2013) *A Very British Murder*, p. 294.

37. P. Rock (1998) *After Homicide* (Oxford: Clarendon Press), p. 4 cited in D'Cruze, Walklate and Pegg (2011 edition) *Murder*, p. 1. For similar opinion see Leyton (1995) *Men of Blood*, p. 8 and J. Carter Wood (2006) 'Criminal Violence in Modern Britain', *History Compass*, Vol. 4, No. 1, pp. 77–90 at p. 80.

38. For further discussion of these various categories of homicide see A. Gekoski (1998) *Murder by Numbers: British Serial Sex Killers since 1950: Their Childhoods, Their Lives, Their Crimes* (London: Andre Deutsch), pp. 16–17; Masters (1994) *On Murder*, p. 42 and Vronsky (2004) *Serial Killers*, p. 8 and p. 11.

39. See D'Cruze (2010) 'Murder and Fatality', p. 103 and P. Jenkins (1988) 'Serial Murder in England 1940–1985', *Journal of Criminal Justice*, Vol. 16, pp. 1–15 at pp. 5–6.

40. For further discussion of the modern fascination with serial killing and serial killers see Gekoski (1998) *Murder by Numbers*, p. 17, pp. 20–21 and p. 23.

41. Masters (1994) *On Murder*, pp. 42–43.

42. For agreement on this see Carter Wood (2006) 'Criminal Violence', p. 77; Spierenburg (2010 edition) *A History of Murder*, p. 1; Brookman (2005) *Understanding Homicide*, p. 1; Rock (1998) *After Homicide*, p. 9 and D'Cruze, Walklate and Pegg (2011 edition) *Murder*, p. 1. It is interesting to note that two of the best-selling criminology textbooks about modern Britain do not contain a specific chapter on homicide – see E. Carrabine, P. Cox, M. Lee and N. South (2002) *Crime in Modern Britain* (Oxford: Oxford University Press) and M. Maguire, R. Morgan and R. Reiner (eds) (2012 edition) *The Oxford Handbook of Criminology* (Oxford: Oxford University Press).

43. For examples of work that call for a better contextual understanding of homicide see D. Wilson (2009) *A History of British Serial Killing: The Definitive Account from Jack the Ripper* (London: Sphere), p. xi and p. 23; K.D. Haggerty (2009) 'Modern Serial Killers', *Crime, Media, Culture*, Vol. 5, pp. 168–87 at pp. 173–84 and S. Wade (2011) *Notorious Murders of the Twentieth Century: Famous and Forgotten British Cases* (Barnsley: Wharncliffe Books), p. 5.

44. Haggerty (2009) 'Modern Serial Killers', p. 169.

45. An observation also made by John Carter Wood in relation to the study of violence in modern Britain more broadly – see Carter Wood (2006) 'Criminal Violence', pp. 77–90.

46. See respectively Hair (1971) 'Deaths from Violence in Britain', pp. 5–24; Gurr (1981) 'Historical Trends in Violent Crime', pp. 295–353; Stone (1983) 'Interpersonal Violence', pp. 22–33; Cockburn (1991) 'Patterns of Violence in English Society', pp. 70–106 and Eisner (2001) 'Modernization, Self-Control and Lethal Violence', pp. 618–33.

47. For further discussion see Dorling (2006) 'Prime Suspect', pp. 7–8 and Spierenburg (2010 edition) *A History of Murder*, p. 216.

48. For further discussion see Dorling (2006) 'Prime Suspect', p. 4; Leyton (1995) *Men of Blood*, p. 129; Brookman (2005) *Understanding Homicide*, Chapters 6 and 7; D'Cruze, Walklate and Pegg (2011 edition) *Murder*, p. 15 and Chapter 3 and A. Ballinger (2000) *Dead Woman Walking: Executed Women in England and Wales, 1900–1955* (Dartmouth: Ashgate).

49. For further discussion of this see D'Cruze, Walklate and Pegg (2011 edition) *Murder*, p. 15 and Chapters 5 and 6; Morris and Blom-Cooper (1964) *A Calendar of Murder*, pp. 279–80; Leyton (1995) *Men of Blood*, p. 133; D'Cruze (2010) 'Murder and Fatality', p. 101; Dorling (2006) 'Prime Suspect', p. 4; Gekoski (1998) *Murder by Numbers*, p. 30.

50. One theory of many suggested by Peter Vronsky in his work (2004) *Serial Killers: The Method and Madness of* Monsters (New York: Berkley), Chapter 1.

51. For further discussion see Wilson (2009) *A History of British Serial Killing*, pp. 19–20 and p. 23; Dorling (2006) 'Prime Suspect', pp. 3–4; Spierenburg (2010 edition) *A History of Murder*, pp. 207–8, pp. 212–13 and p. 218 as well as E. Leyton (1986) *Hunting Humans: The Rise of the Modern Multiple Murderer* (Toronto: McClelland and Stewart).

52. For a fuller discussion of these findings see D. Wilson (2009) *A History of British Serial Killing: The Definitive Account from Jack the Ripper* (London: Sphere).

53. See the reference to these works in notes 31 and 43 above. See also D. Wilson (2006) *Serial Killers: Hunting Britons and Their Victims, 1960–2006* (Winchester: Waterside Press).

54. For further discussion of these typologies see D'Cruze, Walklate and Pegg (2011 edition) *Murder*, p. 33; R.M. Holmes and S.T. Holmes (1998 edition) *Serial Murder* (London: Sage) and especially Vronsky (2004) *Serial Killers*, Chapter 4.

55. Honeycombe (2009) Murders of the Black Museum.

56. See Jenkins (1988) 'Serial Murder', p. 6.

57. Gekoski (1998) *Murder by Numbers*, p. 8.

58. For further discussion see D'Cruze, Walklate and Pegg (2011 edition) *Murder*, Chapter 2.

59. For further discussion see B. Jarvis (2010) 'Monsters Inc.: Serial Killers and Consumer Culture', in C. Greer (ed.) *Crime and the Media – A Reader* (London: Routledge), pp. 351–63. It is interesting to note that the University of Central Lancashire established an Institute for Dark Tourism Research in 2012. Details of this can be found at http://dark-tourism.org. uk/ (Accessed 11th November 2017).

60. For further discussion see Gekoski (1998) *Murder by Numbers*, p. 7; Wilson (2009) *A History of British Serial Killing*, p. 275 and Wade (2011) *Notorious Murders*, p. 5.

61. The subjectivity of media attention in this regard is something considered by David Wilson in Chapter 5 of his work (2011) *Looking for Laura: Public Criminology and Hot News* (Hook: Waterside Press).

62. For evidence of the extensive and ongoing popular fascination with Ted Bundy and Peter Sutcliffe see respectively K.M. Sullivan (2009) *The Bundy Murders: A Comprehensive History* (Jefferson: McFarland) and M. Bilton (2012) *Wicked Beyond Belief: The Hunt for the Yorkshire Ripper* (London: Harper Press).

63. *Manchester Evening News*, 10th January 1975.

64. *Ibid.*, 19th July 1975.

65. See *Ibid.*, 21st July 1975 and *The Guardian*, 21st July 1975.

66. *Manchester Evening News*, 22nd July 1975.

67. *The Guardian*, 26th July 1975.

68. *Manchester Evening News*, 9th March and 10th March 1976 and *The Guardian*, 10th March 1976.

69. *Manchester Evening News*, 10th March 1976.

70. *The Guardian,* 21st July 1976.

71. *The Guardian*, 3rd September 1976; *The Times*, 3rd September 1976 and the *Daily Mirror*, 3rd September 1976.

72. For further detail see N. Appleyard (2009) *Life Means Life: Jailed Forever – True Stories of Britain's Most Evil Killers* (London: John Blake), pp. 178–79 and D. Clayton (2013) *Manchester Stories* (Ayr: Fort Publishing), pp. 67–71.

73. Appleyard (2009) *Life Means Life*, p. 174.

74. According to a Home Office Pathologist operating in the second half of the twentieth century, the biting of victims was not uncommon in modern sexually aggravated murders in Britain – see K. Simpson (1978) *Forty Years of Murder: An Autobiography* (London: Harrap), pp. 270–78. For more on Neville Heath see S. O'Connor (2014) *Handsome Brute: The True Story of a Ladykiller* (London: Simon and Schuster).

75. For further discussion see Appleyard (2009) *Life Means Life*, p. 174. See also newspaper accounts of evidence given by Colin Hardy at Hardy's trial such as that in the *Manchester Evening News*, 20th April 1977.

76. *Ibid.*, pp. 174–75. See also Dr G. Garrett and A. Nott (2001) *Cause of Death* (London: Robinson), p. 144. See also accounts of the evidence given by Shelagh Farrow at Hardy's trial from the *Manchester Evening News*, 20th April 1977 and 27th April 1977 and in J. Jonker (2003 edition) *Victims of Violence* (London: Headline), pp. 172–80.

77. See Appleyard (2009) *Life Means Life*, pp. 176–77 and Garrett and Nott (2001) *Cause of Death*, pp. 137–38. See also newspaper accounts of the confession recounted at Hardy's trial such as that in the *Manchester Evening News*, 20th April 1977 and 27th April 1977 as well as the *Daily Mirror*, 21st April 1977.

78. See Garrett and Nott (2001) *Cause of Death*, p. 140 and Appleyard (2009) *Life Means Life*, pp. 173–74. See also newspaper accounts of the confession recounted at Hardy's trial such as that in the *Manchester Evening News*, 20th April 1977 and 27th April 1977.

79. Appleyard (2009) *Life Means Life*, p. 175 and Garrett and Nott (2001) *Cause of Death*, pp. 144–46. See also newspaper accounts of the confession recounted at Hardy's trial such as that in the *Manchester Evening News*, 20th April 1977.

80. See for instance the *Daily Mirror*, 27th November 1976; the *Manchester Evening News*, 25th April 1977 and 26th April 1977 and Garrett and Nott (2001) *Cause of Death*, pp. 147–48.

81. *Manchester Evening News*, 22nd April 1977.

82. See for instance the testimony of Dr Archibald Campbell reported in the *Manchester Evening News*, 27th April 1977.

83. See *The Times*, 27th April 1977.

84. See *The Times*, 3rd May 1977.

85. See the *Daily Mirror*, 3rd May 1977 and Garrett and Nott (2001) *Cause of Death*, p. 133.
86. *Ibid.*
87. See D. Wilson, H. Tolputt, N. Howe and D. Kemp (2010) 'When Serial Killers Go Unseen: The Case of Trevor Joseph Hardy', *Crime, Media, Culture*, Vol. 6, No. 2, pp. 153–67 at pp. 154–55 and especially Y. Jewkes (2004) *Crime and the Media* (London: Sage), pp. 40–55.
88. G. Orwell (1984 edition) *The Decline of the English Murder* (London: Penguin), pp. 16–18.
89. See Clayton (2013) *Manchester Stories*, p. 74 and the *Manchester Evening News*, 24th April 2012.
90. See N. Weir (2011) *British Serial Killers* (Bloomington: Authorhouse), p. 266.
91. See Garrett and Nott (2001) *Cause of Death*, p. 149.
92. See the details provided in the *Manchester Evening News*, 20th and 21st April 1977.
93. Attempts were made by the victims' families to bring Shelagh Farrow to justice for her part in the three murders that took place, but she had gleaned immunity from prosecution from the authorities in return for her testimony at Hardy's trial. See House of Commons Debates, 11th November 1977, Vol. 938, cc255-6W and Jonker (2003 edition) *Victims of Violence*, pp. 179–80 and pp. 183–84.
94. See *The Guardian*, 15th December 1981 and *The Times*, 15th December 1981.
95. House of Commons Debates, 14th December 1981, Vol. 15, cc13-14W.
96. *R v. Trevor Joseph Hardy* (2008) EWHC 1165 (QB). For further discussion see *The Times*, 23rd February 2008 and the *Manchester Evening News*, 24th April 2012. The ruling for Hardy and for 47 other prisoners in receipt of 'whole-life' sentences was confirmed after an appeal to the European Court of Human Rights – see the *Daily Mirror*, 18th January 2012.
97. See the *Manchester Evening News*, 28th of September 2012 and the *Oldham Evening Chronicle*, 28th September 2012. See also Clayton (2013) *Manchester Stories*, pp. 74–75.
98. For further discussion see Wilson, Tolputt, Howe and Kemp (2010) 'When Serial Killers Go Unseen', pp. 160–63.
99. Weir (2011) *British Serial Killers*, p. 264.

100. See *The Times*, 3rd May 1977 and Garrett and Nott (2001) *Cause of Death*, p. 163.
101. Jonker (2003 edition) *Victims of Violence*, p. 124 and p. 133.
102. For more on Hardy's evident lack of emotion or remorse see *ibid.*, p. 169.
103. See the references at note 72 above in addition to the *Manchester Evening News*, 3rd May 1977.
104. For further discussion see M. Bilton (2012) *Wicked Beyond Belief: The Hunt for the Yorkshire Ripper* (London: Harper Press).
105. Dorling (2006) 'Prime Suspect', p. 9.
106. The author has already begun a book-length project for Palgrave on this subject entitled *A History of Homicide in Britain from 1600 to the Present*.

3

Serious Property Offending in the Twentieth Century

Lucy Williams and Barry Godfrey

1. Introduction

The twentieth century has been recognised by academics, police officers, and even criminals themselves as a time in which the nature of property crime underwent significant and unprecedented change. Two world wars, severe economic depressions, rapid social change, and a technological revolution provided the backdrop for one hundred years in which 'classic' techniques of robbery and burglary began to be supplemented and replaced with smash-and-grab raids, train heists, armed bank jobs, and eventually, electronic crime.

Echoing a scene that would be familiar to any viewer of the popular 1970s police drama 'The Sweeney', *The Guardian* reported a dramatic 'heist' in 1979:

> In what police later called "a smooth, professional job" the men used chainsaws and sledgehammers to break into the van's safe before escaping down a deserted road .... As the security van skidded to a halt an orange Vauxhall Cavalier rammed into its back. At least four men, wearing balaclava helmets and carrying rifles and pistols jumped out of the two vehicles. One man fired his shotgun into the van's off-side front tyre and another ripped off its aerial, while other members of the gang ran back down the

road to the head of the queue of cars which had begun to form. They disabled five cars and a lorry by slashing their tyres, and taking the ignition
keys and throwing them into roadworks nearby … they cut through the
van's safe, removing £380,000, and drove off in a third vehicle – a blue
Transit van. The whole operation took four minutes.[1]

This kind of robbery has come to dominate the public imagination
and serious property crime is much more synonymous with daring and
violent robberies than with white-collar fraud, which is far more prevalent. This chapter provides an overview of some of the key changes in
the nature of all serious property crime, alongside recorded criminal
statistics. Although we devote some thought to the last decades of the
twentieth century, the social, cultural, and technological revolution of
the digital age makes a direct comparison with property crime in earlier
decades difficult. The world of digital identity theft, electronic banking
fraud, and credit-card scams could, without doubt, occupy several chapters on its own. As such, our main analytical focus here is the changing
rates and nature of serious property crime in the first three-quarters
of the twentieth century. What becomes clear is that whilst the practice of carrying out serious property crime may have been altered by
new technologies (motor-aided crime, increased availability of guns),
rates of serious property crime were not vastly altered from those of the
previous century until social upheaval and economic changes in post-
war Britain and again in the last quarter of the century produced the
socio-economic conditions that created a large rise in serious property
offending.

2.   Chronology

a)   Definition and Legal Context

The offence of burglary, or breaking and entering, is complete when a
person either forces entry into a building (a residential or commercial
dwelling) or enters a property without the permission of the owner with
an intent to steal property therein.[2] In 1968 the offence was redefined

under the Theft Act, but the offence remained essentially the same as originally defined by common law. Like burglary, robbery has been long understood by the courts and by the general public as a serious offence which must be prosecuted in the higher courts on indictment. Robbery is the taking of property by force or threat of force. Indeed force or threat of use of force must be present in order for the offence to be made out. Both offences always and continue to attract long prison sentences, especially if the offence was committed at night.

Unlike burglary and robbery, which are clearly defined in a small amount of legislation, fraud offences encompass a variety of criminal acts. Fraud stretches from cheating and gaining property or goods by false pretenses or false representation, to major organised property crime involving the theft by deception of hundreds of thousands of pounds. Fraud was dealt with in both the minor and the higher courts, but could also be treated as a civil offence (tort) when it involved the breaching of a contract through deceit. In the nineteenth century fraud mainly consisted of coining offences, counterfeiting and joint-stock company frauds, but, in the twentieth century, the courts dealt with insurance frauds and large-scale financial irregularities. By the end of century, fraud trials took place daily in Britain's highest courts.

b)   Trends in Incidence and Explanations Offered

The annually published criminal statistics show that the scale of serious property offending was fairly consistent between the start of the twentieth century until World War Two (see Figure 3.1 below). Both the 1914 to 1918 and 1940 to 1945 series of statistics were affected by the difficult circumstances caused by war. Nevertheless, if they reflect the real level of offending, the two World Wars appear to mark something of a watershed for serious crime. Indeed there have been a number of apparent watersheds noted by both social and police commentators which all seemed to herald a new approach to burglary, robbery and serious fraud in the twentieth century. The annually published judicial and criminal statistics can be used to investigate some of the claims of 'watershed moments'.[3]

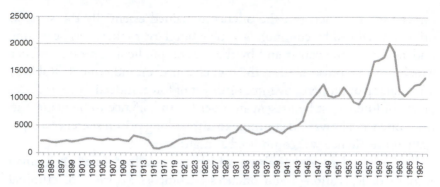

Figure 3.1   Serious Property Offending, England and Wales, 1893–1968[4]

As Figure 3.1 above shows, it was not until late into the 1920s and '30s that prosecution rates of serious property crime began to exhibit significant change. The interwar period was a period of 'social turmoil and turbulence' which 'saw crime increase at the rate of approximately 5 per cent a year.'[5] The rise was partly attributed to returning demobilised soldiers after the First World War.[6] Some men, William Meier rightly points out, already had criminal records and returned to their pre-war activities, but their numbers were swelled by other servicemen returning to find little more than poverty and unemployment (see Figure 3.2 below):

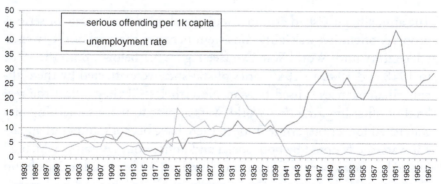

Figure 3.2   Unemployment Rates (%) and Serious Property Offending (per 1000 population)[7]

In the 1930s, continued unemployment and widespread poverty caused by the 'Great Depression' contributed to an interwar 'crime wave'.[8] The punishments for property crime were somewhat toughened up in the interwar period, mainly at the behest of those passing sentence. Sir Henry Dickens, an Old Bailey Judge, stated in 1929 that he 'had tried a good many of these [fraud] cases ... and I am getting tired of them'.[9] The judges were determined to put down 'that class' of offence and penal servitude became the norm for fraudsters, as it already was for burglars and robbers. However, rates of serious property crime doubled between 1929 and 1932, the peak period of interwar unemployment. Considering the long run of data presented in Figure 3.2 above, however, the interwar crime wave seems gentle in comparison to the post-war crisis in serious property offending. In both 1941 and 1942, the annual numbers of thefts committed by juveniles alone nearly topped 45,000.[10] The more serious offence of breaking and entering only ever reached 15,000 at its height in 1945, but had nevertheless risen steadily throughout the war period (see Figure 3.3):

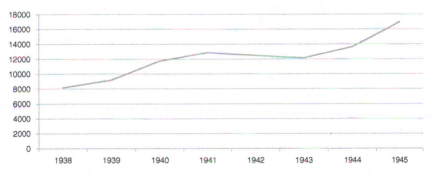

Figure 3.3   Breaking and Entering Offences Committed by Juveniles, England and Wales, 1938–1945[11]

Between 1939 and 1945, recorded instances of crime rose from a yearly 303,771 to 478,394. This constituted 'a rise of 57 per cent in seven years.'[12] In the years before the war, the increase in crime had been more gradual, and 'the war saw a marked quickening in pace' when it came to rising rates of crime, particularly in the last two years of the war.[13] The rise in crime may have been due, in no small part, to the 'severe strain' and lack of manpower facing the depleted police force, and their struggle to contain the 'black market' created by the war.[14] Crimes connected with black market trading dominated the years of the Second World War: offences that Thomas referred to as 'war surplus crime'.[15] These crimes could range from trading in counterfeit or illegally purchased ration coupons to the co-option of deserters or ex-servicemen into pulling off large-scale heists of rationed goods. Thomas notes 'in times of severe shortages, it was not hard to make criminals of those who had never thought of themselves as such.'[16] In desperation one magistrate suggested that men in reserved occupations who had committed burglaries should be sent to the Front.[17] However, it was just as likely to be servicemen already serving in the armed forces who took part in robberies (both at home or abroad whilst on active service).[18]

Figures 3.1 and 3.2 suggest that the Second World War was a significant watershed in the nature of robbery and burglary. In the five years between 1941 and 1946, the rate of robberies in the greater London area almost doubled, and burglaries tripled.[19] Similar, if smaller, increases occurred throughout the rest of the country too. In the interwar years, thieves had been required to sell their stolen wares cheaply. In the time of rationing, there were vast profits to be made fuelling the black market. Stolen goods for the first time could be sold above the market price.[20] Smithies suggests that 'warehouse and lorry theft became highly organised as the war proceeded, and receivers with good business connections were able to dispose of considerable quantities of goods.'[21] The market for the robbery of high-end luxury items like diamonds and furs depleted, and instead there were large sums of money to be made in providing everyday items that the populace were being deprived of. Lucrative robberies were being carried out not just for rationed food items or petrol, but also alcohol, tobacco, 'clothing, cloth, razor blades, soap, and electrical products.'[22] Supplying in-demand items to the black market was a safer, easier, and more lucrative way to dispose of stolen goods.

As Figure 3.4 shows, burglary rates rose steeply during and immediately after the Second World War, and then continued to rise much

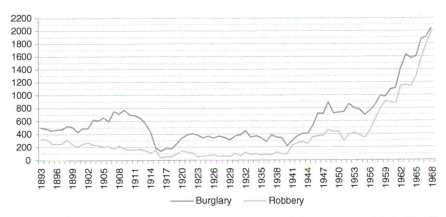

Figure 3.4   Rates of Burglary and Robbery, England and Wales, 1893–1965[23]

more steeply again in the 1960s. There is a similar pattern with robbery, where again the rise was extremely rapid from the mid-1950s.[24] Although Scottish statistics were compiled in slightly different categories to those from England and Wales, again a similar trend can be discerned (see Figure 3.5).

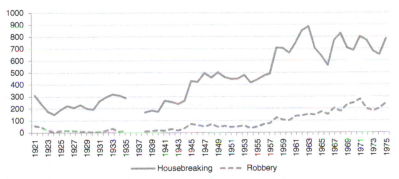

Figure 3.5   Rates of Housebreaking and Robbery, Scotland, 1921–1975[25]

When the shortages created during the Second World War receded, affluent liberalism promised a weary populace material fulfilment. Those on the margins of society sought to achieve this affluence via acquisitive crime.[26] The consumer boom of the 1950s and '60s, and the pervasive attitude that times had never been so good, created a demand for consumer goods and all of the benefits that post-war affluence could provide.[27]

In the two decades after the Second World War, trains carrying the Royal Mail cash, and precious materials were tempting targets for both professional and amateur criminals, as the case study later in the chapter illustrates.[28] Mail robberies slowly declined as transportation methods changed towards the end of the 1960s and road took over rail. Robbers also perpetrated armed hold-ups on premises where large amounts of cash were stored. Teams of robbers would use coercion and violence to subdue a workforce and have cash handed over, ready to be loaded into a waiting 'getaway' vehicle. The Mark 2 Jag gained a reputation among criminals and law enforcement alike as a fast and reliable car; the 3.8 litre model went from 0 to 60 in 8.5 seconds and achieved a top speed of 125 mph with enough room for five adults (just right for a team of bank robbers, or, alternatively, the Flying Squad). The Ford Transit Mark I was introduced in 1965, and it is estimated that 95 per cent of all robberies (involving vehicles) used Transits.[29] The Mark II Transit was introduced in 1978 for the police to use as a high-speed vehicle in order to even out the playing field. They were then used by the regionalised crime squads (introduced to constitute a nationwide network of intelligence and surveillance in the hope of stemming the tide of serious organised and violent property crime).[30]

In the 1970s, technological innovation moved in favour of the forces of law and order with increased security introduced into the banking and commercial arena. Wages were paid electronically into bank accounts rather than in brown envelopes directly to the employees, and there was less need to freight huge amounts of cash around the road system. The introduction of trained armed police also made robbery more risky and heavy penalties were introduced for armed heists.[31] A heightened focus by the authorities on preventing the theft of cash or goods in transit saw a reduction in armed robbery and commercial burglaries, but an increase in street robberies.[32] During this time Britain saw not only a spike in reports and prosecutions for property crime, but also media and political outrage about the 'mugging crisis'. Following the murder of a London pensioner in a mugging gone wrong in 1972, and over a year of sensationalist media coverage, the courts were gearing up to 'declare' war on those responsible for violent street property crime.[33] Those held responsible for the 1970s crime wave in violent personal robberies were not, on the whole, the typical white working-class gangsters that had preoccupied the police in past decades, but were, instead, small numbers of young Afro-Caribbean men who became the centre of a moral panic.[34]

The period from the mid-1980s to the end of the twentieth century saw very large increases in crime and 'notwithstanding drops in recorded levels in the recent years [these] remain at a historically high level.'[35] In fact, just as 'between 1945 and 1970 the nation's recorded crime had more than tripled', between 1971 and 2001 it more than tripled again.[36] The most notable change in the nature of serious property crime in the last decades of the twentieth century was the shift from physical to virtual. As lives and businesses have shifted from the 'analogue' to the 'digital' in the last few decades, personal and work lives, business transactions, and consumer habits have all come to rely on a complex and ever-expanding network of electronic devices and online communication. Electronic offences became a feature of financial crime long before the advent of the Internet on which so much of life and financial crime could now be argued to hinge. As the world had changed to become more digital, so too had the nature of property crime.[37] Credit-card fraud and illicit bank transfers came to replace the robbery of wage vans on payday, and in turn have been replaced by Internet banking fraud, identity theft and a range of digital scams. A shift in how money was handled and financial business occurred took place. The later decades of the twentieth century saw the advent of virtual payments and Internet-based credit and debit transactions. Just like violent street robbery, the credit card crime, identity theft and bank fraud did not require skilled groups of professionals working together on meticulously planned jobs. Instead, hugely profitable financial crime could be carried out by a lone expert with the right equipment.

3. Historiography

The history of ideas around burglars and robbers stretches back to the mid-nineteenth century. Mayhew and Binney, and a host of other Victorian commentators, described the training of juveniles into a life of crime in the criminal 'rookeries', the specialised taxonomy of burglars, dippers, sneak thieves, safe-crackers and so on, and the unique tools of the trade that each type of property offender used to ply their trade.[38] The descriptions of a professional class were stated with authority, but the reality was that much of the assertions about professionalisation were not evidenced and were largely illusionary. Similar myth-making about the professionalisation of property offenders continued into the late nineteenth and early twentieth century. It is telling that many ideas arose from fictional portrayals of dashing and adventurous burglars and robbers. 'Raffles the Burglar! Raffles the Thief!' was a hugely popular fictional character, second only to Conan Doyle's 'Sherlock Holmes'.[39] The image of a skillful cat-burglar, dedicated to professional expertise, was inflected in the national media and in the colourful descriptions of real cases. Sergeant Leeson, an East End detective, asserted that he had arrested the original 'cat burglar' in the early 1900s.[40] However, there were many contenders for that title. Even some 40 years after the first Raffles story appeared, his name was still being coined: 'A Would-Be Raffles' appeared at Salford juvenile court when a 16-year-old admitted 40 burglaries in an attempt to imitate the legendary thief.[41]

It is only the relatively recent work of Hobbs, Levi and Taylor which have brought a greater academic focus to the development of professional and organised crime in the twentieth century.[42] Similarly, until recently, there has been little work on the role that wartime conditions have played in developing criminal networks of serious property offenders operating across the UK. Studies by Smithies, Emsley, and Adey et al., are likely to be supplemented by the new raft of work being undertaken on twentieth-century crime, but the historiography of serious property offenders will still not be substantive.[43] Possibly the lacuna is because serious property offending, until the 1970s, was very similar in character to that of the nineteenth century. For example Raphael Samuel's collaborative writing with Arthur Harding described how Harding stole from shops and formed networks of burglars, receivers and handlers in both pre– and post–World War One England: 'Most of Harding's robberies involved van-dragging (jumping onto moving vehicles and pulling off the goods for confederates to pick up)', but he also carried out street robberies using violence: 'A lot of garroting went on … you had to be tall to do it. You would come up to a man from behind, put your arms round his throat, with your fists on his throttle. If it went on for more than a few seconds he would choke, so you had to be skilled.'[44] Edward Smithies argued that robbers and thieves in the 1930s continued to practice the same traditional modes of robbery as had Harding and his ilk.[45] Burglaries continued to be committed by local men, most often on the private homes of the well-off. Predominantly, burglars in this period made a living from the easy pilfering to be made in middle-class homes. Few burglaries involved high-value thefts of jewellery, artworks and antiques.

The practice of fraud was also fairly unchanging as the first half of the twentieth century unfolded. The 'con men' (swindlers and tricksters) described in Detective Inspector Percy Smith's 1938 catalogue of the fraudsters that he had come across in his career were very similar in character to the swindling clerks, commercial travellers, agents and 'Mr Pooters' perpetrating frauds in the nineteenth century.[46] The *modus operendus* for fraud was essentially the same, and the people carrying it out were similar in class, gender and occupation as they had been before World War One. Smithies argues that it was not until after the 1930s that there was a significant shift away from the Victorian origins of property crime towards a 'new "technology" of property offending', mainly involving mobile offenders in fast cars.[47]

However, despite contemporary panic that armed gangsters in automobiles were visiting a reign of terror on Britain's cities in the interwar period, there was, in reality, only a gradual shift away from targeting private residences towards shop breaking and the raiding of commercial properties. Offenders in the 1930s took advantage of the availability of cars, and the spreading suburbanisation of Britain, to commit robberies and burglaries further from home. Highly mobile and able to work in the city or at a rural country house, such thieves were prolific and difficult to catch. Whilst the image of these burglars had shifted, and their targets evolved, this kind of property crime nevertheless followed the pattern of previous decades in so much as robbery and burglary continued to be the preserve of single offenders or very small groups involved in simple private thefts. However, contemporary commentators, if not many modern historians, noted that the socio-economic conditions created by World War Two created unprecedented changes in the operation and scope for serious property crime.

Wartime commentators, politicians and senior police officers became predominantly concerned with two features: the black market which created opportunities for very large-scale robberies and the apparent rise in juvenile offending. The onset of the war initially saw a slight decrease in crime as young men joined the armed forces. However this effect did not last for long. Men who had not gone to fight, and new waves of juvenile offenders, found multiple profitable criminal opportunities in wartime Britain, as modern authors such as Roodhouse, Emsley, and Adey et al. note.[48]

The wartime crime wave continued after World War Two, due both to the shortage of jobs for returning soldiers and the fact that rationing did not finally end until 1954. Individuals without the official documents, or those who could not find a job in a difficult post-war economy, still needed to eat. Meier provides evidence to suggest that in the final years of the war, deserters constituted between 5 and 7.5 per cent of all persons arrested.[49] Yet the generalised shortages and difficulties occasioned by the war had a far more long-reaching and diverse impact on property crime. Material hardship caused by the war, most notably in relation to food and clothing, arguably continued until the end of rationing in 1954 and thus, to some extent, the crimes of robbery and burglary that evolved in wartime continued for almost a decade after. Whilst the demand for rationed items remained high, there was only so much the authorities could do to combat crimes that, to some extent, enjoyed public support. It was hard to collect information on raids and the offenders or 'spivs' responsible for fuelling the black market whilst so many relied upon their proceeds. As Donald Thomas noted 'the only cure for spivery was the abolition of shortages.'[50]

If the ending of rationing closed off one market, the Assistant Commissioner of the Metropolitan Police, Sir Richard Jackson, suggested a new time had arrived. He stated that 'If I were asked to give a single date for the opening of a new era ... I would suggest May 21st 1952'. This date was the day of the Eastcastle Street robbery, the large-scale theft of bank notes from a London General Post Office.[51] Whilst not the first of its kind, the robbery was important from the perspective of the example it set to similar groups of thieves.[52] The Eastcastle Street Robbery showed that prior planning and meticulous organisation really could pay. This new brand of robberies combined serious preparation with the targeting of high-value goods in transit and the free use of violence.[53] Violence was not only more frequently used but was also more deadly due to the use of guns.

Owning a gun was not illegal in the first part of the twentieth century; most farmers owned shotguns, and a lot of men owned pistols that they had been issued (or found, or stolen) during World War One. Others simply bought their guns. Arthur Harding reminisced, 'I got my first gun about 1904. I remember I fired it in a crowd against a man named Sawyer ... I don't know how I missed but the bullet went up in the air ... I wanted a gun more for protection than for anything else. You could buy a gun then for about 4s or 5s – automatics hadn't come in.'[54] As the British newspapers contemplated the possibility that guns could be used in routine robberies, especially after American 'gangster' movies had glamorised violent crime, the media called for harsher penalties for armed robbery:

> "Hold-Ups" and violence are strewn so lavishly over the news columns in these days that a recluse, drawing his impressions of a post-war society mainly from the newspapers, might be led to assume that firearms are as common as lamp-posts and the use of them as familiar as it is in the films. ... It is possible that the war has left us with more fools who are ready to follow a fashion than do desperadoes who are resolved on bloodshed. ... It makes it all the more necessary for judges and magistrates to treat the mere production of a firearm as a grave offence in itself.[55]

However, although they may have been plentiful in the interwar period, firearms were rarely discharged in the commission of robbery. This changed somewhat after the end of World War Two. Meier contended that from the end of the war until the end of rationing in 1954, 'post-war thieves displayed novel tendencies towards the use of violence in large-scale thefts, due in part to the participation of deserters and ex-servicemen'.[56] Just as with the interwar period, after 1945, returning servicemen had taken pistols and ammunition as souvenirs as they left a defeated Germany. Demobilised soldiers could also keep hold of their guns or sell them on to those that had need of them, and, as a result, 'Firearms rarely seen in pre-war robbery were everywhere.'[57]

The scale of the problem was acutely illustrated by the 1946 amnesty for illegal firearms that yielded over 75,000 weapons and 2,000,000 rounds of ammunition in London.[58] It was not only the availability of weapons that made post-war robbery more likely to be violent. There is evidence to suggest that one cultural and psychological impact of a long and bloody war was that thieves were more inclined to use extreme force. Meier suggested that crime had taken on the 'characteristics of war itself.'[59] Thomas goes further than this arguing that 'some men who had learnt the arts of war continued to exercise them in the new peace.'[60] He suggests that 'some robbers who were to spend many years in Prison might have made a good living by honest means. Yet leading a bank raid, blowing a safe, let alone hijacking a mail train brought the high-octane excitement of active service.'[61] As Emsley noted, the popular 1960 film *League of Gentlemen* visualised this attitude in its depiction of a demobilised highly-skilled group of officers who carry out a daring raid with fast cars, machine guns and military precision. Violent armed robbery seemed appealing even to those who had taken no part in the war. Meier argues that national service in the 1950s made a new generation of young men familiar with guns.[62] Post-war robbery heralded 'the emergence of a new kind of criminal who belonged to "as tough and cunning a crop of hoodlums Britain ever knew."'[63] These new crooks were perceived as twice as dangerous not only because they were armed, or because of their organisational skills, but also because criminals were motorised.

The interwar period was the start of a time in which burglary and burglars became increasingly mobile.[64] The police seemed helpless to stop a new and growing boom in armed and mobile robberies:

> "Robbery Under Arms" – The police, it is stated, are forming armed patrols of motor-cyclists in order to deal with the frequently reported thefts of motor cars. Scotland Yard takes the view that these thefts are the work of one gang under central control – a campaign planned, no doubt, by some descendant of Sherlock Holmes. The Guardian Leader went on to suggest that the police use guns and fast cars to combat this rising tide.[65]

Burglars and robbers were now faster, better equipped and highly mobile, making them much harder to catch. For the first time, criminals could offend in one part of the country and live in another. The police were placed at a disadvantage like never before. As Meier noted, 'Motor cars mechanised criminal activity enabling it to spread through the country and be undertaken on a mass scale.'[66]

These mobile offenders were a breed apart from the 'smash and grab' adventurers of the interwar period described by Smithies: 'Under cover of fog, motor bandits carried out a lightning smash-and-grab raid at the jewellers shop. … Two men drove up to the shop in a dark-coloured touring car. One of them, it is stated, smashed a window with a hammer and snatched a tray of diamond and sapphire rings.'[67]

Post–World War Two offenders turned their attention away from the relatively small gains to be made in the burglary of private houses and small-scale smash-and-grab jewellery raids to the theft of large quantities of commercial merchandise from shops, factories and warehouses. Spoils for these robbers might be huge numbers of gems and precious metals from Regent Street jewellers, or a consignment of fur coats or other high fashion from a tailor's warehouse. Typically, for these offences, a small number of men would drive a car into the front of a shop or the doors of a warehouse and proceed to load the vehicle with available goods. Within a few minutes they could be speeding to a safe location where the car could be abandoned and the goods divided. The benefits of this kind of robbery were clear: the speed and convenience of such raids increased the potential for the size of a haul and severely reduced the likelihood of apprehension.

Even when audacious robberies occurred in broad daylight with police nearby, officers on horse or foot were no match for organised criminals speeding away in a car.[68] The police scrambled to motorise themselves but were small in number and power compared to mobile thieves. Nevertheless, when burglary decreased by 16 per cent in 1935, the police put it down to the Map and Statistics Office guiding police cars (or 'Q cars') to the scene of the crime much more quickly, as well as the introduction of the Flying Squad who devoted their attention to preventing and investigating property crime.[69] A decade later, immediately after the war and until 1949, the Metropolitan Police in London established the Ghost Squad after recognising the unprecedented rise in crime statistics after the war.[70] Detectives in the squad were responsible for collecting information on serious offenders, trailing suspects and preventing incidents of serious and organised crime. Quickly following this pace, similar operations were developed elsewhere in the country. Even after its demise as a unit, the activities undertaken by the Ghost Squad continued to form an important part of specialist policing in the second half of the twentieth century.[71] Yet even the greatest innovations of policing continuously struggled to keep up with mobile offenders until the 1970s and '80s when the police got faster cars and a kind of parity was achieved.

Historians of the 1950s and '60s, however, still lagged behind. There is still a paucity of literature on crime in this period. Although Louise Jackson's work has now revealed the world of youth culture and youth 'deviance' in the 1960s coffee bars, a comprehensive review of property crime in the later post-war period remains to be written. It was only in the 1970s when the media and a small number of influential university academics took an interest in the putative connections between race and crime that robbery again began to be studied in detail. Replacing concerns about armed and mobile teams of professional robbers, the spectre of 'mugging' by young black men presented a new 'crisis' for the media and police to tackle in the 1970s. Whilst, as with any crime, it is hard to know exactly how prominent muggings were in this period, Stewart Hall's exhaustive analysis of the mugging panic suggested that the true peaking of crime in the period was between 1955 and 1965.[72] Thus by the time true concern about this offence arose in the early 1970s, its greatest increase had already passed. As Hall, Jefferson, and others revealed, concern over mugging was far more closely linked to racial tensions and anxiety over social change than an actual change in the incidents of crime or those responsible for it. Moreover, from an historical perspective we know that there was nothing particularly new or innovative about this kind of robbery. Definitions vary, but to a large extent the forceful robbery of men and women on the street by muggers was little different from the 'garrottings' that had terrorised England more than one hundred years earlier in the 1860s. Under different guises and using different methods, violent robbery from the person had been a continuous feature on the criminal landscape, as Pearson and others have noted.[73]

Street mugging and small and disorganised forms of violent robbery continued into the 1980s and beyond, and persuaded the public that robbery was essentially a low-level street-level offence. Although a number of armed bank robberies occurred in later decades, they were few and far between. In some ways technology changed so comprehensively in the final quarter of the twentieth century that even established thieves were unprepared to meet it. The methods and operations of notorious professional criminals of the 1950s and '60s, such as the Krays and Richardsons, seemed redundant and curiously old-fashioned by the 1970s, as the following case study illustrates.

4. Case Studies

It is impossible to identify one single case which exemplifies the serious, organised and professional property offender. As the above sections have explained, there were significant divergences in the operation and treatment of burglary, robbery and fraud in the twentieth century. Whereas fraudsters were often (though not by any means exclusively) drawn from the middle classes, or at least from those who had access to the means to commit fraud (access to business accounts, credit facilities and so on), robbers and burglars tended to rely on physical prowess and brute force. Moreover, there was a vast difference between those street robbers who demanded with menaces the handing over of fashionable trainers, or mobile phones, or wallets, and the teams of armed robbers who preyed on wage vans. This section will therefore focus mostly on a few notorious 'characters' who seem to exemplify and typify the most serious property offenders, those who secured a place in the public imagination whenever the topic of serious property crime arose. Perhaps the most famous group of professional offenders in the twentieth century were The Great Train Robbers of 1963 who held up the Glasgow to London Mail Train. 'In a world in which major crime is usually sordid as well as brutal, the train robbery made excellent family reading. If not heroes they were anti-heroes. The very use of the archaic word 'robber', with its medieval romanticism, implied an heroic mould.'[74] They did not possess the sophistication of Raffles, but they did have an assumed dashing and panache with which they carried out their 'caper'. The gang got away with over £2m; however, they were all subsequently arrested. Evidence found by Buckinghamshire police, forensically examined, secured the capture and conviction of most of the gang, something which often escapes public memory. So too does the injury of the train driver who later died of his injuries. The idea of a band of brothers daringly raiding a train seemed not only to preserve something of wartime camaraderie (discussed earlier) but also the spirit of eighteenth-century highwaymen or Butch Cassidy and the Sundance Kid.

However, even professional robbers did not operate within the same group for robbery after robbery. Robbers were individualists who would team their own skills with that of others on an *ad hoc* basis if an appealing opportunity presented itself. Laurie Taylor's ethnographic study of London's criminal underworld confirmed this picture of a complex sub-culture of professionalism, violence, gambling and very close relationships between men who made their living from serious crime[75] – men who were hidden in a secret and shadowy world. However, they keyed into a long tradition of public imagination. Taylor's 1980s villains were considered to be the descendants of 1960s 'faces'. At the top of the 1960s crime families were the Kray twins, Ronnie and Reggie, who were reviled (and admired) for their use of serious violence in running their property crime-based operation.[76] In fact they had started out with one of the longest running types of serious frauds, the 'Long Firm' game, in the 1950s not the 1960s. This type of fraud had originated in the nineteenth century, but continued well into the twentieth century.[77] They only turned to violence once they had created a network of organised offenders working in East London. Their rivals, the Richardson Brothers, and their henchman 'Mad' Frankie Fraser, operated south of the River Thames in the 1960s. Fraser himself had started out robbing shops during the blackout conditions of World War Two. Although their sphere of influence was away from the Kray twins 'turf', it was the simmering resentment that existed between London's two premier crime families that caused the downfall of both 'empires' and the imprisonment of most members of the London 'firms'.[78]

The Kray twins and the Richardsons loomed large in the media, but their unusually large 'firms' were rare in the 1960s. Like the 1970s and '80s networks that Taylor (1985) and Hobbs (1989, 2001) studied, they were a relatively small part of the picture. As stated earlier, the world of the professional robber was heterogeneous in its makeup. With huge profits to be made, the perpetrators of large-scale robberies and the people involved in particular jobs could range from 'small-time thieves "thinking big" to the hard men who were prepared to take on an armoured truck.'[79] For example, Ronnie Biggs (one of the Great Train Robbers) managed to escape justice for decades, living in Brazil and evading extradition. In 2001 he returned to the UK, and prison, where he remained until released due to his failing health in 2009 (he died in 2013). Needing to find money to live in Brazil he performed many publicity stunts, adding to the idea of glamorous villains 'living it large' abroad.[80] However, what has now largely been forgotten is that Biggs was no criminal mastermind. Neither was he a part of the professional group of serious robbers. He was a bit-part player – a small-time thief who was peripheral to the robbery and who would not be remembered if he had not carried on with his Brazilian escapades for so long.

As Emsley reminds us, most robberies were small scale and the term 'organised' crime was little used until the closing decades of the twentieth century.[81] Moreover, as Hobbs noted, some groups of offenders fall easily into the category of professional organised crime – safe crackers in the 1950s, armed robbers in the 1960s and '70s, drug dealers in the 1990s – but others do not.[82] The street robbers who stole trainers in the 1980s or mobile phones in the 1990s were scarcely professional, and the small robberies committed regularly by young men in the 1970s and '80s was evidence of 'disorganised' rather than organised crime. Professional, dedicated, and skilled burglars and robbers did exist, and World War Two could be seen as a turning point, when serious property offenders became 'networked', which allowed larger and larger 'jobs' to be carried out. However, this world had largely evaporated by the 1970s and '80s. The large-scale robberies once carried out by the Krays, Richardsons and the Great Train Robbers, are now a rare and infrequent event. For example, the 'Brinks-Mat heist in 1983 was almost greeted as a return to a by-gone age. On the 26th of November 1983 an organised gang of robbers broke into a warehouse at London's Heathrow Airport. Expecting to bag a haul of around £3m (which would still have been a considerable robbery), they found over £26m worth of gold bullion, diamonds and cash. With the help of an inside man they gained access to the vault (they had poured petrol over warehouse staff threatening to light a match if their demands were not met). Some, but not all, members of the gang were subsequently arrested (not all were convicted). In a curious return to the heyday of armed robbery, however, the gold bullion was partly laundered through Charles Frederick 'Charlie' Wilson, one of the 1963 Great Train Robbery gang (the treasurer) who had 'retired' to Spain. His skills may have eroded in retirement since he managed to lose £3m of the bullion. In 1990 a young British man knocked on the front door of his hacienda north of Marbella and shot Wilson dead. Over the next three years, four more shootings were connected to the Brink's-Mat raid, and the robbery went down as a serious but anomalous event in the history of 1980s crime. As far as organised crime went, the drug trade offered more opportunities for profit than the drama and risk of armed robberies. That era of serious property offending by teams of burglars and robbers, described in the first sections of this chapter, had gone.

5.   Conclusion

The property crime that had typified the Victorian period continued to dominate the landscape of crime until the First World War. Burglars targeted residences; robbers carried out street-thefts (mainly in the urban areas where anonymity gave them some protection); fraudsters carried out acts of deception (prosecuted as gaining property by false pretences) and a few carried out larger Long-Firm swindles. Serious property crime remained steady (with the exception of the World War One period) until the interwar period when slight, but nonetheless noticeable, changes in how and what property offenders were targeting occurred. However, World War Two could be seen as one of the first significant turning points for property crime. The black market created the conditions for large-scale robbery from warehouses and factories, and the networks of distribution that were forged created a large (if loose) network of organised criminals. This could be said to be the start of organised and professional crime, even if that is sometimes overstated. The introduction of fast cars allowed armed gangs of criminals to commit what was essentially the 'highway robbery' of wages vans; the police were obliged to try and catch them in equally fast motor vehicles. When modern banking technology meant that wages were paid directly into employee accounts, the volatile trade in high-speed mobile robbery declined. Aside from a few high-stakes burglaries and robberies, such as the Great Train Robbery and the Brinks-Mat job, most robberies in the later 1970s and '80s returned to small-scale street offences. Indeed one could say that the prevalence of domestic burglaries and street robberies in the later decades of the twentieth century returned the character of serious property crime to its earlier form – small-scale disorganised crime. The evolution of technology has doubtlessly been one of the most important defining factors in both the rates and nature of serious property crime during the twentieth century.

Notes

1. *The Guardian*, 19th October 1979.
2. In Scotland, the term 'housebreaking' is used.
3. Trends are similar for Scotland, as discussed later in the chapter.
4. Figures for property crime with violence taken from judicial statistics for England and Wales, annually published from 1856.
5. C. Hale (1998) 'The Labour Market and Post-war Crime Trends in England and Wales', in P. Carlen and R. Morgan (eds) *Crime Unlimited? Questions for the 21st Century* (Basingstoke: Palgrave Macmillan), pp. 30–56 at p. 31.
6. C. Emsley (2013) *Soldier, Sailor, Beggarman, Thief: Crime and the British Armed Forces since 1914* (Oxford: Oxford University Press).
7. Unemployment rates taken from J. Denman and P. McDonald (1996) 'Unemployment Statistics from 1881 to the Present Day', *Labour Market Trends*, January, pp. 5–18 at pp. 6–7.
8. W.M. Meier (2011) *Property Crime in London, 1850 to the Present* (Basingstoke: Palgrave Macmillan), p. 57.
9. *The Times*, 5th July 1929. The Long Firm begins with the fraudsters placing small regular orders with wholesalers and ensuring that they are paid promptly. Larger orders are then placed, and when the goods are delivered, they are quickly sold at 'knock-down' prices. They then shut the operation down, fleeing with the profits, and leaving their debts to the wholesaler unpaid. The statistics for 1928 showed that the losses to trade through fraud amounted to £28,000,000.

10. In fact, prosecution figures reveal that post-war robbery was also dominated, almost exclusively, by young men (below the age of 30) and that robbery would often be their first offence – see Meier (2011) *Property Crime in London*, p. 121.
11. Figures taken from P. Adey, B. Godfrey and D. Cox (2016) *Crime, Wartime and Control: Protecting the Population of a Blitzed City, 1939–1945* (London: Bloomsbury).
12. E. Smithies (1982) *Crime in Wartime: A Social History of Crime in World War II* (London: G. Allen & Unwin), p. 2.
13. *Ibid.*
14. *Ibid.*, p. 5.
15. D. Thomas (2005) *Villains' Paradise: Britain's Underworld from the Spivs to the Krays* (London: John Murray), p. 61.
16. *Ibid.*, p. 37.
17. *Manchester Guardian*, 7th January 1940.
18. Emsley (2013) *Soldier, Sailor, Beggarman, Thief, passim.*
19. Meier (2011) *Property Crime in London*, p. 110.
20. *Ibid.*, p. 115.
21. Smithies (1982) *Crime in Wartime*, p. 71.
22. *Ibid.*, p. 59.
24. From the 1950s, crime in general rose steadily at around ten per cent a year, see Hale (1998) 'The Labour Market and Post-war Crime Trends', p. 31.
23. Figures taken from the annually published judicial statistics for England and Wales.
25. Figures taken from the annually published judicial statistics for Scotland.
26. *Ibid.*, p. 111.
27. Hale (1998) 'The Labour Market and Post-war Crime Trends', p. 31.
28. Thomas (2005) *Villains' Paradise*, p. 309.
29. This was estimated by *Top Gear* BBC Television (10th July 2005). This rather dubious source does at least confirm the public image of the Transit as favourite choice of armed robbers, and it is probably not too far from reality.
30. Thomas (2005) *Villains' Paradise*, p. 169.
31. C. Emsley (2011) *Crime and Society in Twentieth-Century England* (Harlow: Pearson), p. 101.
32. Meier (2011) *Property Crime in London*, p. 130.
33. S. Hall, C. Critcher, T. Jefferson, J. Clarke and B. Roberts (1978) *Policing the Crisis: Mugging, the State and Law and Order* (London: Macmillan), p. 11.
34. S. Cohen (1972) *Folk Devils and Moral Panics: The Creation of the Mods and Rockers* (London: MacGibbon and Kee).

35. Hale (1998) 'The Labour Market and Post-war Crime Trends', p. 33.

36. Thomas (2005) *Villains' Paradise*, p. 467.

37. R. Bryant and S. Bryant (eds) (2014) *Policing Digital Crime* (London: Ashgate).

38. For summaries of these discourses see D. Taylor (2010) *Hooligans, Harlots, and Hangmen* (London: Praeger), *passim* and B. Godfrey and P. Lawrence (2014) *Crime and Justice since 1750* (London: Routledge), *passim*.

39. R. Bleiler (2014) 'Raffles: The Gentleman Thief', *Strand Magazine* (http://www.strandmag.com) (Accessed 30 September 2017) and E. Moss (2014) '"How I Had Liked This Villain! How I Had Admired Him!": A.J. Raffles and the Burglar as British Icon, 1898–1939', *Journal of British Studies*, Vol. 53, No. 1, pp. 136–161.

40. A. Leeson (1934) *Lost London: The Memoirs of an East End Detective* (London: Stanley Paul and Co.), pp. 185–190.

41. *Manchester Guardian*, 5th May 1944.

42. See respectively D. Hobbs (1989) *Doing the Business: Entrepreneurship, the Working Class, and Detectives in the East End of London* (Oxford: Oxford University Press); D. Hobbs (1995) *Bad Business: Professional Crime in Modern Britain* (Oxford: Oxford University Press); D. Hobbs (2001) 'The Firm: Organisational Logic and Criminal Culture on a Shifting Terrain', *British Journal of Criminology*, Vol. 41, pp. 549–560; M. Levi (1981) *The Phantom Capitalists: The Organisation and Control of Long-Firm Fraud* (London: Heinemann International) and L. Taylor (1985) *In the Underworld* (London: Guild Publishing).

43. See respectively Smithies (1982) *Crime in Wartime*; Emsley (2013) *Soldier, Sailor, Beggarman, Thief* and Adey, Godfrey and Cox (2015) *Crime, Wartime and Control*.

44. R. Samuel (1981) *East End Underworld: Chapters in the Life of Arthur Harding – Volume Two* (London: Routledge and Kegan Paul), pp. 111–112.

45. Smithies (1982) *Crime in Wartime*, pp. 44–46.

46. See P. Smith (1938) *Con Man: The Personal Reminiscences of Ex-Detective Inspector Percy J. Smith, Late of Scotland Yard* (London: Herbert Jenkins Ltd) and H. Shore (2015) *London's Criminal Underworlds, c. 1720 – c. 1930: A Social and Cultural History* (Basingstoke: Palgrave Macmillan).

47. Smithies (1982) *Crime in Wartime*, p. 40.

48. See *Smithies (1982)*; M. Roodhouse (2013) *Black Market Britain 1939–1955* (Oxford: Oxford University Press); Emsley (2013) *Soldier, Sailor, Beggarman, Thief* (Oxford: Oxford University Press), and Adey, Godfrey and Cox (2016) *Crime, Wartime and Control.*

49. Meier (2011) *Property Crime in London*, p. 113.
50. Particularly in the areas of clothing and petrol, where rationing continued up to 1949 and 1950 respectively, see Thomas (2005) *Villains' Paradise*, p. 73.
51. R. Jackson (1967) *Occupied with Crime* (London: Harrap and Co. Ltd), p. 129.
52. Meier (2011) *Property Crime in London*, p. 118.
53. *Ibid.*, p. 119.
54. Samuel (1981) *East End Underworld*, p. 117.
55. *Manchester Guardian*, 20th April 1920.
56. Meier (2011) *Property Crime in London*, p. 111.
57. Thomas (2005) *Villains' Paradise*, p. 10.
58. *Ibid.*, p. 10.
59. *Ibid.*, p. 27.
60. *Ibid.*, p. 4.
61. *Ibid.*
62. Meier (2011) *Property Crime in London*, p. 125.
63. *Ibid.*, p. 109.
64. Smithies (1982) *Crime in Wartime*, pp. 45–47. There are other clear developments in the nature and exercise of robbery in the interwar period that must be acknowledged also, even if they remain an example of minority practice. The techniques and methods used by safe crackers adapted to utilise the tools of modernity, including the use of special trucks to transport stolen safes.
65. *Manchester Guardian*, 25th August 1919.
66. Meier (2011) *Property Crime in London*, p. 42.
67. *Manchester Guardian*, 16th November 1929. In the 1930s as well, smash-and-grab gangs – such as the Elephant and Castle gang – utilised fast cars to carry out their raids. See A. Brown (2013) *Inter-war Penal Policy and Crime in England: The Dartmoor Convict Prison Riots, 1932* (Basingstoke: Palgrave Macmillan), p. 99.
68. Meier (2011) *Property Crime in London*, p. 64.
69. *The Observer*, 23rd April 1935.
70. Emsley (2011) *Crime and Society*, p. 132.
71. *Ibid.*, p. 162.
72. Hall, Critcher, Jefferson, Clarke and Roberts (1978) *Policing the Crisis*, p. 14.
73. *Ibid.*, pp. 9–10. See also G. Pearson (1883) *Hooligan: A History of Respectable Fears* (London: Macmillan) and Godfrey and Lawrence (2014) *Crime and Justice since 1750*.

74. *The Guardian*, 18th December 1965.

75. Taylor (1985) *In the Underworld,* passim.

76. *Ibid.*, pp. 147–168.

77. For further discussion see Levi (1981) *The Phantom Capitalists* and Shore (2015) *London's Criminal Underworlds, c. 1720 – c. 1930.*

78. Hobbs (1989) *Doing the Business*, pp. 53–61.

79. Thomas (2005) *Villains' Paradise*, p. 309.

80. As did, of course, the criminals like Ronnie Knight and Howard Marks who 'retired' to Spain in the 1970s and 1980s.

81. Emsley (2011) *Crime and Society*, pp. 21–22.

82. Hobbs (1995) *Bad Business,* passim.

4

Racial Hate Crime in Modern Britain

David Nash

1. Introduction

The twentieth century has arguably seen the protection of individuals and minorities as a particularly fundamental growth area of police work. Where the nineteenth century perhaps only encountered minorities as public order problems, or in the context of other crimes, the twentieth century saw them as victims of criminal activity in their own right. Nineteenth-century society regularly thought in terms of the 'criminal classes' and thought of criminals themselves as members of some sort of collective form of aberration from society. By the first third of the nineteenth century the state had admitted both the desirability and possibility of intervening to protect vulnerable groups, such as children and factory workers. But it was only in the twentieth century that British society moved towards safeguarding the rights and identities of groups based solely on their characteristics.

One part of this book, and indeed an aim of this chapter, is to show how changes in the legal landscape have transformed some areas of criminal law and the very conception of criminal justice and its purpose. In the area of discrimination and hate crime, an inclusive definition of citizenship has vastly altered over the course of the twentieth century. In the earlier part of the century, the state was arguably complicit in policies, actions and attitudes that were discriminatory to say the least. By the end of the century, the state had started to develop elaborate methods of defining, detecting, policing, punishing, rehabilitating and educating its population about the evils of, and the damage done to society by, racial hate crimes. Whilst the state did not actively participate in racial hate crimes in Britain, it could certainly be said that at times it was complicit in policies and attitudes that marginalised individuals and groups, perhaps even creating conditions in which prejudice could flourish. Moreover, as we shall discover, a range of feelings and responses such as ignorance, complacency, mistaken assumptions, indifference and insensitivity grew in importance. All these contributed to a situation in which problems evident in the last two decades of the twentieth century have only really begun to reach resolution in the initial decades of the twenty-first century. Yet the onward course of such attitudes through history is by no means linear nor consistently liberalising. This may be demonstrated by a subsequent historian who seeks to analyse the history of prejudice and hate crime in the wake of Brexit.

This chapter highlights the history of racially motivated hate crime, since this was the category of offence which really drove the development of the concept in Britain. This is of course not to say that other areas of discrimination such as disability and cultural lifestyles that attract prejudice did not exist or lacked significance. Indeed, it is a feature of the phenomenon's history that the state's confidence to reach out to new minorities in need of help built upon previous successes in this area.[1] Nonetheless, it would be true to say that discrimination around race has probably been the most important driver of legal developments in Britain in this field during the twentieth century.

Establishing patterns in hate crime perpetration with any degree of certainty can be difficult. There is likely to be an abnormally large dark figure of unrecorded crime which neither policing practitioners nor historians are ever likely to uncover. Likewise, it is equally possible that crimes with a 'hate' content or context may be recorded without this thoroughly crucial element to the crime being noticed. It is also regularly noteworthy that national incidents of one kind or another can provoke spikes in hate crime activity. From an initial focus upon race in the early 1980s, by 2004 the Metropolitan Police Service has expanded its definition to include: 'Any incident that is perceived by the victim, or any other person, to be racist, homophobic, transphobic or due to a person's religion, belief, gender, identity or disability.'[2]

The collection of data relating to instances of racial hate crime is still surprisingly in its infancy and was only seriously systematised by the very end of the twentieth century. This has gone hand in hand with policing developments so that, on occasions, it can be difficult to ascertain whether an increase in racially motivated hate crime (as occurred between 1996 and 2001) is actually 'real', or is a detection panic indicating police attention and action which has been motivated by new priorities.[3] Nevertheless, some interesting patterns from which we can draw some general conclusions do start to emerge from particular studies. In recording anti-Semitic incidents in London between 2001 and 2004 for instance, researchers noticed that these incidents occurred where the targeted community was numerous in number, in actual locations that ostensibly belonged to that target community (in this case schools and synagogues) and that many of these incidents were essentially opportunistic in nature.[4] Only approximately one in ten of the recorded incidents appeared to target individual people, leaving most to be confined to assaults upon property, buildings or presumably general expressions of hatred in community space (e.g. posters, graffiti, etc.).[5] Whilst much political motivation in these crimes was, to a degree, self-evident, there were very few examples of organised politically extreme groups.

Males in the victim sample were targeted disproportionately by male hate crime perpetrators with females generally making a much smaller proportion of both samples.[6] In approximately a third of incidents, no perpetrator was ever identified and only one incident in ten resulted in proceedings against a suspect.[7] Perpetrators in three-fifths of the incidents (approaching 50 per cent) were neighbours or occasionally business associates of the target, with the largest proportion falling within the 41–60 age range.[8] The study's conclusions noted that much of the public's perception of hate crime against Jews was sensationalised and was associated with their sufferings as a result of the holocaust and attitudes in regard to Zionism. This study was keen to point out that it had uncovered both the simplicity and the ubiquity of random and everyday events involving hate crime, Such findings posed something of a challenge to models of 'hate' which saw it linked to political extremism and extremist groups in the main.

As it suggested, such episodes were arguably far more easily policed than the random, opportunist everyday remark that potentially lurked around every corner.[9]

2.   Chronology

a)   Definition and Legal Context

As many lawyers point out, it is scarcely illegal to hate a group or set of individuals. Yet it is also acknowledged that hate crime remains an age-old problem with a clear history of its own stretching back to the ancient world.[10] Many schools of legal thinking argue it is the duty of the law to intervene when that hatred manifests itself as crimes harmful to individuals, groups or societies. This tends to explain why so much of the framing of hate crime as a concept sees it as an adjunct or aggravating factor that affects how a crime is viewed, and is likely to influence sentencing policy for the individuals convicted.[11] Hate crime is generally defined as something that 'represents official recognition of the harm of inter-group aggression and the importance of applying sanctions against it'.[12] Individuals indulge in hate crime because they have a bias against the victim which is a perception of difference or otherness. Their dislike of, or aversion to, the victim is based not upon them as individuals, but instead they are seen as 'representative of a group perceived as possessing a reviled set of characteristics.'[13] Within the nexus of hate crime the perceived scale of the activity is somewhat important. This can range from mischievous juvenile acts through to more serious political actions with consequences that may well far exceed the injury of individual victims.

The goal of a hate crime is to send a clear message to the victim, which is intended to establish, or re-establish, hierarchies in which the perpetrator re-assigns the victim to a clearly subordinate role through targeted denigration. This idea of the perpetrator somehow 'sending a message' is quite crucial to how the crime itself is conceived. Indeed, this also explains why so many hate crime incidents are associated with other words and actions, themselves often labelled 'hate speech'. To combat this, the goal of anti–hate crime legislation and policies is to somehow reassure the victim that society will not tolerate such actions. Whether this, in practice, is a simple or a complex matter varies between respective incidents. Certainly the whole mechanism of hate crime places considerable responsibility upon the state to restore a destabilised situation, and to re-establish feelings of safety amongst those affected by such crimes.

Two things highlight hate crimes as different. Firstly, they have an historical continuity that makes them remarkably similar over many centuries. Indeed it is a feature of such crimes that they are able to draw explicitly from past ideas, idioms and incidents. Secondly, hate crimes are different because they can involve the complicity of authority and institutions in societies that have not in the past, or do not now, recognise their cogency and the damage they do to societies. In a sense it takes a recognition that the harm done by such crimes itself becomes a part of their definition. This also means that the whole issue of definition has been an important part of the concept's history. This has frequently been a barometer of how seriously the issue is taken and it also reflects the ebb and flow of policing and government awareness of the issue. Ostensibly, one self-evident element in the concept's history has been an obvious learning curve in how to manage such issues carefully. An inclusive definition, for example, might involve labelling a great many crimes (such as theft) with a racial motive that would distort the perception of such incidents and likewise unhelpfully feed racial stereotypes of who commits crimes and why. Alternatively, an exclusive and narrow definition potentially leads to significant under-reporting and can thus be construed by victims as both a reason not to trust or respect policing authorities, or indeed to consider them actively or incipiently racist.

The legal evolution of this concept has itself been piecemeal and there is no recognisable pattern to its official adoption. Likewise, decisions about who to include under its protection and the precise reasons for this are often unclear. This means the history of hate crime's development is almost entirely reactive, with those groups achieving protection having done so generally speaking through a mixture of accident, legislation to remedy previous wrongs uncovered by scandal or government investigation, the attention of the press and the respective power and influence of individual pressure groups. In many respects, this represents an important part of the history of legal and social developments in the areas of law, crime and policing.

Hate crimes can occur in many forms. Much policing and literature about it, however, has associated the display of hate with an aggressive desire to convey the message – what we might describe as an 'in your face' approach to conveying disapproval, hate and reasserting subordination. It ought also to be recognised that the crime has mutated to embrace other forms and methods of conveying messages. The onset of cyber hate crime, for instance, has placed distance between perpetrator and victim and produced a more anonymised space which allows predators to use hate crime idioms to oppress individuals. Whilst some of this has been used to target groups known to be victims of other forms of hate crime, one special feature of this development has been the manner in which individual women have been targeted with hate style language by social and sexual predators.[14]

b)   Race Hate Crime and Its History

The nineteenth century witnessed considerable immigration from Ireland and the Irish as an ethnic group were, for the most part, assimilated into British society. This emerges as a success story, especially when their numbers are compared to those of other ethnic groups who emigrated to Britain. Although there were anti-Irish disturbances and a plethora of negative stereotypes about the inferiority of the Irish, some have argued these appeared as part of the construction of British identity.[15]

Anti-Semitism and the attitudes that go with it have a long history in most of western Europe. In Britain the small Jewish minority was more or less tolerated after the early modern period.[16] This began to change in the last quarter of the nineteenth century when the number present in Britain roughly trebled in size, or grew seven fold, depending on which estimate is to be believed.[17] These newcomers were also considered to have been politically radicalised so that their presence appeared to represent a political, cultural, social and economic threat to the prosperity of the indigenous urban working class. In the last years of the nineteenth century considerable extra-parliamentary pressure built up and the Aliens

Order of 1905 effectively ended a non-interventionist approach to immigration which had prevailed up to this point. Although primarily aimed at this new influx of immigrants, the order focussed upon economic criteria using powers to exclude those who did not have the means to subsist adequately, as well as those who fell into vagrancy or required poor relief within a year of entry to Britain. These restrictions became stronger in 1914 upon the outbreak of war where aliens were suddenly considered to pose a threat to national security – a consideration that would come and go in the mind of government during the twentieth and twenty-first centuries. After the end of hostilities the 1920 Aliens Order confirmed the broad provision of the 1905 Order, but also required entry into the country to be at an approved port and for immigrants to be in possession of a work permit. This Act also gave the Home Secretary powers to deport individuals whose presence was not considered to be in the public interest.[18] Although such legislation displays economic motives, it nonetheless shows government acceptance of the fear that immigration can generate amongst the most economically vulnerable members of society and a willingness to restrict it when necessary or convenient. Some analyses have described such attitudes and measures as 'State racism'.[19]

Economically trying times were also the backdrop to the most virulent organised 'unofficial racism' directed against Jews in the twentieth century which appeared in the interwar period.[20] The Imperial Fascist League, led by Arnold Leese, preached a strongly anti-Semitic message that appeared to borrow ideas and forms from Nazi propaganda. This was followed by a more popular and mainstream organisation the British Union of Fascists (BUF) whose membership may have reached 50,000 by early 1934.[21] It was especially active in the East End of London and this eventually led to a confrontation with Jewish and left-wing groups in 1936 in what became known as the 'Battle of Cable Street'. A BUF march of 2000 individuals scheduled to go through the East End under police protection found its way hindered by roadblocks and a crowd of 20,000 anti-fascist demonstrators. This latter group was what would now be termed a rainbow coalition of Jewish activists, Communists, Socialists and Irish Dockers. Eventually the march dispersed as the BUF melted away to Hyde Park leaving the anti-fascists at the scene and clashes with the police ensued. This was perhaps the first instance in which the role of the police appeared to have a political dimension amongst those opposed to their protection of a racist march, whilst it is also clear that a police presence intended to preserve public order looked ambivalent to observers and participants alike. This was perhaps an indication that the police force would regularly be cast as the agents of control and enforcement of the unpopular, as well as facing questions about the attitudes its serving officers would periodically display.

Targeted violence against black communities in Britain has substantially been a product of the twentieth century. It was a feature of the post–First World War period which brought black settlers to Britain and there were some outbreaks of violence notably in the ports of London, Bristol, Liverpool, South Shields, Hull, Glasgow and Cardiff.[22] The last of these included an almost total breakdown of law and order in 1919, which was stimulated by a mob of unemployed workers protesting about the employment of black seamen.[23] The long established and continuing immigration of the Catholic Irish into the East End of Glasgow to take up employment in the mining and textile industries led to similar ethnic tensions. Eventually, as the century wore on, sectarianism became located in areas of public confrontation most notably in the metropolitan football culture, particularly associated with the two Glasgow teams Rangers and Celtic.[24]

Britain's post-1945 shortage of labour was partly answered by immigrants from the Commonwealth and aided by the passage of the 1948 British Nationality Act. Although a 'colour bar' existed preventing the entry of black workers into certain trades, there was little widespread hostility to their arrival at least at first. There were occasional, but isolated, outbreaks of violence between mobs of white protestors and black and Asian workers stretching between the late 1940s and late 1950s.[25] By the 1960s, black immigration into Britain had become a serious political issue and the subject of government legislation. The early part of the decade saw curbs upon immigration in the shape of the Commonwealth Immigrants Act of 1962, followed by the Race Relations Act of 1965, which made generalised attempts to limit prejudice in public contexts. However, the latter of these did create a mechanism to hear such cases in the shape of the Race Relations Board and also created the offence of incitement to racial hatred which also applied in Scotland but not

Northern Ireland.[26] The subsequent Race Relations Act of 1968 extended and built upon the precedents set in the 1965 Act and these were further enhanced by the later 1976 Race Relations Act. Interestingly, this acquired a more proactive reputation through its replacement of the Race Relations Board with the newly created Commission for Racial Equality which was also given greater powers. The change of name itself seemed to signal a change in intention behind combatting racial prejudice.

Indeed, it was this last body that was instrumental in lobbying successive Home Secretaries about the problem of racially motivated violence as a terrifying (often politically motivated) upsurge in race-related attacks occurred in the late 1970s and early 1980s. What seems to have been important was the role of the Commission in presenting hard statistical data to government and its effectiveness as a lobbying tool.[27] Certainly this trend towards multi-agency knowledge and approaches seemed like one method of removing what was becoming something of a dangerous and poisoned chalice for the British police. Having sole responsibility for policing racial incidents (especially after the Scarman Report of 1981) seemed almost counterproductive. The encroaching reach of other agencies, untainted by the problems encountered by the police, seemed to offer an olive branch to beleaguered communities, whilst also sharing some of the burden. However, as we will discover in the context of our case study, the police unfortunately still had some difficult tasks to accomplish whilst other agencies found themselves with limited reach and effectiveness.

Hate crime legislation, although quite recent in origin, has been the heir to a number of supranational declarations emanating from the United Nations, such as Article 1 of the 1945 United Nations Charter. These were partly enacted in piecemeal fashion in the Race Relations Acts mentioned above and section 95 of the 1991 Criminal Justice Act, the 1995 Disability Discrimination Act, the 1998 Human Rights Act and the Race Relations (Amendment) Act of 2000. Subsequently, the Equalities Act of 2010 incorporated the provisions of both the Disability and Race Relations Acts.[28] The creation of legal apparatus which incorporated the idea of increased penalties for crimes motivated by prejudice was a central part of the 1998 Crime and Disorder Act, later augmented by the Anti-Terrorism, Crime and Security Act of 2001. This last Act

allowed for the extension of sentences in episodes where racial aggrava-
tion could be proved to be present.[29] Responding to some public order
concerns, the Act was later amended to also cover issues of distress, alarm
and harassment.

Race hatred also developed from an unexpected quarter in the shape
of religious hatred and blasphemy. By the middle of the twentieth century, common law precedents about blasphemy from the evolution of
English law still remained in place, but their antiquity protected either
the preferred Christian confession of the seventeenth/eighteenth-century
state or upheld protection only for a broader conception of Christianity.
This was discriminatory and simply no longer adequate, since migration
and decolonisation multiplied the presence of other religions in almost
all Western countries.

A particular catalyst in bringing these issues to a head was the Salman
Rushdie affair in the early 1990s. Salman Rushdie produced *The Satanic
Verses*, a novel which, whilst an imaginary work of fiction, contained
passages considered insulting to the Islamic religion.[30] The matter was
considerably debated and many Western advocates of free speech and
publishing took an uncompromising stand. An attempt to implement
the Common Law of Blasphemous Libel in Britain to protect Islam from
Rushdie's apparent attacks met with a rebuttal from the then Minister of
State at the Home Office, John Patten, who maintained the law would
only protect the established Anglican Church.[31] Nonetheless, despite its
manifest failure to mobilise legal solutions to the hurt this ethnic and
faith community felt, this attempt did highlight that legal protection for
simply one religion had become untenable in the modern world. Such
an issue became compounded in Britain when the harmonisation of
laws with European standards gradually made Western blasphemy laws
no longer fit for purpose. In Britain attempts were made by the government to discuss such laws, notably in 2003 when a House of Lords
Select Committee considered what should be done about the unacceptable condition of Britain's blasphemy legislation and its failure to protect
ethnic minorities.[32] One option mentioned in these discussions was the
possibility of borrowing elements of the Indian Criminal Code, legislation which focussed upon preserving public order through the action of
protecting buildings and sacred objects. These had protected the Indian

subcontinent's ethno-religious communities, and the Code's relevance in the English context seemed to make possible the removal of blasphemy laws and their replacement with laws against religious hatred. Whilst equalising the status of religions before the law, the problems in implementing such solutions prevented the Select Committee from offering a viable course of action.

In any event, Britain acquired laws against religious hatred before the Common Law of Blasphemous Libel was finally repealed as a result of an opposition amendment to the Criminal Justice and Immigration Bill of 2008. Religious hatred was finally dealt with under the Racial and Religious Hatred Act of 2008 which amended the 1986 Public Order Act to create the offence of stirring up hatred against persons on religious grounds. Both the intention and impact of these pieces of legislation effectively demonstrated how far governments and policing authorities had begun to link religious and racial hate crime together.

3.   Historiography

Many scholars consider the hate crime concept to have originated in North America and to have gained impetus from those campaigning against discrimination around sexual orientation. This was aided by other organisations seeking similar recognition and a growing interest from the American academic world.[33] Alongside this, scholarship recognised that there was something of a 10- to 15-year time lag before its status was recognised in Britain.[34] A full and nuanced history of hate crime's development and implementation currently remains to be written to a great extent. Certainly there are important research questions that may well motivate this in the future. For example, we need to know what the relationship between growing post-war perceptions of human rights and the rise of the hate crime agenda actually was. Also it would be useful to better understand the relationship between minority pressure groups and the power brokers in policing, government, the media and the third sector, who were capable of persuading government to act and legislate. Furthermore, in assisting with the recognition of oppressed groups, it would be good to establish how far policy became reactive to situations and incidents, when compared with how far policing and community agencies were prepared to innovate or indeed borrow models that worked from other areas of activity.

The literature currently available is predominantly sociological in nature and its brief surveys of the past give some small, often unrelated, hints about its history.[35] The most developed historical work on aspects of hate crime has been the examination of sectarian tensions in Scotland which has ethno-religious characteristics to it. Scholars such as Steve Bruce have noted that the impact of sectarianism has been exaggerated, largely through irresponsible media attention and hysteria.[36] Others, such as Tom Devine, indicate that it has had a far more lasting legacy but was coming to be a thing of the past.[37]

Scholars, such as Barbara Perry, note the fundamental aspect of hate crime as being perpetrated by those who belong to dominant social groups against those that have marginal or less than mainstream status within society.[38] Some, such as Iganski and Lagou, also believe that attention aimed at rectifying these kinds of offences has always been urgent because, since they assault the identity of individuals, they are most keenly felt and inflict disproportionate damage upon the individual and wider societies. Beyond this is the vexed issue of punishment since the impact of sentencing policies for offenders appears unproven, so that instead reflection upon the culpability of the offender is sometimes touted as a way forward.[39] Perhaps related to this assessment of hurt and harm have been arguments that examine the effectiveness of restorative justice as a method of reforming the miscreant and re-establishing respect for the victim.[40] Scholars, such as Gerstenfeld, also advocate policies that enhance the status and campaigns of such individuals and groups in their quest to become accepted as mainstream.[41] Related to this is a tendency to research and argue for the 'next' relevant group to be included in the list of those capable of suffering hate at the hands of dominant groups. In Britain, this recognition has focussed upon the so-called 'five strands' of race, religion, sexual orientation, gender identity and disability. Although accepting this typology, Chakraborti notes that the categories overlap and that a sensible recognition of this is important in planning government or multi-agency responses to the problem.[42] Certainly Britain's history has meant that recognition of hatred against races would predate the recognition of other identities. Nonetheless some, such as Garland and Hodkinson as well as Mason, have sought to make the argument for the gradual inclusion of other groups and this will clearly be a feature of much future work.[43]

In focussing upon the effectiveness or otherwise of actual hate crime legislation, scholars like Iganski have noted the relatively low level of prosecution and conviction. This tends to lead to conclusions that the emotive treatment of 'hate' fails to deal effectively with manifestly lesser crimes and misdemeanours.[44] One other trend in the pertinent scholarship has been to note that, despite concerns about high-profile incidents (such as those linked to blasphemy or international violence), a considerable majority of hate crime incidents are of an everyday nature involving individuals close to, or even within, the community context of the victim.[45] It is also scarcely surprising that a similar pattern emerges from homophobic hate crime.[46]

Some ideas that could be called part of the historiography of hate crime are themselves sometimes snippets picked up from official documentation. These then enter the public domain as a plausible and cogent idea. One example of this process was the so-called 'Bad Apple' thesis, which was an explanation given for individual policemen harbouring racist ideas and exhibiting racist behaviour. This concept appeared dramatically in the Scarman report into the Brixton riots which attacked the poor conduct of individual officers and their role in creating a 'myth of the hostile police', further feeding perceptions of police harassment of black minorities.[47] This idea then almost had a life of its own in the hands of commentators and journalists.

When considering the development of hate crime scholarship, work on the history of racism and race relations in Britain fills in some of the general historiographical lacunae. Benjamin Bowling, for instance, analyses the conceptualisation of racism as a new crime occurring at a time when other issues of 'accountability, consultation, liaison, co-operation and co-ordination' were pressing issues for policing agencies, making these two factors work together in producing solutions.[48] He sees violent racism as emerging fully in the 1970s, with '1981 being the defining moment when it explicitly achieved public recognition when important agencies began to respond to the problem of racial violence in the aftermath of the Toxteth/Brixton riots and the revelations of the Scarman Report into these events.'[49] There was also a significant collapse in confidence that the British police force could tackle new challenges, alongside a souring of confidence in how they were handling the old ones.[50] After the Greater London Council (GLC) intervention in London, this eventually produced the triumph of the 'multi-agency approach' to tackling racially motivated violence which by 1968 he describes as 'virtually unassailable'.[51] A focus upon race as the driver for the recognition and tackling of hate crimes in Britain produces two strands of historiography.[52] One history is characterised by studies of the alienation of whole communities that protested and rioted between 1980 and the early 1990s. This concentrates on the wide social consequences of exclusion and the impact upon society of these troubles.[53] However, the Stephen Lawrence case has also directed much subsequent work into looking at the arrival of hate crime policies and their apparent effectiveness.[54] One offshoot of this latter case and its impact has been an historical re-appraisal of race and ethnic experiences and identity formation at a more individual level, alongside more sophisticated histories of individual ethnic communities and their own relationships with the host community.[55]

What these distinctions point to is the absolutely pivotal nature of the Lawrence case and the shadow it casts across thinking and policy in this area. This shadow has not been diminished by time, the impact of new investigations into the facts or indeed the power of new revelations coming from these. It is to this landmark case that we now turn.

4. Case Study

On 22nd April 1993, Stephen Lawrence, a black 18-year-old, had been with his friend Duwayne Brooks all afternoon and was waiting at a bus stop in Eltham, East London at 10.30 pm.[56] Stephen went to see if the bus was coming and saw a group of between four and five white youths approaching him. When Duwayne called out to him, one of the group shouted 'What, what nigger?' The group then rapidly 'engulfed' Stephen, and during this melee he was stabbed twice by one or more of the group.[57] Stephen Lawrence was thus the victim of a fatal unprovoked hate crime attack. Although several individuals witnessed the attack from a distance, including Duwayne Brooks, none of these could actively identify those responsible. Nonetheless, this crime would eventually be reported as a 'joint enterprise'.[58]

A day after the murder, a note was left in a local telephone box listing four people who the informant indicated were involved – Neil and Jamie Acourt, Dave Norris and Gary Dobson.[59] After some disquiet about the time taken to scale up the investigation, the four were arrested along with a fifth man Luke Knight. It was Knight and Neil Acourt who were charged with murder.[60] A month later, the Criminal Prosecution Service was forced to drop the charges on the grounds that identity parade evidence, which was key to the prosecution's case, was unreliable and thus inadmissible.[61] When the inquest into Stephen Lawrence's death was held at the end of 1993, the Coroner adjourned it when the Lawrence family's lawyer, the renowned radical barrister Michael Mansfield, suggested there was important specific new evidence to consider from witnesses identifying all the defendants.[62] By the following spring however, the Criminal Prosecution Service had also reviewed this evidence but did not consider it sufficient to bring charges against the suspects.

Angered and outraged by this turn of events, Stephen's parents, Neville and Doreen Lawrence, bypassed the Criminal Prosecution Service and launched their own private prosecution in the autumn of 1994 – this time against Neil Acourt, Luke Knight and Gary Dobson. This private prosecution for murder, under the 1985 Prosecution of Offences Act, eventually reached a verdict in 1996 which was in line with the Criminal Prosecution Service's original decision which declared the identification evidence as inadmissible. During the period leading up to this verdict, the Metropolitan Police had begun to amass evidence against Dobson, Acourt and Knight's racist tendencies and their regular recourse to violent language.[63] A year later, the inquest into Stephen Lawrence's death was resumed and concluded with a verdict of unlawful killing. Unequivocally, the coroner described the Lawrence murder, as a 'completely unprovoked racist attack by five white youths'.[64] Nonetheless, the Lawrence family were scarcely any nearer to the point of achieving justice or an end to their anguish. This seemed especially the case since the failure of the private prosecution meant the individuals could, at that time, not be required to stand trial again for this crime due to the double jeopardy laws which prevailed at that period.[65]

Frustrated at the verdict, the *Daily Mail* took the law into its own hands the day after the conclusion of the inquest, printing a front page headline which bluntly accused the five men outlined in the private prosecution of having committed the murder. The newspaper openly invited them to sue for libel if they could prove that the accusation made was false.[66] Whilst clearly a form of trial by journalism, it was evident that the newspaper spoke for many involved in the legal proceedings, and also for many members of the wider public at large. The failure of the police and the legal apparatus of the country to provide satisfactory justice inevitably meant that the spotlight was to fall on these institutions in the months and years that followed. Scarcely a month passed before it was announced that the Police Complaints Authority had instructed the Kent Constabulary to investigate the conduct of those involved in the investigation team, and the wider structures that supported it. This was in response to the Lawrence family's conviction that the initial investigation had been 'bungled'.[67] When it eventually reported nine months later, in a 459-page report, it highlighted weaknesses and criticised some procedural decisions but, at this time, stopped short of voicing criticism of the Metropolitan Police's culture and orientation towards dealing with racist hate crimes. This failure to read the situation and address it was later to be highlighted by subsequent events and further investigation.[68]

The pressure on the Metropolitan Police continued when, in the summer of 1997, the Home Secretary Jack Straw announced a formal judicial inquiry (the Macpherson Inquiry) into the death of Stephen Lawrence. This inquiry was an official manifestation of the widespread dissatisfaction with the inadequacy of police approaches to the case. The inquiry would further probe the conduct of the policing authorities involved in the case, with the aim of sharpening insight and also seeking to learn the lessons evident from how the case was handled. As a part of the inquiry the five suspects were compelled to give evidence or face prosecution. They also received poor treatment from the crowd waiting outside the venue when their answers were considered unhelpful and evasive.[69] A few months later pressure on the Metropolitan Police Commissioner Sir Paul Condon finally paid off, with the Lawrence family receiving a carefully worded apology from the force admitting omissions and failings in procedure.[70] In truth Sir Paul Condon almost certainly had no choice since he was likely to have been made aware of what the Macpherson Inquiry was likely to conclude.

When the Macpherson Report was published in February 1999 it caused a considerable furore, since it squarely accused the Metropolitan Police of having institutionalised racism within its ranks, its procedures and its culture. This appeared evident in both obvious and covert forms and pervaded almost all areas of its activities. It could even be hidden from officers themselves through the assumptions that both training and experience may have given them. Indeed it suggested

> There is no doubt whatsoever but that the first Metropolitan Police Service (MPS) investigation was palpably flawed and deserves severe criticism. Nobody listening to the evidence could reach any other conclusion. This is now plainly accepted by the MPS. Otherwise the abject apologies offered to Mr and Mrs Lawrence would be meaningless.[71]

The report itself made damning reading. It reflected the frustration of the whole ethnic minority community and addressed their concerns about their treatment by the whole British police force throughout the country. It was perceived as a 'clarion call' and it was hoped that it had the potential power to effect 'the debate about policing and racism that has been transformed by this Inquiry.'[72] In making this statement, the Macpherson Report also rebuffed the claims of the Metropolitan Police Commissioner that the Inquiry was in the business of 'stage-managing' its procedures and, by implication, its conclusions. Instead, the Commission replied with the assertion that

> the harm to the relationship between police and the black community was the result of police failures, and the answers to the questions rather than the nature of the questioning. It is of central importance that the Commissioner and his officers should recognise and accept this fact.[73]

This was not to be the last awkward exchange between the Metropolitan Police, government investigatory mechanisms and the Lawrence family. Indeed the Macpherson Report went out of its way to implicate the

Metropolitan Police in forms of indigenous and instinctively racist behaviour. It also made a point of quoting Doreen Lawrence's reaction which outlined what might be regarded as the prejudiced assumptions from which wider and deeper social ills were constructed. She said:

> Basically we were seen as gullible simpletons. This is best shown by Superintendent Isley's comment that I had obviously been primed to ask questions. Presumably, there is no possibility of me being an intelligent black woman with thoughts of her own who is able to ask questions for herself. We were patronised and were fobbed off ....No black person can ever trust the police. This idea is not preconceived. It is based on experience and people who have had bad experiences with the police.[74]

Many such statements were rounded off by both Neville and Doreen Lawrence hoping that the articulation of their grievances would make the Inquiry advance the cause of effective policing of the black community and racist violence. Throughout the Macpherson Report there are sections which appear in bold to highlight the array of inadequate procedures, personal failings and mistakes made by both junior and senior police officers. What became especially noteworthy, and indeed was something that made the Stephen Lawrence Inquiry and its aftermath something of a watershed, was the recognition that racism could potentially be tacit and that a simple lack of training was far more important than previously appreciated. What the report called 'race relations awareness' appeared to be rudimentary at best and it noted that, up to this point, it scarcely had merited serious consideration by the Metropolitan Police Service. In describing the actions of one officer for instance, the report noted that his instinctive urge 'to treat everyone the same' was a barrier to his recognition that what had happened to Stephen Lawrence was a racist killing. It also noted that his interpersonal skills required sharpening and stressed that this officer had been given no training in dealing with either of these issues:

> Although he had worked in multicultural societies and areas throughout his service and believed that he treated everybody in the same way his lack of sensitivity and his inaction, particularly at the hospital, betrayed conduct which demonstrates inability to deal properly with bereaved

people, and particularly those bereaved as a result of a terrible racist attack. He failed to deal with the family appropriately and professionally. This was unwitting racism at work.[75]

This kind of criticism would persistently reappear in later evidence, notably when another officer surmised that because the accused had attacked whites in the past he did not, by definition, consider that 'the attack was purely racist'. He also believed 'to this day that that was thugs, not racism, just pure bloody minded thuggery.'[76] This view was found by the Inquiry to be considerably widespread and was later reported as instrumental in the failure of the black community to report manifestly racially motivated violence.[77] Another witness claimed that racism was instrumental in the tendency of the police to 'assume that such attacks are drug related', whilst a further commentator saw the prevalence of a 'canteen culture' of racism as preventing meaningful attempts to address the issue.[78] When taken together, all of this served to indicate an almost complete breakdown of police and family liaison relations, something which would have been crucial in eliciting an earlier and more successful outcome in the Stephen Lawrence case.[79]

Opening the can of worms that incipient racism represented meant that it was inevitable that the Inquiry would range far and wide in search of evidence. When it lighted upon the extremely controversial policy of 'stop and search', the Inquiry discovered statistics from 1997–1998 which suggested that black people were on average five times more likely to be stopped and searched.[80] From this they noted that 'the majority of officers who testified before us accepted that an element of the disparity was the result of discrimination.'[81] The story was depressingly similar over the reporting and assimilation of information regarding racist incidents, and the web of distrust again appeared all too pervasive.[82]

There also appeared to be a lack of urgency, organisation and leadership from middle-ranking and senior officers at the murder scene leading the Inquiry to declare: 'The lost opportunities for full and proper searches and investigation during the first hours after Stephen Lawrence's murder are to be deplored.'[83] It also emerged that crucial information gleaned from telephone calls from the public was not always passed on in officer briefings and thus not acted upon. In addition, the decision to arrest the accused was enacted on the 7th of May 1993, with evidence that had been available to the police as early as the 24th of April.[84] Interestingly, this issue was finessed by the Inquiry Report by suggesting the unsuitability of the officer taking the decision to arrest, whilst acknowledging that he may have felt unwilling to act sooner because of the press and media attention that the case had evidently attracted.[85]

The Inquiry's report highlighted its belief in 'fundamental errors' and 'a combination of professional incompetence, institutional racism and a failure of leadership by senior officers.'[86] Evidence also appeared of profoundly flawed procedures around such mechanisms as identity parades that did not serve the cause of justice in the least.[87] In trying to break down this spectacularly growing obstacle, and move attitudes to hate crime policing and detection forward, the report made no fewer than 70 recommendations which ranged from procedural issues to recommending some sweeping changes in the law to combat hate crime and the climate which promoted it. The recommendations self-consciously addressed government as well as the police service and called for strategies to investigate, prevent and record racist incidents and to encourage full participation from the relevant communities affected by such episodes. This was also to be aided by much greater levels of sophisticated training of family liaison officers, better briefed about hate crime, and the targeted recruitment of ethnic minority officers.[88] Policing standards were to be improved by ensuring officers were fully aware of responsibilities in this area and expectations that they would discharge these professionally. This was to be enacted through giving Her Majesty's Inspectors of Constabulary greater powers of inspection. This was to be immediately implemented in a full examination of the Metropolitan Police Service and its guidelines and procedures which were recommended to be overhauled and revised.[89] The Inquiry also argued that, henceforth, police operations should be governed by the full force of the Freedom of Information Act to provide both transparency and accountability. Importantly the Inquiry recommended a redefinition of a 'racist incident', something which took the power of defining it away from the policing authorities to now make this reside with the victim. Henceforth this was to be 'any incident which is perceived to be racist by the victim or any other person.'[90]

Procedures for family liaison and victim support services were also required to back this new approach of being more proactive in protecting communities and communicating with them. Several recommendations also suggested clearer and tighter regulations governing the conduct of the Criminal Prosecution Service, especially requesting that the organisation's decision-making processes be more readily communicated to the families of victims.[91] One specific set of recommendations was labelled 'Training'. These sought to put in place a strategy whereby racism awareness training was mandatory amongst uniformed police officers, Criminal Investigation Department and police civilian staff. This area was also given a much more positive slant, intending that this should actively extend into 'valuing cultural diversity' and that the Metropolitan Police Service would be stringently monitored around its compliance with such provisions. The formulation, tabling and reach of police complaints procedures was to be overhauled and made more user friendly for those who had legitimate grievances. The avoidance of such incidents, so the Inquiry believed, might well be aided through the application of a more stringent selection of police officers for promotion to inspector level and above.[92] The ethnic minority presence within the police service was also deemed a high priority, as was a programme of extending racism awareness into the school curriculum through education initiatives which would be enforced by OFSTED inspection.[93] The whole report was finished off with a general plea for the police, local government and what it termed 'relevant agencies' to be involved in 'promoting cultural diversity and addressing racism and the need for focused consistent support for such initiatives'.[94] The clear intention and the eventual effect of this was to ensure that all in society would henceforth take hate crime considerably more seriously. Eventually 67 of the 70 recommendations would be implemented, and much was accomplished by bringing public bodies, including the police and immigration service, under the provisions of the 1976 Race Relations Act through the provisions of the Race Relations Amendment Act (2000).[95]

Despite this outcome, the quest for justice for Stephen Lawrence and his family appeared to have run out of steam when, in May 2004, the Criminal Prosecution Service announced that it ruled out any intention of conducting another trial on the evidence that was currently available. However, a chink of light appeared when the legal principle of 'double jeopardy', which had previously prevented individuals from being prosecuted for the same crime twice, was scrapped by the Home Secretary David Blunkett in April 2005, partly after demands made as a result of the Stephen Lawrence case.[96] Media pressure also continued and a BBC documentary screened in July 2006 raised further concerns about the evidence. This was hard hitting enough to persuade the Metropolitan Police to, once again, carefully review the evidence at their disposal, although the police eventually declined to pursue the allegations.[97] The power of this documentary was combined with new developments in forensic science and the fresh approach of a new investigator, Detective Chief Inspector Driscoll. From here, it became possible that popular demands that the case be pursued to a satisfactory conclusion might well be met.[98] However, it took until the middle of 2010 before this evidence was considered sufficient by the Court of Appeal to bring Gary Dobson and Dave Norris to trial. The trial eventually commenced at the end of 2011 and forensic evidence was to prove crucial linking both Dobson and Norris to the murder, with clear indications that Stephen Lawrence's DNA was on their clothing. After two and half days of deliberation, the jury convicted Dobson and Norris in the first week of January 2012. Both received life sentences with a recommendation that Dobson and Norris serve 15 years 2 months and 14 years 3 months respectively.

The Stephen Lawrence case greatly exposed the issues of prejudice and the failure to address, orientate services and actively tackle hate crime in almost all levels of policing and judicial action. The tenth anniversary of the Macpherson Inquiry did present a picture of some lessons learned and improvements undertaken, but it was arguably too little and too late. Doreen Lawrence had been galvanised by the family witnessing inaction and ineptitude and began to question the level of service black Britons could expect from the police service in the wake of 'hate crime'.

By the middle of 2015, although the Stephen Lawrence case was ostensibly solved, a further shadow was cast over the investigation by accusations that one or possibly more officers involved in the case were corrupt and were alleged to have 'shielded' the killers of Stephen Lawrence in the first days after his murder. This was further evidence that the Stephen Lawrence case had become an embodiment of a series of failings evident from the character of late twentieth-century society, its policing and race awareness cultures. As the press report outlining this final revelation suggested:

> The case is one of the most important in the modern history of the British criminal justice system, having sparked inquiries, reforms of the police and challenges to racial attitudes in Britain.[99]

These words scarcely underestimate the importance of this case for the genesis of the concept of hate crime and its wider recognition as an important social phenomenon. It dramatically showed up the sheer unpreparedness of late twentieth-century British society to recognise and deal with what had been a series of flashpoints that had attended the consequences of post-war immigration into Britain. What might be termed years of hate crime toleration had been somehow 'managed' because they were merely flashpoints which were ostensibly extinguished or burned themselves out. The problems with right-wing organisations such as the National Front in late 1970s London and which culminated in the death of Blair Peach, the riots in Toxteth in 1981, and the Brixton and Broadwater Farm riots of 1985, were all incidents where policing and the state were considered to have failed black immigrant communities.[100] To add to such incidents were ongoing problems associated with the so-called 'sus' laws of the 1970s, phenomena which re-emerged in the 'stop and search' policies of the 1990s.[101] All were warnings to contemporary police services, and the governments of the day, that they were systematically ignoring the needs of ethnic minorities who had a right to be respected and policed just as other citizens were.

Ironically, the Stephen Lawrence case did not reach a dramatic flashpoint as the others listed here achieved. Instead it was, perhaps, the blow-by-blow nature of the case's revelations that were piled increasingly upon one another that fed gradual public disquiet about the whole approach of policing and policy to racially motivated violence. Despite the efforts of good police officers, they were let down by the inattention, poor attitude and, shockingly, the wilfulness of other officers. What felt, perhaps, a more savage indictment was the realisation that quite so many police procedures, working practices and standing orders appeared to be so manifestly unfit for purpose. These exposed that police awareness of racial issues and recognition of the needs of ethnic minority groups were some-how locked in the dark ages. The investigation of the Stephen Lawrence case broke open this hidden cache of complacent and occasionally actively racist attitudes in police culture. As such, the case had dramatically exposed the actions of the police in minute and too often embarrassing detail, enabling the public to view detailed accounts of incompetence and casual racism, with both of these sometimes blended together. Thus, the case asked questions about the whole nature of policing and whether British society was getting the policing service it desired and deserved. As Brian Cathcart, in his authoritative volume about the Stephen Lawrence case, put it:

> Ideas such as unconscious or institutional racism have been thrust into the mainstream while notions that were easier to live with, such as the bad apple theory, have lost much of their authority. It is now less widely accepted that all people should be treated equally and more widely accepted that people should be treated according to their needs. More people see that the need to respect others should not be dismissed as 'political correctness'.[102]

Although, as we have discovered, aspects of the case rumble on beyond the scope of this study, the redefinition of hate crime as something that victims themselves feel was a particularly important step forward.

Henceforth, and armed with this realisation, hate crime began to be seen as a firm priority for government and reforming police services. Thus, our history has shown here the development of a new concept of crime, albeit demonstrating the difficult road that it has travelled in the United Kingdom. The Stephen Lawrence case illuminated the distance that government, policing and the wider values of society had to travel in order to bring justice and civilised treatment to minority groups into the twenty-first century. The Home Secretary, who arguably did most to recognise the importance of the Stephen Lawrence case, also placed it in a viable historical context:

> The pervasive, open racism of the fifties and sixties, the pernicious, sniggering racism of the seventies, eighties and nineties is gone. For that we have to thank Doreen and Neville Lawrence, above all others.[103]

In this statement Jack Straw created a false dawn and it should also be recognised that British society's journey towards justice and civilised treatment is scarcely over. In the years since, some progress has been made in tackling ethnic recruitment to the police (raising it to 4 per cent in pursuit of a 7 per cent target), positive discrimination and better multi-agency tackling of racist incidents.[104] In June 2015, the new Metropolitan Police Commissioner, Sir Bernard Hogan-Howe, admitted that 'there was some justification' to accusations that the force was still, after the revelations of the Stephen Lawrence case, institutionally racist. Moreover, he also confirmed that 'stop and search' figures had also scarcely improved since the mid-1990s and that he could give reasons why this was the case, whilst not being able to either fully explain or justify it.[105] Yet Hogan-Howe also, quite rightly, turned the spotlight away from the police for a moment to reflect on the fact that society as a whole had scarcely broken free from its own poor record of institutional racism: 'You see a lack of representation in many fields – of which the police are one – from judges to doctors, to journalists, to editors, to governments'.[106] It seems that there remains much work to do to make the issue of prejudice and its manifestation in hate crime come even close to a resolution.

5. Conclusion

This chapter has analysed the growth and development of a wholly new area of crime, law and criminological thinking around the issues of race relations and race hatred. This was an issue that had been a part of British society only episodically for the most part of the twentieth century. This obviously grew dramatically in importance during the last 30 years of that century to add significant responsibilities to both policing and the actions of the criminal justice system. In many respects both of these were playing catch up with agendas and expectations that often greatly outpaced their knowledge and mechanisms of response. Indeed, as we have seen, many of the problems created during that period provide evidence of how slowly society's policing and law-making responded to urgent need. The problems that were manifest during these last 30 years of the century have often had to wait until the first two decades of the twenty-first

century to even approach resolution. Sometimes this reflected a growing awareness of the importance of combatting race hatred, sometimes it
reflected the approach of new individuals with better training and competence in such matters. As in some other areas covered by this book,
developments in police work and detection, such as the ability to use
DNA evidence in the Stephen Lawrence case, eventually provided solutions and resolutions to problems that had their genesis in the last quarter
of the twentieth century.

This later resolution of earlier problems indicates that the twentieth-
century history of racial hatred, and attempts to combat this, have been
retarded by a failure to recognise the nature of racially motivated hate
crime. Even indeed how this culture of prejudice can seem to lie even
within public institutions otherwise charged with helping the population
at large. Whilst individuals carry conscious or unconscious prejudice
with them it was also noticeable that policies and procedures often
seemed inadequate in their formulation or were ineffective in practice.
Moreover, hate crime and hate criminals easily attracted newspaper
headlines. The arrival of these new agendas amidst the glare of publicity –
particularly in relation to failures in policy and policing – meant that
the police and other agencies would regularly find themselves looking
over their shoulders. In this they sought to preserve the reputation of
themselves as individuals and the credibility of their own institution, as
the trust they could expect from both immigrant communities and the
wider public was challenged. Meanwhile, the example of Scotland has
indicated a mismatch of perception and reality. One recent report noted
for instance, that although longitudinal studies showed sectarian incidents that could be classed as criminal existed at only a very low level
of incidence, public perception of the issue remained at a constantly
high level since the end of the 1970s. Many still reported the persis-
tence of casual remarks, insulting language and discrimination in the
workplace.[107] By 2012–13 figures for Scotland indicated that sectarian
hate crime had been replaced as the most frequent incident by racially
motivated hate crimes that would be more recognisable south of the
border.[108]

Policing such an area as racial hate crime has – perhaps more than
most other areas covered in this volume – shown up the flaws and inad-
equacies of a whole range of individuals and institutions which have too

often been found wanting in their quest to tackle this area. Nonetheless, progress has been made and by the start of the twenty-first century legislative provision existed for most recognised minority groups who could now expect protection for their beliefs and lifestyle, alongside punishment for those who breached society's covenant of tolerance and respect for all. As we have also seen, criminological scholarship is also engaged upon arguments that seek to extend protection forward for other minority groups and it is very likely such an exploration will continue.

It is also important to note that hate crime came to prominence and public attention in the age of the modern media. So it is less than surprising that radio, television and the printed media have all played a key role in hate crime's evolution in Britain. This can be observed initially in attempts to publicise its existence, right through to commenting upon the views of those who should be constructing and implementing policies to combat the problem. It becomes obvious that, whilst freedom of speech and publication is admirable, in some cases it can have an arguably detrimental effect upon full discussion of the issues involved. A clear example of this arose during the Macpherson Inquiry into the death of Stephen Lawrence. When the Metropolitan Police Commissioner Sir Paul Condon was pressured to acknowledge institutional racism within his force for example, he refused on the grounds that 'it would be easy to please the panel, to please the audience, to walk out of this room so that very superficial media coverage says, "Yes, they have said certain things." I actually think that would be … dishonest, for me to say that just to please you all.'[109] Hate crime is an emotive concept that fuels newspaper stories and publicity and it shows the relationship between policing, the law and public knowledge of this in sharp relief.

Notes

1. See for example J. Garland and P. Hodkinson (2014) '"F**king freak! What the Hell Do You Think You Look Like?" Experiences of Targeted Victimization among Goths and Developing Notions of Hate Crime', *British Journal of Criminology*, Vol. 54, pp. 613–31. See also J. McDevitt, J. Levin and S. Bennett (2002) 'Hate Crime Offenders: An Expanded Typology', *Journal of Social Issues*, Vol. 58, No. 2, pp. 303–17.

2. Metropolitan Police Service (2004) *Hate Crime Policy.* Quoted in P. Iganski (2008) *Hate Crime and the City* (Bristol: Policy Press). The current version of the Metropolitan Police Service Hate Crime Policy is available at http://www.met.police.uk/foi/pdfs/policies/hate_crime_policy_statement_eia_may2015.pdf (Accessed 27th November 2015).

3. P. Iganski, V. Kielinger and S. Paterson (2005) *Hate Crimes against London's Jews: An Analysis of Incidents Recorded by the Metropolitan Police Service 2001–2004* (London: Institute for Jewish Policy Research), p. 1.

4. *Ibid.*, pp. 1–5.

5. *Ibid.*, p. 2.

6. *Ibid.*, p. 3.

7. *Ibid.*, p. 2.

8. *Ibid.*, p. 108.

9. *Ibid.*, pp. 79–81.

10. See B. Bowling (1998) *Violent Racism: Victimization, Policing and Social Context* (Oxford: Oxford University Press), Chapter 1.

11. This distinction between 'pure' hate crimes and those that occur as a consequence of other incidents was made central to early attempts to theorise the concept. See M. Fitzgerald and C. Hale (1996) *Ethnic Minorities – Victimisation and Racial Harassment: Findings from the 1988 and 1992 British Crime Surveys – Home Office Research Study No. 154* (London: HMSO), p. 57.

12. R.J. Boeckmann and C. Turpin-Petrosino (2002) 'Understanding the Harm of Hate Crime', *Journal of Social Issues*, Vol. 2, pp. 207–25, at p. 208.

13. *Ibid.*, p. 208.

14. See D.K. Citron (2014) *Hate Crimes in Cyberspace* (Harvard: Harvard University Press).

15. J. Solomos (2003 edition) *Race and Racism in Britain* (Basingstoke: Palgrave), pp. 38–40.

16. P. Panayi (1994) *Immigration, Ethnicity and Racism in Britain, 1815–1945.* (Manchester: Manchester University Press). Page 115 notes an anti-capitalist anti-Semitism in British radical and left-wing thinking that arguably dates itself back to William Cobbett in the 1830s.

17. Solomos (2003) *Race and Racism in Britain*, p. 41. This suggests a figure of 60,000 in Britain before immigration from Eastern Europe after 1870 transformed this into a figure of between 120,000 and 300,000 by 1914.

18. *Ibid.*, p. 43.

19. P. Panayi (1994) *Immigration*, p. 103.

20. *Ibid.*, p. 122.

21. *Ibid.*, p. 122.
22. J. Jenkinson (2009) *Black 1919: Riots, Racism and Resistance in Imperial Britain* (Liverpool: Liverpool University Press) and J. Jenkinson (1996) 'The 1919 Riots', in P. Panayi (ed.) *Racial Violence in Britain in the 19th and 20th Centuries* (Leicester: Leicester University Press), pp. 92–111.
23. Bowling (1998) *Violent Racism*, pp. 25–26.
24. See W.H. Murray (1997) *The Old Firm: Sectarianism, Sport and Society in Scotland* (Edinburgh: John Donald).
25. Bowling (1998) *Violent Racism*, pp. 29–34.
26. *Ibid.*, p. 35.
27. *Ibid.*, p. 57.
28. N. Hall (2005) *Hate Crime* (Willan: Cullompton), p. 35.
29. *Ibid.*, p. 36.
30. For coverage of this see D.S. Nash (1999) *Blasphemy in Modern Britain 1789–Present* (Aldershot: Ashgate), pp. 258–61 and L. Levy (1993) *Blasphemy: Verbal Offense against the Sacred from Moses to Salman Rushdie* (New York: Knopf Books), pp. 551–67.
31. See the verdict in the *Ex parte* Choudhury case 1 All ER 306. See also Nash (1999) *Blasphemy in Modern Britain,* pp. 259–60. See also M. Tregilgas-Davey (1991) '*Ex parte* Choudhury: An Opportunity Missed', *Modern Law Review*, Vol. 54, No. 2, pp. 294–99.
32. House of Lords Select Committee on Religious Offences in England and Wales First Report (2003). Available at http://www.parliament.the-stationery-office.co.uk/pa/ld200 203/ldselect/ldrelof/95/9501.htm (Accessed 27th November 2015).
33. See Garland and Hodkinson (2014) '"F**king freak!"', p. 615.
34. Hall (2013) *Hate Crime*, passim.
35. The author is currently engaged on a research project which is aimed at producing a comprehensive history of hate crime in Britain.
36. S. Bruce, T Glendinning, T. Paterson and M. Rosie (2005) 'Religious Discrimination in Scotland: Fact or Myth?', *Ethnic and Racial Studies,* Vol. 28, No. 1, pp. 151–68.
37. See the selection of essays in T.M. Devine (ed.) (2000) *Scotland's Shame? Bigotry and Sectarianism in Modern Scotland* (Edinburgh: Mainstream Publishing). For other perspectives see S. Bruce (2004) *Sectarianism in Scotland* (Edinburgh: Edinburgh University Press); M. Rosie (2004) *The Sectarian Myth in Scotland: Of Bitter Memory and Bigotry* (Basingstoke: Palgrave); N. Scotland (2000) *Sectarian Religion in Contemporary Britain*

(Carlisle: Paternoster) and H. Ogasawara (2003) *Performing Sectarianism: Terror, Spectacle and Urban Myth in Glasgow Football Cultures* (London: Centre for Urban Community Research).

38. B. Perry (2001) *In the Name of Hate: Understanding Hate Crimes* (London: Routledge).

39. See Iganski (2008) *Hate Crime and the City* and P. Iganski and S. Lagou (2015) 'Hate Crimes Hurt Some More than Others: Implications for the Just Sentencing of Offenders', *Journal of Interpersonal Violence*, Vol. 30, No. 10, pp. 1696–718.

40. See T. Gavrielides (2012) 'Contextualizing Restorative Justice for Hate Crime', *Journal of Interpersonal Violence*, Vol. 27, No. 18, pp. 3624–43 and A. Kauppinen (2015) 'Hate and Punishment', *Journal of Interpersonal Violence*, Vol. 30, No. 10, pp. 1719–37.

41. P.B. Gerstenfeld (2013) *Hate Crime: Causes, Controls and Controversies* (London: Sage).

42. N. Chakraborti (2015) 'Re-thinking Hate Crime: Fresh Challenges for Policy and Practice', *Journal of Interpersonal Violence*, Vol. 30, No. 10, pp. 1738–54.

43. See Garland and Hodkinson (2014) '"F**king freak!"', passim for an argument that sub cultural lifestyles such as punks and goths should be considered for legislative protection. See also G. Mason (2014) 'Victim Attributes in Hate Crime Law', *British Journal of Criminology*, Vol. 54, No. 2, pp. 161–79 for an argument that violence against those who sexually assault children (paedophiles) should potentially be considered a hate crime.

44. P. Iganski (1999) 'Why Make Hate a Crime?', *Critical Social Policy*, Vol. 19, No. 3, pp. 386–95.

45. See Iganski, Kielinger and Paterson (2005) *Hate Crimes against London's Jews*, passim. See also V. Kielinger and S. Paterson's later study (2007) 'Policing Hate Crime in London', *American Behavioural Scientist*, Vol. 51, No. 2, pp. 196–204 and R. Sibbitt (1997) *The Perpetrators of Racial Harassment and Racial Violence – Home Office Research Study, No. 176* (London: HMSO).

46. Kielinger and Paterson (2007) 'Policing Hate Crime in London', passim.

47. Bowling (1998) *Violent Racism*, p. 81.

48. *Ibid.*, pp. 99–100.

49. *Ibid.*, p. 303.

50. *Ibid.*, p. 65.

51. Bowling (1998) *Violent Racism*, p. 149.

52. Hall (2013) *Hate Crime*, p. 98.

53. See for example A. Beckett (2015) *Promised You a Miracle* (London: Allen Lane); D. Frost and R. Phillips (eds) (2011) *Liverpool 81: Remembering the Riots* (Liverpool: Liverpool University Press); B. Bowling (1998) *Violent Racism;* D. Fassin (2013) *Enforcing Order: An Ethnography of Urban Policing* (London: Polity Press); Lord Scarman (1982) *The Scarman Report: The Brixton Disorders, 10–12 April* (Harmondsworth: Penguin); Centre for Contemporary Cultural Studies (1982) *The Empire Strikes Back: Race and Racism in 1970s Britain* (London: Hutchison); M. Kettle and L. Hodges (1982) *Uprising! Police, the People and the Riots in Britain's Cities* (London: Macmillan) and T. Moore (2015) *The Killing of Constable Keith Blakelock: The Broadwater Farm Riot* (Hook: Waterside Press). See also the items on sectarianism listed in notes 16, 28 and 29. It could also be argued that the impact of the Salman Rushdie case was an offshoot of this since much scholarship concentrated upon the impact of offence upon whole communities. For this see material listed in note 22. For material on the long-term repercussions of the Rushdie case for community relations and responses, multiculturalism and policing see also M. Ruthven (1990) *Salman Rushdie and the Rage of Islam* (London: Chatto and Windus); D. Pipes (2007) *The Rushdie Affair: The Novel, the Ayatollah and the West* (London: Transaction Publishers); P. Weller (2009) *A Mirror for Our Times: The Rushdie Affair and the Future of Multiculturalism* (London: Continuum) and K. Malik (2009) *From Fatwa to Jihad* (London: Atlantic Books).

54. See material cited both above and below in notes 32–37, 49, 88, 94 and 97.

55. See T. Kushner (2004) *We Europeans? Mass Observation and British Identity in the Twentieth Century* (Aldershot: Ashgate); J. Belchem (2014) *Before the Windrush: Race Relations in Twentieth Century Liverpool* (Liverpool: Liverpool University Press); J. Belchem (2007) *Irish, Catholic and Scouse: The History of the Liverpool Irish, 1800–1939* (Liverpool: Liverpool University Press); D. Mason (1995) *Race and Ethnicity in Modern Britain* (Oxford: Oxford University Press). Note that from the 2000 edition onwards the book has a new chapter evaluating the criminal justice system in the wake of the early revelations from the Stephen Lawrence case. For a more critical view of British cultural responses to race and racism see P. Gilroy (2002) *There Ain't No Black in the Union Jack* (London: Routledge).

56. The single most important narrative account of the Stephen Lawrence case up to 1999 and the end of the Macpherson Inquiry can be found in B. Cathcart (1999) *The Case of Stephen Lawrence* (London: Penguin).

57. *The Stephen Lawrence Inquiry: Report of an Inquiry by Sir William Macpherson of Cluny,* Cmd. 4262–1 (1999) (Hereafter *Macpherson Report)*, Paragraphs 1.2 and 1.3. Available at https://www.gov.uk/government/uploads/system/uploads/attachment_ data/file/277111/4262.pdf (Accessed 27th November 2015).

58. *Macpherson Report,* Paragraph 1.5.

59. *Ibid.*, Paragraphs 7.11 and 7.12.

60. *Ibid.*, Paragraph 7.29 and 13.43.

61. *Ibid.*, Paragraphs 21.1–21.22.

62. *Ibid.*, Paragraphs 42.3–42.8.

63. *Ibid.*, Paragraphs 7.33–7.36.

64. *Ibid.*, Paragraph 42.34.

65. *Ibid.*, Paragraph 2.4.

66. *Daily Mail,* 14th February 1997.

67. *Macpherson Report,* Paragraph 2.6.

68. *Ibid.*, Paragraphs 44.9 and 44.10.

69. *Ibid.*, Paragraphs 7.39–7.45 and 42.25.

70. *The Independent,* 22nd October 2011.

71. *Macpherson Report,* Paragraph 2.10.

72. *Ibid.*, Paragraphs 2.15 and 2.17.

73. *Ibid.*, Paragraphs 3.15 and 3.16.

74. *Ibid.*, Paragraph 4.4.

75. *Ibid.*, Paragraph 12.60.

76. *Ibid.*, Paragraph 34.

77. *Ibid.*, Paragraphs 19.35 and 36.10.

78. *Ibid.*, Paragraph 12.64.

79. The *Macpherson Report* devoted an entire chapter to this issue concluding in paragraph 26.37: 'we see here a clear example of the collective failure of the investigating team to treat Mr and Mrs Lawrence appropriately and professionally, because of their colour, culture and ethnic origin.'

80. *Macpherson Report,* Paragraphs 45.8 and 45.9.

81. *Ibid.*, Paragraphs 45.8, 45.9 and 45.10.

82. *Ibid.*, Paragraphs 45.11 and 45.12.

83. *Ibid.*, Paragraph 12.100.

84. *Ibid.*, Paragraphs 13.25 and 13.43.

85. *Ibid.*, Paragraph 15.40. The failure to arrest earlier was also cited as the major error in the case by the Kent Constabulary Inquiry – see Cathcart (1999) *The Case of Stephen Lawrence*, p. 375.

86. *Macpherson Report,* Paragraph 46.1.

87. For problems around identity parades and their proper conduct see *ibid.,* Paragraphs 21.3–21.21.

88. *Ibid.,* Recommendations 18, 19, 23–28, 48–54 and 64–66.

89. *Ibid.,* Recommendations 3 and 4.

90. *Ibid.,* Recommendation 12.

91. *Ibid.,* Recommendations 33, 34, 35, 36 and 37.

92. *Ibid.,* Recommendations 48–59.

93. *Ibid.,* Recommendations 64–69.

94. *Ibid.,* Recommendation 70.

95. 'Stephen Lawrence: How His Murder Changed the Legal Landscape', *The Guardian,* 22nd April 2013. See also items in Chapter Ten notes 50 and 101.

96. *The Guardian,* 12th September 2006.

97. Independent Police Complaints Commission: Investigation Report. Independent investigation into complaints following '*The Boys Who Killed Stephen Lawrence*', 8th May 2012. Available at https://www.ipcc.gov.uk/sites/default/files/Documents/investigation_commissioner_reports/ReviewStephenLawrence.pdf (Accessed 15th February 2017).

98. See *Daily Mail,* 31st July 2015.

99. *The Guardian,* 16th October 2015.

100. See respectively D. Renton (2014) *Who Killed Blair Peach?* (London: Defend the Right to Protest), excerpted in *London Review of Books,* 22nd May 2014; *New Statesman,* 18th September 1981; *The Guardian,* 13th April 1981 and *The Independent,* 23rd October 2011.

101. See C.F. Willis (1983) *Use, Effectiveness and Impact of Police Stop and Search Powers* (London: Home Office Research Unit) and B. Bowling and C. Phillips (2007) 'Disproportionate and Discriminatory: Reviewing the Evidence on Police Stop and Search', *Modern Law Review,* Vol. 70, No. 6, pp. 936–61.

102. Cathcart (1999) *The Case of Stephen Lawrence,* p. 416.

103. *The Guardian,* 22nd April 2013.

104. J. Bennetto (2009) *Police and Racism: What Has Been Achieved 10 Years after the Stephen Lawrence Inquiry Report?* (London: Equality and Human Rights Commission).

105. *The Guardian,* 5th June 2015.

106. *Ibid.*

107. Scottish Government Social Research (2013) *An Examination of the Evidence on Sectarianism in Scotland* (Edinburgh: Scottish Government Social Research). Available at www.scotland.gov.uk/socialresearch (Accessed 28th November 2015), p. 11, p. 13 and p. 14.
108. BBC Scotland News, 'Race Crime in Scotland Falls to Lowest Level in 10 Years', 14th June 2013.
109. Quoted in Cathcart (1999) *The Case of Stephen Lawrence*, pp. 35–60.

5

Offences Against the Person: Child Sexual Abuse

Kim Stevenson

1. Introduction

Reviewing twentieth-century responses to sexual behaviour exposes seismic shifts in how illicit sexual activity was understood, defined and managed. The developing 'sciences' including sexology, psychology, criminology, sociology, feminism and gender theory evolved more nuanced and informed understandings about the nature and impact of sexual violation.[1] This enhanced public awareness and relocated the sexual discourse more prominently into the public sphere. Longstanding social taboos regarding incest, child sexual abuse, rape within marriage and male rape were progressively purged. But society was also forced to acknowledge and confront the existence of sexual activities beyond its comprehension, including the paedophiliac targeting and grooming of children, child pornography and female genital mutilation. Such revelations often manifested themselves through the impulse of moral panics, such as the child sex abuse and paedophile panics of the 1980s and '90s.

The law was slow to respond to the increasing consciousness of child sexual abuse. The Offences Against the Person Act (OAPA) 1861 and Criminal Law Amendment Act (CLAA) 1885 were no longer fit for purpose, requiring the judiciary, with its inherent masculine bias, to 'make the law work'. The all-male courtroom and criminal justice system dominated until virtually the end of the twentieth century. Apart from the gradual introduction of women police officers from c.1918 mentioned by Neil Davie in his chapter in this volume, and female jurors in 1920, female involvement was irrationally unrepresentative given that the vast majority of victims are female.[2] Examples of less than sympathetic 'misunderstandings' by the judiciary and legal counsel regarding the impact of sexual violations, often influenced by enduring Victorian rape myths and gendered stereotypes, proliferated, as did the belief that the evidence of children was unreliable and should not be believed.[3] This chapter focuses primarily on sexual violations committed against children. A similar review on the law relating to rape can be found in an earlier work.[4]

Mid-century, the Sexual Offences Act (SOA) 1956 presented an opportunity to refine the law but it disappointed, mainly restating the existing provisions regarding rape, indecent assault, incest, defilement and procuration. The phenomenon of child sexual abuse had not yet been fully established, therefore there was no legal impetus to review the law. It would take another half century before the Home Secretary, David Blunkett, officially confirmed that the law was 'archaic, incoherent and discriminatory', and for the Sexual Offences Act (SOA) 2003 to recognise the range of sexual offences committed against children.[5]

As we will see in due course, the historiography of twentieth century child sex offending is still being written. For the first half of the century, reliable sources and commentary are sparse. For the second, particularly the 1970s and 1980s, the ongoing disclosures of apparent historic cases of sexual abuse accentuate significant gaps.[6] The extent of recent allegations against ageing celebrities precipitated by the Jimmy Savile Inquiry 2012–2013, and others who held positions of trust in schools and religious organisations, is historically unprecedented. Media investigations have exposed a previously hidden and, for many, unknown world of sexual perversion involving significant numbers of children. Fundamental questions have been raised about the limitations of the law, the criminal justice process at the time such alleged offences were committed and the consequent delayed decisions to prosecute. Twentieth century law reports are peppered with ingenious defences from those accused attempting to avoid liability, or 'justificatory' pleas that their actions should be regarded as a contemporary cultural sexual norm rather than condemned by present-day disapprobation.

2.   Chronology

To understand the twentieth-century context, we need to go back to W.T. Stead's publication of the Maiden Tribute child prostitution scandal in the *Pall Mall Gazette,* 6 July 1885. Until 1841 it was a capital offence to have sexual intercourse with a girl under 12 years, that being the age of marriage.[7] Section 50 OAPA 1861 criminalised carnal knowledge with a girl under 10 years, increased to 13 in 1875, as a felony punishable with a maximum life sentence.[8] The Criminal Law Amendment Bills 1883–85 (initiated by Josephine Butler's campaign concerning the trafficking of young English girls to the Continent) proposed to raise this to 16 years. This proposal triggered major disagreements in the House of Lords about whether young girls deserved or needed such legal protection; some peers believed that it was adult men who needed legal concessions to protect *them* from the 'immoral' advances of underage females.[9] The day after Stead's exposé, the Lords asserted their 'deep conviction' that the Bill 'should become law without delay,' the Government acquiesced not wanting to be seen as disinterested in the protection of young girls.[10]

Section 4 CLAA 1885 confirmed the carnal knowledge of a girl under 13 as a felony and section 5 made the carnal knowledge of girls aged between 13 and 16 a misdemeanour punishable with two years imprisonment. The Act also raised the age of consent for the lesser offence of indecent assault from 13 to 16 years. But the issue of *who* the law was supposed to protect kept resurfacing. In 1893, Jane Tyrrell was convicted at the Central Criminal Court for unlawfully aiding and abetting a man, Thomas Ford, to have carnal knowledge with her while she was aged between 13 and 16. Lord Chief Justice Coleridge quashed her conviction confirming that Parliament could never have intended the 1885 Act to produce such a bizarre result. The case is an early example of the misplaced manipulation of the law that appeared to transfer responsibility onto the child, something that would intensify in the twentieth century.[11]

Despite being heavily contested for the next 40 years, the 1885 threshold of 16 years became progressively recognised as the legal age of consent.[12] The Act only applied to girls; an equivalent age of consent for boys was proposed in the Criminal Law Amendment Bill 1913, but an accompanying clause to increase the age of consent for girls to 18, guaranteed its withdrawal. Equality around both heterosexual and homosexual age of consent was not established until the SOA 2003, underlining the gendered bias that continued throughout the twentieth century.

The CLAA 1885 marked a new development in the criminal law heralding a transition in social and political attitudes that would facilitate much twentieth century protectionist legislation including the Punishment of Incest Act 1908, Children Act 1908 and Children and Young Persons Act 1933. This underpinned a shift in enforcement as the 'persuasive education' of moral campaigners succumbed to the authority of the state and the police. In 1913, the Criminal Law Amendment Committee exerted pressure on the Home Office to permit the appointment of women police officers to take depositions from women and children.[13] The Committee organised a public meeting in 1916 supported by Lady Nott-Bower, wife of the Chief Constable of the City of London Police, who asserted: 'it was a crime and blunder to put a young child in Court when only men could ask questions'.[14] In 1919 (the same year as the Sex Disqualification Removal Act), 50 women were appointed to the Metropolitan Police from which just 2 'were assigned the specific duty of statement-taking from children and young women in relation to sexual offences.'[15] Until their demise, hastened by the Sex Discrimination Act 1975, specialist women police departments combined law enforcement with child welfare protection, a dual role that often generated tensions with their male colleagues and Watch Committees.[16] With equality there was periodic, but not universal, provision of specially trained officers, male and female, to deal with sexual offences. In 1986 Greater Manchester Police set up the first specialist sexual offence unit, but there was no national mandate until the instigation of Sexual Assault Referral Centres in 2011.[17]

It is worth briefly mentioning the difficulties experienced by child victims when called as witnesses in the criminal court. Children were regarded as neither reliable nor competent witnesses and, as victims of sexual abuse, even less likely to be believed. From 1779, children were only permitted to give evidence on oath and provided they could demonstrate sufficient understanding of the likely implications of 'burning in hell' if they did not tell the truth.[18] In the first half of the nineteenth century, trials were often postponed while children could be quickly 're-educated' in their religious knowledge and responsibilities ensuring they could then testify on oath.[19] In 1885, Shaftesbury challenged the Government to relax the rule that children under 12 years must give sworn evidence, something that would not be achieved for another 100 years. He secured an amendment to the CLAA 1885 which permitted girls under 13 years to give unsworn evidence, but a proviso was added that an accused person could not be convicted unless her evidence was corroborated by other independent evidence implicating him. The Children and Young Persons Act 1933 allowed all children under 14 to give unsworn evidence where they possessed sufficient intelligence to justify its reception and understood the duty to tell the truth. Critically, the proviso was retained and not removed until 1988; it was not until 1991 that all children under 14 were automatically allowed to give unsworn evidence.[20] The common law further required that the judge must give an additional corroboration warning regarding the testimony of anyone alleging a sexual offence, child or adult; this was also removed in 1988. After considerable criticism about the treatment of children in court, and the publication of the Pigot Report in 1989, the Youth Justice and Criminal Evidence Act 1999 finally ameliorated many of the practical and formal difficulties of giving evidence, authorising the introduction of screens, video links, pre-recording initial disclosures and the removal of wigs and gowns.[21] However, it would take another 20 years before section 28 of the Act, authorising the use of video recorded cross-examination of child witnesses to avoid the need for physical presence in the courtroom, would be admitted.[22]

The next section of the chronology provides the context for the two case studies both reported in the 1977 law reports: an appeal by a father against his conviction and sentence for committing incest with his 15-year-old daughter, and an appeal by three men against their sentences for engaging in sexual activities with a 14-year-old girl. The two crimes are dealt with separately here as there are significant differences in their origins and legal development. Incest was made a specific crime in 1908 in response to the demands of child welfare campaigners and social reformers, whereas non-familial child sexual abuse was never made the subject of a definitive crime until 2003.

a) Incest

At the time Stead raised public consciousness about continental trafficking, a more serious evil was being uncovered closer to home. In 1883, the Reverend Andrew Mearns, secretary of the Congregational Union, wrote an anonymous pamphlet, 'The Bitter Cry of Outcast London'.[23] Stead helped publicise its searing descriptions of the misery of those living in the London slums and references to immoral incestuous relations. Challenging middle-class Victorian morality, Booth commented that 'Incest is so familiar as to hardly call for remark'.[24] Stead's National Vigilance Association aligned with the National Society for the Prevention of Cruelty to Children (NSPCC) (formerly the London SPCC founded in 1883) and demanded legislative reform. Carnal intercourse within the prohibited degrees of consanguinity or affinity could only be punished in the Ecclesiastical courts but was rarely reported in the official record. Occasionally cases can be detected in the newspapers where a charge was brought either under CLAA age of protection provisions or for rape, but rarely with satisfactory detail.[25] For example, in 1908, John Larcombe, 57 years, was indicted at Bristol Assizes for rape on his daughter whose age, unfortunately, is not given. The judge concluded that as his daughter had no choice but to acquiesce there was no evidence of non-consent, highlighting the need for a specific statutory offence.[26]

Incest had been a criminal offence in Scotland since 1567 and, for a short while, in England during the interregnum. Attempts to enact legislation failed in 1899–1900, and again in 1903 and 1907, meeting considerable resistance. The Lord Chancellor; the Earl of Halsbury, was particularly vociferous:

> I regret very much that the nature of this Bill is one which renders it repulsive to everybody to discuss it ... legislation of this character is calculated to do an infinite amount of mischief ... these are cases which it is inadvisable to drag into the light of day.[27]

The Bill was reintroduced in 1908, sponsored by the Bishop of St Albans, who informed the Lords that during the preceding year 42 cases were referred to the NSPCC; Birmingham reported 11 cases, Liverpool 12 and the Metropolitan Police 36. In addition, of the 193 petitions received by the Home Office pleading remission in sentence for rape or carnal knowledge of a girl, 51 were incestuous convictions.[28] This time their Lordships were convinced and the Act was welcomed as a victory by the NSPCC and the NVA. Section 1 prohibited, in the case of a man, carnal knowledge with anyone who to his knowledge is his grand-daughter, daughter, sister or mother, punishable with between three and seven years penal servitude, two years or less with or without hard labour, or life imprisonment if the girl was under 13.[29] Section 2 provided that where a female aged 16 years or over *permits* a man she knows to be her grandfather, brother, son or father to have carnal knowledge with her by her consent she also commits an offence; the penalty is identical to section 1 except there is no life imprisonment where the male victim is under 13.

The age thresholds and 'permissive' aspect reflect the bias towards protecting young girls as it was known that most cases involved fathers and daughters. It was not unlawful for a grandmother to have carnal knowledge with her grandson as it was thought there was little risk because she would be beyond child-bearing age; also there was an irrebuttable presumption in law, not abolished until the Sexual Offences Act 1993, that boys under 14 were physically incapable of sexual intercourse.[30] Despite the Act stipulating that the consent of the Director of Public Prosecutions was required (to avoid claims of blackmail), on average 56 cases were prosecuted annually. There was also a marked increase in the number of prosecutions for indecent assault against children as the Children Act 1908 permitted summary trial for such offences. The Incest Act required all cases to be held *in camera* so details of the trial proceedings could not be reported in the press. Even in the official law reports, cases are not immediately apparent. Henry Hedges was sentenced to 10 years at Maidstone Assizes in 1909 for 'forcible connexion' with his 15-year-old daughter. The report highlights the keywords 'rape, fresh complaint and corroboration considered' but there is a note from the Lord Chief Justice in brackets, 'This appellant must have been convicted under the Incest

Act.' The Court of Criminal Appeal dismissed his appeal holding that his daughter's evidence was corroborated by the examining doctor who confirmed that her hymen was broken with injuries consistent with frequent sexual intercourse.[31]

Apart from the repeal of the *in camera* rule in 1922 no substantive changes were made to the law until the SOA 2003. Sections 1 and 2 of the 1908 Act were simply renumbered as sections 10 and 11 respectively in the consolidating SOA 1956 and 'carnal knowledge' replaced by the more modern term 'sexual intercourse'. In 1977, 295 cases were reported to the police though only 4 out of 10 were prosecuted.[32] That year the case of *Whitehouse* highlighted a fundamental problem when a father was found not to have broken the law when he incited his 15-year-old daughter to have sexual intercourse with him (see Case Study 1). Section 54 Criminal Law Amendment Act 1977 was quickly rushed onto the statute books to fill this lacuna. By the end of the century hardly any prosecutions were brought. In 1987, 184 males were proceeded against but this had dropped to just 25 by 1997, for females the figures were 6 and 1 respectively.[33] The two offences were now seriously outdated, with the traditional nuclear family being supplanted by looser family structures. The SOA 2003 introduced new offences of familial sexual abuse expunging the stigmatisation of 'incest' from the law and extending liability to aunts, uncles, cousins, step-parents, adoptive parents, fosterers and other full-time carers.[34]

b) Child Sexual Abuse

Until the second half of the twentieth century, the problem of child sexual abuse appears to have been largely unknown and unacknowledged in the press and public discourse. Some public and professional awareness did emerge, primarily amongst child welfare campaigners and early feminists, but it was repeatedly repressed due to a combination of factors including the incest taboo, 'Freudianism, sexual modernism and gender politics ... leading to a long history of cultural denial.'[35] The silence was eventually broken as a result of the feminist campaigns of the 1970s against domestic violence.[36] Lacking any scientific identification, the phenomenon gradually materialised from within the generic classification of physical abuse: firstly through the battered baby syndrome, then non-accidental injury, child abuse and finally child sexual abuse. Similarly, the descriptor 'paedophile' mutated from child molester, pervert and child abuser. It was virtually unheard of until the moral panics of the early 2000s fuelled, after Sarah Payne's murder, by the *News of the World*'s naming and shaming crusade to 'out' all convicted paedophiles.[37]

The nebulous nature of child sexual abuse was further reinforced by the fact that there was no specific crime of sexually abusing a child. Instead, where penile penetration occurred, perpetrators were charged (under section 6 SOA 1956) with unlawful sexual intercourse with a girl aged under 16, which still carried a maximum sentence of just two years (see Case Study 2). Young men under 24 years were still permitted to claim the 'young man's' defence introduced by the CLAA 1922 if they reasonably believed the girl to be over 16 years. This provision was introduced as a concession to young men who might be 'deceived' by young girls. The life sentence was retained for sexual intercourse with girls under 13 (section 5 SOA 1956), but there were no equivalent provisions for boys. Sexual touching could be prosecuted as an indecent assault whether committed against boys or girls under 16, but either non-consent from the victim or hostile intent by the abuser using threats or violence needed to be proved to secure a conviction.[38]

Unsurprisingly, there are very few cases in the historical record of women charged with sexual offences against boys, and none of women sexually assaulting girls until the SOA 2003 made all sexual assaults gender neutral. The Central Criminal Court depositions feature a rare 1900 example where Florence Kennard was charged with indecently assaulting a nine-year-old boy she appears to have induced to have sexual intercourse with her, but the papers focus more on the conflicting medical evidence as to how he became infected with gonorrhoea.[39] The problem of no equivalent age of consent for boys is illustrated in a 1930s case, *R v Hare*. Margaret Hare was charged at the Central Criminal Court with three counts of indecent assault on a boy aged 12. She admitted inducing him to have sexual intercourse with her and his testimony was corroborated by the fact he was infected with a venereal disease. Ingeniously, the prosecution charged Hare under section 62 OAPA 1861, originally drafted to criminalise adult male same-sex activities or 'unnatural' crimes: 'whosoever shall attempt to commit the said abominable crime or shall be guilty of any assault upon any male person.' Hare's female barrister, Miss Venetia Stephenson, sought to stop the case on the grounds that section 62 was restricted to 'unnatural' offences (sodomy). This was dismissed as Hare had already admitted to engagement in sexual intercourse (albeit not sodomitical) and the jury found her guilty. On appeal, Stephenson argued that 'whosoever' only applied to male perpetrators. Justice Avory dismissed this argument too: 'there can be no reason for saying that a woman cannot be guilty of indecent assault upon another female or a male.'[40] Unfortunately there is no evidence of this precedent being used subsequently.

The requirement that an indecent assault must constitute a hostile physical assault or battery exercised the judiciary in a number of cases in the 1950s. In *Fairclough v Whipp*, Whipp was collecting water by the banks of a canal in Clitheroe near four young girls aged between six and nine. He exposed his penis as the nine-year-old passed him and said to her 'Touch it', which she did. Lord Chief Justice Goddard agreed with the Clitheroe magistrates that Whipp had indecently *invited* the child to touch him but as there was no evidence of non-consent, no assault had occurred.[41] The same reasoning was applied in *DPP v Rogers*.[42] Rogers put his arm around his daughter and led her upstairs, she neither objected nor resisted. He then exposed his penis and told her to masturbate him, she obeyed although she did not wish to do so. Again, Goddard confirmed the commission of an indecent act but not an assault as Rogers had not used any force, threats or compulsion, nor could he be liable for incest as sexual intercourse had not occurred.

Parliament responded by passing section 1 Indecency with Children Act 1960 to address the problem of apparent 'consent' to indecent assault. The provision was ill-conceived making it an offence for a person to commit an act of gross indecency with or towards a child under 14 years or incite a child under that age to commit such an act. The penalty was meagre by today's standards, a maximum of two years imprisonment or six months if convicted summarily. The use of the word 'gross' related to the age of the child not the grossness of the indecent act, though the provision did at least apply to both male and female offenders.[43] Yet again the measure proved ineffectual and it was not long before defence counsel sought to exploit the provision.

In 1968, in another rare example, Dulcie Mason, a married woman (age not given) was indicted at Shropshire Assizes with nine counts of indecent assault committed on six boys aged 14 to 15 who visited her house either singularly or in groups. Sometimes she suggested sexual intercourse, sometimes they did, typically she would kiss and touch them beforehand. Justice Veale was convinced that all the boys were 'entirely willing parties':

> There was no threat, no gesture, no pulling of the boy, no reluctance on his part .... I have no doubt that a woman who passively permits sexual intercourse at the suggestion of a boy of fifteen is not assaulting the boy.[44]

His comments reflect the legal presumption that on attaining the age of 14 boys were physically capable of sexual intercourse, and so implicitly had the mental capacity to make such decisions. Mason was therefore acquitted of indecent assault and could not be convicted of gross indecency as all the boys were over 14 years of age. Further challenges were made in cases like *Speck* in 1977 where an eight-year-old girl approached the accused and placed her hand on his trousers touching his penis. Speck made no attempt to remove the girl's hand and left it there for five minutes achieving an erection. The Court of Appeal allowed his appeal against conviction as he had not done an 'act with or towards' a child, he had simply remained inactive.[45] Ultimately, the offence was replaced by sections 9 to 13 SOA 2003 which criminalises all forms of sexual touching and activity with a child under 16.

The last two decades of the twentieth century were marked by a seemingly never-ending media onslaught of horrific child sex abuse scandals, the details and extent of which are still being exposed today, and most beyond the comprehension of right-minded citizens. Evidence of wide-scale systematic and institutional abuse in children's homes first came to light with the Frank Beck affair in the 1980s affecting nearly 250 children. Holding a senior position in Leicester Social Services, Beck was able to recruit other members of his paedophile ring and deflect any allegations of sexual abuse referred to him. Then, ironically on the centenary of Stead's shocking expose, came the Cleveland crisis in 1987 triggering the largest moral panic of the century and highlighting fundamental problems in the management of child sexual abuse. Lady Justice Butler-Sloss who chaired the subsequent inquiry identified a serious breakdown in child protection responses where the police, social services and the medical profession prioritised interagency rivalries and distrust over the welfare of children. Between February and July 1987, 125 children were identified as being sexually abused, discovered through overzealous interventions by social services and by well-meaning doctors using now discredited anal dilation diagnostic techniques. These 'investigations' resulted in many children being taken into care. In her report recommending that the welfare of the child must be paramount, Butler-Sloss refused to single out any one agency, holding them all jointly culpable for the crisis.[46]

In 1991, social workers in Rochdale were condemned for ignoring the report when 20 children were removed from their families on the basis of anonymous telephone allegations of satanic abuse and a 6-year-old boy's ghostly fantasies.[47] Similar crises alleging ritual abuse occurred in South Ronaldsay, Ayrshire, Strathclyde and Nottingham in the early 1990s. A government commissioned report examined 84 cases of alleged satanic abuse between 1987 and 1991. No evidence was found to substantiate any such claims, exposing the myth of ritual abuse and blaming self-proclaimed experts for inflaming such moral panics.[48] The century ended with the revelation of a number of high-profile international child grooming and Internet pornography investigations. These included Operation Cathedral and 'the Wonderland Club' whose members were personally required to contribute 10,000 indecent photographs of children. By January 2001 three-quarters of a million paedophiliac images had been retrieved by police investigators.[49]

3. Historiography

As highlighted in the introduction, the historiography of child sexual abuse from a crime history perspective is far from complete. There is a huge amount of literature about the impact and effects of twentieth-century child sexual abuse and child protection procedures, largely written by those in the disciplines of child studies, child psychiatry, child psychology and sociology but with some contributions from legal academics, criminologists and historians. Child sexual abuse is now such a multifaceted phenomenon, and multi-disciplinary issue, that its historiography presents a major challenge. An informative overview is Olafson's comprehensive interdisciplinary survey, ambitiously synthesizing over 160 references and leading texts.[50]

Behlmer first drew attention to the reluctance of the state to interfere with the privacy of family life and reflect on the role of child reformers from 1870 to 1908, this was developed further by Hendrick in his surveys of child welfare and constructions of childhood in the nineteenth and twentieth centuries.[51] Works on the history of sexuality such as Porter and Hall and Davenport-Hines cover much broader periods, or only make brief reference to twentieth-century child sexual abuse.[52] Brown and Barrett focus on twentieth-century child prostitution extending Walkowitz's nineteenth-century analysis, and Waites covers the shift from the age of sexual protection to consent, but the emphasis is more on sexual (and especially homosexual) autonomy than abuse.[53] Jeffreys offers a typically robust and informative feminist perspective on the role of women's organisations in the protection of young girls during the late nineteenth and early twentieth century.[54] As yet, there is no twentieth-century equivalent to Jackson's seminal work *Child Sexual Abuse in Victorian England* which comprehensively integrates historical, legal, criminological and medical perspectives, but Jackson is currently redressing the balance leading an Economic and Social Research Council funded project tracking child sexual abuse in England and Wales from 1918 to 1970.[55] Jackson has also done much to uncover the role of the Metropolitan Women Police from 1919 to 1969,[56] but child sexual abuse was only just starting to enter the public consciousness at the end of this period, and criminal justice responses had not yet fully grasped or engaged with the developing phenomenon.

A useful starting point in understanding the history of child sexual abuse is Carol Smart's overview from 1910 to 1960, confirming 'that this has been a much neglected period' in terms of detailed scholarship on the subject. Smart explores four discursive fields – medical, political, legal and psychoanalytic – to assess the extent to which 'child sexual abuse as a form of harm ... varied in content and over time'.[57] She is particularly scathing of the role of the law suggesting that 'it was the criminal trial and its attendant procedures which prevented any wide-scale reconceptualisation of the harm of child sexual abuse.'[58] For analysis of the later moral panics and how these were portrayed in the media, Critcher, and Marsh and Melville, provide detailed commentary.[59] Cleveland MP Stuart Bell and journalist Beatrix Campbell track the unfolding events of the Cleveland crisis as experienced in real time from their individual perspectives. Bell invokes comparisons with the Salem witch trials, a theme taken up by LaFontain's *Speak of the Devil* based on her 1994 government review of organised and ritual abuse.[60]

The historiography of incest is even more limited as reports of actual cases are elusive, partly because of the sensitivity of the material but also the early twentieth-century ban on publication. The Victorian commentaries of Mearns, Shaftesbury and Booth are widely available and interrogated in Wohl's *Sex and the Single Room*.[61] Jeffreys has explored potential links between incest and child prostitution, and Wolfram has examined the impact and effect of incestuous activities within family relationships and from the perspective of the debates around eugenics offering some significant insights.[62] Victor Bailey's two-part discussion in the *Criminal Law Review* remains the definitive account of the passage of the 1908 Act, published in 1979 before the digitisation of parliamentary reports and newspaper archives, and a critique of the law at that time.[63] Although Scotland was the first to make incest a religious vice and crime (based on Mosaic Law) in 1567, there does not appear to be any significant Scottish, or indeed Welsh, historiography that draws on archival sources. Leeming tracks the reasons for its reform in 1986 but from a highly theoretical and jurisprudential perspective.[64] Thus, there are significant gaps in understandings of how incest and child sexual abuse were managed and prosecuted in the wider cultural context, particularly in the first half of the twentieth century (something that this author is now investigating) and in relation to the Scottish and Welsh experience.

4. Case Studies

The following case studies, based on two criminal appeals published in the law reports, further illustrate the limitations of the law and its effective application in practice. In both cases the appellants, adult males convicted of unlawful sexual acts committed against young girls, sought to avoid their respective culpability by attempting to transfer some responsibility onto the complainants. In the first, challenging the illegality of incest by exploiting a loophole in the law and in the second, by invoking the kind of stereotypical beliefs that prevailed in the late nineteenth and early twentieth centuries – that men needed to be protected from the 'seduction' of young girls.

a) Case Study 1

On 16 August 1976 Arthur Whitehouse pleaded guilty at Stafford Crown Court to two offences of inciting his 15-year-old daughter to have sexual intercourse with him and was sentenced to two years imprisonment.[65] The sentence took into account three previous convictions in April 1975 for offences of incitement to commit incest and one offence of incitement to commit gross indecency when his daughter was aged 11 and 13. He escaped a custodial sentence and was given three concurrent 15-month sentences suspended for two years, which he had now clearly breached. Whitehouse appealed against his 1976 conviction (despite pleading guilty) and sentence on the grounds it was too severe as he had never used any threats or force against his daughter, had never indecently assaulted her and there was never any likelihood that incest would take place. The judge, granting leave, thought the two-year sentence 'markedly excessive' though to our twenty-first century understandings of child sexual abuse and sentencing practice it might appear derisory.

Exceptionally, the Court of Appeal considered that Whitehouse might have been unlawfully convicted in 1975 of crimes that did not exist and allowed him to appeal against these even though the appeals were time barred. At 15, Whitehouse's daughter was below the age of culpability to commit incest under section 11 SOA 1956: 'for a woman of the age of 16 or over to permit a man whom she knows to be her ... father ... to have sexual intercourse with her by her consent.' At common law, the crime of incitement required inciting another person to commit a crime, as she was legally incapable of committing a crime, Whitehouse could not be guilty of inciting her. Lord Justice Scarman, allowing the appeal, concluded that he had therefore been convicted of a crime not known to the law. Whitehouse could not be indicted for rape or indecent assault as his daughter had 'consented' to her father's abuse; nor could he be convicted of inciting a child to commit an act of gross indecency with him under the Indecency with Children Act 1960 as the child has to be under 14 years. Whitehouse could not be charged with defilement under the 1956 equivalent of the 1885 provision of carnal knowledge with a girl aged between 13 and 16 years, as in 1922 an amendment had imposed a prosecution limit of 12 months from the date of commission of the offence. Hence in its inability to suitably punish Whitehouse, the law was shown up to be the proverbial 'ass', requiring Parliament to urgently enact section 54 Criminal Law Amendment Act 1977 which created a new offence for a man to incite a girl under the age of 16 who he knows to be his daughter, grand-daughter or sister to have sexual intercourse with him, punishable with a maximum two-year sentence.

b) Case Study 2

On 18 February 1977, Derek Taylor 26 years, David Roberts 22 years and Geoffrey Simons 28 years, all pleaded guilty at Nottingham Crown Court to having unlawful sexual intercourse with a 14-year-old girl contrary to section 6 Sexual Offences Act 1956.[66] The charges were sample offences as all admitted in written statements that each had had sexual intercourse with the girl on numerous occasions. Taylor and Simon were sentenced to four months imprisonment and Roberts to two months, all three appealed against their sentences. Their applications were refused but it is the comments of Lord Justice Lawton in the Court of Appeal that are of interest.

Lawton confirms that the circumstances of the case are 'very disturbing,' he expressly describes the girl as 'undoubtedly a wanton' at least four times on the basis that she was sexually experienced before she met any of the applicants and kept a diary of her sexual exploits. She apparently approached the men who admitted they knew how old she was and that she attended school. Taylor was a married man whose wife was pregnant at the time, Roberts married after severing his relationship with the girl and Simons was a bachelor. The court presumed that *she* was the corrupting influence concluding that the men had 'succumbed to her seduction' and had not corrupted her in any way. On the contrary, the fact that she had engaged in what Lawton says 'has come these days to be known as oral sex' confirmed that she was already debauched, they had merely 'increased the degree to which she was debauched' and 'treated her as the village whore'. Lawton affirms that the law exists for the protection of young girls and is particularly necessary in the case of wanton girls. The sentences were therefore appropriate as 'the evil they were doing was to confirm her in her wantoness.' The commentary is illustrative of the contemporary attitudes and perspectives that prevailed at the time, but parallels can be drawn with a more recent case in 2011 involving six adult footballers and two 12-year-old girls, one of whom was also condemned as sexually experienced at a young age.[67] In both cases the girls were shamed without any attempt to consider the underlying factors as to why they might be sexually experienced, with little condemnation of the responsibility of adult men to reject an underage girl's attempts at seduction. Echoes of Victorian and Edwardian cultural norms and attitudes towards girls found to be sexually experienced therefore resonate throughout the twentieth century and well into the twenty-first. These are reflected in the numerous prosecutions for child sexual exploitation involving organised networks comprising groups of young men from particular ethnic backgrounds, as epitomised in the ongoing investigations by the Independent Inquiry into Child Sexual Abuse in Rotherham, Oxford and Rochdale. Such perceptions are disturbing as they undermine understandings of the meaning of, and what constitutes, child sexual abuse. Compared to 2011, in 1977, there was hardly any public rhetoric or specific legislation targeting child sexual abuse, yet despite the enactment of the SOA 2003, and greater awareness and education about the incidence and effect of child sexual abuse, it is disturbing that the judicial response was not all that different. There still appears to be an inherent assumption that men need protection from the advances of young girls rather than a presumption that they take full responsibility for their actions.

5.   Conclusion

The unparalleled scale and diversity of twentieth-century sexual abuse would be unimaginable to any Victorian child carer, and inexplicably, at the time of writing, revelations of abuse perpetrated in the last century show no signs of drying up. Constant reports in the media of the extent of historical institutional abuse in the 1960s, '70s and '80s are overwhelming and the issue cannot be adequately addressed here. On 13 January 2014, Sir Anthony Hart opened the Historical Institutional Abuse Inquiry in Northern Ireland, then the largest independent statutory inquiry in the United Kingdom to investigate claims of physical and sexual abuse in children's homes and juvenile justice occurring between 1922 and 1995.[68] In May 2014, Scottish victims demanded a similar national inquiry triggered by the unspeakable sexual violence at St Ninian's Christian Brothers School in Fife. David Sharpe, abused in the 1960s when he was a ten-year-old pupil at the school, stressed the fundamental failure of society to protect him and others, 'This is not a church issue, it's much deeper than that. This is about councils, social workers, the judiciary and government. Every victim or survivor in Scotland deserves answers.'[69] In North Wales, Operation Pallial was launched in 2013 to deal with 140 allegations of 'significant and systematic' historical sexual abuse at children's homes between 1963 and 1992.[70] All of these have since been superseded by the Independent Inquiry into Child Sexual Abuse in England and Wales which opened in July 2015 and has attracted considerable controversy ever since in respect of its remit, cost and leadership.[71] Thus, the historiography of twentieth-century child sexual abuse is far from complete and remains a work in progress. In particular, more attention needs to be focussed on the Scottish and Welsh experience and their respective cultural contexts. The extent of reported and unreported sexual violation committed during the second half of the twentieth century is undeniably an unprecedented phenomenon, and one that requires historians to objectively reflect back upon to fully contextualise and realise its significance.

Notes

1. See E. Olafson, D. Corwin and R. Summit (1993) 'Modern History of Child Sexual Abuse Awareness: Cycles of Discovery and Suppression', *Child Abuse and Neglect*, Vol. 17, pp. 7–24 at pp. 8–10.
2. For a general historic overview see S. Brownmiller (1975) *Against Our Will, Men, Women and Rape* (New York: Simon and Schuster). Ministry of Justice statistics averaged across 2009/10, 2010/11 and 2011/12 estimate 85,000 females and 12,000 males per year are the victim of serious sexual assaults: Ministry of Justice, Home Office and Office for National Statistics (2013) *An Overview of Sexual Offending in England and Wales*. Available at https://www.gov.uk/government/publications/an-overview-of-sexual-offending-in-england-and-wales (Accessed 12th November 2017). The number of reported sexual offences has increased dramatically since this Overview was published largely because of the ongoing *Independent Inquiry into Child Sexual Abuse* (https://www.iicsa.org.uk) (Accessed 12th November 2017). In the year ending March 2015, there were 88,106 recorded sexual offences, an increase of 37 per cent on the previous year, see *An Overview of Violent Crime and Sexual Offences* (11 February 2016), part 8. Available at https://www.ons.gov.uk/people populationandcommunity/crimeandjustice/compendium/focusonviolent-crimeandsexualoffences/yearendingmarch2015/chapter1overviewofviolent-crimeandsexualoffences#sexual-offences (Accessed 12th November 2017).
3. See K. Stevenson (2017) 'Children of a Very Tender Age Have Vicious Propensities': Child Witness Testimonies in Cases of Sexual Abuse', *Law, Crime, History*, Vol. 1, pp. 75–97; K. Stevenson (2000) 'Unequivocal Victims: The Historical Mystification of the Female Complainant in Rape Cases', *Feminist Legal Studies*, Vol. 8, pp. 346–66; J. Spencer and R. Flin (1993) *The Evidence of Children* (London: Blackstone Press).
4. K. Stevenson (2010) '"Most Intimate Violations": Contextualising the Crime of Rape', in A.-M. Kilday and D. Nash (eds) *Histories of Crime: Britain 1600–2000* (Basingstoke: Palgrave), pp. 80–99.

5. D. Blunkett (2002) *Protecting the Public* (Home Office Consultation Paper, Cmnd. 5668), Foreword.

6. For example, *The Times* has led an investigation into the number of boys subjected to abuse in private and church schools, '130 Private schools in child abuse scandal', *The Times*, 20th January 2014; 'Schools for Scandal', *The Times*, 21st January 2014, in addition to the allegations made against well-known 1970s TV presenters such as Stuart Hall, Rolf Harris, Jimmy Savile, Dave Lee Travis, etc.

7. Statute of Westminster 1275; Elizabeth I lowered it to 10 (Act of 1576) but it reverted back to 12 in the OAPA 1828.

8. Section 4 OAPA 1875. The Age of Marriage Act 1929 increased the age to 16.

9. Parliamentary Papers, House of Lords, 25 June 1883, cols.1390–91, especially the comments of Lord Norton and the Earl of Milltown.

10. The National Archives (TNA): HO45/9547/59343/I/82.

11. *R v Tyrrell* (1894) 1 QB 710.

12. Confirmed CLAA 1922, SOA 1956, SOA 2003. See K. Stevenson (2017) '"Not Just the Ideas of a Few Enthusiasts": Early Twentieth Century Legal Activism and Reformation of the Age of Sexual Consent', *Cultural and Social History*, Vol. 14, pp. 219–36. Currently there is debate about whether it should be reduced to 14 or 15 years.

13. *The Times*, 17th July 1914.

14. *The Times*, 15th March 1916.

15. L. Jackson (2003) 'Care or Control? The Metropolitan Women Police and Child Welfare, 1919–1969', *The Historical Journal*, Vol. 46, No. 3, pp. 623–48 at p. 627.

16. *Ibid.*, passim.

17. In 2008, Solicitor General Vera Baird and Home Secretary Jacqui Smith guaranteed nationwide provision; 'Government Making Real Progress on Rape Convictions', *The Times*, 21st February 2008; Home Office Press Release, 'More Funding Announced for Sexual Assault Referral Centres,' 7th October 2008; Home Office Press Release, 'New Measures to Support Victims of Sexual Assault,' 15th April 2009.

18. *R v Brasier* (1779) 1 Leach 199.

19. See Stevenson (2017) 'Child Witness Testimonies in Cases of Sexual Abuse'.

20. Section 34 Criminal Justice Act 1988; section 52 Criminal Justice Act 1991.

21. Special Measures Directions under section 17 Youth Justice and Criminal Evidence Act 1999. See also Judge Pigot (1989) *Report of the Home Office Advisory Group on Video Recordings* (London: HMSO).

22. Ministry of Justice Press Release, 'Greater protection for rape victims and children at risk of grooming', 19th March 2017.

23. Reproduced in P. Keating (ed.) (1978) *Into Unknown England 1866–1913: Selections from the Social Explorers* (Glasgow: Fontana Collins), pp. 91–111.

24. W. Booth (1890) *In Darkest England and the Way Out* (London: Funk and Wagnalls), p. 65.

25. See K. Stevenson (2016) '"These are Cases Which it is Inadvisable to Drag into the Light of Day": Disinterring the Crime of Incest in Early Twentieth-Century England', *Crime History and Societies*, Vol. 20, No. 2, pp. 31–54.

26. *The Times*, 23rd November 1908.

27. Parliamentary Papers, House of Lords, 16 July 1903, col. 820–824.

28. Parliamentary Papers, House of Lords, 2 December 1908, Incest Bill 2nd Reading, col.1408.

29. Punishment of Incest Act 1908.

30. *R v Waite* (1892) 2 QB 600 at 601 per Lord Coleridge CJ.

31. *R v Henry Hedges* (1910) 3 Cr App R 262.

32. V. Bailey and S. McCabe (1979), 'Reforming the Law of Incest', *Criminal Law Review*, Vol. 14, pp. 749–64 at p. 749.

33. Home Office (July 2000) *Setting the Boundaries* (Home Office Communication Directorate) para. 5.2.3.

34. Section 25 SOA 2003: Sexual activity with a child family member; section 26 SOA 2003: Inciting a child family member to engage in sexual activity.

35. Olafson, Corwin and Summit (1993) 'Modern History of Child Sexual Abuse', p. 8.

36. C. Smart (2000) 'Reconsidering the Recent History of Child Sexual Abuse, 1910–1960', *Journal of Social Policy*, Vol. 29, No. 1, pp. 55–71 at p. 56.

37. C. Critcher (2002) 'Media, Government and Moral Panic: The Politics of Paedophilia in Britain 2000–1', *Journalism Studies*, Vol. 3, No. 4, pp. 521–35.

38. See *R v Lock* (1872) 2 LCRRR 10 per Kelly at p. 12; *Fairclough v Whipp* (1951) 35 Cr App R 138.

39. *R v Florence Kennard*, Central Criminal Court, 12 March 1900, TNA: CRIM1/60/2.

40. *R v Hare*, Court of Criminal Appeal (1934–39) Cox's Criminal Cases 64. Section 62 was repealed and replaced by sections 15 and 16 SOA 1956.

41. *Fairclough v Whipp* (1951) 35 Cr App R 138, see also *R v Burrows* (1952) 35 Cr App R 180 where Burrows exposed himself to a young boy.

42. *DPP v Rogers* (1953) 1 WLR 1017 and also *R v Sutton* (1977) *Criminal Law Review*, 569.

43. Not to be confused with section 11 CLAA 1885 which created an offence of committing an act of gross indecency with another male criminalising homosexual acts, a rare example of a case involving two young boys is *R v Baskerville* (1916) 2 KB 658.

44. *R v Mason* (1968) 53 Cr App R 12 at 18.

45. *R v Speck* (1977) 2 All ER 859.

46. Home Office (1987) *Report of the Inquiry into Child Abuse in Cleveland* (London: HMSO) Cmnd 4991.

47. *Daily Telegraph,* 8th March 1991 and *The Independent,* 8th March 1991.

48. Department of Health (June 1994) *The Nature and Extent of Organised and Ritual Abuse* (London: HMSO).

49. BBC News website, 10th January 2001.

50. Olafson, Corwin and Summit (1993) 'Modern History of Child Sexual Abuse Awareness', especially pp. 7–10.

51. G. Behlmer (1982) *Moral Reform in England 1870–1908* (Stanford, CA: Stanford University Press); H. Hendrick (1994) *Child Welfare: England 1872–1989* (London: Routledge); H. Hendrick (2003) *Child Welfare: Historical Dimensions Contemporary Debate* (Bristol: Policy Press).

52. R. Porter and L. Hall (1995) *The Facts of Life: The Creation of Sexual Knowledge in Britain 1650–1950* (New Haven and London: Yale University Press) and R. Davenport-Hines (1990) *Sex, Death and Punishment: Attitudes to Sex and Sexuality in Britain since the Renaissance* (London: Collins).

53. A. Brown and D. Barrett (2002) *Knowledge of Evil: Child Prostitution and Child Sexual Abuse in Twentieth-Century England* (Cullompton: Willan); M. Waites (2005) *The Age of Consent: Young People, Sexuality and Citizenship* (Basingstoke: Palgrave).

54. S. Jeffreys (1997) *The Spinster and Her Enemies: Feminism and Sexuality 1880–1930* (Melbourne: Spinifex).

55. L. Jackson (2000) *Child Sexual Abuse in Victorian England* (London: Routledge); L. Jackson (2015) 'Child Sexual Abuse in England and Wales: Prosecution and Prevalence 1918–1970', *History and Policy*, 18 June 2015. Some work has been done on the Scottish context see for instance R. Davidson (2001) '"This Pernicious Delusion": Law, Medicine and Child Sexual Abuse in Early Twentieth-Century Scotland', *Journal of the History of Sexuality*, Vol. 10, No. 1, pp. 62–77 and R. Davidson and G. Davis (2012) *The Sexual State: Sexuality and Scottish Governance, 1950–1980* (Edinburgh: Edinburgh University Press).

56. See Jackson 'Care or Control?', passim.

57. Smart (2000) 'Reconsidering the Recent History of Child Sexual Abuse', p. 68.

58. *Ibid.*, p. 66.
59. Critcher (2002) 'Media, Government and Moral Panic', pp. 521–35 and I. Marsh and G. Melville (2011) 'Moral Panics and the British Media', *Internet Journal of Criminology*, pp. 1–21.
60. S. Bell (1988) *When Salem Came to the Boro* (London: Pan Books); B. Campbell, (1988) *Unofficial Secrets* (London: Virago) and J. LaFontain (1998) *Speak of the Devil: Tales of Satanic Abuse in Contemporary England* (Cambridge: Cambridge University Press).
61. A. Wohl (1978) 'Sex and the Single Room: Incest among the Victorian Working Classes', in A. Wohl (ed.) *The Victorian Family* (London: Croom Helm), pp. 197–215.
62. Jeffreys (1997) *The Spinster and Her enemies;* S. Wolfram (1987) *In-Laws and Out-Laws: Kinship and Marriage in England* (Beckenham: Croom-Helm); S. Wolfram (1983) 'Eugenics and the Punishment of Incest Act 1908', *Criminal Law Review*, pp. 308–16.
63. V. Bailey and S. Blackburn (1979) 'The Punishment of Incest Act 1908: A Case Study of Law Creation', *Criminal Law Review*, Vol. 14, pp.708–18. Also see Bailey and McCabe (1979) 'Reforming the Law of Incest', pp. 749–64.
64. W. Leeming (1996) 'New Taboo? Some Observations on the Late Arrival of Changes in the Law of Incest in Scotland', *International Journal of the Sociology of Law*, Vol. 24, pp. 313–36.
65. *R v Whitehouse* (1977) QB 868.
66. *R v Taylor* (1977) 64 Cr App R 182.
67. K. Stevenson (2012) '"It Is What 'Girls of Indifferent Character' Do ..."
Complications Concerning the Legal Age of Sexual Consent in the Light of R v C (2011)', *Journal of Criminal Law*, Vol. 76, pp. 130–39.
68. Full details of the inquiry can be found at http://www.hiainquiry.org/index.htm (Accessed 12th November 2017).
69. *Scottish Daily Record*, 27th May 2014.
70. *BBC News*, 29th April 2013.
71. For example, 'Anger at inquiry judge's absence', *The Times*, 4 August 2016; 'Child abuse survivors' group "gives up" on public inquiry', *The Times*, 13 June 2017; 'Victims "silenced" by child abuse inquiry', *The Times*, 14 June 2017; '£35m child abuse inquiry is yet to publish report', *The Times*, 28 June 2017, etc.

6

Anarchism, Assassination and Terrorism in Modern Britain

Johannes Dillinger

Liberty which is to be enjoyed on the top of a barrel of gunpowder with a lighted match ... is a somewhat ... questionable blessing.[1]

1. Introduction

This chapter aims at providing a short survey of terrorist activity in Britain in the twentieth century. We will begin the discussion with a short definition of terrorism. Even though the focus of this chapter is on the twentieth century, we need to have a brief look at nineteenth-century terrorists in order to understand the longer historical context of terrorism in Britain.[2] The rest of the chapter will follow the development of terrorist activities in Britain in a roughly chronological fashion. The chapter will focus largely on the IRA as for the most part of the twentieth century, it was by far the most serious terrorist threat Britain had to face and because arguably it created a series of precedents for much of the terrorist activity beyond the twentieth century. Indeed, as we will note in the case study of this chapter, new terrorist threats arose as a consequence of very late twentieth-century political developments and built upon these earlier precedents.

Terrorism is notoriously difficult to define. For the purposes of this chapter it will suffice to define terrorism as a form of irregular violence, including threats of violence committed by non-state actors as part of a 'bottom-up' fight against a state. Terrorism has a political aim, even if this political aim is disguised in religious terms – a fight for a theocracy would still be a political fight because theocracies are a form of political state. Terrorist violence is both instrumental and symbolic at the same time. It tries to inflict harm but also wants to provoke specific responses from specific audiences.[3] This communicative aspect of terrorism makes the history of this topic essentially the history of the 'dialogue' between the terrorists and the authorities. This chapter will therefore pay particular attention to the development of anti-terrorist legislation in modern Britain.

2.   Chronology

a)   The Invention of Catastrophic Terrorism in Nineteenth-Century Britain and the Rise of a New Narrative

Terrorism in Britain was first and foremost Irish terrorism. The 'Fenians' (i.e. the Irish Republican Brotherhood) and their American supporters (the Fenian Brotherhood, founded in 1858, after 1867 known as Clan na Gael) were radical advocates of an independent Irish state.[4] Contemporaries were quick to realise that the Fenians' terrorist strategy was very different from that adopted by Continental European anarchists. In contrast to the latter, the Fenians did not make the assassination of political leaders their main aim. In a way reminiscent of modern Al-Qaeda assaults, they attacked public buildings with a certain symbolic character and at least accepted willingly that they were likely to hurt or kill numerous civilians randomly in the process. Two bombing campaigns in 1867–1868 and 1881–1885 targeted prisons, barracks, tunnels, the Glasgow gasworks, the Liverpool town hall, the London underground, the 'Times' building, Mansion House, the House of Commons, Scotland Yard and the Tower.[5] In 1876, Irish terrorists even had two of the world's first submarines built and hoped to use them to bring Britain to heel. Thus, the Fenians have the questionable distinction of being 'pioneers' of the modern catastrophic terrorism that randomly attacks civilians.[6] Even though the authorities had speculated about the possibility of catastrophic terrorism from the late Middle Ages onwards – including creating panic with a number of false alarms – the Irish terrorists of the nineteenth century turned this most atrocious form of political violence into a reality.[7] Thus, London became the prime target of a new form of political crime. Political criminals that targeted civilians especially in the metropolitan area quickly became part of the political imagery of popular culture. Mysteries or spy thrillers that featured terrorists intent on the mass murder of civilians developed into a subgenre of British sensation literature in the late nineteenth century.[8]

Even though the Metropolitan Police had been warned, they failed to prevent the bombing of Clerkenwell Prison in 1867 that killed 12 individuals. Evidently, the British police needed to reorganise to fight the terrorists. In a slow administrative process, the Special Branch of the Metropolitan Police was established between 1881 and 1887.[9] Special Branch was a new type of police force quite distinct from the Irish Branch of the Metropolitan Police. It was supposed to work secretly, outside of normal police structures. It was answerable to the Home Secretary directly, not to the Commissioner of the Metropolitan Police. What is more, Special Branch had the authority to work at the national level, while the rest of the British police force was organised into regional units. The creation of Special Branch was a decisive step in the modernisation of British security forces in which the state acquired unprecedented new powers. Some problems apparently inherent in the structure of anti-terrorist forces almost immediately began to plague Special Branch. For instance there was an administrative confusion about the new police organisation. In addition, there were some questionable practices instigated by the new service including the use of *agents provocateurs* who helped the Fenians plan a bomb attack on the celebrations for Queen Victoria's Golden Jubilee in 1887.[10] Special Branch remained in existence and continued its operations until 2006.

The British government remained remarkably calm in the face of the Fenians' attacks, probably because the terrorists luckily failed to kill or maim many people. Their access to dynamite was restricted and visitors found it quite difficult to enter the Houses of Parliament. Otherwise, the prevailing liberal climate prevented new anti-terror legislation, even though parts of the press did demand closer surveillance and were willing to accept the restriction of individual rights.[11]

The Fenians almost eclipsed other violent extremists. Today many regard the Suffragettes uncritically as heroines, but some of their actions could arguably be described as terrorism. The early twentieth century witnessed considerable terrorist activity by some of these women's-rights extremists. The low points of the Suffragettes' fight came in the spring and summer of 1914. Suffragettes randomly attacked railway lines and a variety of public buildings. Among others, they bombed the church of St Martin-in-the-Fields in London, Lisburn's Christ Church Cathedral as well as Westminster Abbey. Attacks on the Penistone water reservoir and the house where Robert Burns had been born failed. Rather untypically for British terrorism, radical Suffragettes even contemplated the assassination of a political leader, David Lloyd George. Only the outbreak of the First World War stopped this terrorist campaign. The Suffragette radicals caused considerable material damage and willingly accepted the possibility of casualties.[12]

Anarchism constituted another threat. In 1894, the French anarchist Martial Bourdin died when a bomb he had built exploded prematurely in Greenwich Park. Anarchist plots to build bombs were discovered in 1892 and 1894. In 1897, a bomb probably made by an anarchist group detonated in a London train.[13] Even though there was clearly an anarchist threat in late nineteenth-century Britain, the authorities failed to take it very seriously. It is rather telling that the government simply ordered the unit of Special Branch that dealt with Irish radicals to monitor anarchist activity as well. Most of the anarchists came from the Continent. Many had fled to London to escape from persecution. Even though sections of the public watched the activities of immigrants with radical political ideas with some apprehension, most of the problematic newcomers had no plans to attack any British targets. This was certainly due to the fact that the country had become a relatively safe haven for dissidents from the more authoritarian states on the Continent. They were allowed to form numerous clubs and associations. It would have been foolish to provoke a British government which was already under pressure from Europe to deal less leniently with political radicals.

Very like Karl Marx, the German arch-anarchist Johann Most preached the idea of the violent struggle against the state, and was one key example of the kind of dissident who had fled to England. He was only sentenced for seditious libel when his newspaper *Freiheit* [Freedom] openly applauded the assassination of the Tsar in 1881.[14] Matters began to change slightly shortly before the First World War when Latvian dissidents in London resorted to crime to finance their activities. The Tottenham Outrage of 1909, which was in essence a shoot-out between the police and East European anarchists that left 25 people wounded and a policeman and a 10-year-old boy dead, caused a short-lived sensation. The Sidney Street Siege, a protracted gunfight between the police and Latvian dissidents turned burglars in January of 1911, made headlines mainly for the questionable involvement of Home Secretary Winston Churchill. It did not actually herald a new approach by the British government vis-à-vis refugees with a problematic political background.[15]

Nevertheless, the anarchists who sheltered in London had few sympathies for the city that protected them. London was obviously the centre of an 'imperialist' and capitalist superpower. The anarchist press raved against this 'vampire city' that for them represented exploitation.[16] Britain, and especially London, developed an ambiguous identity in this situation. They were the safe havens of dissenters and radicals of various descriptions, inspiring criticism and mistrust. At the same time, Britain and London became the obvious targets for terrorist activities. The narrative of the liberal refuge of radicals that is also the embodiment of everything they reject, and thus their prime target, originally described both Britain and its own metropolitan area. Today, this narrative is often used to describe the status of the entire Western world vis-à-vis (Jihadist) terrorism.

From the second half of the nineteenth century onwards, this basic narrative has had two implications. Firstly, terrorism was seen as an urban threat: It was said to thrive and to target society mainly in large cities like London. Secondly, a certain paternalistic attitude has always been part and parcel of this narrative. The terrorists come from a minority group that somehow feels 'short-changed'. The disaffected – such as foreigners, the poor, the uneducated, religious minorities and of course combinations of these – provide the recruitment pool for terrorist masterminds. Rightly or wrongly, from the nineteenth century onwards, first London and Britain, and then the West, assume that what they see as the weaknesses in their economic and cultural systems are the breeding grounds for terrorists. This concept of terrorism led Britain and the West to see terrorist attacks – at least to a certain degree – as substantially 'their own fault'.[17] In this way, nineteenth-century Britain provided not only the 'model' for twenty-first-century catastrophic terrorism but also a detailed and powerful narrative that explained terrorist activities.

b)   The Rise of the IRA and the Angry Brigade

Dissatisfied with the partition of the country and de Valera's eventual relatively moderate stance, the IRA commenced a series of terrorist attacks. Styling itself the government of Ireland, the IRA declared war on Britain in January 1939. During the next 14 months, a series of bombings across England caused considerable damage and left a number of people dead or injured. During the Second World War the IRA tried in vain to get support from the German Reich for their terrorist endeavours.[18]

Parliament reacted to this declaration of war in a most decisive manner. New legislation directed against Irish terrorism, the first of its kind in British history, was rushed through Parliament in ten days. The Prevention of Violence (Temporary Provisions) Act of 1939 was supposed to help fight 'violence designed to influence public opinion or government policy with respect to Irish affairs; and to confer extraordinary powers on the Secretary of State.'[19] The wording of the Act was deliberately vague, allowing the security forces some considerable leeway. Any person 'concerned in the preparation or instigation' of terrorist violence could be subjected to considerable coercion. Suspects had to have their photographs taken and to register with the local police. Any suspicious person could be permanently exiled from Britain at the discretion of the Home Secretary. Any police officer could arrest and detain anyone he 'reasonably' suspected to be engaged in the preparation or instigation of terrorist violence. Although the Act was meant as an emergency measure, it was allowed to remain in force until 1954.[20]

Apart from the fight against Jewish radicals in Palestine in the second half of the 1940s, post-war Britain experienced a phase of relative calm as far as terrorism was concerned.[21] Around 1970, however, an anarchist group that called itself the 'Angry Brigade' exploded a number of bombs. The 'Angry Brigade' was an ultra-leftish, but not 'orthodox' Communist group like the Action Directe in France or the Rote Armee Fraktion (Red Army Faction) in Germany. The British grouping criticised Communists for being too dogmatic. The Angry Brigade presented itself in a number of 'communiques' as fundamentally anarchist and completely action-oriented. It attacked industry and representatives of the state, as well as targeting what it regarded as symbols of 'consumerism' such as the Miss World Contest and a London boutique: 'The only thing you can do with modern slave-houses called boutiques is WRECK THEM.'[22] Several members of the Angry Brigade were sent to jail in 1972. A revival of the group in the early 1980s was short-lived, but had enough criminal energy to launch a bomb attack on the Conservative Party at its annual summer conference in Brighton. One of the 'communiques' of the Angry Brigade threw some most instructive light on the motives behind their attack: 'We are bored ... and very tired of keeping the peace.' The entertainment value of terrorism for well-to-do young people should not be underestimated.[23]

c) Between Terrorism and Civil War: The Heyday of the IRA

Yet, it was not anarchism but the return of the Irish radicals that made Britain a primary target for terrorist attacks in the second half of the twentieth century. The labels 'Catholic' and 'Protestant' often used to describe the opposing parties in the Northern Ireland conflict are not entirely wrong, but they are misleading. The IRA was essentially a leftist group; it did not have any religious aims. IRA statements talked about nationhood and socialism, not really about denomination.[24] The notorious Green Book, the training manual used by the Provisional Irish Republican Army (known colloquially as the Provos), mentioned religion neither among the long term, nor among the short-term objectives of the organisation. The word 'Catholic' is not even in the book.[25]

The 'Troubles' were a very typical conflict between different ethnic groups competing for influence in the territory they both inhabited. They had more in common with the fight of radical Basque separatists in Spain than with Muslim fundamentalist terrorism (Jihadism). In the context of Irish terrorism 'Catholic' and 'Protestant' are but simplistic labels used for the inhabitants of Northern Ireland who have predominately ethnic Irish ancestors (and tend to have a Catholic background) and for the inhabitants of Northern Ireland who have predominately ethnic English or Scottish ancestors (and tend to have a Protestant background). The 'Protestants' are the descendants of immigrants from the British mainland who were settled in the North of Ireland by the English monarchy in the seventeenth century. In contrast to earlier immigrants, they remained a group apart.[26]

After the creation of Eire and Ulster, the British-Irish majority in the North formed its own administration. With the economic recovery and the political and social reforms of Prime Minister Terence O'Neill, a new 'Catholic' middle class began to establish itself in Northern Ireland in the 1960s. Inspired by the civil rights movement in the United States, members of this new middle class began to protest against the perceived discrimination against the 'Catholics'. This, in turn, led to violent reactions from a minority of 'Protestants' who attacked protesters and torched the houses of 'Catholics' who had dared to move into the better 'Protestant' neighbourhoods. In 1966, the terrorist Ulster Volunteer Force was founded to defend 'Protestants' against a suspected 'Catholic' coup. The summer of 1969 witnessed extremely violent riots. As 'Protestant' officials controlled the police, it was effectively an entirely partisan organisation and behaved in this fashion. The Civil Authorities Act (Special Powers Act) of 1922 had granted the Stormont government sweeping powers, such as the right to ban organisations and meetings, censure publications, arrest suspects and enter and search private homes.[27] Thus, it was difficult to see how 'Catholic' demonstrators could defend themselves against a state that treated them as 'second rate citizens'.

The old IRA failed to react because infighting about Marxist dogma paralysed the organisation. Defying the Dublin leadership of the IRA, radicals in Belfast established a new splinter group first known as the aforementioned Provos. The Provos soon eclipsed the old IRA completely and usurped its name. Almost simultaneously with the creation of the new IRA, the British government dispatched troops to Northern Ireland to restore peace. The IRA made the complete withdrawal of all British troops from Northern Ireland their primary aim, to be followed by the creation of an independent united socialist republic of Ireland. When the British government promised to grant the reforms demanded by the civil rights movement in August 1969, it was too late. The IRA quickly assumed the role of a substitute police force and barricaded so-called 'no go' areas in Northern Ireland, which neither the regular police nor the British troops could enter. This helped the IRA to win support and to develop its structure.[28] At least for some time, the IRA terrorists managed to control and to defend certain territories like a guerrilla army; they might even have had the potential for forming state-like structures. While the IRA was only able to take the first steps in that direction, Sendero Luminoso, the Tamil Tigers and ISIS would later manage to establish government-like control over considerable territories for a prolonged period of time. British terrorism presented in a nutshell what terrorism in general could be capable of.

As early as August 1971, the government of the Northern Irish Prime Minister Brian Faulkner pushed through a law that allowed the security forces to arrest and interrogate suspects without pressing charges. This so-called 'internment without trial' was difficult to reconcile with human rights and the British 'habeas corpus' tradition. Significantly, the British Prime Minister Edward Heath failed to recall Parliament from the summer holidays to discuss the issue. Even though internment was said to be a short-term measure, it was nonetheless used until 1975 and was only finally abolished in 1998. 'Catholics' instinctively condemned internment as just another form of discrimination because, in the event, more than 90 per cent of the people interned were 'Catholics'.[29]

According to the Royal Ulster Constabulary, more than 1500 people were killed by terrorists between 1971 and 1976.[30] The Provo's terrorist attacks on mainland Britain began in October 1971 with the bombing of the London Post Office Tower. This was followed by an attack on a pub in Aldershot frequented by soldiers. The claim that the IRA targeted politicians, security and military personnel only and took pains not to hurt civilians is one of the many propagandistic myths woven around this organisation: from the very beginning of its fight onwards, it willingly accepted the possibility of 'collateral damage'.[31]

On Sunday, 30th January 1972 in the Bogside area of Derry, Northern Ireland, British troops opened fire on civil rights protesters, killing 13 individuals. 'Bloody Sunday', as the episode came to be known, helped to strengthen the IRA because the British authorities handled investigation of the case very badly. In April of 1972, an official inquiry headed by Lord Chief Justice Widgery exonerated the soldiers involved. The management of 'Bloody Sunday' was, at the time, perceived by many as a clumsy attempt to whitewash a crime by the British government, and, as the Savile Report published in 2010 suggests, rightly so. The situation deteriorated further in July 1972, when, following violent provocations from the IRA, British troops launched a surprise attack on the 'no go' areas. This so-called Operation Motorman, the biggest military operation in Ireland since the 1920s, was a success. However, on the advice of Stormont, the British government followed Motorman with a significant number of internments without trial.[32] In reaction to the *de facto* civil war that went on in Northern Ireland, the British government took direct charge in 1972. Stormont was thereafter suspended. The 1973 Northern Ireland Emergency Provisions Act included a large part of the 1922 Special Powers Act. Amendments now restricted the defendant's right to silence.[33]

d) Organisation, Counter-Organisation and Negotiation

The extreme violence of the conflict in the early 1970s reflected the IRA's conviction that the British would be unable or unwilling to sustain a war-like fight for more than a couple of months. By 1976, after fruitless secret talks with representatives of the British government, the terrorists began to realise that their appraisal of the situation had been wholly erroneous. They ended the phase of most intense, insurgency-like violence and implemented the new strategy of a 'Long War' (i.e. a drawn-out series of terrorist attacks resembling a war of attrition). As the Irish Republican News put it: 'There is no quick solution to our British problem.'[34]

Spectacular early low points of the 'Long War' were the murder of the elderly Lord Mountbatten, a member of the royal family, together with two children, aged 14 and 15, in 1979; the Hyde Park and Regent's Park bombings in 1982; and the attack on the Conservative Party Conference in Brighton in 1984.[35] However, the assassinations of Mountbatten and of Conservative politicians in Brighton were the exception rather than the rule for IRA terrorism on the British mainland. There were comparatively few English victims of the IRA with a high political profile. For example, an ill-prepared mortar attack on Downing Street failed in 1991.[36] While a number of public figures from Northern Ireland were assassinated during the 'Troubles', Irish terrorists were never willing (or able) to make political leaders from mainland Britain their prime targets. Following the Fenian pattern, the IRA seemed less interested in the assassination of national leaders than in assaults against government institutions and the British public.

The early 1990s witnessed a certain diversification of the IRA's campaigns. The Baltic Exchange and the Bishopsgate bombings in 1992 and 1993 demonstrated a shift in the IRA's strategy. The terrorists had realised that attacks on London as a centre of finance could potentially damage Britain's economy. Other integral parts of the 'Long War' were propagandistic activities like the 1981 hunger strike. The IRA understood that it was imperative for them to win visible support from the civilian population in order to uphold the claim that they acted to deliver the will of the Irish people. Still, the bilateral policy of 'Armalite and ballot box' that tried to intimidate the (British) public and to win mass support for the IRA at the same time did not work as such. Rather, it demonstrated that legal political activity was an option for IRA sympathisers. Thus, it helped to strengthen the organisation's political branch, Sinn Féin.[37]

With the beginning of the 'Long War', the IRA re-grouped. It gave up its old army-like structure and formed small cells. Among these cells were Active Service Units (ASU) consisting of a commanding officer and four volunteers who carried out the actual attacks.[38] These volunteers were supposed to know only one commanding officer; this officer was supposed to know only one superior. This tight structure however did not prevent British intelligence from making considerable inroads into the ranks of the IRA. Neither did it keep the IRA from splintering into insubordinate offshoots. The Continuity IRA was formed in 1986 when parts of the organisation opposed Sinn Féin taking up seats in the Irish parliament.

The Continuity IRA itself split at least once.[39] The Real IRA, founded in 1997, consisted of adherents of the old IRA strategy that opposed the peace talks. This grouping was responsible for the Omagh atrocity of 1998.[40] The Irish National Liberation Army (INLA) is a 1974 offshoot of the old IRA that nevertheless did not join forces with the Provos. In much the same way as this, the 'Protestant' terrorist groups multiplied.[41]

The fight against terrorism began to have considerable impact upon the British legal system. Under pressure from the public, new laws against terrorism that gave the security forces ever more power were rapidly passed by Parliament after especially atrocious attacks. For instance, the Birmingham pub bombings of 1974 provoked the Prevention of Terrorism Act.[42] Given the IRA terror of the preceding years, new anti-terrorist legislation had probably been overdue. However, it took the shock of the Birmingham episode to influence Parliament to pass an act that at the time even the Home Secretary called 'draconian.'[43] After the Omagh bombing, the Criminal Justice (Terrorism and Conspiracy) Act (1988) was passed. This Act extended the powers of arrest and restricted the right to silence even further, subjecting travellers crossing the border into Northern Ireland to closer scrutiny by the law-enforcement agencies. The testimony of a single police officer was sufficient evidence for a suspect's membership in a terrorist group to be considered proven.

Even though these measures were supposed to be emergency legislation and as such temporary, they stayed in place for many years.[44] The 1984 Prevention of Terrorism Act made it possible for the Secretary of State to keep suspects in custody for a maximum of five days without bringing a charge.[45] Then, in 1989, the Prevention of Terrorism Act cracked down on the financiers of terrorism. This prescribed imprisonment of up to 14 years and unlimited fines for people who helped terrorists financially or failed to inform on persons who did so. The new Act repeated much of the provisions of the earlier laws, but in contrast to them, it did not have a final date clause.[46] The British state grew stronger than it had ever been. Its fight against terrorism clearly eroded civil and human rights in its wake.

Questionable legal practices emerged in the courts in the last third of the twentieth century. In 1975, the so-called Diplock courts were introduced. These replaced trial by jury with trial before a single judge for Irish terrorists. It comes as no surprise that the Diplock courts relied heavily on confessions extracted by dubious methods. In another development in 1978, the European Court of Human Rights condemned the security forces of Northern Ireland for the use of interrogation techniques that violated the European Convention on Human Rights. These courts had been notoriously willing to hear the testimony of 'supergrasses'. Judges accepted as highly reliable evidence the statements of terrorists turned informers who named their former accomplices. Merely on the word of individual supergrasses, dozens of suspects were convicted.[47]

Perhaps unsurprisingly, some serious miscarriages of justice occurred during the 'Troubles'. The most prominent cases being those of the 'Birmingham Six', the 'Guilford Four' and the 'Maguire Seven'. All of the individuals involved were sentenced for IRA-related bombings in 1975/76. After spending years in jail, these prisoners had to be released when a Court of Appeal declared their convictions unsafe and unsatisfactory in 1989 and 1991 respectively. Even though the mere fact that the appeals were granted was a triumph of the British legal system, it goes without saying that the scandals of the unsafe convictions did nothing to enhance the credibility of the fight against terrorism. Co-operation between security forces and 'Protestant' terrorist groups had long been suspected. After the Good Friday Agreement, investigations proved that some of these allegations were correct.[48]

The fight against terrorism not only influenced the British legal system, but it began to change British cityscapes. Private investors felt that they needed to protect themselves from terrorists. After the attacks on London, attempts were made to 'design-out' terrorism from parts of the city. Physical barriers and blast protection provision were installed. In the last decade of the twentieth century, well over 1500 surveillance cameras were placed in the Square Mile alone. Evidently, anti-terrorist measures were an important security element in London well before another centre of world trade was attacked on 9/11.[49]

Until the middle of the 1990s, Irish terrorist groups kept up a steady stream of attacks. They began to peter out when Gerry Adams led Sinn Féin into peaceful negotiations with representatives of Northern Ireland, and the IRA eventually declared a ceasefire in 1997. When referenda in both Irish states ratified the Good Friday Agreement in 1998 it became obvious that no terrorist group could still seriously claim to express the will of the people. Still, it took not the two years originally agreed upon, but more than seven to disarm the IRA.[50] As was to be expected, splinter groups that do not respect Sinn Féin's authority still fight on in the present day.[51] Here, the developments reveal a generic problem in this area of policing and governance in Britain most clearly. When we see terrorism and counter-terrorism as a kind of dialogue between the government and the terrorists, it is at times difficult to decide who actually speaks on the terrorists' side and what precise level of authority they may have. Terrorist groups are not well-disciplined armies; they simply do not have the equivalent of a responsible, clearly defined and generally acknowledged high command or government. This has made all negotiations with the Irish terrorists problematic and questions (the great successes of the 1990s notwithstanding) many over-confident assumptions that Irish terrorism is or could be a thing of the past.

One of the reasons why the fight keeps flaring up from time to time are the tempting economic possibilities of terrorism. Their illegal and therefore secretive nature makes it practically impossible for terrorist groups to finance themselves without engaging in even more criminal acts. The interconnectedness of terrorism and mafia-like organised crime is therefore not a sign of the 'deterioration' of terrorist groups, but instead a trait that is inherent in their structure. Irish terrorism provides very good examples of this. The IRA seems never to have covered more than 50 per cent of its expenditure with donations. Even though it received very considerable sums from Irish-Americans via the fundraising organisation Irish Northern Aid Committee (NORAID) it further resorted to illegal activities to make money from the very start. Irish terrorists engaged in racketeering, bank robbery, smuggling, fraud and trade in counterfeit goods.[52] Partly for the purpose of money laundering, the IRA invested money in pubs, guesthouses, video stores and taxi companies.[53] According to estimates published by the Northern Ireland Select Committee in 2002, the illegal income of Irish terrorist groups was several hundred per cent higher than the running costs of their operations.[54] One of the reasons why some Irish terrorist organisations continue to exist then, even though political solutions have been found for many of the old grievances, is that they are now integral parts of the structures of organised crime.[55]

e)   Other Ethnic Terrorists, Animal Rights Terrorists, Foreign Terrorism

There was some activity by regional terrorists from Scotland during the twentieth century. The Army of the Provisional Government of Scotland and the Scottish National Liberation Army launched a number of attacks on the British state and its representatives, exploding bombs that threatened private persons and committing bank robberies. However, the Scottish terrorists neither matched the aggression and perseverance of the Irish radicals, nor did they provoke similarly massive reactions from the state. The same can be said about Welsh regional terrorism.[56]

A specific kind of terrorism which originated in Britain was that which stemmed from animal rights groups. They regularly resorted to terrorist violence targeting animal hunts, laboratories that experiment on animals and their suppliers as well as the meat industry. From the 1970s onwards, members of the Animal Liberation Front have launched a number of arson and bomb attacks under different *noms de guerre* that seriously injured a number of people. One animal rights group even desecrated a grave and stole a corpse to blackmail the family of the deceased who were guinea pig breeders – a low point even for terrorism.[57]

The siege of the Iranian embassy in 1980 demanded not only a close co-operation between MI5 and the police but also the first use of the Special Air Service (SAS) in Britain. It became obvious that Britain had become a major target for terrorists from the Near and Middle East. Most of these terrorists, among them the Abu Nidal group, attacked Britain for its continued support of Israel. MI5 established its counter-terrorism branch in 1984.[58] Even though the debate about the incident continues, the worst terrorist attack that ever took place in Britain was probably an act of state-sponsored terrorism that primarily targeted the United States. In December 1988, a Pan Am jumbo jet crashed into the Scottish small town of Lockerbie. All 259 people on board as well as 11 individuals from the town died. Two Libyan agents had placed explosives on the plane at the order of dictator Colonel Muammar Gaddafi. The bombing was a response to the United States destroying Libyan ships and planes in the Mediterranean and American airstrikes against the Libyan mainland launched from British bases. The fact that the plane crashed over Britain was probably part of the terrorists' plan as there had been severe tensions between Britain and Libya prior to the incident.[59]

f)   Not Just 'Troubles' Anymore: Terrorism as a Permanent Threat

The history of terrorism in Britain entered a completely new phase in 2000. Prior to the 9/11 atrocities, a new Terrorism Act came into force. With the exception of the 1989 Act, all the previous laws against terrorism had been (at least nominally) temporary. All had been designed to deal with the situation in Northern Ireland. The 2000 Terrorism Act was a permanent and general measure against all terrorists. For the first time in modern history, the British legislature unambiguously acknowledged the fact that terrorism came from a variety of perpetrators and that it was here to stay. New threats emerged due to political relationships being placed under strain by the dynamics of international politics. As a result of this, some terrorist groups sought targets on the British mainland and their tactics and organisational structures inherited elements from previous IRA activity. Terrorism and counter-terrorist measures thus ceased to be seen as weapons in what was in effect a civil war in Northern Ireland and were now regarded as problems in a category of their own.

The Terrorism Act strengthened the British state enormously. It created new offences like openly supporting terrorist groups and seeking or giving training for terrorist activities in Britain or elsewhere. The police were given greater power to 'stop and search'. Any person suspected to be a terrorist could be held by the police without charge for two full days. With the assent of a judge, the detention could be extended to seven days. The Act listed several proscribed terrorist organisations, among them not only Irish ones, but Jihadist groups based in the Near or Middle East including Al-Qaeda as well as the 'Kurdistan Workers' Party' (PKK) and the Basque separatist ETA.[60]

The 2001 Anti-Terrorism, Crime and Security Act was rushed through Parliament in a couple of weeks after the 9/11 attacks. The Act increased security for nuclear facilities, research institutions housing dangerous substances and airports. It allowed the freezing of the assets of suspects right at the beginning of the investigation. The Act sought to integrate the concepts of terrorism and hate crimes as it demanded harsher punishments if violent crime was motivated by racial or religious hatred. The 2001 Act allowed the detention and deportation of foreigners outside the normal court system and based on secret evidence. Some parts of the law were criticised for being incompatible with the European Convention on Human Rights. In 2004, the Joint Committee on Human Rights expressed concern that the law might have a 'corrosive' effect on the rights of the individual vis-à-vis the state.[61]

President George Bush Junior presented the war in Afghanistan and Iraq as an integral part of the 'war on terror' he had declared after the 9/11 mass murder. As Britain was the chief ally of the United States in these conflicts, it was to be expected that Jihadist groups would target the UK. Indeed, only weeks after the attacks on New York and Washington, the English Muslim Richard Reid tried, unsuccessfully, to detonate a bomb hidden in his shoe during a flight to North America.[62]

After 9/11, the budgets of SIS and MI5 increased dramatically. Still, some of the new funds were reserved for the fight against the IRA who were still regarded as a major threat. In 2003, the Director General of MI5 explained that the British fight against Irish terrorism had created 'systems for terrorist protection ... that are the envy of the world.'[63] Still, new concrete measures were needed. As early as 2003, the Association of Chief Police Officers developed a new tactic against suicide terrorists called 'Operation Kratos' (κρατος Greek = power, powerful deed). Once a situation had been declared an 'Operation Kratos', control shifted from the officer at the scene to a superior in a control room with quick access to more pertinent information, enabling the authorities to order a 'shoot-to-kill' directive if necessary.[64]

3.   Historiography

The title of the standard volume edited by Louise Richardson and Robert J. Art *Democracy and Counterterrorism: Lessons from the Past*[65] might stand for the still prevailing approach to the history of terrorism: It is not so much historical research that tries to understand the past as such but rather the attempt to utilise the past in order to achieve the twin aim of preventing terrorist attacks without compromising Western liberties.

There is no standard historical overview that deals with all of the very different terrorist groups active in Britain in the twentieth century. A longue durée perspective that brings the various terrorist threats in Britain together has been established in legal and administrative history. Two recent volumes by Laura Donohue provide surveys of the state's reaction to terrorism in modern Britain.[66] A critical appraisal of the consequences the fight against terrorism has had for society is an integral part of the historiography of British terrorism. In 1993 – still in the context of Irish terrorism, and well before the first major Jihadist attacks on Britain – Paddy Hillyard's book about the practical consequences of the 1989 Prevention of Terrorism Act addressed all the major points that still shape the debate about counter-terrorism today.[67]

MI5 and MI6 were founded in 1909. However, the secretive nature of their work has made it difficult for historians to gain access to primary sources about the development of these institutions. The most prominent historical accounts of MI5 and MI6 are 'official' histories, 'insider' stories or questionable journalistic accounts. These studies deal mostly with administrative developments and the careers of various members of these administrations. Even though all of these works prove that the challenge of Jihadist terrorism after 9/11 changed the work of the intelligence services profoundly, they emphasise that the encounters with various terrorist threats were just some of the many factors that have shaped the development of these agencies.[68] A first history of counter-terrorism in Britain, with a decidedly comparative approach, has suggested that the historical experience of relative stability prevented the British authorities from over-reacting against terrorist attacks.[69]

Unsurprisingly, most authors who deal with terrorism rather than counter-terrorism focus on individual terrorist groups. Most of the historiography of British terrorism so far has focussed on the IRA. Most of the accounts are juridical or quasi-journalistic in nature. The majority of the authors approached the topic not so much with an audience interested in history in mind but for an audience interested in practical politics, political science, law and law enforcement. A longue durée perspective on Irish terrorism in Britain has only been adopted in recent years.

It proved to be difficult to see the Fenians and the IRA together as they are separated by the watershed of the Irish Revolution.[70] Given the fact that the 'Troubles' were a long drawn-out conflict, the standard works by Paul Bew and Gordon Gillespie accompanied an ongoing process.[71] It is most telling that Bew, one of the foremost historians of the 'Troubles', has been directly involved in Irish politics and therefore clashed with Gerry Adams.[72] Cultural history has only just begun to discover terrorism, especially IRA terrorism, as a topic.[73]

Muslim fundamentalist terrorism in Britain is such a recent phenomenon that it has not yet fully turned into a topic for historians. Much of the literature on Jihadism in Britain still hovers between history, political science, criminology, polemics and propaganda.[74] The focus seems to be on the social and cultural conditions that allegedly breed terrorism and on the state's sometimes problematic responses to the Islamist threat.[75] The most comprehensive study seems to be Hannah Stuart's statistical and biographical survey of Jihadism in Britain between 1998 and 2015.[76] On the whole, overviews of the history of terrorism might reserve a chapter for Britain and the 'Troubles', but they tend to focus on the most recent history of the United States rather than on the comparatively long history of terrorism in the United Kingdom.[77] Comparisons between the IRA and Jihadism begin to emerge. Most focus on counter-terrorist laws and measures – or most recently, the British experience of negotiations with terrorists – rather than on the structural dissimilarities and similarities between the terrorist groups themselves.[78]

4.   Case Study

On the 7th of July 2005, one day after the decision to hold the 2012 Olympic Games in London, four Jihadists attacked the city's public transport system. Bombs exploded in quick succession on three subway trains and on a bus killing 52 innocent people and injuring over 700 more. What quickly became known as 7/7 was the first terrorist suicide attack within Britain.[79] Three of the four terrorists were second generation British citizens of Pakistani origin. The fourth, Germaine Lindsay, was a Jamaican-born British resident, the only member of the group that had not been brought up a Muslim but was a recent convert.

There was nothing in the killers' social backgrounds to suggest anything out of the ordinary. Mohammed Sidique Khan worked in a primary school as mentor for pupils from immigrant families. Shehzad Tanweer was a student. He had graduated in sports science. Eighteen-year-old Hasib Hussain was a student, too. Lindsay was an unemployed carpet fitter.[80] Nevertheless, two of the four terrorists had attracted the attention of MI5 before. One was on an American 'no-flight' list. Khan at least had contacts with Muslim radicals in Asia and had spent some time in training camps there. He clearly was the group's leader. Even though the group had had contact with radical organisations in Asia they were not simply the foot soldiers doing the dirty work for a large international conspiracy. Rather, the group worked on its own.[81] Evidently, Jihadism had become a domestic problem.

7/7 questioned the old terrorism narrative but failed to eliminate it from the public mind. If the four terrorists had felt somehow suppressed or short-changed by British society, they had little objective reason to do so. If they were disaffected, they had disaffected themselves. As the statements left by the terrorists before their suicide attacks proved, they had seen themselves as soldiers who brought the war Britain fought in the Middle East back to England's own doorstep. In a perverse parody of democratic thought, they claimed that they were entitled to hold every British citizen responsible for the attacks on Muslims that the democratically elected British government had ordered – events they denounced as war crimes.[82]

Four more bombs were found in London only two weeks later. A police action aimed at stopping a suspected suicide bomber ended in the death of an innocent civilian. The situation crucially had not been designated 'Kratos'.[83] In 2007, another Jihadist coup to attack Glasgow Airport was unsuccessful. The perpetrators were intellectuals well established in Britain.[84] British Jihadism had demonstrated that seemingly ordinary persons from the vast and ill-defined pool of sympathisers and supporters of Muslim fundamentalism could radicalise themselves quickly and start devastating terrorist attacks with very little effort. The cowardly slaughter of civilians had cost the IRA some of the support of their sympathisers. This was apparently not the case with Muslim terrorists.

During the inquest of the 7/7 incident, a spokesperson for MI5 was obliged to point out what he might have thought was obvious: 'Many individuals [are] involved in Islamist extremism but that is not the same as planning terrorist attacks.'[85] The government seems to have disagreed. In August 2005, Prime Minister Tony Blair announced that new and even stiffer anti-terror laws were now necessary. He made it clear that he was willing to ignore norms concerning human rights if they stood in the way of implementing these new measures against terrorism.[86] The Terrorism Act of 2006 created further new offences. Statements that could be understood as direct or indirect encouragement for terrorist acts were made punishable by up to seven years' imprisonment. This regulation clearly targeted radical Muslim preachers and terrorists' 'mentors' like Khan. However, the law might be seen as interfering with the freedom of expression. The period a suspect could be held without charge was extended to 28 days provided a judge reviewed the case every 7 days.[87] Plans to extend the period of detention without charge to 42 days were dropped from the 2008 anti-terror act after some debate. Given the fact that the security forces had failed to prevent the Jihadist campaign of 2005, it was deemed expedient to merge the old Special Branch with the Anti-Terrorist Branch of the Metropolitan Police to form the Counter-Terrorism Command. From 2007 onwards regional counter-terrorism units of the British police came into existence.[88] The old focus on London was finally overcome. The lesson the government learned from 7/7 was clearly that they had to cast their net wider. Thus the state defined 'terrorism' in even broader terms and gave the police even more leeway.

7/7 might become a milestone in the history of terrorism in Britain. The Jihadist took the catastrophic terrorism the Fenians had 'invented' to a new low point. They did not even try to attack government institutions or symbols of the state but aimed exclusively at mass civilian casualties. The cowardly slaughter of civilians had cost the IRA some of the support of their sympathisers. This was apparently not the case with Muslim terrorists' with 'As already suggested civilian casualties had a detrimental effect upon support for the IRA, a situation that later did not apply to Muslim terrorism. Opinion polls conducted between July 2005 and November 2006 suggested that about 100,000 British citizens considered the 7/7 attacks justified.[89] This polarisation of opinion around such events indicated that terrorism's capacity to damage consensus also served to restrict freedoms. As the unfortunate death of a civilian at the hands of policemen in the aftermath of 7/7 demonstrated, counter-terrorist measures were clearly a potential threat to civil rights not only in Northern Ireland but in mainland Britain, too.

5.   Conclusion

Britain seems to have been something of a laboratory of terrorism and counter-terrorism in the modern era. Terrorists with a number of different ethnic, religious and ideological agendas have attacked the country in its recent history. It witnessed the first campaign of catastrophic terrorism and created a strong narrative about the origins of terrorism connected with it. Britain experienced a decades-long fight against a terrorist group in the form of the IRA that ended in a slow peace process. The fact that even after the peace settlement Irish terrorism is unlikely to disappear totally is another important lesson about terrorism to be learned from Britain. The British state has certainly risen to the challenge of terrorism. It adapted remarkably quickly to the decline of Irish terrorism and the rise of Jihadism. During the nineteenth and twentieth centuries, anti-terrorist laws focussed on Irish terrorism. They were supposed to be temporary. However, they had a marked tendency to become permanent and paved the way for the new developments of the twenty-first century. With the Terrorist Act of 2000, British anti-terrorist legislation overcame its regional focus and much of its temporary nature. These measures could not prevent Jihadist aggression in Britain, but they did help to prepare the country for the fight against this new type of domestic terrorism. Terrorism has emphatically changed Britain. The delicate balance between security and personal freedom, between the enhanced powers of the police and traditional civil liberties that had long been an issue for Northern Ireland rather than for mainland Britain became an urgent problem for all Britons. As such the terrorist provocation has strengthened the British state vis-à-vis private individuals enormously.

Notes

1. *The Times,* 24th November 1883.
2. J. Dillinger (2008) *Terrorismus* (Freiburg: Herder), pp. 21–27 and J. Dillinger (forthcoming) 'Early Modern Forerunners of Terrorism and Nineteenth-Century Historians', in C. Dietze and C. Verhooeven (eds) *Oxford Handbook of the History of Terrorism* (Oxford: Oxford University Press).
3. Dillinger (2008) *Terrorismus,* pp. 9–21.
4. B. Porter (1987) *The Origins of the Vigilant State* (London: Weidenfeld & Nicolson), p. 26.
5. *Ibid.,* pp. 27–28 and p. 30.
6. Porter (1987) *The Origins of the Vigilant State,* p. 26.
7. Dillinger (forthcoming) 'Early Modern Forerunners'.
8. A. Taylor (2012) *London's Burning: Pulp Fiction, the Politics of Terrorism and the Destruction of the Capital in British Popular Culture, 1840–2005* (London: Continuum), pp. 46–75.
9. R Wilson and I. Adams (2015) *Special Branch: A History* (London: Biteback) and Porter (1987) *The Origins of the Vigilant State,* pp. 35–67.
10. Porter (1987) *The Origins of the Vigilant State,* pp. 85–88.
11. *Ibid.,* pp. 30–32.
12. S. Webb (2014) *The Suffragette Bombers: Britain's Forgotten Terrorists* (Barnsley: Pen and Sword Books).
13. 'Dynamite Explosion at Aldersgate', *Lloyd's Weekly Newspaper,* 2nd May 1987.
14. Wilson and Adams (2015) *Special Branch,* pp. 39–51; H. Becker and A. Graf (eds) (2006) *Johann Most* (Berlin: FU) and Porter (1987) *The Origins of the Vigilant State,* pp. 101–18.
15. D. Rumbelow (1973) *The Houndsditch Murders and the Siege of Sidney Street* (London: Macmillan).
16. Taylor (2012) *London's Burning,* pp. 54–55 with verbatim quotes, pp. 162–73.
17. *Ibid.,* pp. 164–77.
18. E. Stephan and M. Hull (2003) *Irish Secrets: German Espionage in Wartime Ireland, 1939–1945* (Dublin: Irish Academic Press) and M.L.R. Smith (1997 edition) *Fighting for Ireland?* (London: Routledge), pp. 56–91.
19. http://www.schedule7.org.uk/wp-content/uploads/2014/01/1939_POV_bill.pdf (Accessed 10th October 2017).
20. http://www.schedule7.org.uk/history/1939-prevention-of-violence (Accessed 10th October 2017).

21. D. Cesarani (2009) *Major Farran's Hat: Murder, Scandal and Britain's War against Jewish Terrorism* (London: Heinemann).
22. Verbatim quotes from Communique 8 (1971) found in J. Weir (ed.) (1985) *The Angry Brigade 1967–1984* (London: Elephant Editions), p. 31.
23. *Ibid.*, p. 28.
24. B. Hanley (2010) *The IRA: A Documentary History 1916–2005* (Dublin: Gill & Macmillan), pp. 182–85.
25. http://cain.ulst.ac.uk/othelem/organ/ira/ira_green_book.htm   (Accessed 10th October 2017).
26. P. Waldmann (1989) *Ethnischer Radikalismus* (Opladen: Westdeutscher Verlag).
27. L. Donohue (2001) *Counter-Terrorist Law and Emergency Powers in the United Kingdom* (Dublin: Irish Academic), pp. 16–40.
28. T. Taylor (2002) 'United Kingdom', in A. Yonah (ed.) *Combating Terrorism: Strategies of Ten Countries* (Ann Arbor: University of Michigan Press), pp. 187–243 at pp. 199–200; L. Richardson (2007) 'Britain and the IRA', in R. Art and L. Richardson (eds) *Democracy and Counterterrorism: Lessons from the Past* (Washington: US Institute of Peace Press), pp. 63–104 at pp. 63–72 and P. Bew and G. Gordon (1993) *Northern Ireland: A Chronology of the Troubles, 1968–1993* (Dublin: Gill and Macmillan).
29. http://news.bbc.co.uk/onthisday/hi/dates/stories/august/9/new sid_4071000/407184.stm (Accessed 11th October 2017); Taylor (2002) 'United Kingdom', p. 219 and Richardson (2007) 'Britain and the IRA', p. 87.
30. Taylor (2002) 'United Kingdom', pp. 200–201. For a more detailed account see M. Sutton (1994) *An Index of Deaths from the Conflict in Ireland, 1969–1993* (Belfast: Beyond the Pale).
31. T. Brain (2010) *A History of Policing in England and Wales from 1974* (Oxford: Oxford University Press), pp. 21–25.
32. Hanley (2010) *The IRA*, pp. 170–71 and Richardson (2007) 'Britain and the IRA', pp. 68–70 and pp. 85–87; Taylor (2002) 'United Kingdom', pp. 219–20 and J. Bew (2014) 'Mass, Methods, and Means: The Northern Ireland "Model" of Counter-Insurgency', in D.M. Jones, M.L.R. Smith and C. Ward Gventer (eds) *The New Counter-Insurgency Era in Critical Perspective* (Basingstoke: Palgrave), pp. 156–73 at pp. 159–62.
33. Richardson (2007) 'Britain and the IRA', p. 84.
34. *Republican News*, 9th December 1978.
35. *An Phoblacht*, 18th October 1984 and B. O'Brien (2005 edition) *The Long War: The IRA and Sinn Féin* (Dublin: O'Brien Press).

36. Hanley (2010) *The IRA*, p. 204.
37. Brain (2010) *A History of Policing*, pp. 21–25 and p. 88 and O'Brien, *The Long War*.
38. E. Moloney (2002) *The Secret History of the IRA* (London: Penguin).
39. M. Frampton, (2010) *The Return of the Militants: Violent Dissident Republicanism* [International Centre for the Study of Radicalisation and Political Violence (ICSR)]. Available at http://cain.ulst.ac.uk/othelem/organ/docs/frampton10icsr.pdf (Accessed 11th October 2017).
40. 'Ulster Carnage as Bomb Blast Targets Shoppers', *The Guardian,* 16th August 1998. Available at https://www.theguardian.com/uk/1998/aug/16/northernireland.henrymcdonald1 (Accessed 11th October 2017).
41. A. Richards (2007) 'The Domestic Threat: The Cases of Northern Ireland and Animal Rights Extremism', in P. Wilkinson (ed.) *Homeland Security in the UK: Future Preparedness for Terrorist Attack since 9/11* (Abingdon: Routledge), pp. 81–114 at pp. 81–98.
42. For more details about this see C. Scorer (1980) 'The United Kingdom Prevention of Terrorism Acts, 1974 and 1976', *International Journal of Politics*, Vol. 10, No. 1, pp. 105–11.
43. C. Walker (1986) *The Prevention of Terrorism in British Law* (Manchester: Manchester University Press), pp. 22–24.
44. L. Donohue (2001) *Counter-Terrorist Law and Emergency Powers in the United Kingdom, 1922–2000* (Dublin: Irish American Press), pp. 306–55.
45. http://www.legislation.gov.uk/uksi/1984/418/pdfs/uksi_19840418_en.pdf (Accessed 11th October 2017).
46. http://www.legislation.gov.uk/ukpga/1989/4/pdfs/ukpga_19890004_en.pdf (Accessed 11th October 2017).
47. L. Donohue (2008) *The Cost of Counterterrorism* (Cambridge: Cambridge University Press), pp. 33–56.
48. Richardson (2007) 'Britain and the IRA', pp. 88–90 and Brain (2010) *A History of Policing*, pp. 16–19, pp. 170–72 and pp. 183–85.
49. J. Coaffee (2009) *Terrorism, Risk and the Global City: Towards Urban Resilience* (Farnham: Ashgate), pp. 205–29.
50. Richardson (2007) 'Britain and the IRA', pp. 91–97.
51. *The Daily Mirror*, 5th March 2001.
52. Jane's Intelligence Review, 25th October 2002 and Richardson (2007) 'Britain and the IRA', p. 74 and Richards (2007) 'The Domestic Threat', p. 83, p. 88, pp. 91–92, p. 94, p. 96 and p. 98.
53. Richardson (2007) 'Britain and the IRA', p. 74.
54. Richards (2007) 'The Domestic Threat', p. 99.

55. Richardson (2007) 'Britain and the IRA', p. 74; Hanley (2010) *The IRA*, p. 209 and Richards (2007) 'The Domestic Threat', pp. 86–99.

56. Walker (1986) *The Prevention of Terrorism*, pp. 15–16 and p. 121 and Dillinger (2008) *Terrorismus*, p. 36.

57. Richards (2007) 'The Domestic Threat', pp. 100–108; R. Monaghan (1997) 'Animal Rights and Violent Protests', *Terrorism and Political Violence*, Vol. 9, pp. 106–16 and R. Monaghan (1999) 'Terrorism in the Name of Animal Rights', *Terrorism and Political Violence*, Vol. 11, pp. 159–68.

58. C. Andrew (2010) *The Defence of the Realm: The Authorized History of MI5* (London: Penguin), p. 600, p. 686, pp. 700–703 and pp. 734–35.

59. Andrew (2010) *The Defence of the Realm*, pp. 700–703 and pp. 746–48; Brain (2010) *A History of Policing*, pp. 149–50; Taylor (2002) 'United Kingdom', p. 206 and P. Jenkins (2003) *Images of Terror: What We Can and Can't Know About Terrorism* (New York: Aldine de Gruyter), pp. 11–15.

60. http://www.legislation.gov.uk/ukpga/2000/11/contents (Accessed 12th October 2017) and M. Head (2011) *Crimes against the State* (Farnham: Ashgate), pp. 188–90 at p. 196.

61. http://www.legislation.gov.uk/ukpga/2001/24/contents (Accessed 12th October 2017) and Head (2011) *Crimes against the State*, pp. 194–97 and Richardson (2007) 'Britain and the IRA', pp. 97–98.

62. Brain (2010) *A History of Policing*, p. 330.

63. T. Hennessey (2011) *Spooks: The Unofficial History of MI5* (Stroud: Amberley); N. West (1982) *A Matter of Trust: MI5 1945–1972* (London: Weidenfeld & Nicolson), pp. 217–25 and N. West (2016) *At Her Majesty's Secret Service* (Barnsley: Frontline), pp. 191–92.

64. Brain (2010) *A History of Policing*, p. 330 and pp. 357–60.

65. R. Art and L. Richardson (2007) (eds) *Democracy and Counterterrorism: Lessons from the Past* (Washington: US Institute of Peace Press).

66. L. Donohue (2001) *Counter-Terrorist* and L. Donohue (2008) *The Cost of Counter-Terrorism* (Cambridge: Cambridge University Press).

67. P. Hillyard (1993) *Suspect Community: People's Experience of the Prevention of Terrorism Acts in Britain* (London: Pluto).

68. Andrew (2010) *The Defence of the Realm*; Hennessey (2011) *Spooks*; West (1982) *A Matter of Trust*; West (2016) *At Her Majesty's Secret Service*; A. Vilasi (2013) *The History of MI6* (Bloomington: Author House) and G. Thomas (2010) *Inside British Intelligence* (London: JR).

69. F. Fowley (2013) *Countering Terrorism in Britain and France: Institutions, Norms, and the Shadow of the Past* (Cambridge: Cambridge University Press).

70. For a typical perspective see Hanley (2010) *The IRA* or D. McKittrick and D. McVea (2001) *Making Sense of the Troubles* (London: Penguin). An exception from the rule are the overviews in A. Oppenheimer (2009) *IRA: The Bombs and the Bullet* (Dublin: Irish Academic Press) and S. Hewitt (2008) *The British War on Terror* (London: Continuum), pp. 9–29 that focus on weapons technology.

71. P. Bew and G. Gillespie (1993) *Northern Ireland: A Chronology of the Troubles, 1968–1993* (Dublin: Gill & Macmillan) and P. Bew and G. Gillespie (1996) *The Northern Ireland Peace Process, 1993–1996* (London: Serif).

72. *Irish Times*, 6th May, 2014 and *Belfast Telegraph* 12th May, 2014. For the background see P. Bew (2005) 'The Role of the Historical Adviser and the Bloody Sunday Tribunal', *Historical Research*, Vol. 78, pp. 113–27.

73. Taylor (2012) *London's Burning,* passim.

74. One of the largely neutral accounts that uses historical arguments is P. Wilkinson (ed.) (2007) *Homeland Security in the UK* (London: Routledge)

75. L. Malik (2010) *From Fatwa to Jihad: The Rushdie Affair and Its Aftermath* (New York: Melville).

76. H. Stuart (2017) *Islamist Terrorism: Analysis of Offences and Attacks in the UK (1998–2015)* (London: Henry Jackson Society).

77. A very short selection of titles must suffice here: Head (2011) *Crimes against the State*; R. Law (2009) *Terrorism: A History* (Cambridge: Polity) and B. Hoffman (2006) *Inside Terrorism* (New York: Columbia University Press).

78. See for example R. English (2009) *Terrorism: How to Respond* (Oxford: Oxford University Press); Wilkinson (2007) *Homeland Security*; Hewitt (2008) *British War* and Donohue (2001) *The Cost of Counterterrorism*, pp. 33–66. For negotiations see J. Powell (2014) *Talking to Terrorists* (London: Bodley Head).

79. Powell (2014) *Talking to Terrorists*, pp. 354–57.

80. Blake (2012) *Policing Terrorism*, pp. 90–91. Available at http://www.bbc.co.uk/news/uk-12537976 and http://www.bbc.co.uk/news/uk-12621385 (Accessed 10th September 2015).

81. Blake (2012) *Policing Terrorism*, pp. 354–57 and http://www.bbc.co.uk/news/uk-12537976 (Accessed 10th September 2015).

82. http://news.bbc.co.uk/1/hi/uk/4206800.stm and https://www.youtube.com/watch?v=7iBEBMrzHpc (Accessed 10th September 2015).

83. Blake (2012) *Policing Terrorism*, pp. 357–60.

84. *Ibid.*, pp. 383–84.

85. http://www.bbc.co.uk/news/uk-12537976 (Accessed 10th September 2015).

86. Richardson (2007) 'Britain and the IRA', p. 99.
87. http://www.legislation.gov.uk/ukpga/2006/11/contents (Accessed 12th October 2017).
88. Brain (2010) *A History of Policing*, p. 361 and p. 377.
89. http://web.archive.org/web/20070814190956/ and http://www.mi5.gov.uk/output/Page374.html (Accessed 2nd September 2015).

7

'Hope I Die Before I Get Old': Social Rebellion and Social Diseases

Clifford Williamson

1. Introduction

This chapter chronicles the development of the anxieties about the impact of modern popular music since its emergence in the mid-1950s. It offers an introduction to the history of popular music since 1955 and the various ways in which it has interacted with the issues of delinquency, deviance and disorder. It will then consider the approaches taken by scholars to the significance of popular music as a contributory factor in patterns of criminality and deviance. Here three themes are discussed. First, we will outline the emergence of popular music as a legitimate subject for historical analysis. Second, we will investigate how the debate on sub-cultures associated with specific popular music genres gained academic credibility via cultural studies. Third, we will delineate the dialogue on deviance as it has developed since the 1950s gradually gaining a foothold in scholarly circles.

The final section of the chapter will look at the case study of the 'pay-party' movement within the rave phenomenon of the mid-1980s and early 1990s. 'Pay-parties' were clandestine events organised via anonymous mobile telephone services where patrons were given directions to a location where they paid for entrance to a so-called 'Acid House rave.' The reasons for focussing on this topic are numerous. First, the panics and anxieties associated with rave were many and related to a variety of issues such as public safety, mass trespass, road safety, mass misuse of drugs, organised crime and antisocial behaviour, to name just a few. Second, the political interest in rave (and in the 'pay-party' movement more specifically) was in excess of any other popular music-associated panics. For instance there would be three different pieces of legislation passed in the UK in 1989, 1994 and 1997 which attempted to control the rave scene: this was an unprecedented number. The debate around rave was about lifestyle, leisure and libertarianism; about the boundaries of behaviour between the legal and the illegal. In some ways, it was also about the normalising of deviance based on individual interpretations of just law and personal freedom and what to do about mass law-breaking. It was estimated that at the height of the rave fad, around 300,000 people consumed MDMA (ecstasy) every weekend.[1] This kind of statistic illustrated how, in some respects, drugs seemed to be becoming a major feature of the behaviours of many young people and this in turn entrenched the notion that a mass drug culture had arrived.

The debate also re-ignited discussion of the generation gap. Furthermore, it raised questions of rural versus urban and suburban communities with the weekend 'pay-party' rave scene largely made up of mobile youngsters from the cities partying in fields in the country. Prominent amongst those who raised concerns about rave parties were MPs from rural Wiltshire and Somerset who felt threatened by these interlopers, as they saw them.[2] The rave scene also emphasised a clash between mainstream culture and a re-emergent counterculture. Ravers found allies in their campaign to resist attempts to limit where they could party in the residual elements of the '60s hippies and the peace convoys which had grown off the back of the anti-nuclear movement and who were now fashioned in the media as 'New Age Travellers.'[3] They too had claimed that their freedom of movement and lifestyle had been curtailed and had been met with violence when they attempted to gather at certain places. Most notably this occurred at Stonehenge in 1985 when more than 400 people were arrested by the Wiltshire police during the so-called 'Battle of the Beanfield'.[4] The rave controversy therefore saw the collision of a whole series of elements not just related to the music but to behaviour, attitudes, lifestyle and drugs. Many of these elements were regarded, especially by those in authority, as an anathema and as deviant threats to the social order. As such, the rave scene, and the 'pay-party' movement more specifically, provides a perfect case study for this chapter and indeed for the book more broadly.

The use of the concept of a 'moral panic' in this chapter is undoubtedly controversial, as the very nature and viability of the concept has been challenged especially in the fields of sociology and criminology over the 40 plus years since the publication of *Folk Devils and Moral Panics*. The theory is not just controversial in that it has been appropriated by scholars from outside of sociology from where the idea emerged, or that it has become a 'catch all' approach to the study of deviancy, especially juvenile delinquency by professionals and amateurs alike. However in that it has itself become, for some critics, an idea which is effectively obsolete in the modern multimedia world, the concept of morality so central to Cohen's approach is no longer based on a single agreed set of standards.[5]

It was an idea, as Stanley Cohen himself reflected that was 'informed by the '60s fusion of labelling theory, cultural politics and critical sociology'.[6] However as time has moved on with the advent of multiculturalism, a more complex media landscape and significant pushback by media-savvy representatives of sub-cultures often vilified as folk devils has somewhat altered the landscape. The classic moral panic as outlined by Cohen is less common or effective in provoking a backlash against those labelled.[7] In the main case study in this chapter we see some of these developments in embryonic form where the music press, DJs, ravers and politically well-connected figures such as Paul Staines were able to mount a significant challenge to the dominant narrative about rave culture.

Although 'moral panics' have become much less commonplace or impactful this does not mean that it is a redundant model of the process of social control. In the period covered by this chapter in the first two-thirds of the twentieth century, the classic moral panic model is very relevant as the print and broadcast media still had a veritable monopoly of control over information, ideas of morality, despite some modifications, still tended towards social conservatism and moral entrepreneurs were still somewhat crude in their bandwagon jumping. Also, it is not as if the moral panic model is without prominent contemporary advocates such as Goode and Ben-Yehuda[8], or that even those critical of the concept such as McRobbie and Thornton wish to see it abandoned. They have called for it to be updated[9] and as Yvonne Jewkes has noted 'it is the theory that refuses to go away.'[10]

There has been a surprising reluctance by historians to engage in the study of the development of the modern mass media and crime. It has been largely left to scholars in the fields of sociology, criminology and cultural studies to do so. There have been many histories of crime and there have been many studies of the history of the mass media yet few have sought to fuse the two together. It took a sociologist, Steve Chibnall, to provide the first major study of the history of crime reporting in his 1977 monograph *Law-and-Order News*.[11] Since then it has largely been the preserve of media studies and criminology to examine the role of the media in shaping of the messages around criminality.[12] These fields have been streets ahead of history in conceptualising, theorising and chronicling crime in the media. Also it has been media studies theorists who have best represented some of the shortcomings of media histories.

Most vocal in this has been James Curran. In his article 'Media and the Making of British Society, c.1700–2000' for *Media History* from 2002, he outlined three weaknesses in the study of the history of the media.[13] First, it was focussed on the media such as newspapers or film and this gives rise to in Curran's words 'fractured and incomplete understandings of the historical role of the media.'[14] Second, it is too focussed on the media itself and analysis of content: 'Media history tends not to illuminate the links between media development and wider trends in society because it is often narrowly focused on the content or organisation of the media.'[15] Third, it is too specialised as a result of the first two developments and led to the discussion of the media being left to non-historians.[16] That it took a non-historian to point out these things should give a further cause for concern and stimulate historians to reclaim the ground, or at least ensure in the future that the interdisciplinary nature of media history is well represented by historians amongst the other scholars in the field, and also by extension the study of the history of the media and criminality.

2.   Chronology

The whole period described as the modern era of popular music (that is from roughly 1955 through to the present day) has been subject to periodic anxieties, or what some observers such as Stanley Cohen have called 'moral panics'.[17] These are episodes where concerns have been voiced about the influence and impact of the performers and sub-cultures associated with various genres of popular music. From the violence associated with the so-called Teddy Boys of the 1950s through to the media outrage over members of reality show pop group One Direction being shown smoking marijuana joints in 2014, politicians, the police and media campaigners amongst others have sought to stigmatise, criminalise or shame such deviancy and to limit the influence they may have had on the behaviours of the nation's youth.[18] The strategies employed in the pursuit of these objectives have been varied from legislation to censorship and from social exclusion through to outright violence against those associated with sub-cultures.

The discussion of popular music alongside other themes in this volume may at first seem trivial. Can the occasional media fascination with the words and behaviours of superficial pop stars and their fans compare with an analysis of terrorism, murder or rape? There does seem to be a major imbalance in terms of scale and severity that we need to bear in mind. For example in 1965, Myra Hindley and Ian Brady were arrested on suspicion of the murder of three children. In the same year all three members of the Rolling Stones were fined £5 each for public urination.[19] As a representation of the polarities of deviance it is hard to find such a wide variation in behaviour. Yet five young men found relieving themselves behind a garage in Romford was world news. However, the issues surrounding popular music in modern Britain have not always been this trivial. They have been serious, momentous and sometimes catastrophic. This section deals chronologically with some of the controversies that have been part and parcel of the era.

a) Pre–Rock 'n' Roll

It is important to start with an awareness that the debates about delinquency and deviance relating to youth and music predate the emergence of rock 'n' roll in the mid-1950s. Indeed, it has been an omnipresent concern stretching back centuries as correcting the behaviours of youth enabled society to properly inculcate in them the standards of citizenship and civilisation. Even in the twentieth century, and particularly after the Second World War, there was a pre-existing dialogue on behaviour as it related to the leisure time and popular culture of youth and the moral development of young people as evidenced by the 1947 Clarke Report *School and Life*.[20] This anxiety was established early in the twentieth century with the popularisation of jazz music in the 1920s, followed by swing music in the 1930s and '40s. Despite the economic difficulties of the time, it was estimated that the wages of young people (those between 14 and 20) rose during the interwar period. Boys saw an increase in salary of 300 per cent, whilst girls enjoyed an uplift of more than 500 per cent at this time.[21] Although the bulk of these wages were handed over to parents to help in the upkeep of the family home, there was still, nonetheless, considerable disposable income amongst British youth to spend on leisure-time activities such as the cinema and the dance hall.[22]

Three themes emerged in the interwar period about the influences that popular music and the activities associated with it had on young people. First, there were anxieties about external cultural influences, particularly those coming from America such as jazz. This was often mixed with racial concerns with one Oxford don describing the new sound as 'Nigger music (that) comes from the Devil'.[23] Second, there were a whole series of fears that the dance hall – the main venue for listening and dancing to jazz – was causing moral and intellectual decline. It was said that men and women dancing in such close proximity would inevitably encourage immorality. Indeed, one dance hall denizen who contributed to various Mass Observation surveys neatly summed up their role by saying 'The chief function of the dance halls is to get young people together' they were locations where 'sexuality could be explored.'[24] The fear of the dance halls could turn into panic. There was one notable case in Cambridge in 1931 where the owner of a dance hall was accused and convicted of running a disorderly house, when a police raid discovered that a number of undergraduates were found in the arms of local women and one even had his hand on a girl's knee.[25] For the most part however there was effective moral policing of the halls, with supervisors stalking the dance floor making sure that there 'was no funny business' going on.[26] What happened after they left the venues was another matter. There were other concerns about the impact of dancing. Book publishers for instance became worried that the dance hall craze was leading to a decline in people reading books,[27] and there was at least one case of dance halls breaking the law prohibiting dancing on a Sunday.[28] The third and final anxiety that emerged during the interwar period related to fears that dance halls would become arenas for street gangs to fight turf wars. It seems that some of this concern was well placed. It was not uncommon for local *Palais de Danse* to be troubled by violence instigated by rival members of local gangs. There were violent incidents recorded in London in 1926 and in 1932. In 1934 in Glasgow there was a murder associated with violence in dance halls in which 13 gang members were charged.[29]

Concerns about dance halls reached their peak in wartime. In both the Great War and in the Second World War dance halls were a major focus for moral campaigners who sought to target unescorted women and dissuade them from frequenting such establishments. However, the exercise of moral control proved to be difficult, as one women pointed out: 'Britain seemed so dull and corny, the Yanks gave us cigarettes and chewing gum and the music was fantastic. ... Who wants to listen to schmaltzy music when you are young and can dance to the "A-train" with the Yanks.'[30] The allure and affluence of American servicemen has undoubtedly become part of the folklore of the Second World War. In Glasgow, religious groups organised volunteers to trawl the cafes, restaurants and dance halls in order to try and persuade young women to leave these venues. Such were the fears over the potential for vice and immorality that at times groups tried to use the police to enforce some kind of moral curfew on women. As was the case in the interwar period, the dance hall could be the scene of violence in the 1940s and '50s. For instance, the US Navy shore patrol regarded the Criterion Dance Hall in Londonderry as the most dangerous location in the city for disorderly behaviour and fighting.[31] Aside from all of these concerns there were again problems with the nature of the dancing. Even more than was the case with previous dances, the jitterbug, with its energetic character and manhandling of the female dancers, was looked upon with horror by some. US *Billboard* magazine claimed that there was a campaign in Britain to ban the jitterbug *from* dance halls and bars with jukeboxes where young people would dance.[32]

What was important about the musical culture of the pre–rock 'n' roll era was the way in which the three themes discussed would be the precursors of concerns writ much larger in the second half of the twentieth century. An analysis of public concerns regarding popular music in the interwar period helps us not only to map out the anxieties which would figure prominently in subsequent decades, but it also demonstrates that fears about behaviour, concerns about delinquency of various sorts and the potentially corrupting influence of American music were well established and entrenched in discourses about popular culture and society by 1945. There would, of course, be differences. Adolescents would become more independent after the Second World War, with many leaving the family home to go into higher education and experiment with new lifestyle choices. For example the number of young people at university had risen from in 50,000 1938/39 to 235,000 by 1970/71.[33] For those who still stayed at home, they would have even greater disposable income. The average income of young manual workers would increase from £2.18s in 1948 to £6.6s.7d. by 1960 and with this came access to technologies which would accelerate access to consumer goods, notably with the advent of transistor radios, cheap vinyl records and modestly priced players for them.[34]

b)   Rock 'n' Roll

After the Second World War in particular, there was an awareness of a gap opening up between the generations. Young people between the ages of 14 and 20 would come to feature prominently in the controversies over popular music. Paul Rock and Stanley Cohen characterised the generational division as being facilitated by the 'relative economic emancipation of working-class adolescents.'[35] Increasing economic independence was joined with a second feature identified by Rock and Cohen, an increasing reliance of some sections of youth on the advice and example of their peers as opposed to their parents as major role models in shaping behaviour.[36] This was seemingly a global or at least a Western trend in socialisation. It was identified in the United States and increasingly elsewhere in the early 1950s. It would, in time, turn the generation gap into a generational schism especially, as we shall see, in the 1960s.

The first identifiable group to emerge from this generational gap in the UK at least, were the Teddy Boys. The 'Teds' came to prominence in the middle of 1953 following a fatal disturbance in Clapham in south London.[37] They were called 'Teds' or the 'New Edwardians' due to the fact that many of the youngsters caught up in the violence were seen to be wearing Edwardian style frock coats; a fashion trend borrowed from upper class ex-army officers who had championed the look as a way to differentiate themselves from the 'spiv' style of suits that predominated in the capital during the post-war period.[38] In the aftermath of the Clapham murder, the media jumped all over the issue and produced a whole series of nightmarish reports on the criminal character and generally deviant nature of the 'Teds'. The moral panic generated by the 'Teds' predated the emergence of rock 'n' roll in Britain. In fact, as Pamela Horn argues, the whole issue of 'misdoing of youth loomed large as focus of public attention' after the Second World War.[39] This was exemplified by the 1949 Mass Observation Report on Juvenile Delinquency and also by the 1955 King George Jubilee Fund Report *Citizens of To-morrow*, both of which looked at the influences shaping the behaviour of Britain's youth.[40]

The fusion of deviance with popular music took place in 1956 with the arrival of the movie *Blackboard Jungle* that had as its main theme juvenile delinquency, but it was not this that caused the controversy. Rather, it was the soundtrack of the film and in particular the track *Rock Around the Clock* by Bill Haley and the Comets that seemed to cause significant unrest with a number of cinemas. When later in the year a movie of the same title was released to cash in on the rock 'n' roll craze, there were a number of disturbances leading to it being banned in Bristol, Ipswich and a number of other places.[41] This collision of popular cultural phenomena would be the template for future concerns and patterns of moral panic.

The response of 'moral entrepreneurs' was multifaceted. There were some who blamed a supposedly lenient criminal justice system for the increasing incorrigibility of youth, pointing to the abolition of birching for young offenders as a result of the 1948 Criminal Justice Act. Indeed, there was an attempt to restore birching in 1961 in the British House of Commons but it did not gain much support.[42] There were those who blamed American cultural imperialism. Then were those that pointed to societal issues such as concerns about National Service with conscription. This issue was seen as the cause of some bad behaviour due to the gap between leaving school for the majority at 15 years of age and eligibility for National Service at the age of 18. This left youngsters with insufficient activities to do with their free time prior to service. However, some individuals maintained the view that National Service had its advantages for youth. As once in the services, there was evidence that individuals such as the Teddy Boys were quite easily turned into good citizens. The perceived lack of youth leadership would be a further major theme in the discussion of 'the Ted scare'. It had been identified by the Kings Jubilee Fund as an issue in 1955, and the 1961 Wotton Report on the Youth Service called for the revitalisation of the organisation as crucial to address the problem of directionless young delinquents as exemplified by 'the Teds'.[43] As with most moral panics, after the initial furore and action, the issue gradually fell out of prominence. 'The Teds' themselves entered adulthood, settled down, or moved on to the next fashion and musical trend.

'The Teds' would never totally disappear however. Some gave up their frock coats for leather jackets to become rockers. Others took their cue from the sartorial precision and dynamism of the New Edwardians and maintained their passion for being well dressed. They started to adopt the 'Italian look' as it was described, with fitted suits and short haircuts drawn from images from the increasingly popular output of Italian cinema. Some even went as far as to adopt the scooters which were omnipresent in Italy by the start of the 1960s. A few stayed loyal to 'the Ted' lifestyle, leaving a residual presence that would remain influential and often referenced in future popular cultural trends. Most notably, the ethos of 'the Teds' would be instrumental in the development of punk rock both in terms of style and in the basic character of the music.

c)   Mods and Rockers

In the study of deviance and delinquency in popular music, the era of the clashes between 'mods' and 'rockers' in the holiday resorts of the United Kingdom during 1964 and 1965 figures very prominently. For Stanley Cohen, they were the focus of his ground-breaking study of the nature of 'moral panics' in modern Britain.[44] For Clive Bloom the 'mods' and 'rockers' lifestyles and behaviour revealed a 'shift in values from those of the austere war generation to the newly affluent baby-boomers.' These youths were, he said, 'trapped between British inertia and unobtainable American opportunity.'[45]

On the last weekend in March 1964, at the seaside resort of Clacton-on-Sea in Essex, a series of disturbances took place between competing gangs of men. The police intervened and nearly 100 were arrested.[46] Most of these arrests were for minor charges relating to criminal damage. However, some were for more serious offences such as assault with a deadly weapon and malicious wounding.[47] Throughout the next few months, there were other examples of similar disorder in other holiday resorts including Bournemouth and Brighton.[48] The men involved were identified as the moderns or 'mods'. They were well dressed and well groomed, taking their style of clothing and distinctive motor scooters from the current wave of popular Italian films. Their adversaries were styled 'rockers'. They too had a distinctive look sporting greased coifs, long sideburns and dressed in leathers, copying the look of American movie stars such as Marlon Brando and James Dean. These two groups were also defined by musical tastes with the 'mods' acolytes of American soul and blues or the new British blues scene led by the Rolling Stones and the Yardbirds while the musical taste of the 'rockers' was much older, as they remained devotees of mid-1950s rock 'n' roll movement.[49]

On the back of the disorder, there was much media sensationalism with the headlines screaming 'Wildest Ones Yet!' in the *Daily Sketch* and the *Daily Mirror* 'Wild Ones "Beat Up" Margate' after a major disturbances at the seaside resort on the weekend of 16/17 May 1964.[50] Urgent questions were asked in the House of Commons to the Home Secretary about the ability of the law to deal with such outbreaks of violence.[51] The Home Secretary initially sought to reassure the House that there was more than enough in terms of legal devices and police to cope with future outbreaks. Yet within weeks there would be a whirlwind of legislative activity which was intended not only to deal with the disorder directly, but also to impact upon the role that 'pep-pills' (such as Drinamyl or purple hearts as they were popularly known) may have played in shaping the behaviour of the youngsters involved in the incidents. Parliament quickly passed the Malicious Damages Act of 1964 and the 1964 Misuse of Drugs Act.[52] Outside of Parliament, there was anxiety at the meaning of the turmoil – what it meant for youth, what it meant for society and what it meant for the future. Even the Pope was to get involved. While addressing 1000 Rovers of the Catholic Scouting Association, Pope John XXIII lamented 'the unhappy faces of the Teddy boys … the Mods and Rockers' which he said revealed 'profound, piteous dramas filled with sorrow, lack of trust, vice, badness and delinquency.'[53]

There were four significant aspects of the 'mods' and 'rockers' episode which are of importance to our study. First, was the class composition of the 'mods', in particular. In a study published in *The Times* newspaper based on those remanded in custody during the disturbances, it was argued that many of the youngsters caught up in violence came from 'respectable' suburban backgrounds.[54] This was a departure from the predominant image of delinquency as a working-class problem as evidenced by the 'Teddy Boys' of the 1950s. The spread of nihilism and hooliganism into the suburban middle classes was regarded with horror. Parents were blamed and they also blamed themselves for the advent of the so-called 'respectable thug'. One parent quoted in *The Times* felt that she had been too lenient in terms of discipline, a fact she now lamented.[55] However, for some, even the usual recourse to corporal punishment was insufficient. Another parent quoted in the article for instance, pointed out that his son was seemingly immune to a 'thrashing'. The second key aspect of the 'mods' and 'rockers' episode related to the impact of the abolition of National Service and whether the two were linked. In the discussions about 'the Teds', there was often reference made to the role of conscription in helping to eliminate antisocial tendencies.[56] Without it there was arguably no effective means of controlling or channeling youthful high spirits or misbehaviour in a positive direction.

The third significant aspect of the disorder was the emergence of open warfare between some popular music sub-cultures.[57] The two groups were identifiable as sub-cultures through dress and mode of transportation, but the major thing that divided them was their musical loyalties. It had always been acknowledged that locality, religion and sports allegiances could spark off disorder, but choice of music was, for the United Kingdom at least, a unique development. A final aspect of the episode that was held to be important and was routinely commented on was the lifestyles of the 'mods' and the 'rockers'. The chairman of the Brighton Council of Youth had compiled a survey based on interviews with over 500 youngsters found in coffee bars over the spring and summer of 1964. The survey discovered that 62 per cent of the 'mods' questioned had tried drugs. The proliferation of drugs amongst 'rockers' was 42 per cent. Sexual attitudes were also surveyed with 73 per cent of male 'mods' claiming to have had intercourse and 28 per cent of females. 'Rockers' seemed to have been less promiscuous (or less willing to admit to being so) with 60 per cent of boys and only 12 per cent of girls claiming to be sexually active. How accurate or reliable the report was is debatable, but according to this survey, youth culture was certainly evolving into one involving 'sex, drugs and rock 'n' roll' or 'sex, drugs and soul' if you were a mod.[58]

d)   The Sixties

After the furore over 'mods' and 'rockers', popular music underwent a considerable cultural transformation and for a short time became a virtuous representation of change. The engine of this change was the global impact of 'The Beatles'. 'The Fab Four', as they were affectionately known, were representative of all the social and cultural changes of the era including the triumph of popular music, the end of deference, the end of elitism in culture and perhaps most significantly, the rise of youth. Moral campaigners found some aspects of the appeal of the band problematic. Beatlemania was sometimes disorderly. The flocks of hysterical teenagers who screamed at every sight of the band were regarded with disapproval. Paul Johnson writing in the *New Statesman* called them 'a collective portrait of a generation enslaved by a commercial machine.'[59] The group had been carefully managed and presented as the cheeky but clean-cut boys next door. It was an image that seduced all aspects of popular culture and society at the time. 'The Beatles' were feted by the popular press and the intelligentsia. With politicians seeking to use a bit of star power in the new age of television politics, the British monarchy too had to bow to Beatle power awarding the band MBEs in 1965 for services to music and business as the UK's best export brand. 'The Beatles' became the kings of swinging London, a city that was achieving global recognition for its cultural trendsetting.[60]

Gradually, however, there was to be a revival of anxieties about the role of popular music as the 1960s progressed. 'The Beatles' themselves had caused some controversy, less so in Britain than elsewhere. In the United States, a comment attributed to John Lennon in 1966 that to some young people 'The Beatles' were bigger than Jesus, provoked a major backlash especially in the Bible belt, with a number of radio stations and churches calling for a boycott of their shows.[61] In Japan, anti-Beatles protests took place from those who abhorred the extent of the influence that Western culture, as represented by 'The Beatles', was now having across Japanese society.[62] More serious was an international incident caused when the band snubbed, or was alleged to have snubbed, the wife of the Philippines President Ferdinand Marcos.[63]

'The Beatles' were able to ride out most of these storms, but their putative rivals 'The Rolling Stones' were not so lucky. 'The Stones' management cultivated an image of menace and danger for the group, best summed up by the slogan: 'Would you let your daughter go out with a Rolling Stone?'[64] Where 'The Beatles' sang 'I Want to Hold Your Hand', 'The Stones' sang 'Let's Spend the Night Together'. In 1965, while 'The Beatles' were getting MBEs, 'The Stones' were up on a charge of disorderly behaviour after three band members were caught by the police urinating against a wall. Found guilty, the three were fined £5 each.[65] More serious for the band was when first Brian Jones, and then Mick Jagger and Keith Richards were arrested for the possession of illegal drugs in early 1967.[66]

The mid-1960s saw increasing political attention given over to the issues relating to the misuse of drugs and their intimate association with the sub-cultures of popular music. In 1961, the United Nations Single Convention on Narcotic Drugs called for action on the cultivation of cannabis. The British government wrote this into law with the 1964 Dangerous Drugs Act and in the same year passed the Drugs (Prevention of Misuse) Act 1964, which targeted amphetamines.[67] In 1966, the Prevention of the Misuse of Drugs Modification Order outlawed LSD.[68] The 1967 equivalent legislation increased the powers of search and seizure available to the police and customs officers.[69] The definitive legislative response to concerns towards recreational drug use was to be the 1971 Misuse of Drugs Act.[70] This Act is still the basis of British drug law today.

It was not just 'The Stones' that found themselves in trouble over drugs, the folk singer Donovan was arrested in 1966. The previously untouchable Beatles had their run-in with the police, with both John Lennon in 1968 and George Harrison in 1970 convicted of possession. Quite why these particular stars were singled out remains controversial. For the likes of Keith Richards it was an attempt by the 'establishment' as he referred to it to clamp down on youth culture.[71] For writers such as Dominic Sandbrook, the crackdown was more as a result of a revolt by middle-class moralists seeking to reverse the permissive tide of the late 1960s.[72]

e)   Punk

The era of punk, from roughly 1975 to 1980, brought a whole series of controversies and issues to the fore covering such themes as obscenity, blasphemy, iconoclasm, racism and antisocial behaviour. Of all of the musical sub-cultures associated with deviance and delinquency, it is punk that is the most synonymous with misbehaviour. Indeed, many of the leading lights of the movement seemed to encourage disorder. The manager of the quintessential punk band 'The Sex Pistols', Malcolm McLaren, himself a former member of King Mob an offshoot of the anarchist group 'Situationist International', promoted the idea of 'cash from chaos'.[73] His outspoken views inspired significant degrees of outrage, ostracism and alienation that were to push some punks onto the peripheries of society, but it was also a movement that gave a sense of identity and a voice to people and groups that seemed to have been bypassed by the mainstream.

The arrival of punk on the national stage in Britain occurred during Bill Grundy's television interview of 'The Sex Pistols' on the *Today* show in 1976. It was to be the start of a firestorm of media outrage which resulted in the band (which was just about to start their 'Anarchy' tour as it was called) being turned into pariahs. Workers at the main EMI record-pressing plant at Hayes refused to handle any 'Sex Pistols' records.[74] University chancellors, student union presidents and local councillors cancelled gigs. 'The Sex Pistols' were scheduled to play 27 concerts on their tour but they ended up being allowed to play only 5.[75] The hysteria of the Grundy aftermath saw traditional arenas of free speech such as universities pretty much forced into censorship. Trades unions, at a time of radical industrial action, also backed their members when they boycotted handling 'Sex Pistols' records.[76] The undoubted impact of this series of events is analysed by Keith Gildart in his work *Images of England through Popular Music*. Gildart argues that the 'Anarchy' tour was not just a moral panic, but it was also 'a particular cultural/political event that formed one response to a sense of change.'[77] 'The Sex Pistols' and punk rock became symbols of a delinquent epoch and of a nation, that for some people at least, had gone from swinging to dystopian within a decade.

Although this initial phase of panic would subside, it would be followed in 1977 by a further series of episodes that would consolidate the impression of punk as anathema and punks as deviant. 1977 was the Silver Jubilee of the accession of Queen Elizabeth II. 'The Sex Pistols' released the track 'God Save the Queen' to coincide with the anniversary. Such a provocative title was bound to be a problem; it was not played on the radio, except on the music show of John Peel, and many of the chain stores refused to stock it.[78] The artwork on the single cover by Jamie Reid featured the Queen with a safety pin through her nose and was accordingly banned from displays.[79] Reid himself was beaten up for his trouble. Despite this, on its release, the record went towards the top of the charts selling 150,000 copies in five days.[80] Punk energised a whole sub-culture to copy and emulate the do-it-yourself ethos with fanzines, self-financed records and shops to distribute them.[81] The success of 'God Save the Queen' was testimony to the power of this underground movement.

It proved impossible for punk in general and for 'The Sex Pistols' in particular to avoid trouble. The release of their album *Never Mind the Bollocks* later in 1977 resulted in charges of obscenity under the Indecent Advertising Act of 1899 being levelled.[82] Interestingly, the case revolved around the meaning of the word 'Bollocks', and not the content of the record more generally. In defence of title, Virgin Records employed as a star witness James Kingsley the Professor of English Literature at Nottingham University. Professor Kingsley discussed the origins and usage of the word from its original meaning as a small ball to an expression of exasperation. He took the title in this context to mean 'Never mind the nonsense, here is The Sex Pistols'.[83] The Magistrate in his own words 'reluctantly' agreed with this interpretation and dismissed all charges.[84] This was the first in a series of obscenity trials relating to punk. For instance, 'The Anti-Nowhere League' and 'Crass' were successfully prosecuted in 1982 and 1984 respectively under the 1959 Obscene Publications Act.[85] All the remaining copies of 'The Anti-Nowhere League' record 'So What' were destroyed. 'Crass' were partially successful on appeal, with only one of their songs 'Bata Motel' from the album *Penis Envy* declared obscene.[86]

The punk movement also highlighted some of the lifestyle alternatives of the 1970s such as squatting and collective living. By 1979 there were an estimated 50,000 squatters in the United Kingdom of whom 30,000 were in London.[87] Almost all of the punk pioneers, including Joe Strummer of 'The Clash' and John Lydon of 'The Sex Pistols' had been a squatter at one time or another.[88] Steve Platt, writing in the monograph *Squatting: The Real Story*, argued that squatting was 'the harbinger of a new style of social and political activity.'[89] Some of those who would eventually be characterised as 'anarcho-punks' would take the quasi-political rhetoric inherent in punk and translate it into direct action. Glasper described them as 'making punk a movement as opposed to merely an outlandish fashion statement.'[90] Worley went further and argued that they were 'the basis for an alternative society.'[91] These punks, sometimes called 'crusties', would eventually find common cause with the remnants of the Free Festival Movement and other outsider movements occasionally characterised as 'new age travellers,' the fate of which will be made clear in the case study in this chapter on rave.

This section has highlighted a selected number of controversies over the period covered in this volume. They are by no means the only concerns over popular music and the sub-cultures associated with them. There was contemporaneous to punk the growing disquiet in some circles about reggae music and the behaviour of the growing number of West Indian youths adopting Rastafarianism as a culture.[92] The years following the high watermark of punk were characterised as the post-punk era and they had their share of anxieties associated with them. They ranged from the growth of 'Oi' a splinter movement which was to become increasing associated with racism and the National Front to the anarcho-punks such as 'Crass' who, as already noted, on a number of occasions fell foul of the authorities over obscenity.[93] Also later in the 1980s was the rise of hip-hop and rap and the frequent clashes over public order, sexism and racism which accompanied this new musical genre.[94]

The main examples highlighted were chosen to illuminate the broad trends of the issues around music and young people. These ranged from concerns about sexual impropriety in the Jazz Age through the delinquency associated with the Teddy Boys, the mass disorder of the mods and rockers era, the growing alarm about the drug culture of the 1960s and the compendium of fears raised by punk. In the case study of rave that follows later in this chapter we see all of these issues collide in a mega panic, which will bring down the wrath of the state and society upon the patron of this new cultural movement.

3.   Historiography

For the most part, the study of popular music has been divided between the 'popular' and the 'professional' or scholarly. 'Popular writing' is that produced by the music press or the fanzine or the Internet fan sites for the consumption of 'fandom', reflecting the obsessions and interests of enthusiasts. This is not to say that they are unimportant or inferior. The music press has been crucial in the chronicling and critiquing of the genre. Indeed, some of this work has attained significant scholarly respect such as the publication *New Musical Express* in Britain or *Rolling Stone* in the United States. Fanzines have also been much used in academic studies and there has been a general acknowledgement that works such as *Sniffin' Glue* or *Boy's Own* are vital insights into the world of the fan, as well as being crucial in their own eras in popularising many music genres notably punk and rave. Matthew Worley summed up the role of fanzines by saying 'punk fanzines served as a product of agency, a means of participation and a platform for creative and political expression.'[95]

Professional scholarship relating to popular music has been gaining creditability over the last 40 years. There are now a number of peer-reviewed journals covering the history of popular music. Notably these include *Popular Music and Society*, which started in 1971, *Popular Music History* established in 2004, and more recently *Rock Music Studies* in 2014.[96] Most are interdisciplinary, mixing musicology, studies of technology and sociology amongst many other forms of academic discipline. In terms of monograph publications, the study of the history of popular music has remained dominated by biographies, 'bandographies' and extended reviews of the works of individual performers or groups or genres.[97] This is not to disparage such outputs as the works of journalists such as Simon Reynolds, Jon Savage and Matthew Collin which are widely quoted in this chapter.

Academia has been very slow in treating the history of popular music seriously. In terms of historical works, there have been very few major publications covering the British music scene. Arguably, there is literally nothing to compare with *All Shook Up* by Glenn Altschuler – a major study on the role of rock 'n' roll in shaping the racial, sexual and generational politics of the United States in the 1950s.[98] Keith Gildart attributes this scholarly reticence on the part of the British to 'the overall "conservatism" of the profession and an orthodoxy suggesting that the role ascribed to popular music and its impact ... owes more to "myth" than "reality".'[99] Gildart himself sought to establish the scholarly legitimacy of the study of popular music with his 2013 monograph *Images of England through Popular Music*. In it he argued that popular music was 'an important cultural, social and political force in post-war English society' and therefore relevant as a factor in understanding identity and social change.[100]

Due to the dearth of scholarly activity in the British context, much of the scholarly work on deviance and popular music has been established in disciplines other than history. It has been in sociology and its latent offspring cultural studies where the issues discussed in this chapter have been initially developed. Starting with Howard Becker's *The Outsiders* in 1963, Stanley Cohen's *Folk Devils and Moral Panics* in 1972, through to Stuart Hall and Tony Jefferson in *Resistance through Rituals* in 1976 and Richard Hebdige's *Subculture: The Meaning of Style* in 1979, we have a substantial literature on the concept and use of moral panics and the deviance associated with certain sub-cultures created as a result of the emergence and popularity of pop and rock music. Although in many cases they have been challenged as scholarly orthodoxy, particularly the works of Cohen and Hebdige, they remain vital staging posts in the emergence of academic interest in the popular music and its followers, as well as establishing the scholarly legitimacy of the field.

It was Cohen who identified the process by which alleged deviant behaviour was identified and addressed.[101] And it was Hebdige who was to chronicle the crucial role played by popular music genre in shaping youth sub-cultures and the sense of identity that was felt by those who were often regarded as pariahs and outsiders.[102] Becker gave shape to the concept of labelling deviants and the consequences of social exclusion, and he also derived the notion of the 'moral entrepreneur' who sought to exploit anxieties about deviance to pursue political or behavioural change.[103] Hall and Jefferson, on the other hand, examined the way in which groups manifested dissent through collective behaviours.[104] All of these pioneering works have laid the basis for further study and their crossover appeal into the historical profession has allowed the topic of popular music to at last be regarded as legitimate in studies of the past.

4. Case Study

During the middle to late 1980s in the United Kingdom, there emerged a new youth sub-culture built around dancing called 'rave' or 'acid house'.[105] It was initially based around nightclubs, but as its popularity grew, promoters began to hire larger venues or rent out warehouses or farm buildings to accommodate the numbers who wanted to dance the night away. As many of the larger venues were outside of the main cities and into the countryside, urban and suburban clubbers formed large twilight and dawn convoys to get to and from the locations. This brought the 'ravers', as they were called, to the attention of the authorities – initially the police and local authorities – due to the noise and disruption said to have been caused and owing to the fact that many of the events were not licensed under existing legislation. The media and other 'moral entrepreneurs' also focussed upon the open proliferation of illegal drugs, most notably MDMA or ecstasy, which was a central feature of the sub-culture.[106]

What became known as the 'rave' or 'acid house' scene comprised three key elements: the music, the event and the drugs. The music called 'house' had emerged in the nightclubs of the American Midwest, most notably in Detroit and Chicago in the mid-1980s. It was a synthesis of electronic beats, sounds and pre-recorded samples mixed by a DJ into elongated beat-driven dance music.[107] The second element was the event: the all-nighter. These were evenings of dancing that lasted well beyond the regular licensed hours of clubs that were popular in the holiday destinations of the Mediterranean, most notably the Balearic Islands of which Ibiza was the most famous. Since the 1960s, Ibiza had been a popular resort for the package holiday crowd but also a bohemian refuge, and in the latter part of the decade it became a vital stop-off on the hippie trail.[108] It retained its hedonistic character into the 1980s when youngsters seeking new thrills rediscovered it. The final element of the 'rave' scene was the role of drugs, especially MDMA (3,4-methylenedioxy-*N*-methylamphetamine). The German pharmaceutical company Merck had developed this substance in 1912, but it never really found a place as a therapeutic treatment and it was used variously as a truth drug, in marriage therapy and in psychotherapy.[109] It did find a place as part of the buffet of drugs in the psychedelic era however, and it was notorious enough in the UK in 1970s to be placed in category A of the 1971 Dangerous Drugs Act in 1977, although it remained legal in the United States till the 1990s.[110] Since the 'mod' era, all-nighters had required artificial energy to keep dancers going. The house scene was no different but the drug of choice had a special contribution to make to the success and notoriety of the sub-culture. Since the early 1980s, MDMA had been popular in the club scene where it was known variously as X-T-C or X or ecstasy.[111] It had the unique qualities of enhancing the music, making the flashing lights more vivid and it produced an empathetic response that helped to create a sense of collective euphoria.[112] Dancers were 'loved up' in the vernacular of the scene and for some it was to be an almost religious experience. Indeed ecstasy was to be instrumental in stimulating a revived interest in alternative spiritualism in elements of the club scene.[113]

According to Simon Reynolds, the first attempt to 'recreate the Balearic' experience was in 1985 at the Project Club in Streatham initiated by the DJ Paul Oakenfold.[114] This was followed in 1987 with the setting up of the first club solely devoted to 'house' called Shoom.[115] It was at Shoom that the iconography and look of 'acid house' took shape with the adoption of the smiley face logo and clubbers in baggy clothes that were either tie-dyed or consisted of luminous day-glo colours. Gradually, across London and in other parts of the United Kingdom, acid house nights were taking place in clubs and new venues were being opened to accommodate the fad. So widespread was the sub-culture that it even had its fanzine called *Boy's Own* which started publication in 1986.[116] The crowds gathering to the scene were a mix of hipsters, celebrities, Ibiza veterans and oddly, football hooligans, known as 'acid casuals' looking for afterhours drinking.[117] The venues also grew from small weekly club nights to all night, every night parties in the larger city centre clubs. Eventually, these too proved to be too small for the numbers involved and so the 'scene' migrated to any larger empty space that could be hired or broken into. Technicians then wired up to the mains to power lights and sound systems and clubbers reached the venues via public transport or walking. The occupation of some of these venues resulted in a crackdown by the police who were gradually to chase the 'pay-parties' (as they came to be called) out of the city and into the suburbs and beyond.[118]

The 'rave scene' was to become particularly vulnerable to organised crime as it required increasing quantities of MDMA to satisfy demand. In the end, it was the only stimulant required as clubbers eschewed alcohol. Early in the 'scene' it had been procured in small amounts by clubbers visiting the likes of Amsterdam and Ibiza and bringing the drug back undetected through customs.[119] Now as the number of clubs mushroomed and the size of the audience increased, it was a big business that could only be satisfied via the networks provided by drug gangs.[120] It was the drug connection that brought the 'scene' to the media's attention with *The Sun* newspaper publishing an exposé of the acid house scene in June 1989.[121] Yet early coverage of the sub-culture was ambiguous as *The Sun* marketed its own line in 'acid house' apparel alongside its reportage of 'rave scene' events.[122]

In 1989, a major development took place that was to transform the politics and legal aspects of the 'rave' scene. Two entrepreneurs of the London acid house parties, Tony Colston-Hayer and Dave Roberts, became frustrated at the crackdown on 'pay-parties' in the capital by the Met police force, and so they decided to take the 'scene' into the countryside.[123] Making use of recently introduced mobile telephones and British Telecom's 'Voice Bank System', they transmitted information to 5000 subscribers to a mailing list about the venues and time of raves.[124] The first took place in April at South Warnborough. There followed a summer of such events characterised as the 'Second Summer of Love'.[125] Clubbers not only made use of new technology but also the recently completed M25 orbital motorway around London to gain easy access to the Home Counties. Interchanges to the M4 opened up possible venues in the south and west of England, setting off a firestorm of local protests such as in Wortham in Kent in the late summer of 1989 – where locals said they were subject to an 'Acid House Ordeal' when ravers descended on their locality.[126]

During the 1984–85 Miner's Strike in Britain, to counter 'flying pickets' from striking coal areas reaching collieries in other locations, the Association of Chief Police Officers (ACPO) had formed a liaison committee which used the national reporting centre to monitor and intercept buses carrying pickets and prevent them from reaching their chosen destinations.[127] A key event in the campaign was the closing of the Dartford tunnel in Kent to flying pickets. The supervising officer at that time was Chief Superintendent Ken Tappenden, by 1989 he was Commander in North Kent (an area bisected by the M25). At his behest, a 'Pay-Party Unit' was created which used all of the know-how gleaned from the Miners' Strike, to counter the party organisation strategies of Roberts and Colston-Hoyer.[128] The use of intercepts, of phone tapping or the restrictions of movement, all considered highly dubious when they were used in 1984–1985, were now freely deployed to stop convoys of teenagers partying. For many, this episode evidenced that there was some kind of culture war being fought in Britain between youth and the older generations. In many ways it was an updated skirmish in a battle fought by successive waves of young people throughout the century as chronicled by many other examples in this chapter. What stood out in the era of the pay-party was the comprehensive character of the intervention by the state, with policing strategies more readily recognisable from major industrial disputes employed to suppress the raves. It would see legislation introduced on an unprecedented scale to counter the movement, as will be discussed below, and the longevity of the panic extended from 1988 until 1997. Concerns about mods and rockers fizzled out within a few months of the first seaside incidents; punk had its most significant period under the microscope from the middle of 1976 till the end of 1977, but rave would continue to raise anxieties for nearly a decade.

Throughout the first half of 1989, there were a slew of headlines that would eventually force the Thatcher administration to support legislation intended to crack down on the 'pay-party' movement. In March there was the first reported death associated with ecstasy.[129] There were also reports of fraud. In one case, bogus party organisers had sold 15,000 tickets at £15 a head for a party that was supposed to take place at Thorpe Park. There was no such event however, and the fraudsters absconded with an estimated £225,000.[130] The 'scene' also became associated with other nefarious activities as it was claimed that partygoers had looted a petrol station in Essex on the way to a rave.[131] During the summer, and in response to an outrage over a raucous acid house party in Berkshire, the Home Secretary (Douglas Hurd) signalled that there could be further action after he called for a full report into this event and others like it. The Chief Superintendent of Aylesbury Police also called for new legislation to deal with the problems caused by the parties.[132]

The first move towards a crackdown was made by the police when, after the annual Conference of the Association of Chief Police Constables on 2nd October 1989, a new intelligence unit was created to address the lack of co-ordination between police forces as partygoers crossed jurisdictional lines between police authorities. Seven forces were to co-operate in this venture Kent, Essex, Sussex, Surrey, Hampshire, Hertfordshire and Thames Valley.[133] At the same time, moves were made to disrupt the ability of party organisers to communicate and promote the location of the venues to ravers for the 'pay-parties' via special rate phone lines. The Independent Committee for the Supervision of Telephone Services instructed the main providers of these services – BT, Mercury and Vodaphone – to end the facility, as it was a breach of the Committee's code of conduct.[134] Every means available was being mobilised to address the 'threat' of acid house parties within the terms of existing legislation and through the 'creative' policing strategies, both again unprecedented actions in the annals of the history of popular music and deviance. When these were shown to be inadequate, the government was to step in and, again in an unprecedented move, act specifically to counter a trend in the popular musical culture of youth.

Despite increasing government interest in the issue, it was to be a private member's bill that would legislate to restrict the rave scene. Graham Bright MP for Luton South introduced a bill in early 1990. His purpose in bringing it forward was that it:

> aims to ensure that our young people can go to parties to dance and enjoy music, confident that they are in a safe environment, without making the lives of nearby residents a misery and endangering their own lives. Stiffer penalties for those who are exploiting them are the readiest way of doing that.[135]

The Entertainments (Increased Penalties) Act 1990 introduced a new range of fines and prohibitions on party organisers under the disparate collection of local authority rules and bylaws. The prospect of legislation had provoked a considerable outcry amongst the 'acid house' community. Coylston-Halter recruited Paul Staines, a weekend raver and a Conservative Party activist with considerable contacts in politics, to help co-ordinate the media side of the 'Freedom to Party Campaign' – a loose coalition of acid house ravers and promoters.[136] The group organised a series of demonstrations in London to raise awareness of the cause and to lobby Parliament. The first demo attracted about 5000 people according to organisers, but the second was a major disappointment with only a few hundred gathering in the capital in the rain.[137]

The fizzling out of the Freedom to Party group was an odd end to what seemed to be the political mobilisation of a mass music subculture. However the group was never that well organised. It was largely the work of Staines and Coylston-Halter who used all the influence they could muster to generate publicity. However, despite the false promise of the first rally, ravers did not seem to be all that political – highlighting the gap between the possibilities for political activism with the general indifference experienced. Worley's conclusion in his study of the failure of the political groups to mobilise punks is also very relevant to the rave scene. He said:

> Rather than secure lasting support, such a focus helped reaffirm notions of individualism and cultural experimentation that lent themselves more to a political fragmentation or disengagement than to activism.[138]

During the passage of the 1994 Criminal Justice Act another attempt was made by the left to mobilise ravers with a similar experience of boom and bust.[139]

The debate on the rave scene was not just a spat between the younger and older generations over the safety of the parties or between the authoritarian right and the liberal left over lifestyle choices. There was also a debate within the right between 'traditional' conservatives and libertarian conservatives. Libertarianism had been gathering pace within the Conservative Party during the 1970s through the likes of the 'Monday Club', 'Committee for a Free Britain' and the 'Federation of Conservative Students'. The most authoritative statement on conservative libertarianism and acid house parties came from the aforementioned Paul Staines in an article for the Libertarian Alliance Political Notes in 1991. He attacked those who he described as the 'Lifestyle Police' and the 'Safety Nazis' for a 'hysterical smear campaign' against 'free market dance party entrepreneurs.'[140] His criticism encompassed what he saw as the totalitarianism of the state which used all manner of repression to stop people having a good time. He decried what he saw as the arcane nature of licensing laws arguing that they were an 'area crying out for Thatcherite deregulation.'[141] The use of the language of the free market and laissez-faire is notable at a time where they were very much dominating intellectual discourse.

The advent of the Increased Penalties Act (IPA) was a decisive moment in the history of the rave scene. The prospect of a fine of £20,000 or a prison sentence was enough to discourage many from promoting 'pay-parties'. Prior to the IPA, fines under existing legislation could be absorbed as legitimate business expenses as a maximum of only £2000 could be imposed, but the prospect of the entire profit from one event being extracted as a penalty proved to be too much for some.[142] Yet as

Collin has argued, although at first glance it seemed that the 'ravers had been utterly defeated' it was also the case 'that raves became integrated into the infrastructure of the entertainment industry.'[143] With more liberal licensing laws enacted in many locations, the way was paved for a new generation of super clubs to allow ravers, in the words of Simon Reynolds, to continue 'the living dream of rave.'[144]

The suppression of the pay-party brought to an end the first and arguably the most important of the panics associated with rave and acid house culture. The state had dealt a considerable blow to the movement. However it would not be completely eradicated, and from 1990 through to 1997 there would be periodic revivals of the anxieties associated with the phenomenon. This would result in further political and judicial action to deal with those who still wanted to dance and take ecstasy. Clauses would be added to the 1994 Criminal Justice Act to outlaw outdoor gatherings where music with repetitive beats was played.[145] In 1997, The Public Entertainment Licenses (Drugs Misuse) Act[146] was passed after a clubber called Leah Betts who had taken ecstasy had died. The cause of death was judged to be *hyponatremia* or water intoxication after falling ill at a nightclub in 1995.[147] The Act sought to close venues where it could be established drugs were being sold. It was however the pay-party panic which was to introduce all the parameters of the debate: illegal assembly, trespass, disorder and drug misuse. There were the key issues, which would shape future action.

5. Conclusion

The 1997 Act brought an end to the long period of the rave panic and indeed to some extent the era of controversy over popular music in the United Kingdom. Although there have been notable episodes of concern such as the aforementioned One Direction scandal, they have not had the same shattering impact on Britain in terms of society, culture and the law. That is not to say that panics over popular music and deviance will not reoccur in the future, but we can look at the twentieth-century period as a definable epoch in which pop music was the main characteristic of youth culture and therefore the priority and obsession of moral campaigners.

Throughout the twentieth century the paradigm of the panics related to popular music was fashioned. In the era of jazz and swing the template was set: with concern expressed about the malign influence of popular music on behaviour, etiquette and sexual morals. The notion of the dance hall as a transgressive venue was also sketched out in this period, with dancing gradually breaking down the physical space between the sexes, and possibly inhibitions as well. Also it could be an arena of violence where street gangs could find another place to fight turf wars. However, early on these venues were, for the most part, well policed by management and chaperones. Violence was uncommon despite the hysteria occasionally generated.

During the post-war period, added to the pre-existing dialogues about deviance and popular music, there was growing consciousness of the power of youth both in terms of numbers via the baby boom but also the independent economic influence of the young wage earner. Greater financial autonomy from the older generation was augmented with an increased tendency to copy others in their peer group, displacing adults and parents. These peer groups or sub-cultures as they were ultimately characterised were more often than not built around tastes in popular music. Starting with the Teddy Boys and followed by a succession of others from mods to rockers to punks to skinheads to Rastas and the increasingly fragmented and numerous other musical sub-cultures, we saw a musical balkanization. It became more private, more exclusive and for those excluded from them they seemed to be sources of anxiety as to the meaning and potential for deviant behaviour of such cliques.

With each successive panic a further element was added to the list of possible delinquent activities. The Teds were associated with violence right from the outset, the mods and rockers with mob violence and confrontation. The musical sub-cultures of the 1960s era were to bring sharply into focus the changing sexual politics of the period and awareness of mass experimentation in recreational drugs. All of which elicited a considerable judicial and political response, with enhanced powers for the police and criminalisation of the narcotics now associated with popular music. Punk brought fears of the degradation of youth; it was associated with nihilism and obscenity. For some these were the symptoms of a collapsing social fabric in an era of multiple social deprivation and mass youth unemployment.

The collision of all of these fears can be seen in the response to the 'acid house' scene. Rave was seemingly pre-programmed to be deviant. It had emerged out of the sexual and drug *demi-monde*. It was inherently hedonistic with pleasure at its heart and ecstasy a pillar of the scene. It exploited darkness to find a place to party. It sought to stay ahead of the authorities by exploiting technology and the transport system, but in doing so aggravated and mobilised powerful local and national vested interests to crack down in an unprecedented manner on the pay-party scene.

From the dance halls to the beaches of seaside resorts to the hard shoulder of the M25, each generation had its own arena of moral conflict in which anxieties and fears about behaviour, morality and civility were discussed and challenged and where popular music was the dominant cause for concern. We can see that these panics generated larger debates about the influences which shaped the behaviour of young people and, in a particular context, about the growing power of shared youth culture as a force in society.

Notes

1. *House of Commons Debates*, 17 January 1997, Vol. 288, c. 526.
2. *House of Commons Debates*, 8 November 1989, Vol. 159, c. 97.
3. A.J. Ivakhiv (2001) *Claiming Sacred Ground: Pilgrims and Politics at Glastonbury and Sedona* (Bloomington: Indiana University Press), p. 89.
4. *The Times*, 3 June 1985, p. 3.
5. K. Thompson (1998) *Moral Panics* (London: Routledge); S. Ungar (2001) 'Moral Panic versus the Risk Society: The Implications of the Changing Sites of Social Anxiety', *British Journal of Sociology*, Vol. 52 (June), pp. 271–91; P.A.J. Waddington (1986) 'Mugging as a Moral Panic: A Question of Proportion', *British Journal of Sociology*, Vol. 37 (June), pp. 245–59.
6. S. Cohen (2011, Kindle edition) *Folk Devils and Moral Panics* (London: Routledge), Loc. 417.
7. See A. McRobbie and S.L. Thornton (1995) 'Rethinking "Moral Panic" for Multi-Mediated Social Worlds', *British Journal of Sociology*, Vol. 46 (December), pp. 559–74.

8. See E. Goode and N. Ben-Yehuda (2009) *Moral Panics: The Social Construction of Deviance* (Oxford: Wiley-Blackwell), Second Edition.

9. McRobbie and Thornton (1995) 'Rethinking "Moral Panic" for Multi-Mediated Social Worlds', p. 572.

10. Y. Jewkes, (2011) *Media and Crime* (London: Sage), p. 85.

11. S. Chibnall (1977) *Law-and-Order News* (London: Tavistock Publications).

12. For example the already discussed Jewkes, *Media and Crime.*

13. J. Curran (2002) 'Media and the Making of British Society, c.1700–2000', *Media History,* Vol. 8, No. 2, pp. 135–54.

14. *Ibid.*, p. 135.

15. *Ibid.*

16. *Ibid.*

17. Cohen (2011) *Folk Devils and Moral Panics.*

18. Howard Becker has characterised the authorities in these instances as 'moral entrepreneurs' – see H. Becker (1997) *Outsiders: Studies in the Sociology of Deviance* (London: Simon and Schuster), p. 179.

19. *The Times*, 2 July 1965, p. 15.

20. Ministry of Education (1947) *School and Life Report of the Central Advisory Council for Education (England)* (London: HMSO), pp. 83–87.

21. D. Fowler (1995) *The First Teenagers: The Lifestyle of Young Wage-Earners in Interwar Britain* (London: Woburn Press), p. 93.

22. *Ibid.*, p.100.

23. Quote from Dr Farrell in B. Morton (1993) 'The World of Popular Music', in C. Bloom (ed.) *Literature and Culture in Modern Britain* – Volume One: 1900–1929 (London: Longman), pp. 215–41 at p. 227.

24. *Ibid.*, p. 189 and p. 190.

25. *The Times*, 1 January 1931, p. 9.

26. Morton (1993) 'The World of Popular Music', p. 187.

27. *The Times*, 4 June 1928, p. 19.

28. *Ibid.*, 6 October 1928, p. 9.

29. *Ibid.*, 6 March 1934, p. 11.

30. J. Savage (2008) *Teenage: The Creation of Youth – 1875–1945* (London: Pimlico), pp. 416–17.

31. Report of the Senior Shore Patrol Officer to Commanding Officer, Marine Barracks, USOB, quoted in L. McCormick (2006) '"One Yank and They Are Off": Interaction between US Troops and Northern Irish Women, 1942–1945', *Journal of the History of Sexuality*, Vol. 15, No. 2, pp. 228–57 at p. 237.

32. *The Billboard*, 24 November 1945, p. 88.

33. D. Butler and G. Butler (2000) *Twentieth-Century British Political Facts* (Basingstoke: Palgrave Macmillan), p. 366.
34. Department of Employment (1971) *British Labour Statistics and Historical Abstract 1886–1968* (London: HMSO), pp. 116–17.
35. S. Cohen and P. Rock (1970) 'The Teddy Boy', in V. Bogdanor and R. Skidelsky (eds) *The Age of Affluence* (Oxford: Macmillan), pp. 288–320 at p. 288.
36. *Ibid.*
37. *Daily Mirror*, 15 September 1953, p. 1.
38. R. Ferris and J. Lord (2012, Kindle edition) *Teddy Boys: A Concise History* (London: Milo), Loc. 63.
39. P. Horn (2010) *Young Offenders* (London: Amberley), p. 211.
40. H.D. Willcock (1949) *Report on Juvenile Delinquency* (London: Mass Observation Society) and King George's Jubilee Trust (1954) *Citizens of To-morrow: A Study of the Influences Affecting the Upbringing of Young People* (London: Odhams Press).
41. D. Kynaston (2009) *Family Britain, 1951–57*. (London: Bloomsbury), p. 654.
42. *House of Commons Debates*, 11 April 1961, Vol. 638, c. 72.
43. Wotton Committee (1961) *The Youth Service in England and Wales* (London: HMSO), p. 36.
44. Cohen (2011) *Folk Devils and Moral Panics*, passim.
45. C. Bloom (2014) 'Teenage Rampage: Mods vs Rockers', *History Today*, Vol. 64, No. 7 from http://www.historytoday.com/clive-bloom/teenage-rampage-mods-vs-rockers-1964 (Accessed 30th June 2015).
46. *The Times*, 30 March 1964, p. 8.
47. *Ibid.*
48. *Evening Argus*, 18 May 1964, p. 1.
49. B. Osgerby (1998) *Youth in Britain since 1945* (Oxford, Blackwell), p. 42.
50. *Daily Sketch*, 18 May 1964, p. 1. *Daily Mirror* 18 May 1964, p. 1.
51. *The Times*, 1 April 1964, p. 10.
52. For more on this see S. Mitchell (2002) 'The Conservative Party and the Threat of Rebellious Youth, 1963–64', *Journal of Contemporary History*, Vol. 4, pp. 1–10.
53. *The Times*, 18 August 1964, p. 1.
54. *Ibid.*, 22 May 1964, p. 7.
55 *Ibid.*
56. *House of Commons Debates*, 1 March 1956, Vol. 549, cc. 1387.
57. Cohen (2011) *Folk Devils and Moral Panics*, p. 1.

58. *The Times*, 22 May 1964, p. 7.
59. *New Statesman*, 28 January 1964 quoted in Osgerby (1998) *Youth in Britain since 1945*, p. 59.
60. *Time Magazine*, 15 April 1966.
61. *The Times*, 5 August 1966, p. 8.
62. See T. Fukuya (2011) *The Beatles' Untold Tokyo Story* (Tokyo: Fukuya).
63. P. Norman (2003) *Shout!: The True Stories of the Beatles* (London: Sidgwick and Jackson), p. 267.
64. P. Norman (2013) *Mick Jagger* (London: Harper Collins), p. 218.
65. *The Times*, 2 July 1965, p. 15.
66. *The Times*, 18 March 1967, p. 1.
67. Dangerous Drugs Act 1964, c. 36; Drugs (Prevention of Misuse) Act 1964, c. 64.
68. *House of Lords Debates*, 4 August 1966, Vol. 276, cc. 1461–65.
69. Dangerous Drugs Act 1967, c. 82.
70. The Misuse of Drugs Act 1971, c. 38.
71. K. Richards (2010) *Life* (New York: Back Bay), p. 225.
72. D. Sandbrook (2003) *White Heat, 1964–1970* (London: Little Brown), p. 526.
73. J. Savage (2001 edition) *England's Dreaming: Sex Pistols and Punk Rock* (London: Faber and Faber), p. 34.
74. K. Gildart (2013) *Images of England through Popular Music* (Basingstoke: Palgrave), p. 179.
75. *Ibid.*, p. 191.
76. *Ibid.*, p. 179.
77. *Ibid.*, p. 178.
78. M. Cloonan (1996) *Banned: Censorship of Popular Music in Britain* (Aldershot: Arena), p. 68.
79. Savage (2001) *England's Dreaming*, p. 349.
80. *Ibid.*, p. 358.
81. For a full discussion of the DIY ethos read M. Perry (2011) *Sniffin' Glue: And Other Rock 'n' Roll Habits* (London: Omnibus) and R. King (2012) *How Soon Is Now? The Madmen and Mavericks Who Made Independent Music 1975–2005* (London: Faber and Faber).
82. *The Times*, 25 November 1977, p. 2.
83. Savage (2001) *England's Dreaming*, p. 425.
84. *Ibid.*
85. M. Cloonan (1996) *Banned: Censorship of Popular Music in Britain*, pp. 77–79.
86. *Ibid.*, p. 81.

87. K. Kearns (1979) 'Intra Urban Squatting in London', *Annals of the Association of American Geographers*, Vol. 69, No. 4 (December 1979), pp. 589–98, p. 589.

88. P. Gilbert (2004*) Passion Is a Fashion: The Real Story of the Clash* (London: Aurum), p. 20; J. Lydon (2014, Kindle edition) *Anger Is an Energy: My Life Uncensored* (London: Simon and Schuster), Loc. 1059.

89. Quoted in N. Waites and C. Wolmar (eds) (1980) *Squatting: The Real Story* (London: Bayleaf Books), p. 14.

90. I. Glasper (2014) *The Day the Country Died* (Oakland: PM Press), p. 8.

91. M. Worley (2012) 'Shot by Both Sides: Punk, Politics and the End of Consensus', *Contemporary British History*, Vol. 26, No. 3, pp. 333–54 at p. 345.

92. *House of Commons Debates,* 16 April 1981, Vol. 3, cc. 472–78.

93. See M. Worley (2013) 'Oi! Oi! Oi!: Class, Locality, and British Punk', *Twentieth Century British History*, Vol. 24, No. 4, pp. 606–36 and Glasper (2014) *The Day the Country Died,* passim.

94. See R. Bramwell (2015) *UK Hip-Hop, Grime and the City: The Aesthetics and Ethics of London's Rap Scenes* (London: Routledge); Cloonan (1996) *Banned: Censorship of Popular Music in Britain,* pp. 87–95.

95. M. Worley (2015) 'Punk, Politics and British (Fan)zines, 1976–84: "While the World Was Dying, Did You Wonder?"', *History Workshop Journal*, Vol. 79, pp. 76–106, p. 100.

96. All three titles are produced independently.

97. See for example P. Guralnick's two-volume biography of Elvis Presley (1995) *Last Train to Memphis* and (2000) *Careless Love* (London: Abacus); D. McNally (2003) *A Long Strange Trip: The Inside History of the Grateful Dead* (London: Corgi) and C. Granata (2003) *I Just Wasn't Made for These Times: Brian Wilson and the Making of Pet Sounds* (London: Unanimous).

98. G. Altschuler (2003) *All Shook Up: How Rock and Roll Changed America* (Oxford: Oxford University Press).

99. Gildart (2013) *Images of England,* p. 5.

100. *Ibid.,* p. 17.

101. Cohen (2011) *Folk Devils and Moral Panics,* passim.

102. D. Hebdige (1979) *Subculture: The Meaning of Style* (London: Routledge), passim.

103. Becker (1997) *Outsiders,* passim.

104. S. Hall and T. Richardson (eds) (1975) *Resistance through Rituals: Youth Subcultures in Post-war Britain* (London: Routledge), passim.

105. S. Reynolds (2008, Kindle edition) *Energy Flash: A Journey through Rave Music and Dance Culture* (London: Faber and Faber), Loc. 1077.

106. *The Sun*, 26 June 1989, p. 1. See J. Ward (2015) *Flashback: Drugs and Dealing in the Golden Age of the London Rave Scene* (London: Routledge).

107. For the evolution of house music and its technical aspects see S. Reynolds (2008) *Energy Flash,* Chapter 1.

108. M. Collin (2010) *Altered State: The Story of Ecstasy, Culture and Acid House* (London: Profile Books), p. 46.

109. R. Davenport-Hines (2001) *The Pursuit of Oblivion: A Global History of Narcotics 1500–2000* (London: Weidenfeld & Nicolson), p. 389.

110. *Ibid.*

111. *Ibid.*

112. *Ibid.*

113. For more on this see S.R. Hutson (1999) 'Technoshamism: Spiritual Healing in the Rave Subculture', *Popular Music in Society*, Vol. 23, No. 3, pp. 55–77.

114. S. Reynolds (2008) *Energy Flash*, Loc. 1077.

115. *Ibid.*, Loc. 1209.

116. *Boy's Own* was self-published in London by Terry Farley, Cymon Eckel and Andrew Weatherall calling themselves the Karma Collective, and it was produced from 1986 until 1992. A complete collection of the fanzine was published by DJbooks.com in 2014.

117. See for example M.C. Flux (2015) *Dirty MC Flux: The Confessions of a Reformed Drug Addict and Soccer Hooligan Who Made It Big on the Dance Scene* (London: Merco).

118. Collin (2010) *Altered State*, p. 90.

119. *Ibid.*, p. 65.

120. *The Times,* 7 November 1988, p. 2.

121. *The Sun*, 26 June 1989, p. 1.

122. *The Sun*, 12 October 1988, p. 15.

123. Collin (2010) *Altered State, p. 91.*

124. *Ibid.*, p. 95.

125. The first was in 1967 – it was another example of the conscious modelling of the rave scene on the counterculture of the '60s.

126. *The Times*, 21 September 1989, p. 2.

127. For a more detailed study of this see the essays in B. Fine and R. Millar (1985) (eds) *Policing the Miners' Strike* (London: Lawrence and Wishart).

128. *The Times*, 17 October 1989, p. 13.

129. *The Times*, 30 March 1989, p. 2.

130. *The Times*, 4 August 1989, p. 4.

131. *The Times,* 25 September 1989, p. 7.

132. *The Times*, 5 October, 1989, p. 1.
133. *The Times*, 17 October 1989, p. 2.
134. *Ibid.*
135. *House of Commons Debates*, 9 March 1990, Vol. 168, cc. 1121–22.
136. Collin (2010) *Altered State*, p. 116.
137. *Ibid.*, p. 124.
138. Worley (2012) 'Shot by Both Sides', p. 348.
139. See Osgerby (1998) *Youth in Britain since 1945,* pp. 91–95.
140. P. Staines (1991) 'Acid House Parties against the Lifestyle Police and the Safety Nazis', *Political Notes – The Libertarian Alliance*, Vol. 55, p. 1.
141. *Ibid.*, p. 4.
142. http://www.bbc.co.uk/news/uk-24971287 (Accessed 29th September 2015).
143. Collin (2010) *Altered State*, p. 127.
144. Reynolds (2008) *Energy Flash*, Loc. 1675.
145. Criminal Justice Act and Public Order 1994, London, 1994 c.33 Clause 63.
146. The Public Entertainment Licenses (Drugs Misuse) Act, London, 1997, c.49.
147. *The Times*, 15 November 1995, p. 6.

8

Organised Crime, Criminality and the 'Gangster'

Heather Shore

1. Introduction

In October 2013, the National Crime Agency became operational. Launched to deal with the United Kingdom's most serious organised crime, it replaced the Serious Organised Crime Agency that had been founded in 2006. According to a statement on the agency's website, the 'NCA is a new crime-fighting agency with national and international reach and the mandate and powers to work in partnership with other law enforcement organisations to bring the full weight of the law to bear in cutting serious and organised crime'.[1] Such developments in the governmental organisation of crime control are a relatively recent development. Hence, the criminologist Dick Hobbs has problematised the way in which the British government and the police have presented organised crime as 'a distinctly contemporary phenomenon, a malady of modernity, and the consequence of recent human activity'.[2] This is a position often echoed by historians and by criminologists. For example, Alan Wright has argued that contemporary organised crime is distinctive from its predecessors, 'Global drug markets, international fraud and other forms of enterprise crime make the old forms redundant'.[3] The impact of globalisation and the rapid development of the Internet on the ability to traffic illegally in all sorts of commodities (money, goods, sex, pornography, people) has substantially altered the organised crime environment.

Historians too have seen organised crime as something of recent provenance. Clive Emsley has pointed to the last third of the twentieth century as a period in which the term 'organised crime' began to be used more frequently in England, implicitly linking the increasing public perception of organised crime to the process of globalisation since the end of the Cold War.[4] Consequently few historians have attempted to address the history of British organised crime.[5] For instance, Alyson Brown has focussed on the serious criminality of interwar criminals; Stefan Slater has written on organised vice; and Mark Roodhouse has explored the impact of the black market around the period of the Second World War.[6] Part of the explanation for the dearth of studies on the development of British organised crime in the twentieth century is not only due to lack of access to archives (for example, in the case of criminal offences the National Archives are closed for the remainder of the lifetime of the individuals involved) but perhaps more significantly the lack of clarity and paucity of definition as to what organised crime means and/or involves.

This chapter will provide some insight into the ways in which those definitions have evolved in Britain during the twentieth century. Part of the problem is the dual nature of organised crime. On one hand, we can trace a chronology of British organised crime that has been helpfully mapped out in recent decades by true-crime writers. On the other hand, much of the organisation of crime remains unknowable and undetected. The 'history' of organised crime is largely based on what we know of those individuals, families and institutions identified and defined by law enforcers, politicians and the press as being organised in nature. This chapter will be constructed of three sections. The first will provide a chronological overview, focussing on the development of the key forms associated with British organised crime. The second section will explore historiographical and criminological approaches. The limited nature of historical research in this area has already been noted. However, this section will also consider the development of the problematic true-crime genre, which has been largely responsible in providing an organised crime 'narrative' on which both historians and criminologists have relied. The third and concluding section will further explore the issues raised in the preceding sections by using two case studies: the first focussing on the gambling and protection rackets connected to the racecourses during the interwar period and the second, on the rise of project crime from the 1950s and '60s.

2. Chronology

The definition of organised crime is far from clear cut. Alan Wright has suggested that there might be a distinction between the ways in which crimes, such as burglary for example, are organised and what we might think of as more professional organised crime activity.[7] Referring to historically contextual definitions, Clive Emsley has suggested that the 'professional criminal', a term which was used from the later nineteenth century, 'was someone of ability who had made a rational choice in his way of life and who skilfully used the expanding opportunities provided by faster communication and new technology'.[8] Hence, the terminology of the 'professional', the 'career criminal' and the organisation of crime were frequently associated with the processes of modernity. Originally the term 'organised crime' was used in connection with terrorism, and particularly in relation to events in Ireland in the 1880s when Fenian activity in Britain had escalated. The language was adopted from the late Victorian period to describe forms of organised rebellion and 'thuggery' and this connection to terrorism continued to be a feature throughout the twentieth century. Thus, by the interwar period, the press frequently referred to the outbreak of racecourse crime in terms of 'terrorism', 'insurrection', 'vendettas' and 'espionage'.[9] By the end of the nineteenth century, the term would be used more specifically to denote systematic criminality. In 1891 Robert Anderson, the Assistant Commissioner of Police, wrote about organised crime in the *Contemporary Review*, noting that 'organized and systematic crime might be stamped out in a single generation'.[10] Anderson suggested a 'crusade against crime', which defined organised crime as something deeply connected to society, to families and to the structures and practices of the criminal justice system.

However, it was not until the interwar years that new paradigms of professional criminality would evolve in public and print discourses and references to organised crime became more prevalent. As Alyson Brown has noted in reference to the 1920s, 'the "motor-bandit" and "smash-and-grab" raiders, were often depicted as new and "modern"; more ruthless and calculating, more inured in crime than their predecessors and more exciting'.[11] This focus on 'new' forms of criminality was reflected in the memoirs of former detectives, which were increasingly common during this period.[12] In such writings, new methods and forms of criminality were closely associated with the organisation and planning of crime. In 1933, ex-Divisional Detective Charles Leach would describe the 'new criminal' of the post-war period:

> brought up on the 'movies' and the 'dogs'; daily swelling the growing army of the new-style criminal, the 'smash-and-grab' artists, the 'cat-burglars', the motor-bandits, the confidence-tricksters, the Legion of the Lost who bend to their nefarious uses the latest attainments of Science as fast as the picked brains of the country evolve them.[13]

Nevertheless, the majority of gang crime in this period adhered to traditional forms relating to gambling, protection, violence and territoriality. As the first case study in this chapter demonstrates, there was wide reporting in the press about violent gang conflicts that broke out on the streets of London and the racecourses of the southeast. There was also significant concern about gang warfare in Sheffield during the 1920s and in Glasgow during the 1930s.[14] However, these concerns were arguably shaped by events in North America. By the early 1930s, the real-life organised crime conflicts of New York and Chicago were being re-interpreted by Hollywood for a worldwide audience. The 'gangster' made his entrance into popular culture and became the personification of the organised criminal.[15]

The American 'gangster' was not the only perceived external influence on British organised crime. At various points in the twentieth century, organised crime was constructed as a problem associated with external forces; not least through the lens of immigration. In part, this was associated with the Jewish immigration of the late nineteenth century. Thus the 'alien criminal' would emerge from immigration 'hotspots', such as East London, and largely from poor Jewish communities. For example, there was concern in the early 1900s about Russian and Polish Jewish gangs. The Bessarabians were mentioned by George Sims in 'Alien-Land', the first chapter of his 1911 publication *Off the Track in London*.[16] They are also widely cited in the context of organised crime in popular histories of gangland. However, the murder that is most famously associated with the Bessarabian Society, as they are referred to, that of Henry Brodovitz at the York Minster Music Hall in November 1902, may have been motivated by internal tensions within the immigrant community rather than by organised crime conflicts.[17] Nevertheless, the context of alienism and the fear of the alien criminal would profoundly shape the construction of press attitudes to organised crime for much of the twentieth century.[18] The 'racecourse wars' discussed below were frequently associated with Anglo-Italian and Jewish communities. Moreover, the cocaine trade of the interwar years, sensationalised through the deaths in 1919 of actress Billie Carleton and in 1922 of dancer Freda Kempton, were understood by contemporaries as intrinsically linked to the alien criminal. In the Kempton case, this was typified by involvement of the flamboyant Anglo-Chinese 'Brilliant' Billy Chang, who would later be sentenced to 14 months imprisonment for drug dealing in 1924, followed by deportation.[19] The trope of alien criminality continued to be linked to immigrants and immigrant communities in the second half of the twentieth century. The Maltese Messina brothers established a prostitution empire in the West End from the interwar period. In the post-war, new groups of immigrants became the target of press and police discourses that linked immigration and criminality. The apparent infiltration of gangs of Yardies and Triads into British society would be associated with immigration from the Caribbean and in urban British Chinese communities in the 1950s. However, at least in the case of the Yardies, Alan Wright sees them originating from the politically charged context of Jamaica in the 1980s, who extended their activities to the international drug trade.[20]

Whilst there were concerns about British gangsterdom in the interwar period, home-grown organised crime was still largely associated with local, territorial groupings with interests in gambling and protection markets. Arguably this began to change from the 1930s. As Dick Hobbs has argued, 'What is normally referred to as "the underworld" relates to the West End of London, Soho, during the late 1930s to the early 1970s, and to extortion and the economic relations of prostitution, gambling, and illegal drinking clubs'.[21] As well as the Messina brothers, this involved 'hardmen' such as Jack 'Spot' Comer, Billy Hill, Albert Dimes and Ruby Sparks, who were active from the 1930s through to the post-war period. The overlapping criminal networks with which these men were involved would have a lasting impact. For instance, in the 1930s, Jack Comer was involved in battles over territory with the White family, who had succeeded the Sabini family in running bookmaking pitches at greyhound and horseracing tracks. He was also apparently involved in an attempted raid on Heathrow Airport in July 1948, which was foiled by the Flying Squad.[22] Billy Hill was a contemporary, associate and subsequent adversary of Comer. Whilst Hill had been active prior to the war, it was the opportunities and entrepreneurial possibilities of the black market during the Second World War which really accelerated his criminal 'career'.[23] Notably, he worked with the zoo owner and gambling club host John Aspinall, at whose casino, the Clermont Club, Hill ran a successful criminal scam defrauding its wealthy clients.[24] Albert Dimes was an Anglo-Italian enforcer from Clerkenwell who had been linked to the Sabini family and was a close associate of Billy Hill.[25] Charles John Sparks, popularly known as 'Ruby', was a burglar and smash-and-grab robber who had also been involved in the notorious Dartmouth Prison Mutiny of 1932.[26] Sparks would work briefly with Hill after another escape from Dartmoor in 1940. Both Comer and Hill were characteristic of the metropolitan hardmen who would predominate the public view of 'gangland' by the post-war period. Certainly, both men were notable for their self-aggrandisement. For example, Comer had his biography written by the pulp-fiction novelist Stephen D. Frances, better known as Hank Janson, and Hill had his biography ghostwritten by the crime correspondent of *The People*, Duncan Webb.[27]

Whilst London was home to groups associated with Hill, Comer and their contemporaries, in the decade after the Second World War, gangs involved in gambling and localised protection rackets were identified in many British cities. For example, Glasgow, which had had a significant gang problem in the 1920s and '30s, was apparently the domain of Arthur Thompson in the post-war period.[28] By the 1950s, the nature of organised crime was changing. Organised robbery involving fire-arms planned and undertaken by groups of 'career' criminals seemed to mark a shift in practices from the 1950s and '60s. Billy Hill was particularly associated with 'project crime' that became a major problem in the 1960s and '70s, due to the easing of financial regulations after the war and what seemed to be the willingness of criminals to use extreme violence. Moreover, criminal entrepreneurs would increasingly supplement the local rackets with which they had traditionally been involved with these more ambitious and larger-scale robberies. Hill was believed to be involved in planning one of the early planned robberies in 1952, the Eastcastle Street robbery, in which the robbers escaped with £287,000.[29] The financial rewards escalated in pace with the ambition and violence deployed by robbers in such crimes, and robberies such as the Great Train Robbery of 1963 and that of the Brinks-Mat warehouse at Heathrow in 1983 epitomised the 'project crimes' of the period, which are discussed in the second case study below.

Whilst 'project crimes' have been defined as involving confederacies of career criminals, family-based crime groups such as the Kray twins of East London and the Richardsons of South London dominate discussions of organised crime in the 1960s.[30] The 'family firms' of this period have been the subject of numerous autobiographies and true-crime studies, and a significant mythology has developed around their activities and legacy. In many ways Reginald and Ronald Kray were carrying on in the tradition of their predecessors Hill, Comer and Dimes, and were involved in the provision of 'protection' and in the club scene of the West End. However, the Krays and the Richardsons were also known for their involvement in Long-Firm frauds. This type of crime involves obtaining goods on credit then disappearing before paying, and selling the goods on to make an illegal profit.[31] Although frauds like this had existed previously, the profits from such crimes were significant by the 1960s; James Morton has suggested that such frauds could expect to net up to £150,000.[32]

During the 1960s, until their final arrest in 1968, the Krays combined their Long-Firm frauds with reputations for violence and the running of their Knightsbridge club, Esmeralda's Barn. As Hobbs has noted, the twins' high-society connections gave them a certain invulnerability which they took every opportunity of flaunting: 'As the 1960s progressed the twins became more impudent in their confrontations with authority.'[33] However, inevitably, internecine power struggles would result in a series of deaths, most notably of George Cornell in 1966 and Jack 'The Hat' McVitie in 1967. The twins were finally arrested in a police investigation led by Scotland Yard Detective Leonard 'Nipper' Read in May 1968.[34] They were tried at the Old Bailey in March 1969, receiving life imprisonment for the murders of Cornell and McVitie.[35]

Whilst other criminal groups, including family firms like the Nash, Dixon and Tibbs gangs attempted to fill the vacuum left by the demise of the brothers, many commentators have seen the prosecutions of the Krays and the Richardsons (who had been arrested in 1966) as marking the end of an era.[36] Alan Wright notes that before the 1970s, 'it was still possible to identify clear links with the "underworld" represented by the Sabinis, Jack 'Spot' Corner and Billy Hill'.[37] In the late decades of the twentieth century in contrast, organised crime relationships were characterised by new forms of criminal enterprise which had ambitions and reach far beyond the predominately local territories of their predecessors. The increasing globalisation of technology, transportation and finance has been mirrored in the growth of new types of enterprise crime. In particular, this meant the growth of the market in drugs. By the 1980s and '90s, a growing demand for drugs in the British night-time economy provided significant openings and opportunities for local groups of criminals, whom by their involvement in drug trafficking became participants in international organised crime markets. Some vestiges of the older model of the 'family firm' remained, and the break between older traditions of extortion and fraud and newer forms of criminal enterprise are far from clear cut.[38]

The Adams family, also known as 'The A team' or the 'Clerkenwell crime syndicate', apparently controlled London crime in the 1980s and '90s, but were alleged to have had dealings with South American drug cartels.[39] The most prolific drug-trafficker in the 1990s was Curtis 'Cocky' Warren who had started as a petty criminal in the street gangs of Liverpool and became the only criminal to have featured on *The Sunday Times* rich list.[40] Warren had connections with Colombian, Turkish, Moroccan and European drugs producers and became the main drug supplier in Britain, moving shipments of cocaine, ecstasy and heroin.

He was arrested by the Dutch police at his home in Sassenheim, in the Western Netherlands, where the police found 'three guns, ammunition hand grenades and crates with gas canisters, 1500 kilos of heroin, 50 kilos of ecstasy and $600,000 in cash'.[41]

3.   Historiography

An academic history of organised crime in twentieth-century Britain does not exist. Partly this is to do with the problematic issues of definition, discussed briefly in the introduction. Consequently, this section will look at three strands in the broader writing and research on organised crime. The first part will focus on the limited amount of work that has been done by historians that (at least loosely) relates to organised crime. The second part will briefly outline some of the key models constructed by criminologists, particularly those who have been historically sensitive to development of organised crime. The final part will consider the proliferation of true-crime during the later twentieth century considering the impact it has had on both historians' and criminologists' explorations of organised crime.

In an article that spans both history and criminology, Philip Jenkins and Gary W. Potter argue that the relative lack of historical studies can be attributed to the dominance of North American structures of organised crime.[42] During the 1960s and '70s, American criminologists saw British organised crime as far more rudimentary, and much less evolved, in comparison to the American context. Joseph Albini, an expert on American and international organised crime, argued that 'Britain had very little organized criminality, either past or present'.[43] Whilst this view has substantially altered, and historians have started to illuminate criminal networks in past urban societies, a more consistent historical analysis remains patchy.[44]

Clive Emsley, in an historical overview of organised crime, notes the important influence of American models, as well as the development of the idea of the 'professional criminal', and the connections made between organised crime and immigrant communities from the late nineteenth and early twentieth centuries similar to North American patterns in the early twentieth century.[45] However, Emsley also points to some forms of organised crime that may be more distinct to the British example, in particular he singles out the importance of the impact of the Second World War on the home front, and the relationship between the armed forces and the black market and other forms of racketeering.[46] The significance of the Second World War is also demonstrated by Mark Roodhouse's work on the black market, which focuses on case studies of Essex and Northern Ireland in order to investigate just how much black market activity there was in Britain both during and after the war. However, Roodhouse argues that the media accusations linking the black market with organised crime were often misplaced: 'Thanks to media portrayals … the public, and on occasion officials, came to associate this "black market" with organized crime, though most black marketing involved established businesses developing an illicit side-line'.[47] In contrast petty criminality and minor fiddles were more characteristic.

In the 1950s, Billy Hill waxed lyrical about the war and its opportunities in his modestly titled biography, *Boss of Britain's Underworld*: 'Some day someone should write a treatise on Britain's wartime black market. It was the most fantastic side of civil life in wartime'.[48] In that book, published in 1955, Hill positioned himself in the pantheon of criminal hardmen, casting his glance back to the 'mobs' of the 1920s. The most notorious, or certainly the most written about, criminal family during the interwar period was the Sabini family, who are discussed below in the first case study. The Sabini gang, as they were known, was headed by Charles 'Darby' Sabini and consisted of several his brothers, as well other members of the Italian community in Clerkenwell. Recent research on the Sabini gang has positioned them very specifically in the context of the post-war concerns about crime, alienism and Englishness.[49] It would be the perceived foreignness of the Sabinis, and also of East End Jewish bookmakers such as Edward Emmanuel, which would confirm the connections made in the press between organised criminal activity and 'the alien'. *The Times* commented on the number of 'Italians and Foreign Jews' present during a fight at Greenford Trotting Track in April 1921.[50] Whilst the Sabinis were rooted very much in their local communities, their enterprises on the racetracks, and in bookmaking, protectionism, and the accusations of police corruption, had a strong similarity to the crime syndicates of transatlantic gangsters.[51] Nevertheless, using the terminology of organised crime to describe the racecourse gangs remains contentious.

Alyson Brown has investigated the criminal lives of men who were inmates in Dartmoor prison in the early 1930s. Some of these men had connections to the London gangs. Brown also traced connections between other London-based criminals, including the notorious Ruby Sparks, who (along with his girlfriend Lillian Goldstein) specialised in 'smash-and-grab' crime.[52] However, Brown is wary of assuming the widespread influence of organised criminality in Dartmoor. She suggests that the more violent, organised criminals tended to stand out because they had 'attained a level of official and public notoriety'.[53] Having said this, Brown argues that the maintenance and continuity of criminal networks whilst in Dartmoor does seem to have been more marked amongst the London prisoners, such networks 'appear to have been quite loose affiliations based on fragmented networks and friendship'.[54] Similarly, Heather Shore notes in relation to the racecourse gangs, the 'fundamentally loose nature of these alliances, with men switching allegiances, or groups joining forces when territorial concerns shifted'.[55]

By the late 1920s transatlantic comparisons were increasingly marked.[56] Events in interwar Glasgow drew vivid comparisons to Chicago.[57] Such comparisons were not entirely misplaced. Andrew Davies's detailed analysis of the Glasgow gangs and the growth of racketeering during the 1930s shows that there was evidence of systematic extortion and protection rackets run by some of the most powerful gangs: the Billy Boys, the Kent Star and the Beehive Boys. However, as his account makes very clear, the picture is confused by the role of the press, both locally and nationally. Thus, in the early 1930s the London-based *John Bull*, published its account of 'Glasgow's Reign of Terror', cementing the impression that Glasgow was Britain's very own Chicago.[58] Davies's work is extremely valuable in providing one of the only detailed insights into how violence and criminality can become intertwined in young working-class men's (and some women's) lives. Work on Sheffield by J.P. Bean paints a very similar picture in terms of the networks that developed around gambling interests and territory, also in the interwar period.[59] Not coincidentally, the Sheffield gangs had been suppressed by Percy Sillitoe in the late 1920s, who went on to become the Chief Constable of Glasgow between 1931 and 1943. Sillitoe's self-perpetuated image as the gang-busting cop undoubtedly contributed to Glasgow's reputation for hardness.[60] Nevertheless, Davies does see Glasgow as distinct, pointing to the density of the urban experience, the impact of long-term unemployment and the specific influence of persistent sectarianism (and with it, violence) in the city.[61]

Whilst the violence linked to gambling and protectionism in interwar Glasgow, London and Sheffield has been subject to historical investigation, the historiography of other strands of organised crime in twentieth-century Britain has been less significant. Two themes in the evolution of 'modern' British organised crime have been the underground commodification of drugs and vice. The latter has been the subject of Stefan Slater's work on prostitution in interwar London. Slater questions some of the mythology around the trade in foreign prostitutes during the interwar period. Concern about foreign prostitutes and white slavery had escalated in the 1930s when two murdered prostitutes were linked to a Latvian pimp, Max Kassel, who was 'believed to be a leader of an international gang of white slave traffickers'.[62] Slater understands such anxieties in the context of broader concerns about immigration, and particularly in relation to the apparent convergence of vice and criminality in Soho, an area with a 'reputation as the habitus of foreigners and a den of vice'.[63] He also points to the importance of the Messina brothers in reinforcing this connection. Despite the significance given to the Messinas' vice empire in many true-crime histories of the underworld: 'Even at the pinnacle of their influence, the Messinas had not much more than 20 prostitutes under their control'.[64] Again, the confluence of sensationalist journalism, public fears and anxieties about 'foreignness' is apparent. This trinity also shapes the concerns about drug-taking and distribution in the interwar period.

Drug control policies in Britain and in the United States date from the early twentieth century. In Britain, regulation grew in part in response to moral panics about cocaine during the interwar period.[65] Whilst Jenkins and Potter have described Soho between the wars as 'the heart of London's drug underworld', this may be a problematic view.[66] Certainly, as Marek Kohn's history has shown, the drug problem was largely written about (and indeed policed) in the context of its perceived connection to 'alien' criminality in the shape of drug dealers such as Brilliant 'Billy' Chang and Edgar Manning. As Lucy Bland has argued, these cases also reflected fears about miscegenation, demonstrated in press coverage of the drug deaths of Billie Carleton and Freda Kempton in 1918 and 1922.[67] This is not to suggest that the organisation of drugs or vice was not prevalent in this period. Paul Knepper has written extensively on the role of the League of Nations and about attempts of contemporaries to grapple with the internationalisation of crime networks, both in the interwar period and in the late Victorian and Edwardian era.[68] However, whilst Knepper posits the importance of late nineteenth-century 'globalisation', he also points to the predominant Western concerns about alien criminality.[69]

As noted in the introduction to this chapter, both historians and criminologists have had occasion to turn to the true-crime genre to fill in the narrative map of British gang crime. True-crime publishing has proliferated from the 1980s. Whilst biographies and memoirs of criminals had been popular in the interwar period, and serious books about murder, such as Truman Capote's *In Cold Blood* (1965) and Norman Mailer's *The Executioners Song* (1979), were landmarks in crime writing, the boom in the British 'gangster' genre is relatively recent.[70] It would arguably be the thirst for publicity by the Kray brothers, Reginald and Ronald, which would feed the demand for true-crime texts about hardmen and professional criminals. In 1967, at the height of their notoriety, they approached writer John Pearson to write their biography. The book that Pearson eventually published in 1972, *The Profession of Violence: The Rise and Fall of the Kray Twins*, was not one that the twins particularly approved of. Whilst it was far from sensational, it can be seen as the blueprint for the wave of true-crime accounts and biographies that would appear over the following decades.[71] The Kray twins have often had a starring role, although other contemporaries are also the subject of such texts that celebrate the hardman, such as Frankie Fraser, Lennie McClean, Freddie Foreman and Bruce Reynolds, the ring-leader of the Great Train Robbery of 1963 described in the second case study below.[72]

The publishing phenomenon of criminal biographies in recent years is not unprecedented; however, the continual and growing popularity of such texts is striking.[73] Former criminal lawyer, James Morton, has contributed significantly with this growth, and has been one of the main authors to provide the historical narrative of British organised crime, along with writers like Robert Murphy and Brian McDonald.[74] Such texts have, to large extent, established the chronological and narrative framework of the British 'underworld'. These books do have some value and often the authors have sourced press accounts and police evidence in an attempt to provide credibility. Indeed, Morton has drawn on the records of the Metropolitan Police in his 'gangland' histories and Brian McDonald has used Old Bailey records. However, they need to be read critically and with some scepticism since their reliability and credibility remains questionable. Evidence is thin or lacking, and there is a tendency to repeat mythologies and indeed to create them. The writing tends to be characterised by a form of hyper-masculinity, the author's 'knowledge' often gained through some proximity or close association to the villains, as Brian McDonald writes in the introduction to *Gangs of London*: 'I am a south Londoner, descended from a celebrated family that inhabited Lambeth and Southwark between the wars and in the years following World War Two, when criminal enterprise had some strange respectability. We knew our villains, even paid homage to some of them, and most people, including the police, accepted them'.[75]

Finally, a significant resource for the more recent history of British crime communities is the work of the criminologist Dick Hobbs.[76] Whilst still reliant on the work of historians and true-crime writers, Hobbs also draws extensively on interviews, providing an ethnographic context to criminal enterprise in the late twentieth century. His most recent book, *Lush Life: Constructing Organised Crime in the UK*, blends ethnography, criminology, history and criminal biography in a detailed survey of British (particularly London-based) organised crime in the twentieth and early twenty-first centuries. He argues that the British concept of organised crime 'should be understood within the context of political change, particularly in forms of global governance, post-industrialisation, unrestrained consumerism, and the intensity of contemporary illegal trading relationships'.[77]

Hobbs notes that the targeting of immigrant cultures predated the use of the term 'organised crime', and that the state responded to fears about alien criminality, by racialising the drug and sex trades and labelling them as organised crime.[78] His discussion of the evolution of what he describes as the 'marquee names of British crime' (including the Sabinis, Billy Hill, Jack Spot Corner, the Krays and the Richardsons) explores the way in which these working-class individuals and groups (often bound by kinship) were essentially entrepreneurs, who exhausted the potential of their own locales by colonising new territories.[79] They did this primarily through violence. Hobbs see the traditional neighbour-hood crime groups as the 'forefathers and cultural chaperones of con-temporary, loose-knit, urban elites', post-industrialisation (from the 1980s) marked a decisive break with the past.[80] However, Hobbs says little about the more recent crime families that have dominated the British organised crime scene, for example the Adams in Clerkenwell and the Noonans in Manchester, as well as individuals like Kenneth Noye in London, Thomas McGraw and Paul Ferris in Glasgow, and Curtis Warren in Liverpool. This suggests that the history of the later twentieth-century evolution of British organised crime, the 'break with the past', remains to be undertaken.

4.   Case Studies

a)   Racecourse Crime

Some of the earliest events to be clearly discussed as organised criminality were the activities of gangs associated with racecourse crime, which became more prevalent from 1919.[81] Racing experienced a surge of popularity dur-ing the post-war period, with attendance at racecourses increasing after 1918.[82] The combination of growing popularity with declining opposition to gambling provided fertile ground for the growth of gambling-related crime. The conflicts involved groups of men from various parts of the country with confrontations frequently taking place on the racecourse, or in close proximity to them. Nevertheless, many of the events described and further investigated by the police took place in local pubs, clubs and streets in London. Indeed, despite the connection to the racecourse, the violence was overwhelmingly perceived as metropolitan.

The criminal activity to which the 'racecourse wars' was collectively applied has some features of organised crime as it has been defined by modern criminologists.[83] Thus they were predominantly territorial conflicts related to the control of gambling and betting on the racecourse, but the evidence suggests that the gangs were involved in a variety of illegal activities, not just betting, protectionism and gambling. The earliest references to problems on the racecourses involving individuals who would go on to be associated with the racecourse wars date from the aftermath of the First World War. In December 1922, an attempt was made by the Metropolitan Police to provide a narrative of key events in the racecourse wars.[84] This account describes a key confrontation between Darby Sabini and the Birmingham Gang (also known as the 'Brummagen Boys') in March 1921, in which Sabini fired a revolver to frighten the Birmingham men off. Sabini was charged with shooting with intent, but acquitted of the offence and fined for possessing a revolver without a permit.[85] The battle lines were roughly drawn between the Sabini gang, also known as the Italian Gang from Clerkenwell, and the Jewish bookmakers on one side and the South London Elephant and Castle Gang and Birmingham Gang on the other.

In June 1921, on returning from a race meeting, the Birmingham men attacked a charabanc carrying bookmakers from Leeds, mistaking them for the Sabinis. This affray became known as the Battle of Epsom, and was widely reported in the national press.[86] By 1922, the violence had escalated, and in that year several confrontations broke out on London streets. For instance, on Good Friday 1922, Elephant and Castle man Fred Gilbert had been slashed at the New Raleigh Club in Jermyn Street, allegedly by members of the 'Italian Gang'.[87] Alfred Solomon, an associate of the Sabinis, was detained, but no further proceedings were taken. Then in July 1922, a confrontation between the 'Birmingham Gang' and 'Italian Gang' broke out on Grays Inn Road. A Detective Rutherford 'happened to be in and about the vicinity ... and endeavoured to effect their arrest'. Rutherford was shot at and several arrests were made of men who were charged with feloniously shooting at a policeman with intent to murder. In August 1922, a further confrontation involving firearms between the 'Italian Gang' and George Sage and Frederick Gilbert (from Camden Town, but affiliated to the Birmingham/Elephant and Castle

Gang) in Mornington Crescent resulted in a number of arrests.[88] Events reached a climax of sorts on the evening of 20th November 1922 when Darby and Harry Sabini were shot at by Augustus and Enrico Cortesi, in the Fratellanza Social Club in Clerkenwell.[89] After the Old Bailey trial of the Cortesi brothers in January 1923, confrontations and affrays continued, however press coverage of the events was rather less vigorous.[90] This would change in September 1924, when Sabini man Alfred Solomon was charged with the murder of a bookmaker named Barnett Blitz in a club shooting.[91] The case was presented as one of self-defence by the defence lawyer, the noted Q.C. Edward Marshall Hall. Solomon had apparently defended himself in a struggle during which Blitz had violently attacked Solomon's associate Edward Emmanuel. Solomon was eventually found guilty of manslaughter and sentenced to three years penal servitude.

The following year saw significant press and political attention to racecourse violence. In particular this would be associated with the crusading Conservative Home Secretary William Joynson Hicks who declared war on the race gangs in the summer of 1925.[92] The *Daily Express* reported on a number of confrontations that had allegedly occurred in London and other parts of the country between March 1924 and August 1925.[93] As a response to these reports, the Commissioner of Police initiated a full investigation into the London affrays which concluded that the *Express* had exaggerated the events and no further action was to be taken.[94]

After the mid-1920s, coverage of the racecourse wars was much more sporadic, although it is probable that there were continuities in gang activity involving networks from the East London, Clerkenwell and Elephant and Castle areas.[95] The newspaper reportage of the gangs, however, was far from the sensational coverage of the key events of the early 1920s. By this time the Bookmakers Association and the Jockey Club had taken measures to more effectively regulate and control betting on the racecourses.[96] Moreover, by the later 1920s, the Sabini gang were much less visible in the British press. Charles Sabini had been threatened with bankruptcy, probably as the result of a failed libel action the previous year.[97] It may be that Sabini's financial problems stymied the family's activities by the later 1920s. Darby Sabini had consolidated his interests in the southeastern racecourses by taking up residence in Hove from

1926. Whilst his brothers remained in London, it may be that removal of the enigmatic Italian gang leader from the metropolis meant that the press lost interest.

Whilst occasional references to racecourse violence, and its main protagonists, would occasionally surface in the 1930s, only in 1936 did the press report racecourse violence with any of their previous vigour. In June 1936, a group of 16 men, described as mostly coming from the Shoreditch, Bethany Green, Hackney and Dalton districts, were charged with frequenting Lewes racecourse to commit felonies.[98] The men were tried at Sussex Assizes and found guilty of wounding Mark Frater, a bookmaker's clerk, and assaulting both Frater and his employer, the bookmaker Alfred Solomon. Both the accused and the victims were men closely connected to the London racing fraternity. According to film historian Steve Chibnall, it was on this event that Graham Greene loosely based his novel, *Brighton Rock*, published in 1938.[99] Another violent confrontation that was widely reported was a fight between two Italian brothers named Camilo and Massimino Monte-Columbo, and a number of other men at the Wandsworth greyhound track. The men that were arrested and charged with the murder were 'racing men' from Clerkenwell – Bert Marsh (also known as Papa Pasquale) and Herbert Wilkins – and they were found guilty of manslaughter at the Old Bailey on 17th of November 1936.[100] In the press, the fight was presented as a result of a quarrel within the Italian gang.[101]

Despite the tendency in the press to isolate these events as the 'racecourse wars' it is clear that they have to be understood as part of a broader evolving set of networks in and around London. During 1936 in London, Jack 'Spot' Comer was (allegedly) taking part in the Battle of Cable Street and Billy Hill was sentenced to four years penal servitude for robbery. Moreover, notorious burglars and robbers like George Ingram and Ruby Sparks had pursued their 'criminal careers' in the 1920s and '30s, in between frequent terms of imprisonment.[102] Thus criminal networks overlapped and, arguably, new forms of criminal organisation encompassed the more formal structures that were developing in relation to metropolitan territory and the gambling and associated protection industry.

b)   Project Crime

It was the seminal work by Mary McIntosh that would define the form of armed robbery that appeared from the 1950s. According to McIntosh, there were four basic types of criminal organisation: *picaresque, craft, project* and *business*.[103] The 'picaresque' form of organisation referred to a permanent gang under one man's leadership, with profits shared according to the member's rank. Craft organisation was 'typical of people performing skilled but small-scaled thefts and confidence tricks'.[104] Business organisation included those involved in extortion and/or suppliers of illegal goods and services, who have gained some degree of immunity from law. Finally, McIntosh defined project crime as the 'organisation, typical of burglars, robbers, smugglers or frauds-men, engaged in large-scale crimes involving complicated techniques and advance planning'.[105] Such crimes were carried out by ad hoc teams of 'specialists' brought together for a specific job.

The methodology of these crimes had evolved, in part, as a response to the introduction of better and more robust safes and locks. Thus the old 'craft' crime, in which cutting devices would be used to outwit the development of new technology such as tumbler locks, was finally defeated and replaced by armed robbery that took the more direct approach of firearms and violence.[106] William Meier has suggested that the rise of this type of robbery can in part be linked to the decline in economic regulations after the war and the rise of affluence that came with economic recovery.[107] However, he also points to the robbers' social and economic backgrounds. Thus the lives of the young men who became involved in armed robbery were often characterised by the experience of wartime evacuation followed by National Service (which trained young men in the practices of violence), early spells of custody in institutions such as approved schools or borstals, a history of escapes from such institutions, as well as an entrepreneurial approach to employment opportunities.[108] Bruce Reynolds, the planner and organiser of the Great Train Robbery, typified this profile, as did his confederate Ronald Biggs. As Reynolds notes in his autobiography, upon arrival at the borstal punishment centre at Wandsworth Prison, 'In the punishment centre, awaiting allocation, I met a very engaging bloke called Ronnie Biggs. Like me, he'd been there before. He had gone to Usk in Monmouthshire, a grim old borstal miles from anywhere. It wasn't his cup of tea and subsequently he left without permission'.[109]

From the 1950s and '60s there would be a series of increasingly high-profile armed robberies, involving significant violence and reaping large financial rewards.[110] The Great Train Robbery of 1963 remains the quintessential project crime of the 'gangland' era.[111] For example, the first earliest reporting of the robbery in *The Times*, on the 9th August 1963, noted that, 'For audacity and skilful planning the Post Office and British Railways cannot recall a parallel to what is widely believed to be the biggest train robbery in the country's history'.[112] The Home Office correspondence, reports and papers, and photographs are now open to the public, as are the records of the trial at Aylesbury Assizes.[113] Moreover, the robbery has become part of the cultural lore of the 1960s, featuring in recent histories of the decade.[114] Perhaps most significantly, in terms of the public understanding of 'project crime', it was an event around which a body of literature would subsequently build, telling the 'story' of the events from the perspective of the robbers.

Author Piers Paul Read published what is regarded as the seminal true-crime account of the robbery in 1978. Read had apparently been approached by the publishers W.H. Allen, who in turn had been approached by the robbers on their release from gaol in 1976. The resulting book, *The Train Robbers: Their Story*, was billed as 'the inside story' of the robberies.[115] Other true-crime accounts of the robbery were written by those involved, including the robbers, Bruce Reynolds and Ronnie Biggs, and the detectives, Malcolm Fewtrell, Jack Slipper and Frank Williams.[116] The sheer notoriety of the 'Great Train Robbery' was due, at least in part, to the flamboyant escapes of three of the robbers. Bruce Reynolds spent five years on the run until he was arrested and sentenced in 1969; Charles Wilson was convicted in August 1963 but escaped from Winson Green Prison in August 1964; Ronald Biggs was convicted in September 1963 and escaped from Wandsworth Prison in July 1964.[117] It would be the contemporary press reporting, as well as the memoirs and autobiographies described above, which would contribute to the robbery's iconic status in the following decades. As Reynolds noted, reflecting at the time, 'The heat was enormous. The daily papers were devoting page after page to the story, increasing pressure on the police. For their part, the Old Bill was throwing everything at the case – dozens of detectives, radio appeals, daily press briefings'.[118]

Other large-scale robberies occurred during the later twentieth century, including the robbery of the Security Express deport (£7 million) and the Heathrow Brinks-Mat robbery (£26 million) in 1983, the Knightsbridge Security deposit robbery (£40–60 million) in 1987 and the City of London Bearer Bonds robbery (£292 million) in 1990. However, in terms of the broader incidence of robbery, Clive Emsley has argued that the statistics for the twentieth century are problematic. Thus, at the start of the century, the number of robberies ranged between 200 and 300 per year. Whilst there were some minor rises and falls in between the wars and in the decade after the Second World War, from the end of the 1950s the figures would rise dramatically to a peak of 74,000 per year in 1995.[119] Whilst Emsley suggests that it is difficult to detect any broad trends in robbery, Dick Hobbs has noted that in the ten years before the Brinks-Mat robbery in 1983, armed robberies had risen by 349 per cent.[120] He argues that these types of large-scale project robberies tended to decline by the later twentieth century. In part this can be explained by further improvements in technology and security, but also because the rewards from drugs became so much more significant.[121] On the other hand, Roger Matthews has argued that the decline can be explained by the decreasing 'attractiveness of commercial robbery'.[122] In particular he points to the effectiveness of policing and sentencing strategies in reducing the number of career criminals who were involved in project crimes: 'The exceptionally long sentences that tend to be meted out to those convicted of armed robbery ensured that, once convicted of this offence, the vast majority of robbers were imprisoned for a considerable length of time'.[123]

5.   Conclusion

This chapter has argued that organised crime in Britain is a relatively modern phenomenon. Whilst illegal activities have long been subject to some form of economic or social organisation, only recently can this be clearly identified as having taken place by larger-scale and systematic means, and with a series of impacts that reach beyond the local to have national and even global repercussions. Nevertheless, there are patterns relating to the organisation of crime that can be identified in historical documentation and in other cultural and social mediums such as the press. This chapter has focussed more specifically on two periods in which concerns about organised crime can be seen to have undergone a marked shift. First, the 1920s, when concerns about the territorial fighting and protection rackets enacted on the metropolitan streets and southeastern racecourses reflected a confection of popular fears around alienism, terrorism and the gangster. Second, the post Second World War period, when new paradigms of organised and professional criminality merged with the more traditional models, and other financial and technological developments enabled opportunities for entrepreneurial criminals to undertake ambitious robberies and frauds. Ultimately, however, as Dick Hobbs suggests, organised crime is a 'shifting terrain'.[124] Its definition is rarely fixed, often fluid, and continues to be shaped from one generation to the next.

Notes

1. http://www.nationalcrimeagency.gov.uk/ (Accessed 30th October 2017).
2. D. Hobbs (2013) *Lush Life: Constructing Organized Crime in the UK* (Oxford: Oxford University Press), p. 13.
3. A. Wright (2006) *Organised Crime* (Cullompton: Willan), pp. 174–75.
4. C. Emsley (2011) *Crime and Society in Twentieth-Century England* (Harlow: Pearson Education Limited).
5. H. Shore (2007) '"Undiscovered Country": Towards a History of the Criminal "Underworld"', *Crimes and Misdemeanours*, Vol. 1, No. 1, pp. 41–68.
6. A. Brown (2011) 'Crime, Criminal Mobility and Serial Offenders in Early Twentieth-Century Britain', *Contemporary British History*, Vol. 25, No. 4, pp. 551–68; A. Brown (2013) *Interwar Penal Police and Crime in England: The Dartmoor Convict Prison in 1932* (Basingstoke: Palgrave Macmillan), pp. 96–128; S. Slater (2007) 'Pimps, Police and Filles De Joie: Foreign Prostitution in Interwar London', *London Journal*, Vol. 32, No. 1, pp. 53–74; M. Roodhouse (2011) 'In Racket Town: Gangster Chic in Austerity Britain, 1939–1953', *Historical Journal of Film, Television and Radio*, Vol. 31, No. 4, pp. 523–41.

7. Wright (2006) *Organised Crime*, p. 2.

8. Emsley (2011) *Crime and Society*, p. 87. F.P. Wensley (1931) *Detective Days: The Record of Forty-two Years' Service in the Criminal Investigation Department* (London: Cassell) and F.D. Sharpe (1938) *Sharpe of the Flying Squad* (London: John Long).

9. H. Shore (2011) 'Criminality and Englishness in the Aftermath: The Racecourse Wars of the 1920s', *Twentieth Century British History*, pp. 1–24, at p. 5.

10. See the commentary in the *Pall Mall Gazette*, 'How Crime Might Be Abolished', 5th January 1891.

11. Brown (2011) 'Criminal Mobility', p. 563.

12. Emsley (2011) *Crime and Society*, p. 87.

13. C.E. Leach (1931) *On Top of the Underworld* (London: Purnell and Sons), p. 3.

14. A. Davies (2013) *City of Gangs: Glasgow and the Rise of the British Gangster* (London: Hodder & Stoughton) and J.P. Bean (1981) *The Sheffield Gang Wars* (Sheffield: D & D Publications).

15. A. Davies (2007) 'The Scottish Chicago? From "Hooligans" to "Gangsters" in Interwar Glasgow', *Cultural and Social History*, Vol. 4, No. 4, pp. 511–27; Roodhouse (2011) 'In Racket Town', passim.

16. G.R. Sims (1911) *Off the Track in London* (London: Jarrold & Sons).

17. *Old Bailey Proceedings*, Trial of Max Moses, Samuel Oreman, Barnet Broziskersy, Killing, Murder, 17th November 1902 (t19021117-41); The National Archives (hereafter TNA): CRIM 1/80/6, Defendant: Moses, Max; Oreman, Samuel; Broziskevaki (sic), Barnett, Charge: Murder and wounding.

18. M. Kohn (1992) *Dope Girls: The Birth of the British Drug Underground* (London: Granta).

19. L. Bland (2013) *Modern Women on Trial: Sexual Transgression in the Age of the Flapper* (Manchester: Manchester University Press), pp. 65–69.

20. Wright (2006) *Organised Crime*, p. 178.

21. Hobbs (2013) *Lush Life*, p. 58.

22. R. Murphy (1993) *Smash and Grab: Gangsters in the London Underworld, 1920–60* (London: Faber and Faber), pp. 95–97.

23. M. Roodhouse (2013) *Black Market Britain: 1939–1955* (Oxford: Oxford University Press), p. 253.

24. D. Thompson (2008) *The Hustlers: Gambling, Greed and the Perfect Con* (London: Pan Macmillan).

25. D. Thomas (2005) *Villains Paradise: Britain's Underworld from the Spivs to the Krays* (London: John Murray), p. 376.

26. A. Brown (2011) 'The Smash-and-Grab Gangster', *BBC History*, January, pp. 42–43 and A. Brown (2006) 'The Amazing Mutiny at the Dartmoor Convict Prison', *British Journal of Criminology*, Vol. 47, No. 2, pp. 276–92.

27. H. Janson (1959) *Jack Spot: Man of a Thousand Cuts* (London: Alexander Moring) and B. Hill (1955) *Boss of Britain's Underworld* (London: Naldrett Press).

28. Davies (2013) *City of Gangs* and Thomas (2005) *Villains Paradise*, pp. 369–70.

29. 'London Mail Robbery', *The Times*, 22nd May, 1952, p. 6 and Murphy (1993) *Smash and Grab*, pp. 112–14.

30. A considerable literature has grown around the family firms of this period, particularly the Kray twins. However, much of it is biographical and auto-biographical and subject to the limitations of the true-crime genre detailed below. A good overview is available in Hobbs (2013) *Lush Life*, pp. 70–81. The definitive study of the Kray twins is by John Pearson – see J. Pearson (1973) *The Profession of Violence: The Rise and Fall of the Kray Twins* (St. Albans: Panther). A follow-up was published after the death of the Krays, J. Pearson (2001) *The Cult of Violence: The Untold Story of the Krays* (London: Orion).

31. M. Levi (1981) *The Phantom Capitalists: The Organisation and Control of Long-Firm Fraud* (London: Heinemann).

32. J. Morton (1992) *Gangland: London's Underworld* (London: Little Brown), p. 107.

33. Hobbs (2013) *Lush Life*, pp. 73–74.

34. 'Arrest of the Kray Brothers', *The Times*, 9th May 1968, p. 1.

35. 'At least 30 years' – Gaol of the Kray Twins', *The Times*, 6th March 1969, p. 1.

36. For the Nash, Dixon and Tibbs crime families, see Morton (2001) *East End Gangland* (London: Sphere) and 'Gang Leader Richardson Gaoled for 25 Years', *The Times*, 9th June 1967, p. 2.

37. Wright (2006) *Organised Crime*, pp. 173–74.

38. D. Hobbs (1998) 'Going Down the Glocal: The Local Context of Organised Crime', *Howard Journal*, Vol. 37, No. 4, pp. 407–22.

39. Morton (2001) *East End Gangland*, pp. 314–17 and P. Gottschalk (2009) *Entrepreneurship and Organised Crime: Entrepreneurs in Illegal Business* (Cheltenham: Edward Elgar Publishing), pp. 17–18. Terry Adams, the leading member of the group, was not arrested until 2007 see 'Britain's "Godfather" Behind Bars', *The Telegraph*, 10th March, 2007.

40. Emsley (2011) *Crime and Society*, p. 102.

41. Gottschalk (2009) *Entrepreneurship and Organised Crime*, p. 75.

42. P. Jenkins and G.W. Potter (1988) 'Before the Krays: Organized Crime in London, 1920–1960', *Criminal Justice History*, Vol. IX, pp. 209–30 at p. 210.

43. J.L. Albini (1986) 'Organized Crime in Great Britain and the Caribbean', in R. Kelly (ed.) *Organized Crime: A Global Perspective* (New Jersey: Rowman and Littlefield), pp. 95–112, cited in Jenkins and Potter (1988) 'Before the Krays', p. 210.

44. Jenkins and Potter (1988) 'Before the Krays', passim.

45. Emsley (2011) *Crime and Society*, pp. 87–108 at pp. 87–88.

46. Emsley (2011) *Crime and Society*, p. 95.

47. Roodhouse (2013) *Black Market Britain*, p. 256.

48. Hill (1955) *Boss of Britain's Underworld*, p. 17 cited in Roodhouse (2013) *Black Market Britain*, p. 15.

49. Shore (2011) 'Criminality and Englishness' and H. Shore (2015) *London's Criminal Underworlds, c. 1725 – c. 1930: A Social and Cultural History* (Basingstoke: Palgrave Macmillan).

50. *The Times*, 4th April 1921.

51. Shore (2011) 'Criminality and Englishness', p. 10 and pp. 13–15 and Jenkins and Potter (1988) 'Before the Krays', pp. 221–22. See also Shore (2015) *London's Criminal Underworlds*, passim.

52. Brown (2013) *Inter-war Penal Policy*, pp. 99–101, p. 104 and pp. 106–9.

53. *Ibid.*, p. 125.

54. *Ibid.*, p. 126.

55. Shore (2011) 'Criminality and Englishness', p. 9.

56. H. Shore (2014) '"Rogues of the Racecourse": Racing Men and the Press in Interwar Britain', *Media History*, Vol. 20, No. 4, pp. 352–67.

57. Davies (2007) 'The Scottish Chicago?', passim.

58. Davies (2013) *City of Gangs*, pp. 192–95.

59. Bean (1981) *Sheffield Gang Wars*, passim.

60. Sir P. Sillitoe (1955) *Cloak without Dagger* (London: Cassell).

61. Davies (2013) *City of Gangs*, p. 2.

62. Slater (2007) 'Pimps', p. 53. Also, S. Slater (2009) 'Prostitutes and Popular History: Notes on the "Underworld", 1918–1939', *Crime, Histoire & Société*, Vol. 13, No. 1, pp. 25–48.

63. Slater (2007) 'Pimps', p. 67.

64. Slater (2009) 'Prostitutes', p. 217. For the Messinas see also, Jenkins and Potter (1988) 'Before the Krays', pp. 214–17.

65. Kohn (1992) *Dope Girls*, passim.

66. Jenkins and Potter (1988) 'Before the Krays', p. 214.

67. Bland (2013) *Modern Women*, pp. 65–69.

68. P. Knepper (2009) *The Invention of International Crime: A Global Issue in the Making, 1881–1914* (Basingstoke: Palgrave Macmillan) and P. Knepper (2011) *International Crime in the Twentieth Century: The League of Nations Era, 1919–1939* (Basingstoke: Palgrave Macmillan).

69. Knepper (2009) *The Invention of International Crime*, pp. 188–91.

70. On crime memoirs see M. Houlbrook (2013) 'Fashioning an Ex-crook Self: Citizenship and Criminality in the Work of Netley Lucas', *Twentieth Century British History*, Vol. 24, No. 1, pp. 1–30.

71. Pearson (1973) *Profession of Violence*, passim.

72. F. Fraser and J. Morton (1995) *Mad Frank: Memoirs of a Life of Crime* (London: Sphere); L. McClean (2003) *The Guv'nor* (London: John Blake Publishing); F. Foreman (2009) *Freddie Foreman: The Godfather of British Crime* (London: John Blake Publishing) and B. Reynolds (1995) *The Autobiography of a Thief* (London: Bantam Press).

73. For evidence of this fascination in earlier periods see L.B. Faller (1987) *Turned to Account: The Forms and Functions of Criminal Biography in the Late Seventeenth- and Early Eighteenth-Century England* (Cambridge: Cambridge University Press).

74. Morton (1992) *Gangland*; J. Morton (1994) *Gangland, Vol. 2: The Underworld in Britain and Ireland* (London: Little Brown); Morton (2001) *East End Gangland*; Murphy (1993) *Smash and Grab*; B. McDonald (2000) *Elephant Boys: Tales of London and Los Angeles Underworlds* (Edinburgh: Mainstream) and B. McDonald (2010), *The Gangs of London: 100 Years of Mob Warfare* (Wrea Green: Milo Books).

75. McDonald (2010) *The Gangs of London*, introduction.

76. D. Hobbs (1995), *Bad Business: Professional Crime in Modern Britain* (Oxford: Oxford University Press); D. Hobbs (1997), 'Professional Crime: Change, Continuity and the Enduring Myth of the Underworld', *Sociology*, Vol. 31, No. 1, pp. 57–72 and Hobbs (2013) *Lush Life*, passim.

77. Hobbs (2013) *Lush Life*, p. 2.

78. *Ibid.*, pp. 56–57.

79. *Ibid.*, p. 58.

80. *Ibid.*, p. 88 and Hobbs (1997), 'Professional Crime', p. 67.

81. A longer version of this section can be found in the chapter on the Sabini gang and the racecourse wars in Shore (2015) *London's Criminal Underworlds*.

82. M. Huggins (2003) *Horseracing and the British*, 1919–1939 (Manchester: Manchester University Press), p. 146.

83. Jenkins and Potter (1988) 'Before the Krays', pp. 221–23.

84. TNA: HO 144/10430, 'Racecourse ruffians: activities of the "Sabini" gang'; 'Memorandum', n.d.

85. TNA: HO 144/10430, 'Metropolitan Police Report', 1st December 1922.

86. TNA: MEPO 3/346, 'Affray at Ewell known as "The Epsom Hold-Up" on 2nd June 1921, following Race Meeting', 1921.

87. See McDonald (2010) *The Gangs of London*, pp. 115–280. For the events of the summer of 1922, see especially pp. 168–77.

88. Detailed accounts of these events can be found in the Home Office file, TNA: HO144/10430 and Shore (2011) 'Criminality and Englishness'.

89. For example: 'Sabini Drama Heroine', *Daily Express*, 29th November 1922 and 'Club Shooting: Girl's Pluck', *Daily Mirror*, 29th November 1922.

90. TNA: CRIM1/209, 'Cortesi, Augustus; Cortesi, George; Cortesi, Paul; Cortesi, Enrico; Tomaso, Alexander, Charge: Attempted Murder', January 1923.

91. *The Morning Chronicle*, 19th November 1924 and TNA: MEPO3/374, 'Alfred Solomon charged with the Wilful Murder of Barnett Blitz'.

92. Reported in the *Evening Standard*, 24th and 25th August 1925 and *Daily Mail*, 24th August 1925.

93. *Daily Express*, 24th August 1925. For Joynson Hicks' campaigns see Kohn (1992) *Dope Girls*, p. 120, pp. 140–41 and p. 149.

94. TNA: HO144/10430, 'Minutes, H.O., August 1925'.

95. For example, TNA: HO144/10430 covers the activities of racecourse ruffians and the Sabini gang until 1929. TNA: MEPO3/374 covers the murder of Barnet Blitz by Alfred Solomon and its aftermath from 1924 to 1931.

96. C. Chinn (1991) *Better Betting with a Decent Feller: Bookmaking, Betting and the British Working Class, 1750–1990* (London: Harvester Wheatsheaf), pp. 181–84.

97. *The Times*, 16th December 1925; 30th June 1926 and 11th June 1926.

98. *The Times*, 10th June 1936; *Empire News*, 14th June 1936 and *Empire News*, 21st June 1936.

99. S. Chibnall (2005) *Brighton Rock* (London: I. B. Taurus), p. 17.

100. TNA: CRIM1/882, 'MARSH, Bert; WILKINS, Herbert Charge: Murder, wounding with intent', 10th November 1936. *The Times*, 17th November 1936; *Daily Mirror*, 18th November 1936 and McDonald (2010) *The Gangs of London*, p. 257.

101. *Daily Mirror*, 18th September 1936 and McDonald (2010) *The Gangs of London*, p. 257.

102. Murphy (1993) *Smash and Grab*, pp. 156–60; Hill (1955) *Boss of Britain's Underworld*, passim and Brown (2011) 'The Smash-and-Grab Gangster', passim.

103. M. McIntosh (1975) *The Organisation of Crime* (London: Macmillan), pp. 28–29.

104. *Ibid.*, p. 28.

105. *Ibid.*, p. 28.

106. R. Matthews (2002) *Armed Robbery* (Cullompton: Willan), pp. 18–19.

107. W. Meier (2011) *Property Crime in London: 1850–Present* (Basingstoke: Palgrave Macmillan), pp. 118–20.

108. *Ibid.*, p. 124 and passim.

109. Reynolds (1995) *Autobiography of a Thief*, p. 43 and Meier (2011) *Property Crime*, pp. 128–29.

110. HC Deb 01 August 1963 vol 682 c125W see http://hansard.millbanksystems.com /written_answers/1963/aug/01/armed-robbery (Accessed 30th October 2017).

111. A very detailed recent account of the robbery is by N. Russell-Pavier and S. Richards (2012) *The Great Train Robbery: Crime of the Century* (London: Weidenfeld & Nicolson).

112. 'Bank Loses £500,000 in Mail Train Raid', *The Times*, 9th August, 1963, p. 8.

113. For example, TNA: HO 242/3 to 242/5; ASSI 13/646 to 13/659. Many of the records of the Director of Public Prosecution (DPP) and of the Metropolitan Police (MEPO) relating to the robbery, are currently closed until the mid-twenty-first century.

114. D. Sandbrook (2006) *White Heat: The Story of Britain in the Swinging Sixties* (London: Abacus), p. 572.

115. P.P. Read (1978) *The Train Robbers: Their Story* (London: Alison Press).

116. Reynolds (1995) *Autobiography of a Thief*; R. Biggs (1994) *Odd Man Out* (London: Bloomsbury); M. Fewtrell (1964) *The Train Robbers* (London: Arthur Barker); F. Williams (1973) *No Fixed Address* (London: W. H. Allen & Co Ltd) and J. Slipper (1981) *Slipper of the Yard* (London: Sidgwick and Jackson).

117. 'Reynolds arrest ends long hunt by Yard men', *The Times*, 9th November 1968, p. 1; '25 years for Bruce Reynolds', *The Times*, 15th January 1969, p. 1; '15-Minute Raid Freed Mail Train Prisoner', *The Times*, 13th August 1964; 'Second Train Robber escapes from Prison', *Guardian*, 9th July 1965, p. 1; 'Home Secretary Orders Escape Inquiry', *The Times*, 10th July 1965, p. 8.

118. Reynolds (1995) *Autobiography of a Thief*, p. 257.

119. Emsley (2011) *Crime and Society*, p. 31. These are figures for robbery more generally (including street robbery), not just project crimes.
120. Hobbs (2013) *Lush Life*, p. 147.
121. *Ibid.*, pp. 147–49.
122. Matthews (2002) *Armed Robbery*, p. 137.
123. *Ibid.*, p. 137.
124. D. Hobbs (2001) 'The Firm: Organizational Logic and Criminal Culture on a Shifting Terrain', *British Journal of Criminology*, Vol. 41, pp. 549–60.

9

Punishment: The Death Penalty and Incarceration

Helen Johnston

1. Introduction

This chapter will examine punishment across the twentieth century. It will discuss the changing contours of punishment across the period by focussing on two areas: the use of imprisonment and the death penalty. Whilst one of the most significant moments of the century with regard to punishment was the end of the death penalty in the mid-1960s, the whole penal system changed considerably at the beginning of the century with an expansion in the use and range of penalties available to the courts. The first few decades of the century witnessed a period of decarceration and is often regarded as the 'golden age of penal reform'. However, after the Second World War and particularly in the last three decades of the century, the reverse occurred. England and Wales witnessed a continual increase in the prison population and at the turn of the twenty-first century had a higher prison population than many other countries in Western Europe.

This chapter will examine these events firstly by documenting the chronology of punishment across the century and then its historiography. If the focus of the early to mid-twentieth century was, as criminologist David Garland has argued, one of 'penal-welfarism',[1] then the focus of the latter decades of the twentieth was a 'law and order' political agenda, followed by a shift towards managerialism and the management of offenders in terms of the risk that they posed to the public and their risk of reoffending. This discussion will be followed by two case studies which provide more detail to two significant events. The first case study puts the death penalty in context by examining what turned out to be the final days of capital punishment in Britain: the execution of Peter Anthony Allen and Gwynne Owen Evans, the last two people executed in England and Wales. The second case study focuses on imprisonment and considers the Mountbatten Report (1966) which examined security in prisons in the wake of a number of high-profile escapes across the country. The recommendations of the Mountbatten Report led to the use of different categorisation of prisoners by security status, from Category A the highest level down to Category D where prisoners can be trusted in lower security or 'open' settings. These categories remain in use in the twenty-first century.

2. Chronology

At the very end of the nineteenth century, the Gladstone Committee (1895) was appointed to examine prisons conditions.[2] Pressure on the Home Office for an inquiry into imprisonment had been growing for a while, as critics not only questioned the severity of the late Victorian prison regimes, but also the administration and leadership of the Prison Commission, then under the charge of Edmund Du Cane. There were a number of concerns: first, experience had taught administrators that despite their best efforts, severely deterrent regimes could not be applied to all prisoners – some due to age or infirmity needed alternative practices. Second, even for the most deterrent prison regimes, the appropriateness of their use was questioned as commentators complained prisoners found themselves with no chance for reformation and little hope for the future. This was particularly highlighted by a set of exposé newspaper articles entitled 'Our Dark Places' which featured in the *Daily Chronicle* in 1894 (thought to have been written by Rev. W.D. Morrison, then the chaplain of Wandsworth Prison) and subsequently by literary scholar and former prisoner Oscar Wilde in his *The Ballad of Reading Gaol*, which mounted a scathing attack on the prison system and was published in 1898.[3] The third concern was that Du Cane had too much power and control, and that as a result the system lacked accountability and was far too bureaucratic.[4] In the end, the Gladstone Committee acknowledged many of the problems but advocated a balance between deterrence and reform. Du Cane resigned. Subsequently, hard labour was replaced with productive labour, convict prisoners could work in association, education was recognised as important to reform, and remission of the prison sentence was introduced for those in local prisons (serving less than two years), along with greater support on release through Discharged Prisoners Aid Societies.

Beyond the prison regimes, the Gladstone Committee is also seen as the platform for much wider and more fundamental changes in the whole of the penal system.[5] The Probation of First Offenders Act 1887 had emerged from work by missionaries, both in the courtroom setting and those working with released prisoners, welfare work and crime prevention in general. The Act applied only to those with no prior convictions, who were convicted of an offence punishable for not more than two years and, if applied, who would be subject to recognizances (with or without sureties). Consideration also had to be given to the youth, character of the offender and the nature of the offence. However, the provision was slow to be taken up, but by the turn of the nineteenth century, it was being used more frequently and the number of missionaries in police courts had expanded and their work was highly regard by magistrates.[6]

In 1900 those convicted in the criminal justice system were dealt with in the following ways: in the higher courts (Assizes and Quarter Sessions) 20 offenders were sentenced to death, 728 to penal servitude (long-term imprisonment), 6430 to imprisonment (less than two years), 61 to other types of custody (reformatory school or inebriate reformatory), 91 were fined, 2 were whipped and 640 were sentenced to recognizances or sureties (under either Probation of First Offenders Act, Summary Jurisdiction Act or other statutes). The summary courts (magistrates courts), where the bulk of offenders were processed (and was similarly the case in the late twentieth century), convicted 616,731 offenders. The overwhelming majority of these offenders, 531,752, were fined. Of the remainder, 63,867 were imprisoned, 3234 were whipped, 1250 were sent to reformatory schools and 14,805 to recognizances or sureties (as above).[7] Although fines were the most common penalty instructed by the courts, many offenders defaulted on payment of fines and this resulted in their imprisonment. The passing of the Criminal Justice Act 1914 had a significant impact on fine defaulters as this legislation allowed people time to pay fines and later provision was made to pay instalments; subsequently large numbers of fine defaulters were removed from the prison system.[8]

The early twentieth century was a 'truly extraordinary period' as the wider changes in the penal system would have a dramatic effect on the system itself as well as the prison population levels therein.[9] In 1907 the Probation of Offenders Act was passed and this introduced formal supervision by probation officers and was extended to offenders who had previous convictions.[10] Three decades later in 1938, there were 29,301 probation orders, most were made in the summary courts, where it had become the most common punishment for indictable offences and accounted for 34 per cent of disposals (with imprisonment and fines at around 17 per cent each).[11]

The first establishment opened was a borstal for young offenders in Kent in 1902, the system developed apace and was formalised by the Prevention of Crimes Act 1908.[12] The creation of these alternative methods of dealing with first offenders – those under 16 years old and those with mental health problems – and giving time to pay fines had a significant impact on the prison population. Over the following decades the prison population would dramatically change. At the time of the Gladstone Committee in 1895, the total daily average prison population in England and Wales was 14,394 although there were 160,117 total commitments to the prison system, as the overwhelmingly majority of sentences were short and experienced in local prisons.[13] By 1908, the daily average prison population was 22,000. Although there were over 200,000 receptions to prisons by this time, three out of four of these were for non-indictable offences or defaulting on fines. By 1938, the daily average prison population was just over 11,000 and this represented the smallest prison population in Europe.[14] On the face of it then, a great deal was achieved in the first half of the twentieth century with regard to the number of people in prison, though as we will discuss in the following sections, this would completely reverse in the later decades of the century.

Views about criminality were largely still based on ideas about individual morality by the late Victorian period, but into the twentieth century there were growing ideas that were underpinned by Social Darwinism about the relationship between biology, heredity and criminality. Positivist criminology, as it was known, did influence some criminal justice and penal policies. For example, policies that were underpinned by categories like 'mental defective' and to some extent those held under sentence of 'preventive detention'.[15] Across Europe, a number of countries adopted arguments based on the relationship between heredity and criminality, but this was not the case in England, although views about criminals were underpinned by notions of degeneracy or mental or physical deficiencies.[16] The 'problem' groups in society were its lowest and unproductive members – often due to biological, physical or mental weakness or degeneracy – and referred to as the 'rough' or the 'residuum'. They were not just criminals, but the poor, lunatics and vagrants. The Victorian 'criminal classes' did still exist, but they were thought to be much smaller in number and therefore were seen as less threatening. The term, the 'residuum' or the 'rough' remained in common usage until the Second World War.[17]

The 1920s and '30s are often seen as the 'golden age of penal reform', led by Prison Commissioner Alexander Paterson. Paterson was appointed in 1922, the same year that an unofficial report on the prison system by two former prisoners, (conscientious objectors in the First World War) Stephen Hobhouse and A. Fenner Brockway, slammed the system for its 'machine-like' rigid operation as well as the debilitating effects of separate confinement on prisoners.[18] Sir Maurice Waller, not Paterson, was chairman of the Commission, but Paterson's view that people should be sent to prison '*as* punishment rather than *for* punishment' became central to the liberal sentiment and symbolic of the mood of penal thought during these decades.[19]

Paradoxically, 1932 was also the year of one of the largest prison disturbances in English prison history – the 'mutiny' at Dartmoor Prison.[20] But rather than destabilising the reform period, the disturbance at Dartmoor – where 150 men took control of the prison, lighting fires and causing serious damage to the buildings – was seen by the investigating committee, led by Herbert Du Parcq, as a localised event. Subsequently, 33 Dartmoor inmates were sentenced to a total of 99 years for their part in the disturbance.[21] Perhaps what this event also hints toward however, is that despite the 'golden age of penal reform', change inside prison regimes was pretty slow in coming. In convict prisons, periods of separation were gradually reduced, though they were not abolished until 1930. Education and recreation were introduced, and talking was permitted at meal times and during exercise, but more generally, improvements were somewhat limited across the 1920s and '30s.[22]

This was similarly the case in the local prison system too, but a larger prison population and a higher turnover of population probably contributed to the enduring nature of severe and deterrent Victorian prison regimes. Thus for the majority of prisoners little changed until the 1920s and '30s. Separate confinement was not abolished until 1931, and criticisms of the rigid and 'machine-like' operation of the system continued.[23] Certain policies directed at women and girls from the end of the nineteenth century onwards also served to engulf some females in semi-penal institutions for criminal offences, but also for reasons of 'immorality', being 'troublesome' or for being 'at risk'.[24]

Just before the outbreak of the Second World War, one of the most significant areas of development occurred. Rooted in commentary and debate from the 1920s and '30s, it was acknowledged that all prisoners did not have to be held in either a secure local or a convict prison but rather they could be held in different security settings. This led to the first 'open' prison, New Hall, Wakefield, opening in 1936.[25] Two World Wars also impacted on imprisonment and punishment. It might be argued that the lasting effect of the First World War and the ensuing devastating loss of life helped to sustain a philosophy of punishment which prioritised reform and rehabilitation, but this was a period in which decarceration had already begun.[26] In the early 1940s, the crime rate and prison population began to increase and the Second World War also had an impact on the physical prison estate. Air raids and bombings occurred in a number of prisons in London and other major cities (Liverpool, Hull and Bristol, for instance), but the first attacks were felt in the borstal institutions in the south of England.[27] The operation of prisons was also effected by changing staff – as large numbers of individuals were called up to regiments, auxiliary staff were called in to help – and through rationing and other restrictions.[28]

Between 1938 and 1946, the prison population increased by 50 per cent. As a result, prisons that had had to be temporarily closed or evacuated due to air raids had to be reopened, and in the post-war period, a programme of expansion began as 17 new prisons and borstals were established.[29] In the midst of this expansion, Lionel Fox began his work as Chairman of the Prison Commission. The post-war period also saw some of the changes proposed in the Criminal Justice Bill 1938 come to fruition. For example, the first open prison for women was established at Askham Grange in 1946, and subsequently the Criminal Justice Act 1948 was passed abolishing the sentence of penal servitude. The subsequent Prison Act 1952 laid down the foundation of prison rules for the remainder of the century. Although the Criminal Justice Act 1948 was seen as a major piece of legislation at the time, it was 'a penological dinosaur, obsolete in its conceptions and largely unadaptable to the changing world of post-war Britain'.[30]

The second half of the twentieth century has seen the continual increase in the prison population which fluctuated in the 1950s between 20,000 and 26,000, then fell to around 22,000 in 1960. After this it began to rise and this upsurge continued for the remainder of the century.[31] British society also witnessed an equivalent increase in recorded crime from the 1950s onwards, although from 1995, this began to decline. Philip Rawlings has characterised this period as the 'end to optimism'.[32] Although the liberal progressive philosophy and practice remained strong in the Prison Commission and continued into the Labour government's policies of the 1960s, a number of problems had been growing nevertheless. As Rawlings notes, on the one hand, the liberal progressive agenda was demonstrated by the prioritisation of the welfare of children who had committed crimes, as well as by revisions to abortion, homosexuality and suicide legislation. On the other hand, the criminalisation of drugs offences and stricter immigration laws also came into force at the same time. Some viewed British society as in moral decline, where the permissive and promiscuous liberal agenda threatened the very fibre of the country, particularly in the case of young people. Teddy boys, cinema wrecking and the mods and rockers clashing in the beach towns of the south coast of England (discussed in more detail in Chapter 7 of this volume) were all examples of how independent and hedonistic youth had too much freedom and lacked discipline. They were also examples of 'moral panics' created by the media.[33]

The 1960s also heralded the end of the death penalty. Pressure for change had been growing for decades and can be traced back to the movement for the abolition of public execution in the early to mid-nineteenth century. After public execution was abolished in 1868, campaigners continued to lobby for the total abolition of capital punishment, but their attempts were defeated a number of the times before the end of the nineteenth century.[34] The drama of the death penalty had been transformed by its privatisation. It had been sanitised and this allowed it to continue in a more tolerable form.[35] Instead of outright abolition then, slow change began to occur in relation to the capital punishment of different groups of offenders. For example, the death penalty was abolished for offenders under the age of 16 in 1908. In 1930 this was extended to those under 18, and in the following year capital punishment was abolished for all pregnant women, although in practice these types of cases had typically been commuted to a life sentence for some time.[36] No one under 18 years old had been executed in the previous 40 years, and the Select Committee on Capital Punishment reporting in 1931 recommended raising the age limit to 21 years, though this was not taken forward.[37]

During the first half of the twentieth century, debate about the use of capital punishment continued and controversial cases drew the attention of the public; it was 'the issue that would not go away'.[38] The National Campaign for the Abolition of Capital Punishment was formed in 1925. The Select Committee on Capital Punishment reported that during the period 1900–1929 there had been 423 people sentenced to death, 327 of them had been reprieved and therefore on average there were 14.13 executions per annum. This Committee recommended the abolition of capital punishment for a period of five years.[39] Again in 1938 there was a free vote in the House of Commons that recommended the abolition of capital punishment but this was not acted upon.[40] Roy Calvert was a key figure in the abolition movement and his book, *Capital Punishment in the Twentieth Century,* was highly influential in the movement to reform. It was subsequently cited in the Lords, during the confirmation of permanency of abolition of the death penalty in 1969.[41]

Member of Parliament Sidney Silverman garnered support for Bills in Parliament to consider the abolition of capital punishment on multiple occasions across this period. In 1948 for instance, his motion for the abolition of capital punishment was carried in the House of Commons but defeated in the Lords. In 1949 a Royal Commission on Capital Punishment began its inquiry, reporting in 1953 that abolition was beyond its remit, and in any event, all of its recommendations were rejected.[42] From the 1950s until the mid-1960s when capital punishment was effectively abolished (suspended in 1965 for five years then abolished in 1969), and despite public opinion being largely in favour of the death penalty, a cluster of high-profile cases hit the headlines and prompted calls for reform and called its use into question.[43] In 1949 for instance, Timothy Evans had been executed for the murder of his wife and child, though by 1953, it had been discovered that they might well have been the victims of multiple murderer John Christie. Christie, who lived in a flat below the Evans' at 10 Rillington Place was convicted of the murders of six women whose bodies had been found in the house, and he allegedly confessed to the murder of Mrs Evans.[44] Earlier the same year, Derek Bentley was executed as an accessory in the murder of a police officer, although he had learning difficulties and epilepsy and his co-accused, Christopher Craig, who actually fired the gun that killed the officer, was not put to death due to his age.[45] Two years later in 1955, the case of Ruth Ellis, who had shot her abusive lover three days after a vicious assault had resulted in a miscarriage, drew hundreds of letters, a petition to the Home Secretary and columns and columns of newspaper reportage, yet she was executed nonetheless at Holloway Prison on the 11th of July. She was to be the last woman executed in England.[46]

In 1963, at a point at which the crime rate had reached an all-time high, changes were also evident in the penal system. The Prison Commission was abolished and became a department of the Home Office.[47] In the prison system, the following two to three decades would be marked by an increasing prison population, overcrowded prison establishments, understaffing, staff unrest and industrial action, poor physical and living conditions (slopping out did not end until 1996) and riots and disorder.[48] There were a number of serious disturbances in the high-security estate (as will be discussed in the second case study in this chapter) and subsequently in local prisons. The backdrop to these problems needs to be understood in the following context. The rise of 'law and order' politics from the late 1970s onwards has resulted from the collapse of the 'rehabilitative ideal' and the conclusion that 'nothing worked' when addressing the problem of crime. This 'law and order' ideology prioritised a tough stance on crime, that offenders should get their 'just deserts', and that they should be dealt with as severely as possible. These views permeated the whole of the penal system. It was suggested by some commentators that a 'new punitiveness' in criminal justice policy could be observed from the mid-1990s. Political views about law and order underpinned the Thatcher government's policies from 1979, but were further accelerated by the subsequent Major government. However, this view was not merely isolated to Conservative government ideology but was maintained to a great extent with the election of New Labour from 1997, as was denoted by its campaign to be 'tough on crime and tough on the causes of crime'.[49] In addition, and in the last ten years of the twentieth century, there also developed a managerialist approach which prioritised cost effectiveness in the administration of criminal justice, a facet of what might be termed the 'new penology'.[50]

3.   Historiography

The standard historiography of punishment in the twentieth century is that punishment became more enlightened and rehabilitative. That we moved away not only from the use of physical punishment, but also from the deterrent regimes of the nineteenth century towards attempts to reform the behaviour of offenders through more progressive and constructive means. Overall this historiography is located within a much longer history of punishment which sees the movement away from the barbaric punishments of the early modern period to the birth of the prison in the early nineteenth century and, ultimately, to the end of the use of the death penalty and other forms of physical punishments in many Western countries by the end of the 1970s.

Traditional or Whig accounts of these changes, for example those by David Cooper, Christopher Hibbert or Sidney and Beatrice Webb, frequently based on the views of the reformers writing at the time, tended to see these changes in punishment in terms of progress.[51] The practices of the past were barbaric, inefficient and haphazard; the 'new' system was measured and rational. These changes were part of the development of a modern civilised society. As Emsley observes, until the late 1970s this was 'the usual narrative of penal history ... inspired by liberal and humanitarian ideals.'[52] Brutal public displays of punishment were barbaric and excessive and this needed to be replaced by a new system which was more measured and ordered – one that only executed certain offenders and did so in private, away from the eyes of public – ultimately leading to the total abolition of the death penalty.[53] This system of punishment would be replaced by the prison, not the disorderly and diseased gaols of the past, but a new prison, an orderly and functional environment where prisoners were given the basics for survival – food, shelter, sanitation – and were put to labour and given religious and moral education through which their behaviour could be altered.[54]

During the 1960s and '70s, a number of writers challenged many aspects of the traditional account. Notably they were concerned with power and social control, many emerging from or influenced by the Marxist social histories of the time. Collectively, these accounts explored questions of power and power relations. They sought to understand the economic and philanthropic motives of 'reformers', as well as the interests of the governing class, state power, authority and regulation. Historians such as Douglas Hay, Peter Linebaugh and Vic Gatrell argued that the law was deeply biased when it came to class and this was exemplified in cases of capital punishment and the operation of mercy.[55]

Unlike traditional accounts that readily accepted the views of the reformers of the period, revisionist writers have questioned the motives and ideology of reformers, examining the consequences of 'reform' for those subject to it, as well as the degree to which motivation can be seen purely in terms of benevolence.[56] A number of authors also located these changes in punishment and the rise of the prison as an 'institution' within a broader understanding of the forces of social control in wider society.[57] Since the revisionist accounts, there has been more nuanced scholarship which has taken a more cultural approach to changing penality.[58] More specifically, the standard historiography of the prison in the first half of the twentieth century is one of progress; a movement away from the deterrent regimes of the Victorian era to a more reforming and rehabilitative penal policy and prison regime. Undoubtedly, the whole penal system changed markedly in the first two decades of the twentieth century as the introduction of probation, more time to pay fines and alternative sentences all contributed to a lower prison population, although the range of penalties to which people were subjected was widened significantly. A great deal of emphasis in these years was placed on addressing issues relating to first-time and young offenders. The first few decades were dominated by a widening of types of punishment that largely resulted in decarceration (fewer people being sent to prison) at least until the 1950s. The focus of punishment had shifted towards the treatment of the offender. For criminologist David Garland, the beginning of the twentieth century was the key moment in the development of the modern penal system as a whole, and one in which the modern 'penal-welfare' complex was established.[59] He sees this period as more important for example than the birth of the prison at the end of the eighteenth and beginning of the nineteenth century, which had been emphasised by many of the revisionist scholars discussed above.

Overall, the history of punishment is not well served in the first half of the twentieth century,[60] and as yet, there is not really a historiography of punishment in the last 50 years of the twentieth century as there is very little historical work on this period, partly due to the closure of archival records. However, this mantle has been taken up by the emergence of sociological and subsequently criminological research, within which there is a considerable scholarship on punishment more widely and on the prison more specifically. In contrast to the first few decades, the last 20 to 30 years of the twentieth century saw the prison system come under increasing pressure from an increasing prison population.[61] It was frequently expressed that the prison, or the penal system more broadly, was 'in crisis'.[62] Indeed some criminologists viewed it as having been 'perpetually' in crisis since the Gladstone Committee at end of the nineteenth century.[63]

It is clear that during the 1960s and '70s, the collapse of the 'rehabilitative ideal' in combination with a high and increasing prison population, staff unrest, poor living conditions and periods of serious disturbances in high-security and subsequently in local prisons across the country, mark out the latter decades of the century as being quite different to the experiences of the early 1900s. The focus of punishment has also shifted. Whilst attention was still on the offender, the late twentieth-century discussion was centred on risk and the management of the risk that offenders pose to the public, especially in terms of reoffending and it was argued that a 'new penology' emerged.

Between 1993 and 2011 the prison population doubled to a zenith of over 88,000 inmates, and at the time of writing the figure for England and Wales stands at around 86,000. England and Wales was not alone in maintaining a high and increasing prison population at this time. Many Western countries experienced these increases. The most notable, 'world leader' in imprisonment rates, the United States, holds more than two million people in prison. This situation is commonly referred to as 'mass imprisonment': a term denoting not only the sheer number of people in prison but within this, the systematic imprisonment of whole groups of the population – young black men.[64] The over-representation of minority groups or indigenous populations was also a concerning feature of imprisonment in England and Wales, as well as Australia and New Zealand at the beginning of the twenty-first century. In 2012, England and Wales had the highest prison population in Western Europe, proportionate to the countries' total populations, expressed as 154 people in prison per 100,000 of the whole population (Scotland's prison population was also 154 per 100,000). England and Wales have topped the league table for Western Europe for a number of years and this seems to be because we send more people to prison and we send them to prison for longer periods of time.[65]

The emergent 'new penology' was one based on risk management and actuarial justice. It underpinned policies such as long indeterminate sentences based on public protection in the UK or the 'Three Strikes' legislation (mandatory life sentence after a third offence) in the United States.[66] Others have observed a 'new punitiveness', a 'populist punitiveness' or a 'punitive turn' since the mid-1990s.[67] In addition to the increasing prison populations, they have noted the increasing punitiveness of sentencing policy and the penal system; the use of 'three strikes' laws, austere prison regimes, greater use of super maximum-security prisons, shaming or public humiliation punishments, electronic surveillance techniques and zero-tolerance policing. These features, which were once exceptional, have become more central to punishment and are being undertaken by those who claim to represent public opinion.[68] The prison, they maintain, is now longer Foucault's social laboratory but 'a container for human goods now endlessly recycled through what has become a transcarceral system of control.'[69] However, whilst 'penal populism' is apparent in some countries, it is not inevitable and other countries in Europe have managed to avoid a similar outcome.[70]

4. Case Studies

a) The End of the Death Penalty – The Executions of Peter Anthony Allen and Gwynne Owen Evans

In August 1868, 18-year-old Thomas Wells became the first person to be executed inside prison, at HMP Maidstone, after the end of public execution in Britain earlier the same year. Ninety-seven years later, Peter Anthony Allen and Gwynne Owen Evans were the last two people executed in Britain, their executions occurring simultaneously at HMP Manchester and HMP Liverpool. By the early 1960s there were around 12 or so executions per year and this had been the case since 1900. All of these executions were for murder convictions (with the exception of wartime treason) and were carried out inside prison walls.[71]

The spectacle of suffering that predominated at public executions during the nineteenth century had been removed, and the execution was restricted in all ways in comparison with earlier decades. Once convicted and inside prison, those sentenced to death were kept separate from all other prisoners. They were held in a condemned cell, they were attended by two prison officers at all times and were under constant observation.[72] Other prisoners and staff were aware of the impending execution sentence, with the condemned being observed alone in the exercise yard or in the cell where they were held. In some prisons, the condemned would be moved to a cell close to the gallows for the final preparations and last ministrations by the prison chaplain. In others, the condemned cell was part of a cluster of cells used for the condemned, for visits and for the gallows.[73]

The execution itself was undertaken by the executioner and his assistant, who would arrive at the prison the day before. The weight and the height of the condemned were made known and the executioner observed the offender unseen. The apparatus was tested and the length of the drop calculated. On the execution day, the equipment was checked again and the rope coiled and chained. At the appointed time the execution party went to the condemned cell, the executioner pinioned the arms of the prisoner and officers led them to the scaffold, standing them over the division of the trap door. The assistant executioner then pinioned their legs, the executioner placed a white sack over their head and the noose around their neck. The executioner then pulled the lever; the medical officer would then check that life was extinct and the body was left to hang for one hour. It was said that the whole process from the executioner entering the cell to the pulling of the lever took between 9 and 25 seconds.[74] After the execution had taken place, the body was removed by officers and the body of the condemned was buried in an unmarked grave in prison grounds.

In the early twentieth century, the prison commissioners were keen for sombre decorum at executions and to avoid the exposure of any 'botched' episodes.[75] The privatisation of execution in 1868 ensured that the 'theatre' of public execution had vanished. After this time, executions were marked by the raising of a black flag at the prison and by the tolling of the prison bell for 15 minutes both before and after the execution was carried out. These markers, signifying that the execution was either imminent or had been carried out, were notably curtailed in comparison to events of the early nineteenth century, but even these were seen as excessive or melodramatic by early twentieth-century standards. Black flags were revoked in 1902. Eventually prison bells only tolled after the execution. By 1925, the press were excluded and instead a death notice was posted on the prison gate.[76] The curtailment of these practices encouraged the Select Committee on Capital Punishment in 1931 to state that:

> Year by year, the death penalty has been withdrawing itself from public gaze. The death bell is no longer tolled; the black flag is no longer raised. If we take away the scaffold as well it is because it is not needed in this new day of social rebuilding. We can build better without it.[77]

Seal argues that instead the capital trial became the 'spectacle', a form of entertainment and the presence or not of a crowd outside the prison on hanging day, a 'constituent part of execution stories'.[78]

All of those executed in the twentieth century, during peacetime at least, were put to death for murder. Between 1900 and 1949, there were 1080 men and 130 women sentenced to death, of whom 621 men and 11 women were actually executed.[79] In many ways the case of Evans and Allen was not exceptional. In July 1964, they had been found guilty of the murder of John Alan West at his home in Workington, Cumbria. At Manchester Crown Court on the 7th July, Allen, aged 21 years, and Evans, aged 24 years, were sentenced to death. The trial had lasted for seven days, and during the proceedings it was said that the two men had attacked West with a cosh and a knife and then stole a gold watch and bank books from the house. The blood-stained knife had been found later at Windermere.[80] West was found in a pool of blood with multiple head injuries by a neighbour who raised the alarm. Tellingly, the victim had been stabbed in the heart. After the passing of the sentence, it was said that the mothers of both of the condemned telegrammed the Queen pleading for clemency, but this was not forthcoming. Lord Parker, Lord Chief Justice said, 'a more brutal murder would be difficult to imagine'.[81] Although in previous decades executions at prisons had gained considerable attention as sites where the debate between those supporting and those against the death penalty would meet, the executions of Allen and Evans (unknown to everyone at the time as the last executions in Britain) did not receive any great attention.

By this time, the Homicide Act of 1957 had restricted executions to certain types of murder, distinguishing between capital and non-capital murder and in this case applying 'murder in the course of theft'. It was reported in *The Guardian* that at Walton Prison two men had kept all-night vigil but there had been no demonstrations at Strangeways. At the time of the execution some 20 individuals had gathered, but it was said that they came to see if there were any protests or demonstrations, rather than wait news of Allen and Evans' fate. In Preston, where both men had been living, a silent vigil of 23 people, led by the curate of Preston Parish Church, was held in the market square.[82] Unsurprisingly, given the diminution of information about executions in the public domain, there were no details of the actual executions reported by the newspapers of the time; they simply noted that the death notice had been posted and reported on whether there was a public gathering outside. Although not a case of national controversy, like the well-known cases of Ruth Ellis or Derek Bentley, there was local debate about the fate of the two men. The abolitionist view was championed by the curate previously mentioned, Reverend Geoffrey Grimes, who campaigned for their reprieve, but the local Conservative councillor, Joe Holden, headed a counter-campaign to ensure their execution. Recalling the events 25 years later, Grimes said:

> Curates were supposed to keep quiet …. I think the vicar must have been on holiday. It was difficult to find sympathy for the two men. You had to believe that all capital punishment was wrong. The main thing that comes to mind is the aggravation and nastiness of people. We were besieged with threatening letters and phone calls. People walked out of church when I spoke of it.[83]

The Homicide Act of 1957 had differentiated between capital and non-capital murder but it was unworkable in practice.[84] There were four types of capital murder: those cases where murders had occurred in the course of a theft, by shooting or causing an explosion, alongside murder during the resisting of arrest or during an escape, and also the murder of a police or prison officer. In theory this was supposed to remove the choice for the judge or Home Secretary, but only resulted in negative public opinion as it was said to encourage somewhat arbitrary decisions.[85] Subsequently, there were other offenders sentenced to death but they had their executions commuted to life imprisonment. By November 1965, in the wake of further consternation and debate, the death penalty was suspended for five years by the Murder (Abolition of the Death Penalty) Act 1965.[86] In 1969, the Houses of Parliament carried the motion to remove the five-year limit on the suspension of the death penalty.[87] Subsequently, in 2003, the British government signed the European Convention on Human Rights and under Protocol 13 removed the power for British legislators to ever restore capital punishment. The objective of this document was to ensure that Europe remains a death-penalty free zone in perpetuity.[88]

b)   Mountbatten Report (1966) and Security Classifications

In 1966, Earl Mountbatten of Burma presented his *Report of the Inquiry into Prison Escapes and Security* to the Home Secretary.[89] The inquiry had been established to investigate a number of prison escapes, notably that of George Blake, and to make recommendations to improve prison security. George Blake had been sentenced to 42 years imprisonment after pleading guilty to five offences under the Official Secrets Act 1911 at the Central Criminal Court in 1961. He was 'no ordinary spy … his crimes were of the most despicable character'.[90] In June 1966 Blake escaped from Wormwood Scrubs prison in London. His escape was high profile but it was one of five high-profile escapes that had occurred from different prisons between August 1964 and 1966.[91] Charles Wilson, one of the Great Train Robbers, who was four months into a 30-year prison sentence, escaped from Birmingham Prison in August 1964. Ronnie Biggs, another of the Great Train Robbers, also serving 30 years, escaped with three other prisoners from Wandsworth Prison in July 1965. In May 1966, nine prisoners escaped whilst being transferred back to Parkhurst Prison after appearing as witnesses in a trial at Winchester Assizes. Then in December 1966, Frank Mitchell – who was a life-sentence prisoner with a long history of offending – escaped from an outside working party at Dartmoor Prison. At the time, the newspapers described him as 'the most dangerous and violent prisoner in custody', though this statement was not officially endorsed by the Mountbatten Report.[92]

The Mountbatten Report was the outcome of the cumulative effect of these escapes and it investigated how each of these escapes occurred, making recommendations and commenting on prison security generally. The report recommended a new system of security classification, categorising prisoners from Category A, who under no circumstances could be allowed to get out of prison, down to Category D, those prisoners who could be trusted to be in open conditions.[93] This system was widely implemented and indeed continues to be used in the twenty-first century. Mountbatten also recommended the building of a new maximum-security prison to hold all Category A prisoners, and a site was already being considered on the Isle of Wight. The government did not adopt this particular aspect of the report, but a subsequent subcommittee lead by the academic Professor Leon Radzinowicz and reporting in 1968, recommended instead that Category A prisoners be 'dispersed' around the prison system in smaller numbers rather than being placed into one maximum-security institution. These prisons were to provide a liberal regime within a secure perimeter.[94] This 'dispersal' system, in the end, began with seven prisons (Albany, Gartree, Hull, Parkhurst, Wakefield, Wormwood Scrubs (D-wing) and Long Lartin). At the time, elements of the Mountbatten Report 'reveal moments of divergence from prevailing welfarist or liberal perspectives and foreshadow the conceptualisation of security as the raison d'etre in prison that was to occur in the mid-1990s'.[95] However, the prevailing belief was still that long-term prison regimes needed to be humane and that measures needed to be put in place to neutralise the negative effects of imprisonment.

In the following decades, putting this philosophy into practice in punitive prison environments was a challenge, and the difficulties in balancing a liberal regime, whilst maintaining order and control, were felt from the 1970s through to the 1990s.[96] Whilst there were no escapes from dispersal prisons for the first 19 years of the new system, there were disturbances at Parkhurst, Albany and Gartree between 1969 and 1972 and incidents including hostage-taking at Albany in 1973. This was followed by a riot at Hull Prison in 1976, which resulted in so much damage that the prison had to be removed from the dispersal system for a year.[97]

Problems continued in the dispersal system into the 1980s and mid-1990s, but by this time punishment and its delivery had become dominated by a 'law and order' political agenda as discussed earlier in this chapter. Security would come sharply into focus again in April 1990, but this time the disturbances were not in long-term prison establishments, but in a local prison: Strangeways in Manchester. The Strangeways riot was the 'worst series of prison riots in the history of the British penal system' and lasted for 25 days.[98] Whilst the riot was still ongoing, Lord Chief Justice Woolf was appointed and set up an inquiry into the disturbances. His subsequent report focussed on Strangeways and five other serious riots that occurred at Glen Parva, Dartmoor, Cardiff, Bristol and Pucklechurch.[99] He recognised the need for a balance between security, control and justice.[100] His report noted that whilst the prevention of escape and the prevention of disruption would contribute towards stability in the prison system, he believed prisoners ought to be treated with 'humanity and fairness to prepare them for their return to the community in a way that makes it less likely that they will re-offend.'[101] Essentially, Woolf was saying that the prison lacked legitimacy in the eyes of the prisoners, and that this was centrally important in not only explaining the present disorder but also preventing future disorder from breaking out. However, only a few years later, escapes from high-security prisons, Whitemoor and Parkhurst, contributed to further security clampdowns across the prison estate. The subsequent Inquiries, Woodcock (1994) and Learmont (1995) led to the development of new practices and procedures based on security and control, including the use of dog patrols, more CCTV, more searches of all people entering prisons, increased security perimeters and tighter controls over prisoner movements, effecting not only high-security establishments, but the whole prison estate and seemingly evident of the 'new penology'.[102]

5. Conclusion

This chapter has examined two areas of punishment across the twentieth century, and what has been discussed is a narrative of contrasts. On the one hand, there were some fundamental changes to punishment across the century that resulted in what many would regard as positive steps, such as the end of the death penalty and the use of a wider range of penalties in the penal system that provide alternatives to the use of imprisonment by the courts. Most of these changes occurred in the first six decades of the century. Whilst the Victorian prison regimes of the early twentieth century might have been slow to change for prisoners, the numbers of those experiencing such prison environments were dramatically different by the 1930s. Whilst it might be argued that the range of penalties available in the penal system (developed in the early century and subsequently) 'widened the net' and led to a greater expansion of ways and methods by which punishment could be inflicted, in the prison system, decarceration occurred. The last four decades of the twentieth century were as remarkable, but for largely the opposite reason. The use of imprisonment as a sanction increased dramatically in the latter decades of the period. By the end of the twentieth century, England, Wales and Scotland imprisoned more people than many other countries in Western Europe, and those we send to prison experience imprisonment for longer periods than before.

Notes

1. D. Garland (1985) *Punishment and Welfare: A History of Penal Strategies* (Aldershot: Gower), p. 5.
2. Gladstone Committee (1895) *Report from the Departmental Committee on Prisons*, (C.7702), Vol. LVI (London: Home Office).
3. Anonymous (1894) 'Our Dark Places', *The Daily Chronicle*, 29th January 1894; O. Wilde (1898/2002) *De Profundis, The Ballad of Reading Gaol and Other Writings* (London: Wordsworth), pp. 115–38.
4. V. Bailey (1997) 'English Prisons, Penal Culture, and the Abatement of Imprisonment, 1895–1922', *Journal of British Studies*, Vol. 36, pp. 285–324; C. Harding (1988) '"The Inevitable End of a Discredited System?" The Origins of the Gladstone Committee Report on Prisons – 1895', *The Historical Journal*, Vol. 31, No. 3, pp. 591–608 and M. Nellis (1996) 'John Galsworthy's Justice', *British Journal of Criminology*, Vol. 36, No. 1, pp. 61–84.
5. Garland (1985) *Punishment and Welfare*, passim.
6. G. Mair and L. Burke (2012) *Redemption, Rehabilitation and Risk Management: A History of Probation* (Abingdon: Routledge); L. Radzinowicz and R. Hood (1990) *A History of the English Criminal Law and Its Administration from 1750: Volume 5: The Emergence of Penal Policy* (London: Stevens); for more on the early history of probation see W. McWilliams (1983) 'The Mission to the English Police Court, 1876–1936', *The Howard Journal*, Vol. XXII, pp. 129–47; R. Gard (2014) *Rehabilitation and Probation in England and Wales, 1876–1962* (London: Bloomsbury); M. Vanstone (2004) *Supervising Offenders in the Community: A History of Probation Theory and Practice* (Aldershot: Ashgate).
7. Judicial Statistics (1902) *Judicial Statistics of England and Wales, for 1900.* [Cd. 953, 1115]: 49; 65.

8. There is very little research in the history of crime or criminological research about the use of financial penalties, despite their prominent use in the criminal justice system. Notable exceptions are P. Young (1989) 'Punishment, Money and a Sense of Justice', in P. Carlen and D. Cook (eds) *Paying for Crime* (Milton Keynes: Open University Press); A.E. Bottoms (1983) 'Some Neglected Features of Contemporary Penal Systems', in D. Garland and P. Young (eds) *The Power to Punish: Contemporary Penality and Social Analysis* (London: Heinemann) and more recently, O'Malley, for overview see P. O'Malley (2013) 'Monetized Justice: Money and Punishment in Consumer Societies', in J. Simon and R. Sparks (eds) *The Sage Handbook of Punishment and Society* (London: Sage).
9. D. Wilson (2014) *Pain and Retribution: A Short History of British Prisons, 1066 to the Present* (London: Reaktion Books), p. 89.
10. Gard (2014) *Rehabilitation and Probation in England and Wales,* passim.
11. Mair and Burke (2012) *Redemption, Rehabilitation and Risk Management,* passim.
12. V. Bailey (1987) *Delinquency and Citizenship: Reclaiming the Young Offender, 1914–1948* (Clarendon: Oxford); W.J. Forsythe (1990) *Penal Discipline, Reformatory Projects and the English Prison Commission 1895–1939* (Exeter: Exeter University Press).
13. H. Johnston and B. Godfrey (2013) 'Counterblast: The Perennial Problem of Short Prison Sentences', *Howard Journal of Criminal Justice,* Vol. 52, No. 4, pp. 433–37 and S. McConville (1995) *English Local Prisons: Next Only to Death, 1860–1900* (London: Routledge), passim.
14. See A. Rutherford (1984) *Prisons and the Process of Justice: The Reductionist Challenge* (London: Heinemann) and Wilson (2014) *Pain and Retribution,* passim.
15. Garland (1985) *Punishment and Welfare,* passim.
16. See for instance Radzinowicz and Hood (1990) *A History of the English Criminal Law and Its Administration from 1750,* passim; C. Emsley (2010 edition) *Crime and Society in England, 1750–1900* (Harlow: Longman) and B. Godfrey, D. Cox and S. Farrall (2010) *Serious Offenders: A Historical Study of Habitual Criminals* (Oxford: Oxford University Press).
17. See for instance G. Stedman-Jones (2013) *Outcast London: A Study in the Relationship between Classes in Victorian Society* (London: Verso) and B. Godfrey (2014) *Crime in England, 1880–1940* (Abingdon: Routledge).
18. S. Hobhouse and A.F. Brockway (1922) *English Prisons To-day: Being the Report of the Prison System Enquiry Committee 1922* (London: Longmans, Green & Co.).

19. S.K. Ruck (ed.) (1951) *Paterson on Prisons: The Collected Papers of Sir Alexander Paterson* (London: Frederick Muller), p. 23.

20. See A. Brown (2013) *Inter-war Penal Policy and Crime in England: The Dartmoor Convict Prison Riot, 1932* (Basingstoke: Palgrave Macmillan); W.J. Forsythe (1990) *Penal Discipline, Reformatory Projects and the English Prison Commission,* passim and Wilson (2014) *Pain and Retribution,* Chapter 4.

21. Brown (2013) *Inter-war Penal Policy,* p. 1.

22. See Forsythe (1990) *Penal Discipline,* passim; B. Forsythe (1995) 'The Garland Thesis and the Origins of Modern English Prison Discipline: 1835 to 1939', *The Howard Journal,* Vol. 34, No. 3, pp. 259–73; Hobhouse and Brockway (1922) *English Prisons To-day,* passim; Rutherford (1984) *Prisons and the Process of Justice,* passim and Brown (2013) *Inter-war Penal Policy,* passim.

23. See for instance Forsythe (1990) *Penal Discipline,* passim; Bailey (1997) 'English Prisons', passim; H. Johnston (2008) 'Reclaiming the Criminal: The Role and Training of Prison Officers in England, 1877–1914', *Howard Journal of Criminal Justice,* Vol. 47, No. 3, pp. 297–312 and Brown (2013) *Inter-war Penal Policy,* passim.

24. For further discussion see S. D'Cruze and L. Jackson (2009) *Women, Crime and Justice in England since 1660* (Basingstoke: Palgrave Macmillan), passim; A. Barton (2005) *Fragile Moralities and Dangerous Sexualities: Two Centuries of Semi-Penal Institutionalisation for Women* (Aldershot: Ashgate), passim and P. Cox (2013) *Bad Girls in Britain: Gender, Justice and Welfare, 1900–1950* (Basingstoke: Palgrave Macmillan), passim.

25. S. McConville (1998) 'The Victorian Prison: England, 1865–1965', in N. Morris and D.J. Rothman (eds) *The Oxford History of the Prison: The Practice of Punishment in Western Society* (Oxford: Oxford University Press), pp. 117–38.

26. See Rutherford (1984) *Prisons and the Process of Justice,* passim and Wilson (2014) *Pain and Retribution,* Chapter 4.

27. Y. Jewkes and H. Johnston (2011) 'The English Prison during the First and Second World Wars: Hidden Lived Experiences of War', *Prison Service Journal,* Vol. 198, pp. 47–51 and Parliamentary Papers, RCP & DCP (1945) *Report of the Commissioners of Prisons and Directors of Convict Prisons for the Years 1939–1941,* Cmd. 6820.

28. Jewkes and Johnson (2011) 'The English Prison', and Report of the Commissioners, 1939–41.

29. K. Soothill (2007) 'Prison Histories and Competing Audiences, 1776–1966', in Y. Jewkes (ed.) *Handbook on Prisons* (Cullompton: Willan), pp. 27–48.

30. T. Morris (1989) *Crime and Criminal Justice since 1945* (Oxford: Basil Blackwell), p. 77.

31. See *ibid.* as well as M. Cavadino, J. Dignan and G. Mair (2013) *The Penal System* (London: Sage), passim.

32. P. Rawlings (1999) *Crime and Power – A History of Criminal Justice 1688–1998* (Essex: Longman), p. 139.

33. See S. Cohen (1972) *Folk Devils and Moral Panics: The Creation of the Mods and Rockers* (London: MacGibbon and Kee) and G. Pearson (1983) *Hooligan: A History of Respectable Fears* (London: Macmillan).

34. D. Taylor (1998) *Crime, Policing and Punishment in England, 1750–1914* (Basingstoke: Macmillan).

35. For further discussion see V.A.C. Gatrell (1996) *The Hanging Tree: Execution and the English People, 1770–1868* (Oxford: Oxford University Press) and J. Pratt (2002) *Punishment and Civilisation* (London: Sage).

36. See Pratt (2002) *Punishment and Civilisation* and B.P. Block and J. Hostettler (1997) *Hanging in the Balance: A History of the Abolition of Capital Punishment in Britain* (Hook: Waterside).

37. *Select Committee on Capital Punishment*, 1931, (15) (London: HMSO), p. 47.

38. Morris (1989) *Crime and Criminal Justice*, p. 77.

39. *Select Committee on Capital Punishment*, 1931, p. 97.

40. For further discussion see Block and Hostettler (1997) *Hanging in the Balance*, p. 97–101.

41. See E.R. Calvert (1928) *Capital Punishment in the Twentieth Century* (London: Putnam's Sons) and also J. Rowbotham (2010) 'Execution as Punishment in England: 1750–2000', in A.-M. Kilday and D.S. Nash (eds) *Histories of Crime: Britain 1600–2000* (Basingstoke: Palgrave Macmillan), pp. 180–202.

42. For further discussion see Morris (1989) *Crime and Criminal Justice* and Block and Hostettler (1997) *Hanging in the Balance*.

43. See Morris (1989) *Crime and Criminal Justice*, passim. For a more detailed discussion on the complexities of public opinion, the media and the death penalty see L. Seal (2014) *Capital Punishment in Twentieth-Century Britain: Audience, Memory, Justice* (Abingdon: Routledge).

44. See the references in note 34 above.

45. See *Ibid.* and C. Emsley (2005) *Hard Men: The English and Violence since 1750* (London: Hambledon).

46. For further discussion see Morris (1989) *Crime and Criminal Justice*, passim; Block and Hostettler (1997) *Hanging in the Balance*, passim; L. Seal (2011) 'Ruth Ellis and Public Contestation of the Death Penalty', *Howard Journal*

of Criminal Justice, Vol. 50, No. 5, pp. 492–504. For further discussion of the women sentenced to death in the twentieth century see A. Ballinger (2000) *Dead Woman Walking* (Aldershot: Ashgate).

47. Morris (1989) *Crime and Criminal Justice*, p. 73.
48. For further discussion see Cavadino, Dignan and Mair (2013) *The Penal System*, passim.
49. *Ibid.*
50. *Ibid.*
51. See the pertinent references at notes 47 and 48.
52. C. Emsley (2011) *Crime and Society in Twentieth-Century England* (Harlow: Longman), p. 201.
53. See for instance D. Cooper (1974) *The Lesson of the Scaffold* (London: Allen Lane) and C. Hibbert (1957) *The Road to Tyburn: The Story of Jack Sheppard and the Eighteenth Century Underworld* (London: Longmans, Green & Co.).
54. For further discussion see S. Webb and B. Webb (1963) *English Prisons under Local Government* (London: Longmans, Green & Co.); J.R.S. Whiting (1977) *Prison Reform in Gloucestershire* (London: Phillimore) and E. Stockdale (1977) *A Study of Bedford Prison, 1660–1877* (Chichester: Phillimore).
55. For further discussion see D. Hay (1975) 'Property, Authority and the Criminal Law', in D. Hay, P. Linebaugh, J.G. Rule, E.P. Thompson and C. Winslow (eds) *Albion's Fatal Tree: Crime and Society in Eighteenth-Century England* (London: Allen Lane), pp. 17–64; P. Linebaugh (1975) 'The Tyburn Riot against the Surgeons', in D. Hay et al. (eds) *Albion's Fatal Tree*, pp. 65–118; P. Linebaugh (1993) *The London Hanged – Crime and Civil Society in the Eighteenth Century* (London: Penguin); V.A.C. Gatrell (1990) 'Crime, Authority and the Policeman-State', in F.M.L. Thompson (ed.) *The Cambridge Social History of Britain 1750–1950, Volume Three* (Cambridge: Cambridge University Press), pp. 243–310 and Gatrell (1994) *The Hanging Tree* (Oxford: Oxford University Press).
56. See for instance M. Ignatieff (1978) *A Just Measure of Pain: The Penitentiary in the Industrial Revolution* (London: Macmillan); M. Ignatieff (1983) 'State, Civil Society and Total Institutions: A Critique of Recent Social Histories of Punishment', in S. Cohen and A. Scull (eds) *Social Control and the State* (London: Martin Robertson), pp. 75–105; D.J. Rothman (1990 edition) *The Discovery of the Asylum: Social Order and Disorder in the New Republic* (Boston: Little, Brown and Co); A. Platt (1969) *The Child Savers: The Invention of Delinquency* (Chicago: Chicago University Press) and S. Cohen (1985) *Visions of Social Control: Crime, Punishment and Classification* (London: Polity).

57. See for instance M. Foucault (1991) *Discipline and Punish – The Birth of the Prison* (London: Penguin); D. Melossi and M. Pavarini (1981) *The Prison and the Factory: Origins of the Penitentiary System* (London: Macmillan); Cohen and Scull (eds) (1983) *Social Control and the State* and Cohen (1985) *Visions of Social Control*. Subsequently, others have developed a Foucauldian approach to women's imprisonment including R.P. Dobash, R.E. Dobash and S. Gutteridge (1986) *The Imprisonment of Women* (Oxford: Basil Blackwell) or to the Prison Medical Service as for example with J. Sim (1990) *Medical Power in Prisons: Prison Medical Service in England, 1774–1998* (Milton Keynes: Open University Press).

58. Some examples are the work of Pieter Spierenburg and that of Randall McGowen such as P. Spierenburg (1984) *The Spectacle of Suffering: Execution and the Evolution of Repression – From a Pre-industrial Metropolis to the European Experience* (Cambridge: Cambridge University Press); P. Spierenburg (1991) *The Prison Experience: Disciplinary Institutions and Their Inmates in Early Modern Europe* (New Brunswick: Rutgers University Press); R. McGowen (1983) 'The Image of Justice and Reform of the Criminal Law in Early Nineteenth-Century England', *Buffalo Law Review*, Vol. 32, pp. 89–125; R. McGowen (1986) 'A Powerful Sympathy: Terror, the Prison, and Humanitarian Reform in Early Nineteenth-Century Britain', *Journal of British Studies*, Vol. 25, pp. 312–34; R. McGowen (1987) 'The Body and Punishment in Eighteenth-Century England', *Journal of Modern History*, Vol. 59, No. 4, pp. 651–79 and R. McGowen (1994) 'Civilising Punishment: The End of Public Execution in England', *Journal of British Studies*, Vol. 33, pp. 257–82. For additional examples see Garland (1985) *Punishment and Welfare*; D. Garland (2002) *The Culture of Control: Crime and Social Order in Contemporary Society* (Oxford: Oxford University Press); Pratt (2002) *Punishment and Civilisation* and P. Smith (2008) *Punishment and Culture* (Chicago: Chicago University Press).

59. Garland (1985) *Punishment and Welfare*, passim.

60. C. Emsley (2005) 'Crime and Punishment: Ten Years of Research, Filling In, Adding Up, Moving On: Criminal Justice History in Contemporary Britain', *Crime, Histoire & Sociétés/Crime, History & Societies*, Vol. 9, No. 1, pp. 117–38.

61. Cavadino, Dignan and Mair (2013) *The Penal System*, pp. 9–30 and Morris (1989) *Crime and Criminal Justice*, pp. 125–43.

62. Cavadino, Dignan and Mair (2013) *The Penal System*, passim.

63. See M. Fitzgerald and J. Sim (1982) *British Prisons* (London: Macmillan), passim.

64. D. Garland (2001) 'The Meaning of Mass Imprisonment', *Punishment and Society*, Vol. 3, No. 1, pp. 5–7.

65. Cavadino, Dignan and Mair (2013) *The Penal System*, p. 14.

66. M.M. Feeley and J. Simon (1992) 'The New Penology: Notes on the Emerging Strategy of Corrections and Its Implications', *Criminology*, Vol. 30, pp. 449–74. Available at http://scholarship.law.berkeley.edu/facpubs/718 (Accessed 18th November 2017).

67. See for instance Cavadino, Dignan and Mair (2013) *The Penal System*, passim; J. Pratt, D. Brown, M. Brown, S. Hallsworth and W. Morrison (eds) (2005) *The New Punitiveness: Trends, Theories, Perspectives* (Cullompton: Willan).

68. *Ibid.*

69. *Ibid.*, p. xiii.

70. See J. Pratt (2006) *Penal Populism* (London: Sage).

71. C. Emsley (2005) *Hard Men: The English and Violence since 1750*, pp. 168–69.

72. For further discussion see J.E. Thomas (1972) *The English Prison Officer since 1850* (London: Routledge & Kegan Paul).

73. S. Hobhouse and A.F. Brockway (1922) *English Prisons To-day*, passim.

74. *Royal Commission on Capital Punishment*, 1949–1953, Cmd. 8932 (London: HMSO), p. 250.

75. McConville (1995) *English Local Prisons*, pp. 409–31.

76. Pratt (2002) *Punishment and Civilisation*, p. 27.

77. *Select Committee on Capital Punishment*, 1931, p. 97.

78. Seal (2014) *Capital Punishment in Twentieth-Century Britain*, p. 66.

79. *Royal Commission on Capital Punishment*, 1949–1953, p. 300.

80. 'Two Sentenced to Death After 7-Day Trial', *The Guardian*, 8th July 1964, p. 6.

81. 'Silent Vigil as Two Men Are Hanged', *The Guardian*, 14th August 1964, p. 18.

82. *Ibid.*

83. M. Engel, 'Enough Rope', *The Guardian*, 12th August 1989, p. 23.

84. See Emsley (2011) *Crime and Society*, passim.

85. For further discussion see Rowbotham (2010) 'Execution as Punishment', passim.

86. Murder (Abolition of the Death Penalty) Act 1965, c. 71. Available at http://www.legislation.gov.uk/ukpga/1965/71/contents (Accessed 18th November 2017).

87. A free vote in both the House of Commons and the House of Lords voted in favour of abolition, with leaders of all major parties voting for abolition, see Emsley (2011), *Crime and Society*, p. 207.

88. http://www.echr.coe.int/Documents/Convention_ENG.pdf (accessed 21 February 2018).

89. Earl Mountbatten of Burma (1966) *Report of the Inquiry into Prison Escapes and Security* (London: HMSO).

90. *Ibid.*, p. 7.

91. *Ibid.*

92. *Ibid.*

93. *Ibid.*

94. Advisory Council on the Penal System (1968) *The Regime for Long-Term Prisoners in Conditions of Maximum Security* (London: HMSO).

95. D. Drake (2012) *Prisons, Punishment and the Pursuit of Security* (Basingstoke: Palgrave Macmillan), p. 40.

96. *Ibid.*

97. *Ibid.* See Parliamentary Papers, *Report of an Inquiry by the Chief Inspector of the Prison Service into the Cause and Circumstances of the Events at H.M. Prison Hull during the period 31st August to 3rd September 1976*, Cmd. 453 (1977).

98. *Prison Disturbances April 1990*, Report of an Inquiry by the Right Honourable Lord Justice Woolf and His Honour Judge Stephen Tumin, Cmd. 1456 (London: HMSO), p. 1.

99. *Ibid.*

100. *Ibid.*, p. 19. See also E. Genders (2008) 'The Woolf Report', in Y. Jewkes and J. Bennett (eds) *Dictionary of Prisons and Punishment* (Willan: Cullompton), pp. 322–23.

101. Cited in Cavadino, Dignan and Mair (2013) *The Penal System*, p. 24.

102. See J. Woodcock (1994) *Report of the Enquiry into the Escape of Six Prisoners from the Special Security Unit at Whitemoor Prison, Cambridgeshire, on Friday 9th September 1994* (London: HMSO) and J. Learmont (1995) *Review of Prison Service Security in England and Wales and the Escape from Parkhurst Prison, Tuesday 3rd January 1995* (London: HMSO). For further discussion see A. Liebling (2002) 'A "Liberal Regime within a Secure Perimeter"?', in A.E. Bottoms and M. Tonry (eds) *Ideology, Crime and Criminal Justice* (Willan: Cullompton), pp. 97–150.

10

Law Enforcement: Policies and Perspectives

Neil Davie

1. Introduction

At the beginning of the twentieth century, Britain's police service was still a relatively young institution. It had been created piecemeal, beginning with London's Metropolitan Police or 'Met', established by Sir Robert Peel in 1829, which replaced the capital's largely amateur and part-time corps of parish constables, watchmen and entrepreneurial thief-takers. Legislation from the 1830s to the 1850s allowed borough and county forces to be established throughout Britain on the London model,[1] though well into the twentieth century they would retain a distinctive organisation and system of local accountability, setting them apart both from each other and from the Met.[2] Established above all in response to elite fears about rising crime levels[3] and the threat to social order posed by the socio-economic and political fallout of the Industrial Revolution,[4] the early days of the 'New Police', as it was known, were dogged by controversy. Complaints about both over- and under-zealous policing were legion, and there was a long-running dispute between central government and local authorities, as well as between political factions within local communities, over such issues as democratic accountability and cost. By 1900, however, the criticism and resistance of those early years had been largely forgotten, and the model of the disciplined, bureaucratically controlled local force, its officers a familiar presence on the streets as they patrolled in organised 'beats', had become accepted (albeit grudgingly and within certain limits by those groups most likely to be on the receiving end of a police truncheon) at all levels of British society.[5]

By any measure, the structure and practice of law enforcement in Britain would change out of all recognition during the following hundred years. The number of separate police forces in England and Wales fell from over 200 to 43; a reduction accompanied by increasing central government control, which in turn brought greater uniformity. By the 1920s, it was being suggested in Whitehall that the British police had been 'transformed from a collection of separate (sometimes very separate) Forces into what amounted, for most practical purposes, to a single Service', with the Home Office 'in effect, a central police authority'. This was an exaggeration, but accurately identified future trends.[6] Practice changed significantly too, if gradually and unevenly, as beat policing gradually gave way to motorised patrols, specialised departments appeared and new forensic identification techniques were introduced. As important in many ways was the changing face of the British police over the century. Women officers joined the ranks from 1914, and in the post-war period, growing numbers of ethnic minority officers were recruited, though proportionally they would continue to remain less numerous than in the wider population. The introduction of both groups was generally met with grudging acceptance by existing police officers, though hostility and discrimination would remain a persistent problem within the service.[7]

These organisational and operational changes were partly a response to the shifting pattern of criminal behaviour during the century (itself a function of broader demographic, socio-economic and cultural trends in the country as well as changes in the criminal law); and partly a function of the adoption of new tools, technologies and strategies in order to bring law-breakers to justice. It is important to emphasise, however, that there was nothing ineluctable about this process. The decision to develop particular tools and technologies and implement particular policing strategies involved making *choices* from among the range of law enforcement options on offer; choices in Parliament, choices in the Home Office, and choices among senior police managers.[8] Even the individual constable pounding the beat or patrolling in a panda car was faced with choices, albeit of a different kind. Indeed, it has been suggested that one of the things that defines policing on the ground (as distinct from other stages in the prosecution and punishment process) is the deliberate *non-enforcement* of the law, with officers choosing to pursue certain types of wrongdoing and turning a blind eye to others.[9] There was also a grey area where the police might intervene to prevent behaviour judged 'disorderly' or 'suspicious', even though no criminal offence had been committed. On this latter point, historian Philip Rawlings observes that, for much of its history, 'the [police] uniform was sufficient to empower almost any action – a house search, an assault, detention in a cell, an order to "move on"'.[10] At each level of the decision-making process then, certain forms of criminal (or even non-criminal, but still 'unacceptable') behaviour were singled out for particular attention, and certain tools and strategies deployed from the range of options on offer in order to address that behaviour.

Those choices were not merely pragmatic and organisational ones, however, although they might be presented as such by the actors involved, neither were they determined exclusively by Britain's political, cultural and institutional traditions. The latter were certainly important, limiting the range of options seen as worthy of serious consideration.[11] Within these parameters, however, there were real choices to be made, and the process was accompanied by debate – at times heated – concerning the causes of crime and the role that law enforcement agencies and their officers should play in preventing wrongdoing and identifying and pursuing offenders. This theme will be explored in detail in the last section of this chapter, which examines shifting opinions on police discretion, as embodied in the 1984 Police and Criminal Evidence Act (PACE). A number of different groups of actors took part in this and other debates on law enforcement in twentieth-century Britain: MPs, government officials, criminologists and other 'experts', and journalists. It is on these debates that this chapter will focus, though it always needs to be remembered, as we noted earlier, that the room for discretion at the sharp end of policing means that there is no simple relationship between the elaboration of policies or objectives in Parliament, the Home Office or elsewhere, and their application on the ground.

In the next section, we shall see that in the late 1950s, after a long period of relative quiescence, debates about the role of the British police took on a new urgency against a backdrop of concern about rising crime rates. Up to that point, it has been argued, 'the modus operandi of the police, their structure and organisation [had] changed little' since 1900. Thereafter, 'the pace of change became hectic'.[12] A key question in these new circumstances was whether the police should be given new powers in order to tackle this apparent crime wave, and if so, what kind of powers? Or were there, on the contrary, grounds for arguing that existing powers were being abused, and that extending the latter would represent a threat to civil liberties? In short, what exactly was the police *for*? From the late 1950s, the search for answers to those questions would be accompanied by what criminologist Robert Reiner has termed 'a babble of scandalous revelation, controversy and competing agendas for reform'.[13] That 'babble' would not let up for the remainder of the century.

2. Chronology

In terms of changes both in police organisation and structure and in wider attitudes to policing, twentieth-century Britain would seem then to break down into two broad periods, with the late 1950s and early 1960s marking a significant watershed. Before considering in detail the reasons for this shift at mid-century, let us turn to the period which preceded it, which has traditionally been characterised as one marked by a broad consensus in British society about the nature and role of its police. There is no shortage of contemporary evidence attesting to support for what was considered a distinctly British or English (the two terms were often used interchangeably in this period) conception of law enforcement. Throughout the first half of the twentieth century, the British frequently congratulated themselves that they possessed 'the best police in the world', though little justification was given for the use of this superlative, beyond the fact that, unlike their counterparts in continental Europe and the United States, the British 'bobby' was said to be uniquely *un*-militarised, *un*armed and *un*-political – a powerful symbol of the consensual and cohesive nature of the country's social and political institutions.[14]

The idea that there existed in the past a 'golden age of policing', with the British bobby, avuncular yet firm, dressed in a high-buttoned blue tunic and helmet reminiscent of Victorian England, dispensing impartial justice – including meting out summary punishment to juvenile ne'er-do-wells with the occasional 'clip around the ear'[15] – remains a seductive one, even today.[16] Many associate this image with the popular fictional character, PC George Dixon, created for a 1950 feature film, and resurrected five years later for the long-running BBC television series, *Dixon of Dock Green*.[17] We shall see in the following section that recent historical scholarship has questioned the ubiquity of this benign attitude to British policing up until the 1950s, particularly among the working class. It is also clear that the description of the British police as un-militarised, unarmed and un-political is at best a partial (in both senses of the term) description of early twentieth-century law enforcement.[18] Nevertheless, even taking these caveats on board, there seems little doubt that during the first half of the twentieth century, the British police did indeed enjoy a measure of cross-party political support and public approbation unmatched either in previous or subsequent periods.[19]

It is also striking that in the period between 1900 and 1955, the police largely escaped the critical attention being given to other domains of the criminal justice system by government ministers, Home Office officials and criminologists. True, as we have noted, there were periodic attempts to rationalise and centralise, usually with a view to tightening Home Office supervision – actions which occasionally sparked friction between central and local government. The First World War and its aftermath is generally considered to have been particularly significant in this respect, bringing as it did the multiplication of Home Office committees, directives and inter-force conferences.[20] There were also calls for the British police to embrace the possibilities offered by developments in forensic science and by new communication technologies, notably the motor car, the telephone and the radio. Indeed, considerable, if uneven, progress was made in each of these areas during the first half of the century.[21]

It would equally be misleading to state that the police service and its officers were entirely free of controversy during these years. From time to time, cases of corruption or of the excessive use of force would surface – the latter generally associated with the policing of industrial disputes or the detention of suspects in police cells. As Rawlings observes, how-ever, '[m]ost allegations were simply dismissed, ignored or never came to light'.[22] In the few instances where police corruption or the use of unjusti-fied force by officers *were* officially confirmed, such abuses were normally put down to the excesses of a few wayward 'black sheep'.[23] Experienced London magistrate Cecil Chapman was probably thus reflecting a com-mon view when he wrote in 1925 that 'When uncontrolled power is put into the hands of men, it is not to be expected that everybody can resist repeated temptation to abuse it.'[24]

However, if we compare debates in the field of law enforcement in the first half of the twentieth century with those in penal policy over the same period, it is immediately apparent that the two fields stand in marked contrast. Whereas the Gladstone Commission of 1895 had ushered in a period of wide-ranging discussion about the type of punishment best suited to particular kinds of offender, with many contributors taking as read that the Victorian prison system was in urgent need of a radical over-haul, there were few calls for similar root and branch reform of the British police. The underlying causes of this contrast are complex, but it seems likely that a key reason why the police largely escaped critical scrutiny during these years was the apparently sharp downward turn in the crime rate during the period 1880–1940. According to the judicial statistics for England and Wales, prosecutions fell across the board, with a particularly significant fall in the number of violent crimes. For example, the number of prosecutions for common assault fell from approximately 33 offences per 10,000 persons in 1871 to about 16 by 1901 and just 5.6 by 1931. Similar, if rather less spectacular, falls can be observed in other areas over the same period. Prosecutions for drunkenness in 1931 were thus only a quarter as many as in 1871, while those for criminal damage fell by two-thirds over the same period.[25]

Interpreting criminal statistics has long been recognised as a particularly hazardous enterprise.[26] A recent synthesis of research on the subject for the early twentieth century by Barry Godfrey describes the official figures of the period as 'manifestly unreliable'. It would appear that a significant but unknown (and probably unknowable) proportion of the apparent fall in the number of crimes committed was the result of changes in the law or in police procedure, rather than any genuine reduction in criminal activity.[27] That being said, Godfrey concludes that even when such distortions are taken into account, the evidence would seem to point to 'a gradual, long-term and uneven decline' in crime during the first half of the twentieth century.[28] Even more important, from our point of view, is his observation that 'Social and public policy between 1880 and 1940 was ... largely driven by the belief that violence was declining, that public disorder was falling, and that the war on crime was well-advanced'.[29]

With crime low and apparently set to continue on its downward trajectory, it is perhaps to be expected that a certain complacency should have set in in law enforcement circles. True, there was a small group of persistent, mostly petty, offenders bucking the downward trend, known significantly at the turn of the century as *the residuum*. Their stubborn refusal to conform to the statistical predictions of their day made recidivists a source of intense medical, penal and criminological speculation throughout the period; one 1908 book on the subject describing them as 'Britain's blot' (complete with evocative black stain on the cover to drive the point home).[30] Yet if Britain had blotted her copybook in this respect, it was more of an irritant than a major source of concern for most commentators and policy-makers. There were those, mainly with links to the Edwardian eugenics movement, who were convinced that an alarming surge in criminal activity was just around the corner (to be perpetrated, apparently, by a growing army of mentally and physically sub-normal habitual offenders), but such doom-laden predictions attracted little support – and were consistently belied by the official crime statistics.[31]

However, a widespread view had become entrenched among specialists by 1900 that the habitual offender, once embarked on a life of crime, was largely impervious to reform, having been driven to law-breaking by irresistible external forces which he or she was powerless to resist. Whether these forces were derived from the social environment, from an individual's physical and psychic constitution or a mixture of the two was a matter of long-running and sometimes acrimonious debate,[32] but many concurred that 'the "criminal" man [was], to a large extent, a "defective" man, either physically or mentally'.[33] The solutions proposed tended to reflect the familiar nature–nurture divide. Some saw no alternative but to sequester large numbers of the criminal or proto-criminal 'feeble-minded'; a few went as far as calling for the 'sterilisation' of such groups, voluntary or otherwise. Others preferred to put their faith in modernised penal institutions, including the new 'borstals' for juvenile offenders, or chose to rely on the beneficial effects of wider educational provision and other state-regulated social welfare remedies. As I have argued elsewhere, these were not necessarily mutually exclusive options; many policy-makers and criminologists agreed that different solutions were required for different kinds of offender.[34]

Seen from a modern perspective, what is striking in these early twentieth-century debates on the best way of tackling crime is that the police were given little more than a walk-on part. There were several reasons for this. As we have just seen, the focus of official and expert attention in these years was on 'defective' habitual criminals, seen as largely immune to conventional crime prevention techniques; at the mercy of environmental or hereditary forces beyond their control. Only increased state intervention, it was reasoned, whether in the medical, penal or social fields, was capable of bringing those destructive forces under control.[35] This was manifestly not a job for the humble bobby on the beat. Not all crime was the work of such persistent offenders of course, though not surprisingly perhaps, both the eugenics movement and the psychiatric profession tended to emphasise (though from very different starting points) the currency of these weak-willed, criminal automatons.[36]

For other types of law-breakers – juvenile offenders, occasional criminals and those committing public order offences – most contributors to the debate were in no doubt that the time-honoured methods adopted by the police were, and would remain, perfectly adequate; particularly, it was argued, when combined with a criminal justice system placing an increasing emphasis on rehabilitation and training. This 'liberal-progressive' approach, as it has been termed, which dominated official thinking in the United Kingdom for the first half of the century, presented itself as the 'modern', 'scientific' alternative to Victorian-style incarceration. It emphasised the importance of the classification of prisoners by psychologists, psychiatrists and social workers, and the need to develop specialised institutions (like open prisons or the borstals referred to earlier) to cater for them. The greater use of suspended sentences, probation and parole, together with a variety of welfare agencies (both state-run and voluntary) was also urged in order to divert offenders away from prison.[37]

For a variety of reasons, this effective marginalisation of law enforcement in debates about criminal justice policy would not last. From the late 1950s, the model of British policing described above would begin to come under strain and by the end of the following decade had been seriously compromised. In some circles at least, as Reiner puts it, the 'plod' was being transformed into a 'pig'.[38] There was no sudden collapse in support for the police, of course, even among those groups most likely to be on the receiving end of police intervention.[39] Nevertheless, from the late 1950s onwards, a number of high-profile cases of corruption (with several high-ranking officers among those implicated), coupled with growing disquiet about heavy-handed policing of civil rights demonstrations and industrial disputes, plus new evidence of excessive force used to interrogate suspects or 'teach a lesson' to 'unruly' youths, heralded a shift in attitudes to law enforcement.[40] It was not so much that standards of police conduct were slipping, or that there were more 'black sheep' manning (if that is the right word) the thin blue line. Rather, it turned out that in the new political and cultural context of post-war Britain, the government, the courts and the public were no longer prepared (or perhaps it would be more accurate to say that they were *less* prepared) to give officers the benefit of the doubt in cases of alleged malpractice, the result, as one senior police officer had put it in 1958, of 'an increasingly critical outlook by a more widely and highly educated public'.[41] Twelve years later, a Police Federation spokesman put it more bluntly, referring to the increasing tendency for his officers to find themselves 'eyeball to eyeball with the fanatics, the lunatics and the hooligans'.[42]

By the standards of later decades, much of the debate around these issues in the 1960s can seem decidedly low-key. However, two parallel developments in these years were to transform the debate and, in time, official thinking on law enforcement. The first of these developments was the growing conviction that contrary to what had been taken as read for the previous half century or more, it now looked as if the war on crime was not being won after all. Once again, official crime statistics took centre stage, 'provid[ing] a basis both for media and political debate, and a benchmark by which policy was assessed, made and remade.'[43] Although research by criminologists and historians in the 1970s was providing a much clearer idea of the limitations of official statistics – indicating that the seven-fold increase in the four decades after 1945[44] was most definitely not to be taken at face value – the general upward arc could not be gainsaid, and indeed, was confirmed by the first results of the victim-based *British Crime Survey* (BCS) when they became available in the early 1980s.[45]

Up until the mid-1960s, with crime still low, the near certainty of detection by the police was still widely seen as the best form of deterrent, whereas it was up to the criminal justice system to provide the penal remedies – whether punitive or rehabilitative (or a combination of the two) – which would bring about a change of heart in the offender. It was this division of labour, as we have seen, which meant that law enforcement was considered largely irrelevant in discussions about the causes of crime. By the 1970s, however, as criminologist Terence Morris notes,

> a mood of pessimism had set in, stimulated by the recognition that even if rehabilitation 'worked' it would be working on so few – by reason of the small proportion of offenders who were apprehended – that it would hardly make a dent in the problem. The enthusiasm then shifted to the idea of *physical methods of crime prevention that targeted all offenders*. For this reason the future social historians may make mention of the last decades of the twentieth century as the time when the modern locksmith, aided by all the advantages of microchip electronics, came into his own.[46]

It might be added that in this new context the police officer 'came into his own' also, though quite what 'his own' *was* would remain a subject of controversy, as we shall see in the last section of this chapter. This is the second development of the period that was to transform debates and official thinking about policing in Britain from the 1960s onwards: a major shift in what have been termed the 'expert narratives' on crime–how crime and crime prevention were conceptualised by government ministers, Home Office officials and academic criminologists.[47] As we have seen, the dominant viewpoint in the first half of the century and up until the 1960s was that criminals were fundamentally different from the rest of the population and were drawn into offending by environmental or hereditary forces beyond their control which resulted in a pathological incapacity to respect the law.[48] This view was challenged by a new generation of academic criminologists and sociologists, steeped in the radical politics of the 1960s, who rejected outright the previous emphasis on individualised, medico-psychological profiling. Although they shared with that earlier perspective the importance ascribed to social deprivation as a cause of crime, the radical criminologists underlined the importance of broader, *structural* causes of offending, particularly those linked to divisions of class, gender and race. They also argued that previous research into crime, in concentrating on the poor and the working class, had largely ignored white-collar crime as well as police malpractice – notably with regard to the black community. Indeed, a series of official inquiries in the 1980s and '90s, as well as a growing body of academic research, provided clear evidence of malpractice in the policing of Britain's ethnic minority communities, though its scale and significance remains the subject of intense debate.[49] Particularly serious, from the point of the view of the police, were the conclusions of the 1999 Macpherson Inquiry into the murder of black teenager Stephen Lawrence that the police investigation had been 'marred by a combination of professional incompetence, institutional racism and a failure of leadership by senior officers'.[50]

Exponents of this new brand of radical criminology often had close links to civil liberties, feminist and anti-racist groups – the growth of which was also a feature of this period – and tended to share with them the conviction that the police were as much the cause of, as the solution to, Britain's apparently growing lawlessness. They pointed to cases like the death of teacher Blair Peach during an anti-racist protest in Southall, London, in April 1979. Police critics were left unconvinced by the subsequent coroner's verdict of 'death by misadventure', and suspected that Peach had died at the hands of one of the Met's anti-riot officers.[51] Indeed, as Robert Reiner points out, this period saw the emergence of a growing gulf between sections of middle-class opinion and the police, the origins of which can be traced to the experience of political protest from the 1960s onwards and the politicization of certain forms of marginal deviance affecting some middle-class people, such as recreational drugs and homosexuality. Although such a stance was by no means universal in middle-class circles, it was, as Reiner points out, 'of enormous significance in converting policing into an overt political issue.'[52]

These radical perspectives on the causes of crime and the role of the police were not the only 'expert narratives' in circulation, however. As criminologist David Garland has noted, there were two main alternatives on offer. The first, emerging at the beginning of the 1980s, drew on a longstanding conception of a pathologically deviant 'criminal class' existing at the bottom of society, wilfully cutting itself off from the law-abiding, hard-working majority of the working class. One of the most well-known exponents of this thesis was American sociologist Charles Murray. His references to an 'underclass', composed of 'people who live in a different world from other Britons', and whose rejection of family values, aversion to work, and lack of respect for the law risked 'contaminating the life of the entire neighbourhood', could have been lifted, almost word for word, from works published in the 1850s and '60s.[53] It would become a common refrain, with minor variations, throughout the 1980s and '90s.[54] As Garland notes:

> This is the criminology of the dangerous other … depicting it [crime] in melodramatic terms, viewing it as a catastrophe, framing it in the language of warfare and social defence. … This view of the criminal other has both ontological and epistemological implications. Being intrinsically evil or wicked, some offenders are not like us. … The appropriate reaction for society is one of social defence: we should defend ourselves against these dangerous enemies rather than concern ourselves with their welfare and prospects for rehabilitation.[55]

Garland's second criminological narrative also emerged at the beginning of the 1980s and became firmly entrenched thereafter in the Home Office.[56] It was, like the first, little interested in the prospects for rehabilitation, though for rather different reasons. Eschewing 'dispositional' theories of crime altogether (that is to say the view that certain people have a disposition to offend and that the key to crime prevention lies in modifying their behaviour), emphasis was placed on what became known as 'situational' crime prevention. This was described by a leading government criminologist of the period as 'a pre-emptive approach that relies, not on improving society or its institutions, but on reducing opportunities for crime'; the aim being 'to increase the effort and risks of crime and reduce the rewards as perceived by a wide range of offenders.'[57] In place of Murray's moral certainties, here we have 'an approach to social order that is, for the most part, amoral and technological', seeking to redesign public space (transport systems, commercial and leisure areas, housing, etc.) in ways that minimise the opportunities for disorder and deviance; an approach that is based not so much on crime control in the traditional sense as on a form of risk management.[58] Situational crime prevention also sets great store by the technologies of electronic surveillance (notably CCTV) and ever more sophisticated forensic identification techniques, both seen as powerful tools for deterring crime and detecting offenders.[59]

What is striking about both the underclass thesis and its later variants, and the pre-emptive situational approach to crime prevention is that they place renewed emphasis on the importance of law enforcement, whether it is a question of deterrence, prevention, 'partnerships' with other public and private bodies, surveillance or aggressive, proactive policing.[60] No longer are the police seen as bit-players in the war against crime, a point to which we will return below. Whether that faith in policing solutions is justified is another matter. As the authors of a recent survey of the subject conclude, 'the police are primarily *managers of crime* and *keepers of the peace*, not a vehicle for reducing crime substantially'. They add: 'Crime is the product of deeper social forces, largely beyond the ambit of any policing tactics, and the clear-up rate is a function of crime levels and other aspects of workload rather than police efficiency.'[61]

3. Historiography

As in other fields of criminal justice history, the historiography of law enforcement in Britain took a radically different direction in the 1970s.[62] Up to that point, research on the history of policing had been relatively limited, and what did exist had been largely confined to studies of administrative and jurisdictional changes, often penned by journalists, civil servants or former officers.[63] This body of work – published during the period of low crime rates and near universal faith in the British model of policing – tended to present the history of law enforcement in the country as one of gradual advance, driven by a group of far-sighted and well-intentioned reformers. Critics of this onward march of reform tended to be dismissed as reactionary or foolish, misguidedly attempting to stand in the way of ineluctable progress towards that golden age of bureaucratic efficiency and public consent.[64] Although the best of this 'Whig' police history, as it is known, provides valuable, detailed evidence of the administrative and legal changes affecting police work from the 1830s onwards, it pays little attention to the broader political and social context; it underestimates the difficulty of achieving and maintaining 'consent', particularly among the working class; and it has little to say about white-collar crime or the darker side of police 'discretion' on the picket line or in the detention cell. This early police history also suffered from a notable geographical bias, with the history of policing outside England largely neglected.[65]

From the 1970s, a group of 'revisionist' historians began to address these issues. As one survey of these debates puts it, '[t]he Whig view was not so much revised as swatted away by the radical historians of the 1970s and '80s.'[66] Sharing some of the theoretical and methodological priorities of the radical criminologists referred to earlier, the revisionists re-wrote police history. They were often inspired, at least initially, by a Marxian paradigm that considered the police not (as Whig scholars had tended to do) as the impartial instruments of a benevolent state, but as the more or less willing agents of 'ruling class' interests; just as the criminal justice system was considered to serve those same sectional interests in the courtroom and the prison cell. This conception drew on the pioneering work of a number of scholars from the 1960s and early 1970s, chief amongst them E.P. Thompson and Michel Foucault.[67] The result was that revisionist criminal justice historians portrayed the 'new police' above all as 'the eyes and ears of ruling elites at the very centers of working-class daily life',[68] playing a pivotal role in the machinery of surveillance and control deemed necessary to create an obedient, subservient workforce of the kind needed for the emerging capitalist economy.

Since the 1980s, local studies of British policing history have proliferated (part of what has been termed an 'explosion of crime history' during the period[69]), bringing empirical and conceptual nuance to the early, rather crude 'social control' model on which much of the early revisionist police history was based.[70] The work of Clive Emsley and his collaborators at the Open University's International Centre for the History of Crime, Policing and Justice has been particularly important in this respect. Emsley's *The English Police: A Political and Social History* (1991) represented a key early synthesis of this new empirical work (including his own major contribution). Other important works followed from this group of scholars,[71] including the authoritative four-volume reference collection published by Ashgate in 2011. The collection's third volume, *Police and Policing in the Twentieth Century*, edited by Chris A. Williams, represents an invaluable resource for students of the subject.[72] We are also gaining a better understanding of the specific trajectories of policing history in Wales and Scotland, and in Ireland, both before and after partition.[73] At the same time, a number of important general works on the history of policing in Britain in the twentieth century have appeared since Emsley's 1991 book.[74] Post-Whig police historians have only rather belatedly ventured into the twentieth century, though it is significant that, in addition to the Williams' collection, two of Britain's most respected specialists in criminal justice history have recently published detailed studies of all or part of the period, providing much-needed syntheses of research in the field.[75] For the moment, the first half of the twentieth century is rather better served by detailed historical research than more recent decades, though this is changing.[76] For the period after 1945, however, it is difficult to make a clear distinction between 'historical' and 'criminological' works. Indeed, a number of criminologists working partly or wholly in the law enforcement field have gone to considerable lengths to ground their research in its historical context, as can be seen from several of the works cited earlier in this chapter.[77] It is to be hoped that such historically informed criminology, just as criminologically informed history, will gain further ground in the years to come.[78]

4.   Case Study

Discretion, as we have noted, is an inevitable part of police work. Indeed, it has been pointed out that 'the police department has the special property … that within it discretion increases as one moves down the hierarchy'.[79] Historically, the thin blue line was just one deep most of the time, with a single police constable patrolling his beat, usually on foot, usually at night. This state of affairs meant that, whatever the theoretical means of oversight in place,[80] in practice, beat constables (like their plain-clothes colleagues in the detective departments) were largely on their own at the sharp end

of policing. This meant that they were able to exercise considerable disure
tion when dealing with transgressors, deciding whether to make an arrest,
issue a warning, or administer the kind of summary chastisement referred
to earlier.[81] While senior officers were aware of the potential for undue
force being used while making an arrest or in a detention cell, and that the
customary perquisites of the bobby on the beat could give way to bribes or
other forms of corruption, it was generally assumed that such abuses were
rare, and that when they did occur, the police could keep its own house
in order. Another long-unchallenged aspect of police discretion, noted by
Barry Godfrey, derived from the fact that particular, well-defined groups
in society were generally held to blame for most of the country's criminal activity. As a result, such groups as drunken men, unruly youths, the
unemployed and 'aliens' were regularly singled out for intensive surveillance and disproportionate coercive force.[82]

For a variety of reasons, some of which have been evoked earlier in this
chapter, by the 1970s each of the aforementioned elements of that consensus was under severe strain. Indeed, by the end of that decade there
was a growing body of opinion in official circles, as well as among lawyers
and criminologists, that 'although a degree of discretion was inevitable,
British law took an unnecessarily permissive stance to police powers by
formulating elastic and vague rules'.[83] While senior officers continued
to maintain that tighter regulation would hamper police effectiveness, a
series of *causes célèbres* in the 1970s and early 1980s uncovered evidence
not only of large-scale police corruption (notably in the Met), but also
of widespread violation of the rules regarding the handling of criminal
evidence and the interrogation of police suspects. An official inquiry in
1977 into the treatment of three teenage suspects arrested in connection
with the murder of Maxwell Confait,[84] and chaired by former high court
judge Sir Henry Fisher, found widespread ignorance among junior police
officers regarding the regulations for questioning and charging suspects.[85]
A subsequent Policy Studies Institute report on policing in London concluded that while 'outright fabrication of evidence is probably rare …
departure from rules and procedure affecting evidence are far more common'; its authors adding that 'There will be no fundamental change as
long as many police officers believe that the job cannot be done effectively within the rules'.[86]

Fisher recommended a wide-ranging inquiry into the subject, a call which was taken up by the Labour government in 1978 with the setting up of the Royal Commission on Criminal Procedure (RCCP). The commission reported in 1981, making a series of recommendations aimed, as it put it, at striking a balance between 'the interests of the community in bringing offenders to justice and ... the rights and liberties of persons suspected or accused of crime'.[87] Indeed, 1981 has been described as 'a major climacteric for the politicization of policing',[88] bringing as it did not only the RCCP Report in January, but also, a few months later, large-scale rioting on the streets of a number of British cities. Although there were a number of deep-seated causes of the unrest, the immediate flashpoint was the breakdown of relations between the police and the country's ethnic minority communities. In the subsequent inquiry (which focussed principally on the disturbances at Brixton in April), Lord Scarman fell short of accusing the police of systematic racism, but did find evidence of 'occasional' racial prejudice among front-line officers. Although senior officers were exonerated in this respect, Scarman did draw attention to what he termed 'errors of judgement' and 'a lack of imagination and flexibility' in the policing of Britain's inner cities.[89]

Following a protracted period of consultation, debate – characterised, according to one specialist, by an atmosphere of 'polarized polemics'[90] – and revision,[91] some of the key recommendations of the RCCP were given legislative form by Mrs Thatcher's second Conservative government with the passage of the 1984 Police and Criminal Evidence Act (PACE). The Act purported to offer that balance between powers and safeguards stressed in the royal commission's report.[92] Such a balance is extremely difficult to achieve in practice, as Reiner explains:

> Rules constructed too loosely undermine the pretensions of criminal procedure to sift out offenders accurately and fairly from innocent people. If they are pitched too restrictively, not only do obviously guilty offenders escape justice but police respect for the rule of law is undermined, with the counter-productive consequence that violations of due process may increase. ... The problem is to place the balance so that there is neither an abandonment by the legal system of its role of protecting just procedures, nor demoralisation of the police through too frequent exposure to Dirty Harry dilemmas.[93]

Was PACE successful in this respect? The thrust of the Act and its accompanying Codes of Practice[94] has been described by jurist David Dixon as an attempt both to 'authorise and regulate' police powers.[95] On the first point, the new legislation provided for the first time explicit authorisation for the police to encroach on individual liberty in various ways, including stop and search, search of premises, and detention of suspects in custody during a police investigation; replacing at a stroke a complex web of common law rules and local bye-laws. Dixon points out that:

> the police had routinely done these things before the new laws, exploiting the gaps and uncertainties in the common law and local legislation, and relying on their targets' ignorance of, or inability to enforce, their rights. What was new was that the police now had clear authorisation for such practices.[96]

'However', he goes on:

> the new laws did not merely legalise what the police had always done or provide new powers. In defining police powers, the law both clarified them and set their limits. For example, if the police were authorised to detain suspects between arrest and charge, such detention was made subject to specific time limits. In addition, new powers were complemented by rights for suspects which were to be shifted from the airy rhetoric of judicial neglect to specific rules on, for example, access to legal advice.[97]

One of the most contentious of the police powers covered by PACE relates to the power to stop and search members of the public. Earlier in the century, as we have seen, the police uniform was often considered justification in itself for sweeping powers to search, detain, and even assault suspects. The context was now very different. Section 1 of the 1984 Act extended police stop and search powers,[98] but added an accompanying obligation on officers to act on the basis of 'reasonable suspicion'[99] and to keep detailed records of all stops. Failure to comply was made a disciplinary offence, and the courts were given wide discretion to exclude evidence from stops which did not meet all the above criteria.[100]

As a number of criminologists have pointed out, the existence of rules governing police behaviour in no way guarantees their application in the face of incompetence, prejudice or both.[101] Indeed, the disproportionate presence of blacks and Asians in the stop and search statistics compared with whites (respectively nearly seven times and twice as numerous, according to figures from 2009[102]) continues to raise concerns about racial profiling. Whatever the relative contribution of overt discrimination to this pattern (as distinct from socio-economic, demographic or other factors[103]), it is clear that a perception of injustice with regard to stop and search policy continues to undermine public support for the police, contributing to what the 1999 Macpherson Inquiry termed a persistent 'climate of distrust' towards its officers within Britain's ethnic minority communities.[104] Indeed, in many ways, Lord Macpherson's report and the subsequent polarised reactions to its publication may be taken as a telling symbol of that 'babble of scandalous revelation, controversy and competing agendas'[105] which has come to dominate late twentieth-century analysis and debate on law enforcement in Britain. More generally, however, the verdict on PACE has been rather more positive, though most researchers concede that its impact on police practice has been uneven and patchy.[106] On the plus side, they point, in particular, to the existence of stronger safeguards with regard to the treatment of suspects in custody and to the more vigorous exercise of judicial oversight of police procedure by the courts.[107] However, both criminologists and front-line police officers point to a major shift in law enforcement priorities since the second half of the 1990s. Indeed, Reiner argues convincingly that by the end of the decade, the notion of 'balance' between police powers on the one hand and safeguards for suspects and prisoners which had been enshrined (albeit imperfectly) in PACE had given way to what he calls 'a rhetoric of modernization to *rebalance* [the criminal justice system] in favour of victims, supposedly justified by a new era of exceptional insecurity and threat.'[108] This emphasis on foregrounding victims versus offenders (with the latter urged to take responsibility for their own actions rather than seek 'excuses' for their wrongdoing) and on the grave danger posed to British society by crime, disorder and (since 2001) terrorism, are part of what has been termed a 'crime control consensus' throughout the United Kingdom since the mid-1990s,[109] itself part of a transnational trend towards greater 'punitiveness' in criminal justice policy in recent decades.[110] The implication is that previous criminal justice policy (including PACE) was considered somehow out of kilter and ill-suited to the exacting demands of late twentieth and early twenty-first-century law enforcement. In this context, emphasising the need to maintain balance between police powers and the rights of suspects and offenders could be (and was) dismissed by government ministers and officials as both anachronistic and irrelevant. As one specialist remarks, it could be considered equivalent to 'complaining that a game of chess is not being played according to the rules of draughts'.[111]

That new game of chess has been accompanied by a steady stream of legislation since the mid-1990s,[112] extending police powers (including a multiplication of the circumstances in which a stop and search can be made *without* 'reasonable suspicion') and eroding certain of the safeguards contained in the original PACE legislation.[113] It is revealing in this context that a 2002 Home Office review of PACE was given as a remit: 'To ensure that the legislation remains a useful tool *supporting the police and providing them with the powers they need to combat crime*'; a very different conception of the law from that which had surrounded its inception.[114]

5. Conclusion

Clive Emsley brings to a close his study of crime and society in twentieth-century England with the stark observation that '[r]ather than perceiving of the institutions within the criminal justice system as the best in the world, by the last decade of the century, many appeared to have lost faith in them.'[115] The irony here is that the loss of faith to which Emsley refers – which has shown no signs of abating in the new century – has been accompanied by a significant fall in the UK crime rate. As for earlier periods, the exact scale and chronology of the fall remains difficult to evaluate with precision, but the existence of a general downward trend since 1995, evident in both the BCS- and police-derived data, is now firmly established.[116] Clearly then, the improving crime statistics have not heralded a return to the benign image of policing in Britain characteristic of that earlier period of falling or stable rates. Indeed, as criminologist Tim Newburn puts it, whatever the future holds for the British police, one thing we can say with some confidence is that the era in which the public police in England somehow came to symbolise nationhood has passed and will not return …. [T]he policing arrangements associated with Dixon of Dock Green are long gone (including from our imaginations, which may be the only place they ever truly existed). New ways of organising and understanding policing are emerging.[117]

Just what those 'new ways' consist of remains far from clear, and is a subject of lively debate among criminologists, who bandy around such terms as *transnationalisation, civilianisation* and *marketization*, among others.[118] All contributors to the debate emphasise, however, that the tendency of both the British public and politicians to wish to see the police as 'tough, no-nonsense crime fighters' (as the then Home Secretary Theresa May put it in 2011[119]) fails to take into account the wide range of tasks undertaken on the thin blue line and the plurality of bodies, both public and private, currently entrusted with policing functions. These tasks include, as one researcher notes (in what is clearly a far from exhaustive list), not only arresting suspects, holding them in detention, and presenting them to court, but

> paperwork, insurance forms, burglary and stolen car reports, assistance in emergencies, traffic regulation and parking, … chasing wild or escaped animals, disposing of bodies, delivering death notices to families, cleaning up streets of glass and metal after road accidents, and modulating disputes.[120]

Not quite *Dixon of Dock Green*, perhaps, but a reminder that we need to be sensitive to elements of continuity as well as change when taking the long view of law enforcement in twentieth-century Britain.[121] Taking that long view shows no sign of losing its appeal to researchers, whether historians or criminologists. A marked feature of recent work in this field has been a focus on the role of women as criminals, victims and criminal justice professionals, along with an interest in the links between law enforcement on the one hand and youth offending and domestic and workplace-related crime on the other.[122] Clearly, the thin blue line continues to stimulate both breadth and depth of analysis.

Notes

1. It was only in 1856, however, that county and borough forces became mandatory, with the passage of the County and Borough Police Act.
2. A fact which, as Barry Godfrey et al. remark, confirms that 'Despite all the rhetoric, there is not really any single "British way" of controlling police' [B.S. Godfrey, P. Lawrence and C.A. Williams (2008) *History and Crime* (London: Sage), p. 56].
3. Historians have been generally sceptical concerning this apparent crime wave: 'The judicial system since 1805 had been generating spurious evidence, through statistics, that crime was increasing alarmingly. ... We know now that what was increasing in the first half of the nineteenth century was not crime but the prosecution rate, a very different matter' [V.A.C. Gatrell (2008) 'Crime, Authority and the Policeman-State', in F.M.L. Thompson (ed.) *The Cambridge Social History of Britain, 1750–1950, Volume 3: Social Agencies and Institutions* (Cambridge: Cambridge University Press), pp. 243–310 at p. 250].
4. It has been argued that in Scotland there was 'a much broader concept of policing for the public good, the public interest or public happiness, as opposed to concern to avert the ills to come or the maintenance of order', see W.G. Carson and H. Idzikowska, (1989) 'The Social Production of Scottish Policing 1795–1900', in Douglas Hay and Francis Snyder (eds) *Policing and Prosecution in Britain 1750–1850* (Oxford: Clarendon Press), pp. 267–97 at pp. 270–71. Glasgow had its own force as early as 1800, and the city's experience would prove a major influence in the subsequent creation of the Metropolitan Police [D.G. Barrie (2000) *Britain's Oldest Police Force? – A Political and Social History of Policing in Glasgow 1779–1846* (Glasgow: Strathclyde University Press)].
5. For a good introduction to the complex and voluminous literature on this subject, see B. Godfrey and P. Lawrence (2014) *Crime and Justice since 1750* (London: Routledge), Chapter 2.
6. Sir Arthur Dixon, quoted in P. Rawlings (2011) *Policing: A Short History* (Cullompton: Willan), p. 186. On this point, see also C. Emsley (2011) *Crime and Society in Twentieth-Century England* (Harlow: Longman), pp. 155–56.
7. L.A. Jackson (2006) *Women Police: Gender, Welfare and Surveillance in the Twentieth Century* (Manchester: Manchester University Press); J. Whitfield (2004) *Unhappy Dialogue: The Metropolitan Police and Black Londoners in Post-war Britain* (Cullompton: Willan).

8. R. Reiner (2010 edition) *The Politics of the Police* (Oxford: Oxford University Press), p. 70.

9. C.A. Williams (2010) 'Policing the Populace: The Road to Professionalisation', in D.S. Nash and A.-M. Kilday (eds) *Histories of Crime: Britain 1600–2000* (Palgrave: Basingstoke), pp. 160–79 at p. 160.

10. Rawlings (2011) *Policing: A Short History*, p. 155.

11. Reiner (2010 edition) *The Politics of the Police*, p. 70.

12. Emsley (2011) *Crime and Society in Twentieth-Century England*, p. 153.

13. Reiner (2010 edition) *The Politics of the Police*, p. 59.

14. Emsley (2011) *Crime and Society in Twentieth-Century England*, p. 153.

15. See *Ibid.*, p. 159 and the note on this point.

16. Godfrey and Lawrence (2014) *Crime and Justice since 1750*, p. 20; T. Morris (1989) *Crime and Criminal Justice since 1945* (Oxford: Basil Blackwell), pp. 55–56.

17. PC Dixon's first appearance was in the film *The Blue Lamp* (1950), made with the co-operation of the Metropolitan Police. *Dixon of Dock Green* ran from 1955 to 1976 – see Emsley (2011) *Crime and Society in Twentieth-Century England*, pp. 110–12.

18. On this point, see Clive Emsley's astute analysis, based on parallels with the French and US systems of policing, in his book: (1996 edition) *The English Police: A Political and Social History* (Harlow: Longman), pp. 248–61.

19. Reiner (2010 edition) *The Politics of the Police*, p. 69.

20. Emsley (2011) *Crime and Society in Twentieth-Century England*, p. 155 and Gatrell (2008) 'Crime, Authority and the Policeman-State', p. 262.

21. On the question of new communication technologies, Emsley notes, however, that 'the beat officer remained dependant on his whistle and his physical prowess for a generation after 1945' see Emsley (2011) *Crime and Society in Twentieth-Century England*, p. 167.

22. Rawlings (2011) *Policing: A Short History*, p. 160.

23. C. Emsley (2010 edition) *The Great British Bobby: A History of British Policing from the Eighteenth Century to the Present* (London: Quercus), p. 211.

24. Quoted in Emsley (2011) *Crime and Society in Twentieth-Century England*, p. 160.

25. Based on B. Godfrey (2014) *Crime in England 1880–1945: The Rough and the Criminal, the Policed and the Incarcerated* (Abingdon: Routledge), pp. 31–33.

26. C. Emsley (2010 edition) *Crime and Society in England, 1750–1900* (Harlow: Pearson), Chapter 2.

27. Godfrey (2014) *Crime in England*, passim and see the quotation at p. 45. On this issue, see also Emsley (2010 edition) *Crime and* Society, pp. 14–20.
28. Godfrey (2014) *Crime in England*, p. 45.
29. *Ibid.*
30. J.F. Sutherland (1908) *Recidivism: Habitual Criminality and Habitual Petty Delinquency: A Problem in Sociology, Psycho-Pathology and Criminology* (Edinburgh: William Green).
31. M.J. Wiener (1990) *Reconstructing the Criminal: Culture, Law and Policy in England, 1830–1914* (Cambridge: Cambridge University Press), Chapter 6 and N. Davie (2005) *Tracing the Criminal: The Rise of Scientific Criminology in Britain, 1860–1918* (Oxford: Bardwell Press), Chapter 5.
32. Wiener (1990) *Reconstructing the Criminal*, p. 228.
33. See Sir Evelyn Ruggles-Brise's 'Preface' to C. Goring (1913) *The English Convict: A Statistical Study* (London: HMSO), p. 8.
34. Davie (2005) *Tracing the Criminal*, pp. 186–87.
35. Wiener (1990) *Reconstructing the Criminal*, p. 355.
36. N. Davie (2013) 'Lombroso and the "Men of Real Science": British Reactions, 1886–1918', in P, Knepper and P.J. Ystehede (eds) *The Cesare Lombroso Handbook* (London: Routledge), pp. 353–54.
37. D. Garland (1985) *Punishment and Welfare: A History of Penal Strategies* (Aldershot: Gower).
38. Emsley (1996 edition) *The English Police*, Chapter 8 and Reiner (2010 edition) *The Politics of the Police*, pp. 78–80.
39. Survey evidence collected by the Royal Commission on the Police in 1962 revealed that 85.2 per cent of Britain's professional and managerial classes still had 'great respect' for the police, with only slighter lower figures for the skilled working class (81.8 per cent) and among semi- and unskilled workers (81.9 per cent). Figures from Reiner (2010 edition) *The Politics of the Police*, p. 69.
40. Emsley (1996 edition) *The English Police*, pp. 177–80 and Emsley (2010 edition) *Crime and Society*, pp. 250–54.
41. Emsley (2011) *Crime and Society in Twentieth-Century England*, p. 161 and P. Rawlings (1999) *Crime and Power: A History of Criminal Justice 1688–1998* (Harlow: Longman), p. 157.
42. Quoted in Reiner (2010 edition) *The Politics of the Police*, p. 80.
43. Emsley (2011) *Crime and Society in Twentieth-Century England*, p. 21.
44. The total number of indictable offences in England and Wales known to the police rose from 478,394 in 1945 to 3,426,400 in 1985, a seven-fold increase. See Morris (1989) *Crime and Criminal Justice*, Table 7.1, p. 91.

45. M. Maguire (2012 edition) 'Criminal Statistics and the Construction of Crime', in M. Maguire, R. Morgan and R. Reiner (eds) *The Oxford Handbook of Criminology* (Oxford: Oxford University Press), pp. 206–44 at pp. 221–23.

46. Morris (1989) *Crime and Criminal Justice*, p. 106 (author's emphasis added).

47. The term is from Emsley (2011) *Crime and Society in Twentieth-Century England*, Chapter 7.

48. *Ibid.*, p. 145.

49. C. Phillips and B. Bowling (2012 edition) 'Ethnicities, Racism, Crime and Criminal Justice', in M. Maguire, R. Morgan and R. Reiner (eds) *The Oxford Handbook of Criminology* (Oxford: Oxford University Press), Chapter 13.

50. Sir William Macpherson (1999) *The Stephen Lawrence Inquiry: Report by Sir William Macpherson of Cluny* [Cm 4262] (London: The Stationary Office), para. 46.1. On the mixed results of this inquiry, see N. Davie (2007) 'A "Bolt-on Extra to the Police's Work"?: Racism and Policing in the UK since the Macpherson Report', in M. Prum, B. Deschamps and M.-C. Barbier (eds) *Racial, Ethnic and Homophobic Violence: Killing in the Name of Otherness* (Abingdon: Routledge-Cavendish), pp. 83–94; P.A.J. Waddington (2010) 'A Virtuous Exception? The Macpherson Inquiry and Report into the Murder of Stephen Lawrence and Its Investigation', in D. Downes, D. Hobbs and T. Newburn (eds) *The Eternal Recurrence of Crime and Control: Essays in Honour of Paul Rock* (Oxford: Oxford University Press), pp. 183–209. See also chapter Four in this volume.

51. D. Downes and R. Morgan (1996 edition) 'Dumping the "Hostages to Fortune"? The Politics of Law and Order in Post-War Britain', in M. Maguire, R. Morgan and R. Reiner (eds) *The Oxford Handbook of Criminology* (Oxford: Oxford University Press), pp. 87–134 at p. 92. An internal police inquiry at the time, not made public until 2010 (but known to the coroner), concluded that an officer from the Met's Special Patrol Group was indeed 'almost certainly' responsible for Peach's death and recommended the prosecution of those involved ('Blair Peach: After 31 Years Met Police Say "Sorry" for Their Role in His Killing', *The Guardian*, 27th April 2010).

52. Reiner (2010 edition) *The Politics of the Police*, p. 96.

53. Charles Murray (1990) quoted in Emma Bell (2011) *Criminal Justice and Neoliberalism* (Basingstoke: Palgrave Macmillan), p. 94. On the earlier period, see V. Bailey (1993) 'The Fabrication of Deviance? "Dangerous Classes" and "Criminal Classes" in Victorian England', in J. Rule and R. Malcolmson (eds) *Protest and Survival: The Historical Experience* (London: Merlin Press), pp. 221–57.

54. Bell (2011) *Criminal Justice*, pp. 94–97 and J. Welshman (2006) *Underclass: A History of the Excluded, 1880–2000* (London: Hambledon Continuum), Chapters 8 and 9.

55. D. Garland (2001) *The Culture of Control: Crime and Social Order in Contemporary Society* (Oxford: Oxford University Press), p. 184.

56. Emsley notes that by the end of the twentieth century the Home Office's Research Development and Statistics Directorate had become the largest single employer of criminologists in the UK, raising concerns within the discipline about the consequences of the latter's dependence on government agendas and policies for its research [Emsley (2011) *Crime and Society in Twentieth-Century England*, pp. 146–47]. On the latter point, see T. Newburn (2011) 'Criminology and Government: Some Reflections on Recent Developments in England', in M. Bosworth and C. Hoyle (eds) *What is Criminology?* (Oxford: Oxford University Press), Chapter 33.

57. Ronald Clarke (1992) cited in T. Newburn (2003 edition) *Crime and Criminal Justice Policy* (London: Pearson/Longman), p. 103 and R.V.G. Clark (1980) '"Situational" Crime Prevention: Theory and Practice', *British Journal of Criminology*, Vol. 20, No. 2, pp. 136–47.

58. Garland (2001) *The Culture of Control*, p. 183. On 'situational crime prevention', see also D. Downes and P. Rock (2011) *Understanding Deviance: A Guide to the Sociology of Crime and Rule-Breaking* (Oxford: Oxford University Press), p. 231 and passim.

59. I have explored these issues elsewhere in N. Davie (2007) 'Le Retour de l'Homme Criminel? ADN, Criminalité et Déterminisme Biologique', in M. Prum (ed.) *La Fabrique de la 'Race': Regards sur l'Ethnicité dans l'Aire Anglophone* (Paris: L'Harmattan), pp. 235–57; N. Davie (2007) 'Le Bras Long de la Justice? Biométrie, Précrime et le Corps Criminal', in M. Prum (ed.) *Changements d'Aire : De la 'Race' dans l'Aire Anglophone* (Paris: L'Harmattan), pp. 99–124.

60. Garland (2001) *The Culture of Control*, p. 187.

61. T. Newburn and R. Reiner (2012 edition) 'Policing and the Police', in M. Maguire, R. Morgan and R. Reiner (eds) *The Oxford Handbook of Criminology* (Oxford: Oxford University Press), pp. 807–37 at p. 829 (author's emphasis added).

62. Emsley (1996 edition) *The English Police*, p. 277.

63. See for example T.A. Critchley (1967) *A History of Police in England and Wales, 1900–1966* (London: Constable); Sir Leon Radzinowicz (1948) *A History of English Criminal Law and Its Administration since 1750,*

Volume 1: The Movement for Reform (London: Pilgrim Trust) and C. Reith (1943) *British Police and the Democratic Ideal* (London: Oxford University Press).

64. C. Emsley (2007 edition) 'Historical Perspectives on Crime', in M. Maguire, R. Morgan and R. Reiner (eds) *The Oxford Handbook of Criminology* (Oxford: Oxford University Press), pp. 122–38 at pp. 123–24; Godfrey and Lawrence (2014) *Crime and Justice since 1750*, pp. 16–17 and Williams (2010) 'Policing the Populace', pp. 167–70.

65. A. Dinsmor and A. Goldsmith (2005) 'Scottish Policing – A Historical Perspective', in D. Donnelly and K. Scott (eds) *Policing Scotland* (Cullompton: Willan), pp. 40–58 at p. 40.

66. Godfrey, Lawrence and Williams (2008) *History and Crime*, p. 17.

67. M. Foucault (1977 edition) *Discipline and Punish: The Birth of the Modern Prison* (trans. A. Sheridan) (London: Penguin); E.P. Thompson (1963) *The Making of the English Working Class* (Harmondsworth: Pelican); E.P. Thompson (1975) *Whigs and Hunters: The Origins of the Black Act* (London: Allen Lane); D. Hay et al. (1975) *Albion's Fatal Tree: Crime and Society in Eighteenth-Century England* (London: Allen Lane). For the context, see P. Spierenburg (2004) 'Social Control and History: An Introduction', in C. Emsley, E. Johnson and P. Spierenburg (eds) *Social Control in Europe, Volume 2: 1800–2000* (Columbus: Ohio State University Press), pp. 1–21.

68. R.D. Storch (1976) 'The Policeman as Domestic Missionary: Urban Discipline and Popular Culture in Northern England, 1850–1880', *Journal of Social History*, Vol. 9, No. 4, pp. 481–509 at p. 481.

69. Godfrey, Lawrence and Williams (2008) *History and Crime*, p. 18.

70. For example, D. Taylor (2002) *Policing the Victorian Town: The Development of the Police in Middlesbrough c. 1840–1914* (Basingstoke: Palgrave Macmillan); D. Philips and R.D. Storch (1999) *Policing Provincial England 1829–1856: The Politics of Reform* (London: Leicester University Press). On the limitations of the 'revisionist' approach, see Godfrey, Lawrence and Williams (2008) *History and Crime*, pp. 18–20.

71. For example: B. Godfrey, C. Emsley and G. Dunstall (eds) (2003) *Comparative Histories of Crime* (Collumpton: Willan); C.A. Williams (2014) *Police Control Systems in Britain, 1775–1975: From Parish Constable to National Computer* (Manchester: Manchester University Press) and P. Lawrence (ed.) *Policing the Poor: The Making of the Modern Police, Volume 3* (London: Pickering & Chatto).

72. C.A. Williams (ed.) *Police and Policing in the Twentieth Century* (Abingdon: Ashgate).

73. For an introduction to the specifics of policing in Scotland and Northern Ireland, largely outside the scope of this chapter, see T. Newburn (ed.) (2008 edition) *Handbook of Policing* (Cullompton: Willan), Chapters 8 and 9. More detailed historical analyses can be found in: D.G. Barrie (2008) *Police in the Age of Improvement: Police Development and the Civic Tradition in Scotland, 1775–1865* (Cullompton: Willan); A. Goldsmith (2002) 'The Development of the City of Glasgow Police 1800–1939' (Unpublished PhD thesis, University of Strathclyde); J. McGowan (2010) *Policing the Metropolis of Scotland: A History of the Police and Systems of Police in Edinburgh and Edinburghshire, 1770–1833* (Mussleburgh: Turlough); B. Griffin (1997) *The Bulkies: Police and Crime in Belfast, 1800–1865* (Dublin: Irish Academic Press); E. Malcolm (2006) *The Irish Policeman, 1822–1922: A Life* (Dublin: Four Courts Press) and D.J.V. Jones (1996) *Crime and Policing in the Twentieth Century: The South Wales Experience* (Cardiff: University of Wales Press).

74. Emsley (1996 edition) *The English Police*; Emsley (2010 edition) *The Great British Bobby*; Rawlings (2011) *Policing: A Short History*; D. Taylor (1997) *The New Police in Nineteenth-Century England: Crime, Conflict and Control* (Manchester: Manchester University Press); T. Brain (2010) *A History of Policing in England and Wales since 1974: A Turbulent Journey* (Oxford: Oxford University Press). Also of interest are chapters on policing in more general works on criminal justice history: Emsley (2010 edition) *Crime and Society*; Godfrey and Lawrence (2014) *Crime and Justice since 1750* and Rawlings (1999) *Crime and Power*.

75. Emsley (2011) *Crime and Society in Twentieth-Century England* and Godfrey (2014) *Crime in England*.

76. Among the many works that could be cited in this context are: B. Godfrey and D.J. Cox (2012) *Policing the Factory: Theft, Private Policing and the Law in Modern England* (London: Continuum); Jackson (2006) *Women Police*; B. Weinberger (1995) *The Best Police in the World: An Oral History of English Policing* (Aldershot: Scholar Press) and J. Whitfield (2004) *Unhappy Dialogue: The Metropolitan Police and Black Londoners in Post-war Britain* (Cullompton: Willan).

77. Emsley (2011) *Crime and Society in Twentieth-Century England*, p. 237. The works of David Garland, Robert Reiner and Tim Newburn, for example, fall into this category, as does that of John Muncie on youth crime: (2009 edition) *Youth and Crime* (London: Sage).

78. A point of view eloquently expressed by Godfrey, Lawrence and Williams (2008) *History and Crime*, pp. 18–21.

79. J.Q. Wilson (1968) cited in Newburn and Reiner (2012) 'Policing and the Police', p. 809.

80. These included fixed meeting points for beat officers with their superiors or with constables on neighbouring beats. Beat officers were also expected to keep detailed records, indicating exactly precisely where they had patrolled and when. For urban forces, the introduction of Tardis-like blue police boxes in the 1920s, from which beat officers were required to check in by telephone, offered an additional means of supervision (until personal radios made them redundant). By the interwar period, however, a more flexible system of beats, giving greater autonomy to individual officers, made such supervision impractical. This trend accelerated with the generalisation of motorised patrols from the late 1950s [Godfrey (2014) *Crime in England*, pp. 120–21 and p. 134 and Emsley (1996 edition) *The English Police*, pp. 224–40.].

81. Emsley (2011) *Crime and Society in Twentieth-Century England*, pp. 158–59.

82. Godfrey (2014) *Crime in England*, p. 126. See also Reiner (2010 edition) *The Politics of the Police*, pp. 94–96.

83. Newburn and Reiner (2012) 'Policing and the Police', p. 809.

84. For the details of this case, see S.P. Savage and B. Milne (2007) 'Miscarriages of Justice', in T. Newburn, T. Williamson and A. Wright (eds) *Handbook of Criminal Investigation* (Abingdon: Willan), pp. 610–27 at pp. 618–20.

85. Sir Henry Fisher (1977) *The Confait Case: Report by the Hon. Sir Henry Fisher* [HC 90] (London: HMSO).

86. Quoted in Reiner (2010 edition) *The Politics of the Police*, p. 83.

87. (1981) *The Royal Commission on Criminal Procedure Report* [Cmnd. 8092] (London: HMSO).

88. Reiner (2010 edition) *The Politics of the Police*, p. 205.

89. Lord Scarman (1981) *The Brixton Disorders 10–12 April 1981, Report of an Inquiry by the Rt. Hon Lord Scarman, OBE* [Cmnd. 8247] (London: HMSO), para. 4: 62.

90. Reiner (2010 edition) *The Politics of the Police*, p. 215.

91. M. Zander (2012) 'PACE (The Police and Criminal Evidence) Act 1984: Past, Present and Future', *LSE Law Society and Economy Working Paper Series*, 1/2012, pp. 3–4.

92. Reiner (2010 edition) *The Politics of the Police*, p. 212.

93. *Ibid.*, pp. 212–13. C.B. Klockars (1980) 'The Dirty Harry Problem', *Annals of the American Academy of Political and Social Science*, Vol. 452, pp. 33–47. The article's title takes its name from the series of films from the 1970s and '80s, portraying Harry Callahan, a fictional American detective (played by Clint Eastwood), seemingly left with no alternative but to resort to illegal or 'dirty' means to achieve a 'just' outcome.

94. The original five codes contained detailed procedural rules regulating stop and search, search and seizure, detention and questioning of suspects, identity parades, and tape recording of police interviews. Three other codes would follow: on video recording of interviews, on powers of arrest and concerning terrorist suspects see Reiner (2010 edition) *The Politics of the Police*, p. 213.

95. D. Dixon (2008) 'Authorise and Regulate: A Comparative Perspective on the Rise and Fall of a Regulatory Strategy', in E. Cape and R. Young (eds) *The Police and Criminal Evidence Act 1984: Past, Present and Future* (Portland: Hart), Chapter 2.

96. *Ibid.*, p. 29.

97. *Ibid.*, p. 29.

98. Jurist Paul Roberts notes: 'Section 1 of PACE empowers all constables, whether or not in uniform, to search any person or vehicle in a public place … for stolen goods, offensive weapons or articles made or adapted for use in crime.' In addition, 'a raft of subject-matter-specific statutes confers additional stop-and-search powers in relation, *inter alia*, to drugs, protected wildlife, terrorist offences and the security of civil aviation.' Roberts adds, however, that 'the modern trend is towards further extensions and ad hoc additions', see P. Roberts, 'Law and Criminal Investigation', in T. Newburn, T. Williamson and A. Wright (eds) *Handbook of Criminal Investigation*, pp. 92–105 at pp. 102–4.

99. Suspicion has to be connected to some specific characteristic of the individual concerned, and not simply derived from his or her membership of a category (social or ethnic for example) considered 'likely' to offend, see Reiner (2010 edition) *The Politics of the Police*, p. 214.

100. Roberts, 'Law and Criminal Investigation', p. 103 and Newburn and Reiner (2012) 'Policing and the Police', p. 814.

101. J. Lea (2000) 'The Macpherson Report and the Question of Institutional Racism', *The Howard Journal*, Vol. 39, No. 3, pp. 219–33 at p. 223.

102. Phillips and Bowling (2012) 'Ethnicities, Racism, Crime and Criminal Justice', pp. 381–82.

103. There is some evidence, for example, that the particular ethnic groups 'place themselves at risk of being stopped by the police by their differential use of public space' see *ibid.*, p. 383.

104. Macpherson (1999) *The Stephen Lawrence Inquiry*, para. 45.10.

105. Reiner (2010 edition) *The Politics of the Police*, p. 78.

106. *Ibid.*, p. 218; Dixon (2008) 'Authorise and Regulate', pp. 32–33 and Newburn and Reiner (2012) 'Policing and the Police', pp. 814–15.

107. Reiner's survey of the positive and negative consequences of the law is particularly useful, see Reiner (2010 edition) *The Politics of the Police*, pp. 215–17.

108. Reiner (2010 edition) *The Politics of the Police*, p. 222 (author's emphasis added).

109. R. Reiner (2007) *Law and Order: An Honest Citizen's Guide to Crime and Control* (Cambridge: Polity), pp. 124–29; D. Downes and R. Morgan (2007 edition) 'No Turning Back: The Politics of Law and Order into the Millennium', in M. Maguire, R. Morgan and R. Reiner (eds) *The Oxford Handbook of Criminology*, pp. 201–40; L. McAra (2008) 'Crime, Criminology and Criminal Justice in Scotland', *European Journal of Criminology*, Vol. 5, No. 4, pp. 481–504 and C. Hamilton (2014) *Reconceptualising Penality: A Comparative Perspective on Punitiveness in Ireland, Scotland and New Zealand* (London: Ashgate).

110. J. Pratt et al. (eds) *The New Punitiveness: Trends, Theories, Perspectives* (Cullompton: Willan Publishing). Whether this phenomenon is 'new' is another matter.

111. Dixon (2008) 'Authorise and Regulate', p. 35. See also Reiner (2010 edition) *The Politics of the Police*, p. 218.

112. For example: The 1994 Criminal Justice and Public Order Act, the 1997 Police Act, the 1998 Crime and Disorder Act, the 2000 Terrorism Act and the 2001 Criminal Justice and Police Act.

113. For the details, see Reiner (2010 edition) *The Politics of the Police*, pp. 220–22; Newburn and Reiner (2012) 'Policing and the Police', pp. 814–15 and Bell (2011) *Criminal Justice*, pp. 106–13.

114. Quoted in Reiner (2010 edition) *The Politics of the Police*, p. 221 (author's emphasis added). See also Dixon (2008) 'Authorise and Regulate', p. 39 and Zander (2012) 'PACE (The Police and Criminal Evidence) Act 1984, p. 5 and passim.

115. Emsley (2011) *Crime and Society in Twentieth-Century England*, p. 232.

116. Maguire (2012 edition) 'Criminal Statistics', pp. 221–23 and Emsley (2011) *Crime and Society in Twentieth-Century England*, pp. 22–23.

117. T. Newburn (2008) 'The Future of Policing', in T. Newburn (ed.) *Handbook of Policing* (Cullompton: Willan), pp. 824–41 at p. 836.

118. See for example the articles in the 2013 issue of the journal *Criminology and Criminal Justice* (Vol. 13, No. 2) by Karen Bullock, Simon Holdaway, Mike Hough, David Leeney, Andrew Millie and Robert Reiner.

119. Quoted in A. Millie and K. Bullock (2013) 'Policing in a Time of Contraction and Constraint: Re-imagining the Role and Function of Contemporary Policing', *Criminology and Criminal Justice*, Vol. 13, No. 2, pp. 133–42 at p. 139.

120. Peter Manning (1999) quoted in Newburn (2008) 'The Future of Policing', p. 832.

121. A point also emphasised in some of the criminological literature. See for example T. Jones and T. Newburn (2002) 'The Transformation of Policing? Understanding Current Trends in Policing Systems', *British Journal of Criminology*, Vol. 42, No. 1, pp. 129–46 and L. Zedner (2005) 'Policing Before and After the Police: The Historical Antecedents of Contemporary Crime Control', *British Journal of Criminology*, Vol. 46, Nos. 1, 2, pp. 78–96.

122. Emsley (2011) *Crime and Society in Twentieth-Century England*, pp. 235–38 and Godfrey (2014) *Crime in England*.

Further Reading

Chapter 1: Introduction: Crime and Punishment in Twentieth-Century Britain

Adam, A. (2015) *A History of Forensic Science: British Beginnings in the Twentieth Century* (London: Routledge).

Bailey, V. (2014 edition) *Order and Disorder in Modern Britain: Essays on Riot, Crime, Policing and Punishment* (London: Breviary Stuff Publications).

Brown, A. (2003) *English Society and the Prison: Time, Culture and Politics in the Development of the Modern Prison* (London: Boydell Press).

Carrabine, E., P. Cox, M. Lee and N. South (2002) *Crime in Modern Britain* (Oxford: Oxford University Press).

Emsley, C. (2011) *Crime and Society in Twentieth-Century England* (Harlow: Pearson).

Gartner, R. and B. McCarthy (eds) (2014) *The Oxford Handbook of Gender, Sex and Crime* (Oxford: Oxford University Press).

Knepper, P. and A. Johansen (eds) (2016) *The Oxford Handbook of the History of Crime and Criminal Justice* (Oxford: Oxford University Press).

Moore, S.E.H. (2014) *Crime and the Media* (Basingstoke: Palgrave).

Seal, L. (2014) *Capital Punishment in Twentieth-Century Britain: Audience, Justice, Memory* (London: Routledge).

Williams, C.A. (2011) *Police and Policing in the Twentieth Century* (London: Routledge).

Chapter 2: Britain's 'Most Wanted': Homicide and Serial Murder since 1900

Brookman, F. (2005) *Understanding Homicide* (London: Sage).

D'Cruze, S. (2010) 'Murder and Fatality: The Changing Face of Homicide', in A. M. Kilday and D.S. Nash (eds) *Histories of Crime: Britain 1600–2000* (Basingstoke: Palgrave), pp. 100–19.

D'Cruze, S., S. Walklate and S. Pegg (2011 edition) *Murder* (Abingdon: Routledge).

Gekoski, A. (1998) *Murder by Numbers: British Serial Sex Killers since 1950: Their Childhoods, Their Lives, Their Crimes* (London: Andre Deutsch).

Jewkes, Y. (2004) *Crime and the Media* (London: Sage).

Leyton, E. (1995) *Men of Blood: Murder in Modern England* (London: Constable).

Spierenburg, P. (2010 edition) *A History of Murder: Personal Violence in Europe from the Middle Ages to the Present* (Cambridge: Polity Press).

Wilson, D. (2009) *A History of British Serial Killing: The Definitive Account from Jack the Ripper* (London: Sphere).

Wilson, D., H. Tolputt, N. Howe and D. Kemp (2010) 'When Serial Killers Go Unseen: The Case of Trevor Joseph Hardy', *Crime, Media, Culture*, Vol. 6, No. 2, pp. 153–67.

Worsley, L. (2013) *A Very British Murder: The Story of a National Obsession* (London: BBC Books).

Chapter 3: Serious Property Offending in the Twentieth Century

Adey, P., B. Godfrey and D. Cox (2015) *Crime, Wartime and Control: Protecting the Population of a Blitzed City, 1939–1945* (London: Bloomsbury).

Emsley, C. (2011) *Crime and Society in Twentieth-Century England* (Harlow: Pearson).

Emsley, C. (2013) *Soldier, Sailor, Beggarman, Thief: Crime and the British Armed Forces since 1914* (Oxford: Oxford University Press).

Godfrey, B. and P. Lawrence (2014) *Crime and Justice since 1750* (London: Routledge).

Hobbs, D. (1995) *Bad Business: Professional Crime in Modern Britain* (Oxford: Oxford University Press).

Hobbs, D. (2001) 'The Firm: Organisational Logic and Criminal Culture on a Shifting Terrain', *British Journal of Criminology*, Vol. 41, pp. 549–60.

Levi, M. (1981) *The Phantom Capitalists: The Organisation and Control of Long-Firm Fraud* (London: Heinemann International).

Meier, W.M. (2011) *Property Crime in London 1850 – Present* (Basingstoke: Palgrave Macmillan).

Shore, H. (2015) *London's Criminal Underworlds, c. 1720 – c. 1930: A Social and Cultural History* (Basingstoke: Palgrave Macmillan).

Taylor, L. (1985) *In the Underworld* (London: Guild Publishing).

Chapter 4: Racial Hate Crime in Modern Britain

Bennetto, J. (2009) *Police and Racism: What Has Been Achieved 10 Years after the Stephen Lawrence Inquiry Report?* (London: Equality and Human Rights Commission).

Boeckmann, R.J. and C. Turpin-Petrosino (2002) 'Understanding the Harm of Hate Crime', *Journal of Social Issues*, Vol. 2, pp. 207–25.

Bowling, B. (1998) *Violent Racism: Victimization, Policing and Social Context* (Oxford: Oxford University Press).

Cathcart, B. (1999) *The Case of Stephen Lawrence* (London: Penguin).

Gerstenfeld, P.B. (2013) *Hate Crime: Causes, Controls and Controversies* (London: Sage).

Hall, N. (2005) *Hate Crime* (London: Routledge).

McDevitt, J., J. Levin and S. Bennett (2002) 'Hate Crime Offenders: An Expanded Typology', *Journal of Social Issues*, Vol. 58, No. 2, pp. 303–17.

Paterson, S. (2007) 'Policing Hate Crime in London', *American Behavioural Scientist*, Vol. 51, No. 2, pp. 196–204.

Perry, B. (2001) *In the Name of Hate: Understanding Hate Crimes* (London: Routledge).

The Stephen Lawrence Inquiry: Report of an Inquiry by Sir William Macpherson of Cluny, Cmd. 4262-1 (1999). Available at https://www.gov.uk/government/uploads/system/uploads/attachment_data/file/277111/4262.pdf.

Chapter 5: Offences Against the Person: Child Sexual Abuse

Bailey, V. and S. Blackburn (1979) 'The Punishment of Incest Act 1908: A Case Study of Law Creation', *Criminal Law Review*, Vol. 14, pp. 708–18.

Behlmer, G. (1982) *Moral Reform in England 1870–1908* (Stanford: Stanford University Press).

Critcher, C. (2002) 'Media, Government and Moral Panic: The Politics of Paedophilia in Britain 2000–1', *Journalism Studies*, Vol. 3, No. 4, pp. 521–35.

Home Office (1987) *Report of the Inquiry into Child Abuse in Cleveland* (London: HMSO) Cmnd 4991.

Home Office (July 2000) *Setting the Boundaries* (London: Home Office Communication Directorate).

Jackson, L. (2003) 'Care or Control? The Metropolitan Women Police and Child Welfare, 1919–1969', *The Historical Journal*, Vol. 46, No. 3, pp. 623–48.

LaFontain, J. (1998) *Speak of the Devil: Tales of Satanic Abuse in Contemporary England* (Cambridge: Cambridge University Press).

Mearns, A. (1883) 'The Bitter Cry of Outcast London' rep. P. Keating (ed.) (1978) *Into Unknown England 1866–1913: Selections from the Social Explorers* (Glasgow: Fontana Collins), pp. 91–111.

Olafson, E., D. Corwin and R. Summit (1993) 'Modern History of Child Sexual Abuse Awareness: Cycles of Discovery and Suppression', *Child Abuse and Neglect*, Vol. 17, pp. 7–24.

Smart, C. (2000) 'Reconsidering the Recent History of Child Sexual Abuse, 1910–1960', *Journal of Social Policy*, Vol. 29, No. 1, pp. 55–71.

Chapter 6: Anarchism, Assassination and Terrorism in Modern Britain

Bew, P. and G. Gordon (1993) *Northern Ireland: A Chronology of the Troubles, 1968–1993* (Dublin: Gill and Macmillan).

Brain, T. (2010) *A History of Policing in England and Wales from 1974* (Oxford: Oxford University Press).

Donohue, L. (2001) *Counter-Terrorist Law and Emergency Powers in the United Kingdom, 1922–2000* (Dublin: Irish American Press).

Head, M. (2011) *Crimes Against the State* (Farnham: Ashgate).

Hewitt, S. (2008) *The British War on Terror* (London: Continuum).

Porter, B. (1987) *The Origins of the Vigilant State* (London: Weidenfeld & Nicolson).

Richardson, L. (2007) 'Britain and the IRA', in R. Art and L. Richardson (eds) *Democracy and Counterterrorism: Lessons from the Past* (Washington: US Institute of Peace Press), pp. 63–104.

Taylor, A. (2012) *London's Burning: Pulp Fiction, the Politics of Terrorism and the Destruction of the Capital in British Popular Culture, 1840–2005* (London: Continuum).

Taylor, T. (2002) 'United Kingdom', in A. Yonah (ed.) *Combating Terrorism: Strategies of Ten Countries* (Ann Arbor: University of Michigan Press), pp. 187–243.

Wilkinson, P. (ed.) *Homeland Security in the UK: Future Preparedness for Terrorist Attack since 9/11* (Abingdon: Routledge).

Chapter 7: 'Hope I Die Before I Get Old': Social Rebellion and Social Diseases

Altschuler, G. (2003) *All Shook Up: How Rock 'n' Roll Changed America* (Oxford: Oxford University Press).

Cloonan, M. (1996) *Banned: Censorship of Popular Music in Britain* (Aldershot: Arena).

Cohen, S. (2011 edition) *Folk Devils and Moral Panics* (London: Routledge).

Davenport-Hines, R. (2001) *The Pursuit of Oblivion* (London: Weidenfeld & Nicolson).

Fowler, D. (1995) *The First Teenagers* (London: Woburn Press).

Gildart, K. (2013) *Images of England through Popular Music: Class, Youth and Rock 'n' Roll, 1955–1976* (London: Palgrave).

Glasper, I. (2014) *The Day the Country Died* (London: PM Press).

MacDonald, I. (1994) *Revolution in the Head: The Beatles' Records and the Sixties* (London: Vintage).

Reynolds, S. (1998) *Energy Flash: A Journey through Rave Music and Dance Culture* (London: Faber).

Savage, J. (1992) *England's Dreaming: The Sex Pistols and Punk Rock* (London: Faber).

Chapter 8: Organised Crime, Criminality and the Gangster

Davies, A. (2013) *City of Gangs: Glasgow and the Rise of the British Gangster* (London: Hodder & Stoughton).

Emsley, C. (2011) *Crime and Society in Twentieth-Century England* (Harlow: Pearson Education Limited).

Hobbs, D. (2013) *Lush Life: Constructing Organized Crime in the UK* (Oxford: Oxford University Press).

Jenkins, P. and G.W. Potter (1988) 'Before the Krays: Organized Crime in London, 1920–1960', *Criminal Justice History*, Vol. IX, pp. 209–30.

Roodhouse, M. (2013) *Black Market Britain: 1939–1955* (Oxford: Oxford University Press).

Shore, H. (2007) '"Undiscovered Country": Towards a History of the Criminal "Underworld"', *Crimes and Misdemeanours*, Vol. 1, No. 1, pp. 41–68.

Shore, H. (2011) 'Criminality and Englishness in the Aftermath: The Racecourse Wars of the 1920s', *Twentieth Century British History*, Vol. 22, No. 4, pp. 1–24.

Shore, H. (2015) *London's Criminal Underworlds, c. 1725 – c. 1930: A Social and Cultural History* (Basingstoke: Palgrave Macmillan).

Slater, S. (2009) 'Prostitutes and Popular History: Notes on the "Underworld", 1918–1939', *Crime, Histoire & Société*, Vol. 13, No. 1, pp. 25–48.

Wright, A. (2006) *Organised Crime* (Cullompton: Willan).

Chapter 9: Punishment: The Death Penalty and Incarceration

Ballinger, A. (2000) *Dead Woman Walking: Executed Women in England and Wales, 1900–1955* (Aldershot: Ashgate).

Block, B.P. and J. Hostettler (1997) *Hanging in the Balance: A History of the Abolition of Capital Punishment in Britain* (Hook: Waterside).

Brown, A. (2013) *Inter-war Penal Policy and Crime in England: The Dartmoor Convict Prison Riot, 1932* (Basingstoke: Palgrave Macmillan).

Cavadino, M., J. Dignan and G. Mair (2013 edition) *The Penal System: An Introduction* (London: Sage).

Emsley, C. (2011 edition) *Crime and Society in Twentieth-Century England* (Harlow: Longman).

Forsythe, W.J. (1990) *Penal Discipline, Reformatory Projects and the English Prison Commission 1895–1939* (Exeter: Exeter University Press).

Garland, D. (1985) *Punishment and Welfare: A History of Penal Strategies* (Aldershot: Gower).

Pratt, J. (2002) *Punishment and Civilisation: Penal Tolerance and Intolerance in Modern Society* (London: Sage).

Seal, L. (2014) *Capital Punishment in Twentieth-Century Britain: Audience, Memory, Justice* (Abingdon: Routledge).

Wilson, D. (2014) *Pain and Retribution: A Short History of British Prisons, 1066 to the Present* (London: Reaktion Books).

Chapter 10: Law Enforcement: Policies and Perspectives

Dinsmor, A. and A. Goldsmith (2005) 'Scottish Policing – A Historical Perspective', in D. Donnelly and K. Scott (eds) *Policing Scotland* (Cullompton: Willan), pp. 40–61.

Emsley, C. (1996, second edition) *The English Police: A Political and Social History* (Harlow: Longman).

Emsley, C. (2010, revised edition) *The Great British Bobby: A History of British Policing from the 18th Century to the Present* (London: Quercus).

Garland, D. (2001) *The Culture of Control: Crime and Social Order in Contemporary Society* (Oxford: Oxford University Press).

Newburn, T. (2008, second edition) 'The Future of Policing', in T. Newburn (ed.) *Handbook of Policing* (Cullompton: Willan), pp. 824–40.

Newburn, T. and R. Reiner (2012, fifth edition) 'Policing and the Police', in M. Maguire, R. Morgan and R. Reiner (eds) *The Oxford Handbook of Criminology* (Oxford: Oxford University Press), pp. 806–37.

Rawlings, P. (2002) *Policing: A Short History* (Cullompton: Willan).

Taylor, D. (1997) *The New Police in Nineteenth-Century England: Crime, Conflict and Control* (Manchester: Manchester University Press).

Williams, C.A. (ed.) (2010) *Police and Policing in the Twentieth Century* (Abingdon: Ashgate).

Zedner, L. (2005) 'Policing Before and After the Police: The Historical Antecedents of Contemporary Crime Control', *British Journal of Criminology*, Vol. 46, No. 1, pp. 78–96.

Index

A

Abolition of the Death Penalty
    Act (1965), 259
Abortion, 7
Abu Nidal, 163
Acourt, Jamie, 105
Acourt, Neil, 105
Actus reus, 33
Adams family, 220, 227
Adams, Gerry, 161, 167
Adey, Peter, 74, 76
Albini, Joseph, 221
Aliens Order Act (1905), 96–97
Aliens Order Act (1920), 97
Allen, Peter Anthony, 244, 256
Altschuler, Glenn, 195
Allen, Peter Anthony, 23
Al-Qaeda, 150, 164
Amnesty International, 14
Anarchism, 150, 152–53, 155
    Angry Brigade, 155
Anderson, Robert (Assistant
        Commissioner of Police),
        215
Animal Liberation Front, 163
Angry Brigade, 155
Anti-Nowhere League (band), 193
Anti-Semitism, 96–97

Anti-Social Behaviour Order
    (ASBO), 12
Anti-Terrorism, Crime and Security
        Act (2001), 99–100, 164–65
Army of the Provisional Government
        of Scotland, 163
Art, Robert J., 165
Askham Grange Open Prison, 249
Association of Chief Police Officers
        (ACPO), 165, 199, 200
Avory, Justice Horace, 134

B

Bailey, Victor, 138
Barrett, David, 137
'Battle of Epsom', 228
'Battle of the Beanfield', 178
'Battle of Cable Street', 97–98
Bean, J.P., 223–24
The Beatles (group), 189–90, 191
Beck, Frank, 135–36
Becker, Howard, 195–96
Beehive Boys gang, 223
Ben-Yehuda, Nachman, 179
Behlmer, George, 137
Bell, Stuart, 138
Bentley, Derek, 13, 251, 259

Betts, Leah, 203
Bessarabians, 217
Bew, Paul, 167
Billboard, 183
Billy Boys gang, 223
Birmingham gang, 228
'Birmingham Six', 5, 161
Blackboard Jungle, 185
'Black market, 76, 84
Blair, Tony, 169
Blake, George, 260
Bland, Lucy, 225
Blasphemy Laws, 20, 100–01, 103
    repeal in England and Wales, 101
    Rushdie, Salman, 100–01
        Satanic Verses, 100–01
Blom-Cooper, Louis, 38
'Bloody Sunday', 158
    Widgery, Lord Chief Justice John
        Passmore, 158
Bloom, Clive, 187
The Blue Lamp, 16
Blunkett, David, 112, 126
Bookmakers Association, 229
Booth, William, 130, 138
Bourdin, Martial, 152
Bow Street Runners, 15
Bowling, Benjamin, 103
Brady, Ian (active 1963–1965), 13,
        17, 42, 181
Bright, Graham, 201
Brink's-MAT raid (1983), 17, 83–84,
        85, 219, 233
Brighton Rock, 16, 230
British Crime Survey (BCS), 280
British Nationality Act (1948), 98
British Union of Fascists (BUF), 97
Brixton Riots (1981), 104
Brixton Riots (1985), 113

Broadwater Farm riots (1985), 113
Brockway, A. Fenner, 247
Brown, Alyson, 137, 216, 223
Bruce, Steve, 102
Bundy, Ted, 44, 50
Burglary, 19, 66–67, 70–72, 74, 75,
        78–79, 85
    media depictions of, 72–74,
        77–78
    rates of, 70–72
Butler, Josephine, 127
Butler-Sloss, Lady Justice Anne
        Elizabeth Oldfield, 136

C

Calvert, Roy, 250
Campbell, Beatrix, 138
Campbell, Christina, 47–48
Capital Punishment, 13, 23, 250–51,
        256–59
    Abolition of the Death Penalty
        Act (1965), 259
    Bentley, Derek, 13, 251, 259
    Ellis, Ruth, 13, 251, 259
    Evans, Gwynne Owen, 23, 244,
        256
    Evans, Timothy, 13, 251
    Hanratty, James, 13
    National Campaign for the
        Abolition of Capital
        Punishment, 250
    Royal Commission on Capital
        Punishment (1949), 251
Cathcart, Brian, 114
Chakroborti, Neil, 102
Chang, Brilliant 'Billy', 217, 225
Chibnall, Steve, 180, 230
Child abuse, 8

sexual abuse, 132–36, 140–42
    Cleveland scandal, 136, 138
    historiography of, 136–38,
        142–43
    problems with evidence, 129, 136
    Rochdale scandal, 136, 141
Children Act (1908), 128, 131, 132
Children and Young Persons Act
        (1933), 128, 129
Christie, John Reginald Halliday
        (active 1943–1953), 40, 251
Churchill, Winston, 153
Citizens of Tomorrow, 185
City of London Bearer Bonds robbery
        (1990), 233
Civil Authorities Act (Special Powers
        Act) (1922), 156, 158
Clarke Report School and Life (1947),
        182
The Clash (band), 193
Cockburn, James, 41
Cohen, Stanley, 179, 180–81, 184,
        186–87, 195–96
Coke, Sir Edward, 33
Collin, Matthew, 203
Coleridge, Justice John Duke, 127
Colston-Hayer, Tony, 198, 199, 201
Comer, Jack 'Spot', 218, 219, 220,
        227, 230
Commonwealth Immigrants Act
        (1962), 98
Condon, Sir Paul (Metropolitan
        Police Commissioner),
        106–07, 117
Confait, Maxwell, 286
Conservative Party
    Committee for a Free Britain, 202
    Federation of Conservative
        Students, 202

Contemporary Review, 215
Cooper, David, 252
Cornell, George, 220
Cortesi brothers, 229
Craig, Christopher, 251
Crass (band), 193, 194
    prosecution of, 193
Crime
    and gambling, 22, 227–30
    career crime, 22
    celebrity criminal, 17
    child abuse, 8
    cybercrime, 8
    detection of, 5
        role of experts in, 5
    fraud, 8
        Long Firm, 219–20
    gang violence, 19, 21–22, 75, 183
        immigrant gangs, 216–17,
            222–23
    hate crime, 7
    historiography of, 1–2, 32,
        36–39, 40–44, 48–50, 54,
        68–81, 83, 101–04, 136–38,
        142–43, 165–67, 179–80,
        193, 194–96, 201–03,
        213–14, 217–18, 221–27,
        252–56, 283–85
    history of, 2–3
    marginal groups and, 3
    media and, 14–16
    organised crime 19, 21–22,
        213–41
        historiography of, 213–14,
            217–18, 221–27
    and popular writing, 40–41, 43
    prevention of, 5
    primary sources for, 2
    project crime, 22, 219, 231–33

Crime – *continued*
  property crime, 6, 65–89
    Historiography of, 73–81
    trends in, 67–73, 76, 79
    media coverage of, 72–73
    mugging, 80–81, 85
    and violence 72–73, 231
  prostitution, 22, 127, 224
  protection rackets, 22
  sex crimes, 7, 125–47
  technological developments in, 8, 66, 73
  technological developments preventing, 72, 161, 272–73, 283
Crime and Disorder Act (1998), 99
Crime Desk, 15
Crimewatch, 15
Criminal Investigation Department (CID), 111
Criminal Justice Act (1914), 246
Criminal Justice Act (1948), 185, 249
Criminal Justice Act (1991), section 5, 99
Criminal Justice Act (1994), 202, 203
Criminal Justice Act (2003), 50
Criminal Justice (Terror and Conspiracy) Act (1988), 160
Criminal Justice and Immigration Bill (2008), 101
Criminal Justice System, 6–7, 126–27, 129, 245–46
  criticism of, 7, 126–27
  miscarriages of justice, 161
  public opinion of, 7
  victim support, 6
Criminal Law Amendment Act (CLAA) (1885), 125–26, 128, 129, 130

Criminal Law Amendment Act (1922), 133
Criminal Law Amendment Act (1977), 132, 140
Criminal Law Amendment Bill (1913), 128
Criminality 6–7, 15
  psychological understanding of, 5–6
Criminology, 1–2, 5–6, 39, 41, 50–51, 221, 225, 228, 254, 280–81, 288–89
  European influence upon, 5
Critcher, Chas, 138
Crown Prosecution Service, 7
Curran, James, 180
Cybercrime, 8

D

Daily Sketch, 187
Daily Mail, 106
Daily Mirror, 187
Dangerous Drugs Act (1977), 197
'Dark Tourism', 43–44
Dartmoor Prison Mutiny (1932), 218, 247–48
Davenport-Hines, Richard, 137
Davie, Neil, 126
Davies, Andrew, 223–24
Death Penalty, see capital punishment
Devine, Tom, 102
Dickens, Sir Henry, 69
Dickson gang, 220
Dimes, Albert, 218, 219
Diplock Courts, 8, 160–61
Disability Discrimination Act (1995), 99
Dixon, David, 288

Dobson, Gary, 105, 112
Donohue, Laura, 166
Donovan, 191
DPP v Rogers, 134
Driver, Beverley, 46
Drugs
    abuse of, 21, 178, 181, 187–91,
        196–98, 203, 204
    Dangerous Drugs Act (1977), 197
    Drugs Prevention Misuse Act
        (1964), 190
    'Pep-Pills', 187–8
    policies to control, 224–25
        United Nations Single
            Convention on Narcotic
            Drugs (1961), 190
        Prevention of the Misuse of
            Drugs Modification Order
            (1966), 190
    trafficking of, 220–21
Du Cane, Edmund, 244–45
Du Parcq, Herbert, 248

E

East Castle Street robbery (1952), 219
Ecstasy (MDMA), 178, 196–98, 203
Eisner, Manuel, 36, 41
Elephant and Castle gang, 228
Elias, Norbert, 36–37
Ellis, Ruth, 13, 251, 259
Emsley, Clive, 74, 76, 78, 83, 214,
        215, 221–22, 233, 253,
        284–85, 290
England, 7
Entertainments (Increased Penalties)
        Act (1990) (IPA), 201,
        202–03
Equalities Act (2010), 99

ETA, 164
Ethnic minorities 80–98, 109
    and crime, 80, 109
    as victims of hate crime, 96–98
European Convention on Human
        Rights, 165
    Protocol 13, 269
European Court of Human Rights,
    8, 161
Evans, Gwynne Owen, 23, 244, 256
Evans, Timothy, 13, 251

F

Fairclough v Whipp, 134
Farrow, Shelagh, 46–47, 50
Faulkner, Brian, 157
Ferris, Paul, 227
Fisher, Sir Henry, 286–87
Ford, Thomas, 127
Foreman, Freddie, 225
Forensic techniques, 5
    DNA evidence, 116
    graphology, 5
Foucault, Michel, 284
Fraser, 'Mad' Frankie, 82, 225
Fraud, 9, 67, 73, 75, 82, 219
    Long Firm, 219–20
Free Festival Movement, 193
Freiheit (Freedom), 153

G

Gaddafi, Colonel Muammar, 163
Gambling, 22, 227–30
Gang violence, 19, 21–22, 75, 183
    immigrant gangs, 216–17, 222–23
Garland, David, 243–44, 254, 282
Garland, Jon, 103

Gatrell, Vic, 253
Gekoski, Anna, 43
Gerstenfeld, Phyllis, B., 102
Gifford, Hardinge, Earl of Halsbury,
        130–31
Gilbert, Frederick, 229
Gildart, Keith, 192, 195
Gillespie, Gordon, 167
Gladstone Committee (1895),
        244–45, 246, 254, 276
Glasper, Ian, 193
Goddard, Lord chief Justice Baron
        Rayner, 134
Godfrey, Barry, 276–77, 286
Good Friday Agreement, 161–62
Goode, Erich, 179
'Great Train Robbery' (1963), 17, 19,
        81–84, 219, 225, 231–33
    Biggs, Ronald, 83, 231–33, 260
    Reynolds, Bruce, 225, 231–33
    The Train Robbers: Their Story, 232
    Wilson, Charles Frederick
        (Charlie), 84
Greater London Council (GLC), 104
Greater Manchester Police, 128
Grimes, Reverend Geoffrey, 259
Grundy, Bill, 191
Government
    accountability of, 2
    legislation, 6, 13, 98–103, 188,
        190–91
'Guildford Four', 161
Gurr, Ted, 41

H
Haigh, John George (active 1944–
        1949), 40
Hair, Paul, 41

Haggarty, Kevin D., 40
Hall, Edward Marshall Q.C., 229
Hall, Lesley, 137
Hall, Stuart, 80, 195–96
Hanratty, James, 13
Harding, Arthur, 74–75, 77
Hare, Margaret, 133
Hardy, Trevor (1945–2012), 19, 32,
        34, 44–54
    criminological views of, 50–51
Harrison, George, 191
Hart, Sir Anthony, 142
Hate crime, 7, 19–20, 91–124
    definitions of, 94–6
    ethnic minorities as victims of,
        96–97
    historiography of, 101–104
    history of, 96–101
    Racial and Religious Hatred Act
        (2008) 101
    trends in, 93–94
Hatton Garden jewellery raid, 17
Hay, Douglas, 253
Heath, Edward, 157
Hebdige, Richard, 195–96
Hedges, Henry, 131
Hendrick, Harry, 137
Hibbert, Christopher, 252
Hicks, William Joynson, 229
Hill, Billy, 218, 219, 220, 222, 227,
        230
Historical Institutional Abuse
        Inquiry in Northern Ireland,
        142
*Histories of Crime: Britain
        1600–2000*, 2
Hobhouse, Stephen, 247
Hobbs, Dick, 72, 82, 83, 213,
        219–20, 226–27, 233, 234

Hodkinson, Paul, 103
Hogan-Howe, Sir Bernard
        (Metropolitan Police
        Commissioner), 115
Holden, Joe, 259
Holmes, Sherlock, 15–16
Home Office, 7, 11, 23, 100, 151,
        200
Homicide, 18, 31–63
    definitions of, 33–34
    historiography of, 36–39, 40–44,
        48–50, 54
    impact of medicine upon,
        38
    manslaughter, 34, 36–37
    methodologies of, 41
    rerum natura, 33
    trends in, 37–93, 41–42
Homicide Act (1957), 33–34, 37,
        258, 259
Homosexuality, 7
Horn, Pamela, 185
House of Lords Select Committee on
        Religious Offences (2003),
        100–01
Human Rights Act (1998), 99
Hume, Baron David, 35
Hurd, Douglas (Home Secretary),
        200
Hussain, Hasib, 168
Hyndley, Myra (active 1963–1965),
        13, 17, 42, 181

Iganski, Paul, 103
Illustrated Police News, 15
Incest, 130–32
Incest Act (1908), 128

Indecency with Children Act (1960),
        134, 140
Independent Committee for the
        Supervision of Telephone
        Services, 200–01
Independent Inquiry into Child
        Sexual Abuse in Rotherham,
        Oxford and Rochdale, 141,
        142
Indian Criminal Code, 100–01
Infanticide, 34–35, 37
Infanticide Act (1922), 34
Ingram, George, 230
Iranian Embassy Siege (1980), 163
Irish Northern Aid Committee
        (NORAID), 162
Irish Republican Army (IRA), 20–21,
        149, 154–62, 164, 166,
        168–70
    Active Service Units, 159
    Birmingham pub bombings
        (1974), 160
    bombing campaigns, 154, 157–60
    Brighton Bombing, 159
    Continuity IRA, 159–60
    historiography of, 166–67
    hunger strikes, 159
    Irish National Liberation Army
        (INLA), 160
    'Long War', 158–60
    murder of Lord Mountbatten
        (1979), 159
    Omagh Bombing, 160
    Provisional IRA, 155–57, 160
    Real IRA, 160
    Sinn Féin, 159, 161
Irish Republican Brotherhood (IRB),
        Clan na Gael, 150–52
    bombing campaigns, 150–51

J

Jackson, Louise, 80, 137
Jackson, Sir Richard, (Assistant
    Commissioner Metropolitan
    Police), 76
Janson, Hank, 218
Japan, 190
Jefferson, Tony, 195–96
Jeffreys, Sheila, 137, 138
Jenkins, Philip, 221, 224
Jewkes, Yvonne, 179
Jockey Club, 229
Joint Committee on Human Rights,
    165
Judicial statistics, 276–77, 179–80

K

Khan, Mohammed Sidique, 168, 169
Kennard, Florence, 133
Kent Star gang, 223
Knepper, Paul, 225
Knight, Luke, 105
Knightsbridge Security Deposit
    Robbery (1987), 233
Kohn, Marek, 224–25
Kray, Ronald and Reginald, 17, 19,
    81, 82, 219, 225, 227
Kurdistan Workers' Party (PKK), 164

L

Lagou, Spiridoula, 102
Larcombe, John, 130
Law Amendment Act (1996), 33
Law and Order News, 180
Lawrence, Doreen, 105, 108
Lawrence, Neville, 105, 108

Lawrence, Stephen, 20, 104–17, 281
    BBC documentary on the murder
        of, 112
    inquest into death of, 105
        Mansfield, Michael, 105
    Kent Constabulary investigation,
        106
    Macpherson Inquiry, 106–11, 281,
        289
    murder of, 105
        Acourt, Jamie, 105
        Acourt, Neil, 105
        Dobson, Gary, 105, 112
        Knight, Luke, 105
Lawton, Lord Justice Frederick,
    140–41
The League of Gentlemen (1960), 78
Leach, Charles, 216
League of Nation, 225
Learmont Inquiry (1995), 262
Leeming, William, 138
Leese, Arnold, 97
Legislation, 6, 7
Lennon, John, 190
Levi, Michael, 74
Lindsay, Germaine, 167
Linebaugh, Peter, 253
Lloyd George, David, 152
Lockerbie bombing, 163–64
London, 151, 152–54, 161, 201,
        216–17, 226, 227, 230, 286
    security precautions in, 161
    terrorist attacks (7/7), 167–70
Long Firm fraud, 219–20
'Long Firm Game', 82
LSD, 190–91
Luminoso, Sendero, 157
Lydon, John, 193

M

Macpherson Inquiry (1999), 106–11, 281, 289
'Maguire Seven', 161
Malicious Damages Act (1964), 188
Manning, Edgar, 225
Mansfield, Michael, 105
Manslaughter, 34, 36–37
Marsh, Bert, 230
Marsh, Ian, 138
Mason, Dulcie, 135
Mason, Gail, 103
Mass Observation, 182
    Report on Juvenile Delinquency (1949), 185
Matthews, Roger, 233
Maudsley, Robert (active 1973–1978), 42
May, Theresa, 291
McClean, Lennie, 225
McDonald, Brian, 226
McGraw, Thomas, 227
McIntosh, Mary, 231
McLaren, Malcolm, 191
McRobbie, Angela, 179
McVitie, Jack 'The Hat', 220
Mearns, Rev. Andrew, 130, 138
Media, 14–17, 43, 49, 65, 72–73, 77, 106, 112, 126, 180–81
    and serial killers, 43
    fictional portrayals, 16
    film, 16, 43, 77, 78
    internet, 14
    newspaper reporting, 4, 14–16, 77, 106, 113, 152, 185–88, 198, 229–30, 232–33
    radio, 14
    television, 14, 15, 65, 112

'True Crime' genre, 16–17, 225–26, 232–33
Meier, William, 68, 76, 77, 78, 79, 231
Melville, Gaynor, 138
Mens Rea, 33
Messina brothers, 217, 218, 224
Metropolitan Police, 79–80, 105–15, 271
    and 'stop and search' policies, 109, 113, 115, 288
    and 'Racecourse Wars', 229
    corruption in, 112–13
    Counter Terrorism Command, 169
    Flying Squad, 79
    Ghost Squad, 79–80
    Hogan-Howe, Sir Bernard (Metropolitan Police Commissioner), 115
    'institutional racism' within, 107–10, 113–14
    recruitment of ethnic minority officers, 111
    Special Branch, 151
MI5, 165–69
MI6, 166
Miscarriages of justice, 5
    'Birmingham Six', 5, 161
    'Guildford Four', 161
    'Maguire Seven', 161
Misuse of Drugs Act (1964), 188
Misuse of Drugs Act (1971), 191
Mitchell, Frank, 260
Monte-Columbo brothers, 230
'Moors Murders' 13
Moral panics, 18, 39, 125, 136, 177–79, 182–83, 185–87, 204–05

Morris, Terence, 38, 280
Morrison, Reverend W.D., 244–45
Morton, James, 219, 226
Mossoph, Sharon, 45, 47–48, 49
Most, Johann, 153
Mugging, 80–81, 85
Mountbatten Report (1966), 23,
    244, 260–61
Murder, 13, 18, 31–63
  categories of, 39
  legal defences, 34, 35–36
    in Scotland, 35–36
  mass murder, 39
  serial murder, 39–40, 42, 44–54
  spree murder, 39
Murphy, Robert, 226
Murray, Charles, 282–83

N

Nash gang, 220
National Campaign for the Abolition
    of Capital Punishment, 250
National Crime Agency (NCA), 213
National Front (NF), 113, 194
National Service, 185–86, 188, 231
National Society for the Prevention
    of Cruelty to Children
    (NSPCC), 130, 131
National Vigilance Association, 130,
    131
New Age Travellers, 178, 193
Newburn, Tim, 290–91
New Musical Express, 194
New Statesmen, 189
News of the World, 133
Newspaper reporting, 4, 14–16, 77,
    106, 113, 152, 185–88, 198,
    229–30, 232–33

Nilsen, Dennis (active 1978–1983)
    42
Noonan gang, 227
Norris, David, 105, 112
Northern Ireland, 7, 8, 13–14, 142,
    155–62, 164, 167, 170, 183,
    222
  'Bloody Sunday', 158
    Widgery, Lord Chief Justice
      John Passmore, 158
  Diplock Courts, 8, 160–61
  Faulkner, Brian, 157
  Good Friday Agreement, 161–62
  Historical Institutional Abuse
    Inquiry in Northern Ireland,
    142
  internment without trial, 8, 157,
    158
  Irish Northern Aid Committee
    (NORAID), 162
  Irish Republican Army (IRA),
    20–21, 149, 154–62, 164,
    166, 168–70
    Active Service Units, 159
    Birmingham pub bombings
      (1974), 160
    bombing campaigns, 154,
      157–60
    Brighton Bombing, 159
    Continuity IRA, 159–60
    historiography of, 166–67
    hunger strikes, 159
    Irish National Liberation Army
      (INLA), 160
    'Long War', 158–60
    Murder of Lord Mountbatten
      (1979), 159
    Omagh Bombing, 160
    Provisional IRA, 155–57, 160

Real IRA, 160
Sinn Féin, 159, 161
'Operation Motorman', 158
Royal Ulster Constabulary (RUC), 157
sectarianism in, 156
terrorism in, 13–14
Ulster Volunteer Force, (UVF), 156
Northern Ireland Emergency Provisions Act (1973), 158
Northern Ireland Select Committee (2002), 162
Nott-Bower, Lady Louisa, 128
Noye, Kenneth, 227

O

Offences Against the Person Act (OAPA) (1861), 125–26, 133–34
Off the Track in London, 217
OFSTED, 111
Olafsen, Erna, 137
One Direction (group), 181, 203
O'Neil, Terence, 156
'Operation Cathedral', 136
'Operation Motorman', 158
Operation Pallial, 142
Organised Crime 19, 21–22, 213–41
Orwell, George (1903–1950), 49

P

Paedophilia, 136
Pall Mall Gazette, 127
Parker, Lord Chief Justice Hubert, 258
Paterson, Alexander, 247

Patten, John, 100
Payne, Sarah, 133
Peach, Blair, 113, 281
Peel, John, 192
Peel, Sir Robert, 271
Pearson, Geoffrey, 80
Pearson, John, 225
'Pep-Pills', 187–8
Perry, Barbara, 102
Pigot Report (1989), 129
Platt, Steve, 193
Police, 79–80
corruption, 3–4, 112, 275–76
Police Federation, 279
racism in, 20
Police and Criminal Evidence Act (PACE) (1984), 24, 273, 287–90
Police Complaints Authority, 106
Police Five, 15
Policing, 3, 6, 8, 23–24, 109, 113, 128, 164–65, 271–302
accountability of, 4
and surveillance technology, 161, 272–73, 283
Association of Chief Police Officers (ACPO), 165, 199, 200
'bad apple' thesis, 103
Brixton Riots (1981), 104
Brixton Riots (1985), 113
Broadwater Farm riots (1985), 113
corruption, 3–4, 112, 275–76
crime prevention, 5
fictional depictions of, 16, 275, 291
Flying Squad, 79
Forensic techniques, 5
DNA evidence, 116
graphology, 5

Policing – *continued*
  Ghost Squad, 79–80
  historiography of, 283–85
  ideologies of, 7–8
  'Kratos' Operations, 165, 168
  leadership of, 4
  Metropolitan Police, 79–80,
    105–15, 271
    and 'stop and search' policies,
      109, 113, 115, 288
    and 'Racecourse Wars', 229
    corruption in, 112–13
    Counter Terrorism Command,
      169
    Flying Squad, 79
    Ghost Squad, 79–80
    Hogan-Howe, Sir Bernard
      (Metropolitan Police
      Commissioner), 115
    'institutional racism' within,
      107–10, 113–14
    recruitment of ethnic minority
      officers, 111
    Special Branch, 151
  National Crime Agency (NCA),
    213
  'New Police', 271–72
  newspaper coverage of, 4
  phone tapping, 199
  Police and Criminal Evidence Act
    (PACE) (1984), 24, 273,
    287–90
  Police Complaints Authority, 106
  Police Federation, 279
  Police Five, 15
  political dimensions of, 4
  Prosecution of Offences Act
    (1985), 105

  Public Entertainment Licenses
    (Drugs Misuse) Act (1997),
    203
  racism in, 20
  role of, 4
  Royal Commission on Criminal
    Procedure (1981), 23–4, 287
  Scarman, Lord Justice Baron Leslie
    George, 140, 287
    Scarman Report (1981), 99, 287
  Serious Organised Crime Agency,
    213
  'Tottenham Outrage' (1909), 153
  Toxteth Riots (1981), 104
  women officers, 23, 128, 137, 272
Policy Studies Institute report on
    policing in London, 286
Popular Music, 21
  'Acid House Rave', 177–79,
    196–205
    Amsterdam, 198
    Freedom to Party Campaign,
      201
    Ibiza, 197–98
  and dancehalls, 182–3
  and disorder, 21, 177–211
    historiography of, 179–80, 193,
      194–96, 201–03
  fanzines, 194, 198
  and government legislation, 178
  'Mods' and 'Rockers', 186–89, 200
    and seaside violence, 186–87,
      200
  Oi, 193–94
  'pay-parties', 177, 199–200
  Punk rock, 191–94, 204–05
  Reggae, 193, 204
  'rock and roll', 184–86

'Teddy Boys', 181, 185, 186, 188, 194, 204, 249–50
Porter, Roy, 137
Potter, Gary W., 221, 224
Prevention of Terrorism Act (1974), 160
Prevention of Terrorism Act (1989), 160, 164
Prevention of Terrorism Act (2000), 164, 170
Prevention of Violence (Temporary Provisions) Act (1939), 154
Prison Act (1952), 249
Prisons, 9–10, 22–23, 243
  'boot camps' 10
  celebrity prisoners, 11
  conditions in, 10, 11, 251–52, 254–55
  Dartmoor Prison Mutiny (1932), 218, 247–48
  'dispersal' system, 261
  Du Cane, Edmund, 244–45
  Mountbatten Report (1966), 23, 244, 260–61
  open prisons, 9, 249
  overcrowding in, 11
  population statistics, 246–47, 249, 255
  Prison Commission, 249
  prison service, 4
  protests in, 11
  public opinion of, 11
  regimes in prison, 9
Prevention of Crime Act (1908), 13, 246
Prevention of the Misuse of Drugs Modification Order (1966), 190

Prison Commission, 249
Probation of First Offenders Act (1887), 245
Probation of Offenders Act (1907), 246
The Project Club (venue), 197
Property Crime, 6, 65–89
  and violence 72–73
  fraud, 9, 67, 73, 75, 82, 219
    Long Firm, 219–20
  historiography of, 73–81, 83
  'hold-ups', 77
  media coverage of, 72–73, 77
  trends in, 67–73, 76, 79
Prosecution of Offences Act (1985), 105
Prostitution, 22, 127, 224
Public Entertainment Licenses (Drugs Misuse) Act (1997), 203
Public Opinion, 9, 14–17
Public Order Act (1986), 101
Punishment 8–14, 22–23, 185, 243–70
  and eugenics, 277–78
  Anti-Social Behaviour Order (ASBO), 12
  approved schools, 12–13
  borstals, 246, 278
  capital punishment, 13, 23, 250–51, 256–59
    abolition, 23, 34
    abolition campaigns, 13
  community service, 9, 11–12
  historiography of, 252–56
  internment without trial (Northern Ireland), 8, 157, 158
  Mountbatten Report (1966), 23, 244, 260–61

Punishment – *continued*
  'new penology', 255–56
  policies, 8, 9–14, 23
  prisons, 4, 9–11, 22–23, 243
  Probation of First Offenders Act
    (1887), 245
  Probation of Offenders Act (1907),
    246
  public opinion of, 9–12
  recidivism, 244
  shame punishments, 12
  victim reconciliation, 12
  Victorian reformatory school, 13
  youth punishment 13, 22

R

R v Hare, 133–34
R v Speck, 135
'Racecourse Wars', 227–30
Race Relations Act (1965), 98
Race Relations Act (1968), 99
Race Relations Act (1976), 99, 111
Race Relations (Amendment) Act
    (2000), 99, 111
Race Relations Board, 98–99
Racial discrimination, 92–93, 98, 112
Racial and Religious Hatred Act
    (2008) 101
Racism, 91–3, 95–124
Radzinowicz, Leon, 261
Rape, 7, 125, 126, 130
  within marriage, 125
Rawlings, Philip, 249, 253, 276
Read, Leonard 'Nipper', 220
Read, Piers Paul, 232
Reiner, Robert, 274, 279, 281, 287,
    289
Reynolds, Simon, 197, 203

Richards, Keith, 191
Richardson Charles and Edward, 19,
    81, 82, 219, 227
Richardson, Louise, 165
Roberts, Dave, 198, 199
Roberts, David, 140–41
Robbery, 17, 65–66, 70–72, 75–79,
    231–33
  Brink's-MAT raid (1983), 17,
    83–84, 85, 219, 233
  City of London Bearer Bonds
    robbery (1990), 233
  Hatton Garden jewellery raid, 17
  mugging, 80–81, 85
Rock Around the Clock, 185
Rock, Paul, 39, 184
Rolling Stone, 194
Rolling Stones (group), 181, 187,
    190, 191
Roodhouse, Mark, 76, 214, 222
Royal Commission on Capital
    Punishment (1949), 251
Royal Commission on Criminal
    Procedure (1981), 23–24,
    287
Royal Ulster Constabulary (RUC),
    157
Rushdie, Salman, 100–01

S

Sabini Brothers, 22, 218, 220,
    222–23, 227–30
Sage, George, 228
Samuel, Raphael, 74–75
Satanic Verses, 100–01
Saville, Jimmy, 126
Scarman, Lord Justice Baron Leslie
    George, 140, 287

Scarman Report (1981), 99, 287
Scottish Law, 35–36
Scotland, 7, 35, 37–38, 71, 98–99,
        102, 116, 138, 163, 216
   burglary in, rates of, 71
   gangs in, 216, 218–19, 223–24, 227
   Glasgow Airport attack (2007),
        168
   incest in, 130, 138
   infanticide in, 35
   Scottish Law, 35–36
   sectarianism in, 98, 102, 116
Scottish National Liberation Army,
        163
Seal, Lizzie, 258
Secret Intelligence Service (SIS), 165
Select Committee on Capital
        Punishment (1931), 250,
        257–58
Serial Murderers, 39–40, 42, 44–54
   and popular writing, 43
   Brady, Ian (active 1963–1965), 13,
        17, 42, 181
   Bundy, Ted, 44, 50
   Hardy, Trevor (1945–2012), 19,
        32, 34, 44–54
      criminological views of, 50–51
   Hyndley, Myra (active 1963–
        1965), 13, 17, 42, 181
   Sutcliffe, Peter ('The Yorkshire
        Ripper' active 1975–1980),
        17, 42, 44, 52–53
   typologies of, 42
   West, Fred and Rosemary (active
        1967–1987), 17, 42
Serious Organised Crime Agency, 213
Sex Discrimination Act (1975), 128
Sex Disqualification Removal Act
        (1919), 128

Sex Pistols (group), 191–93
   'Anarchy tour', 191–92
   *Never Mind the Bollocks, Here's the
        Sex Pistols*, 192–93
      court case surrounding, 192–93
Sexual Assault Referral Centres, 128
Sexual Offences Act (SOA) (1956),
        126, 128, 132, 133, 140
Sexual Offences Act (1993), 131
Sexual Offences Act (2003), 132,
        133, 135, 141–42
Sexuality, 7, 182, 183, 189, 194, 204
   consent, 7, 8
Sharpe, David, 142
Shoom (venue), 198
Shore, Heather, 223
Sillitoe, Percy, 224
Silverman, Sidney, 251
Simons, Geoffrey, 140–41
Skala, Wanda, 44–48
Slater, Stefan, 214, 224
Smart, Carol, 137–38
Smith, George Joseph (active 1912–
        1914), 39–40
Smithies, Edward, 70, 74, 75, 79
Social Darwinism, 247
Solomon, Alfred, 228–29, 230
Sparks, Charles John 'Ruby', 218,
        223, 230
Speak of the Devil, 138
Special Air Service, 163
Special Branch, 151
Spierenburg, Peter, 31–32
St. Ninians Christian Brothers
        School, 142
Staines, Paul, 179, 202
   Libertarian Alliance Political
        Notes, 202
Stead, W.T., 127, 130

Stevenson, Venetia, 134
Stewart, Lesley (Janet), 44, 46–48
Stone, Lawrence, 41
Staines, Paul, 201
Straw, Jack, 106, 114–15
Strummer, Joe, 193
Stuart, Hannah, 167
Suffragette terrorism, 152
Summary Jurisdiction (Process) Act
      (1881), 245
The Sun, 198
Sutcliffe, Peter ('The Yorkshire
      Ripper' active 1975–1980),
      17, 42, 44, 52–53

T

Tamil, Tigers, 157
Tanweer, Shehzad, 168
Tappenden, Ken, Chief
      Superintendant, 199
Taylor, Derek, 140–41
Taylor, Laurie, 74, 82
Terrorism, 13–14, 20, 149–76, 215
   and Jihad, 153, 156, 164, 165,
      166–70
   Angry Brigade, 155
   animal rights terrorism, 163
   definitions of, 150
   ETA, 164
   Glasgow Airport attack (2007), 168
   'Guildford Four', 161
   historiography of, 165–67
   Lockerbie bombing, 163–64
   Prevention of Terrorism Act
      (1974), 160
   Prevention of Terrorism Act
      (1989), 160, 164

Prevention of Terrorism Act
      (2000), 164, 170
Prevention of Violence (Temporary
      Provisions) Act (1939),
      154
Terrorism Act (2006), 169
Terrorism Act (2008), 169
Theft, 19, 65–89
Theft Act (1968), 66–67
The Times, 188, 231–32
Thomas, Donald, 70, 76, 78
Thompson, E.P., 284
Thornton, Sarah L., 179
Tibbs gang, 220
'Tottenham Outrage' (1909), 153
Toxteth Riots (1981), 104
'Twin Towers attack' (9/11) 164, 165,
      166
Tyrrell, Jane, 127

U

Ulster Volunteer Force, (UVF), 156
United Nations Charter (1945),
      Article I, 99
United Nations Single Convention
      on Narcotic Drugs (1961),
      190
United States of America
   gangster culture of, 216–17, 221

V

Victim Reconciliation, 12
Victorian Reformatory School, 13
Violence, 18–20, 22, 31–63, 103,
      186–88, 231
Vronsky, Peter, 42

W

Waites, Matthew, 137
Wales, 138, 142, 163
Walkowitz, Judith, 137
Waller, Sir Morris, 247
Warren, Curtis 'Cocky', 220, 227
West, Fred and Rosemary (active 1967–1987), 17, 42
Whitehouse, Fred, 139–40
Widgery, Lord Chief Justice John Passmore, 158
Wilde, Oscar, 244–45
Wilkins, Herbert, 230
Williams, Chris A., 285
Wilson, Charles, 260
Wilson, David, 42, 51–52
'Wonderland Club', 136
Woodcock Inquiry (1994), 262

Woolf, Lord Chief Justice Harry Kenneth, 261–62
Worley, Matthew, 193, 194, 201–02
Wotton Report on the Youth Service (1961), 186
Wright, Alan, 213, 215, 217, 220

Y

Yardbirds (group), 187
Youth Justice and Criminal Evidence Act (1999), 129
Youth, 12–13, 22, 80, 182
    consumption patterns of, 182–84, 187, 189, 205
    offending 12–13, 22, 80, 278
    violence, 186–89
    Wotton Report on the Youth Service (1961), 186

JUN 0 8 2018

CPSIA information can be obtained
at www.ICGtesting.com
Printed in the USA
LVHW06s1117200518
577856LV00018B/155/P